Magnetic Resonance
Angiography

Magnetic Resonance Angiography

A Practical Approach

Editor

E. KENT YUCEL, M.D.

Associate Professor of Radiology
Department of Radiology
Boston University Medical Center
Boston, Massachusetts

McGRAW-HILL, INC.

Health Professions Division

New York   St. Louis   San Francisco   Auckland   Bogotá   Caracas   Lisbon
London   Madrid   Mexico City   Milan   Montreal   New Delhi
San Juan   Singapore   Sydney   Tokyo   Toronto

MAGNETIC RESONANCE ANGIOGRAPHY
A Practical Approach

1 2 3 4 5 6 7 8 9 0   KGPKGP   9 8 7 6 5 4

ISBN 0-07-072695-7

This book was set in Times Roman by Ruttle, Shaw & Wetherill, Inc.
The editors were Jane Pennington and Muza Navrozov;
the production supervisor was Richard Ruzycka;
the index was prepared by Lillian Rotberg;
the cover was designed by José Fonfrias.
Arcata Graphics/Kingsport was printer and binder.

Library of Congress Cataloging-in-Publication Data

Magnetic resonance angiography : a practical approach / editor, E.
    Kent Yucel.
        p.   cm.
    Includes bibliographical references.
    ISBN 0-07-072695-7
    1. Angiography.   2. Blood vessels—Magnetic resonance imaging.
    I. Yucel, E. Kent.
    [DNLM: 1. Cardiovascular System—radionuclide imaging.
    2. Magnetic Resonance Imaging.   3. Angiography.   WG 141.5.R3 M196
    1995]
    RC691.6.A53M338   1995
616.1'307548—dc20
DNLM/DLC
for Library of Congress   94-3649

To Tamsin, Morgan, and the twins

Veniet tempus quo posteri nostri tam aperta nos nescisse mirentur.
—SENECA

Contents

Contributors*

Philip A. Blaustein, M.D. [4]
Staff Radiologist
Department of Radiology
HCA L. W. Blake
Parrish, Florida

Georg M. Bongartz, M.D. [5]
Associate Professor of Radiology
Department of Clinical Radiology
University of Muenster
Muenster, Germany

Richard P. Cambria, M.D. [14]
Division of Vascular Surgery
Associate Professor of Surgery
Massachusetts General Hospital
Harvard Medical School
Boston, Massachusetts

Thomas G. Di Salvo, M.D. [11]
Fellow, Cardiac Unit
Massachusetts General Hospital
Harvard Medical School
Boston, Massachusetts

Charles L. Dumoulin, Ph.D. [3]
Research Scientist
GE Corporate Research and Development
Schenectady, New York

Robert R. Edelman, M.D. [8]
Director of MRI Division
Department of Radiology
Beth Israel Hospital
Associate Professor of Radiology
Harvard Medical School
Boston, Massachusetts

R. Gil Gonzalez, M.D., Ph.D. [4]
Director of MRI Division
Department of Radiology
Massachusetts General Hospital
Assistant Professor of Radiology
Harvard Medical School
Boston, Massachusetts

Daryl R. Gress, M.D. [6]
Director of Neurovascular Service
Department of Neurology
Assistant Clinical Professor of Neurology
University of California at San Francisco
    School of Medicine
San Francisco, California

George J. Hunter, M.D., B.S., F.R.C.R. [7]
Instructor in Radiology
Harvard Medical School
Massachusetts General Hospital
Boston, Massachusetts

John A. Kaufman, M.D. [10, 12]
Instructor in Radiology
Harvard Medical School
Division of Vascular Radiology
Assistant in Radiology
Massachusetts General Hospital
Boston, Massachusetts

James R. MacFall, Ph.D. [9]
Assistant Professor
Department of Radiology
Duke University Medical Center
Durham, North Carolina

Warren J. Manning, M.D. [8]
Assistant Professor of Medicine
Assistant Professor of Radiology
Harvard Medical School
Associate Director of Noninvasive Cardiac Imaging
Beth Israel Hospital
Boston, Massachusetts

Patrick T. O'Gara, M.D. [11]
Associate Professor of Medicine
Director, Coronary Care Unit
Massachusetts General Hospital
Harvard Medical School
Boston, Massachusetts

Eléonore Paquet, M.D., F.R.C.P.C. [7]
Associate Professor of Medicine
University of Montreal
Montreal Heart Institute
Montreal, Canada

* The numbers in brackets following the contributor name refer to chapter(s) authored or co-authored by the contributor.

Dennis L. Parker, Ph.D.   [2]
Associate Professor of Radiology
Department of Radiology
University of Utah
Salt Lake City, Utah

Martin R. Prince, M.D., Ph.D.   [10, 12]
Assistant Professor of Radiology
Co-Director, Division of MRI
University of Michigan Medical Center
Ann Arbor, Michigan

Richard L. Robertson, Jr., M.D.   [4]
Neuroradiologist
Department of Radiology
Children's Hospital
Boston, Massachusetts

Bettina Siewert, M.D.   [8]
Fellow in Radiology
Beth Israel Hospital
Boston, Massachusetts

Michael S. Silver, Ph.D.   [1]
Philips Medical Systems
Shelton, Connecticut

Lorraine K. Skibo, M.D.   [17]
Chief, Section of Vascular
    and Interventional Radiology
Palo Alto VA Medical Center
Assistant Professor of Radiology
Stanford University Medical School
Palo Alto, California

H. Dirk Sostman, M.D.   [9]
Professor and Vice Chairman
Department of Radiology
Duke University Medical Center
Durham, North Carolina

Ralph Weissleder, M.D., Ph.D.   [16]
Department of Radiology
Director, MR Pharmaceutical Program
Massachusetts General Hospital
Assistant Professor of Radiology
Harvard Medical School
Boston, Massachusetts

Pamela K. Woodard, M.D.   [9]
Resident
Department of Radiology
Duke University Medical Center
Durham, North Carolina

E. Kent Yucel, M.D.   [10, 12, 13, 15]
Department of Radiology
Boston University Medical Center
Boston, Massachusetts

Preface

Over the last few years, magnetic resonance angiography (MRA) has begun to make the transition from being an investigational technique practiced at a few academic centers to a crucial tool in the diagnosis of vascular disease throughout the body. No longer limited to the carotid arteries and intracranial vasculature, MRA has proven utility in the evaluation of the veins and arteries of the trunk and extremities. Nonneurologic applications can be expected to increase rapidly as newer techniques, such as gated time of flight and segmented turbo-gradient echo, become more widespread on commercial systems. To keep up with the growing importance of these peripheral applications and because the techniques suitable for different anatomic areas can be quite different, separate chapters have been devoted to the thoracic aorta, extremities, renal and visceral arteries, and veins.

Although not clinically relevant at the present time, recent advances in MR technology have made coronary and pulmonary MRA a real possibility for the first time. Further advances will be necessary for these applications to make the transition to the clinical realm, but because of their growing importance, we are fortunate to have chapters on these areas contributed by leaders in their respective fields. Beyond the development of more advanced hardware and software, the development of blood-pool contrast agents for MR promises to revolutionize how we perform MRA studies in the near future, and no text on MRA would be complete without an introduction to this exciting area.

One of the things that makes MRA a tool of such growing importance is the enthusiastic reception it has received from referring clinicians. They see in MRA an opportunity to obtain much of the information they need to manage their patients without subjecting them to the risks, expense, and discomfort of conventional angiography. I have asked respected clinicians in the fields of neurology, vascular surgery, and cardiology who are also familiar with the uses of MRA to present their views of how this emerging technology plays a role in their current practice and where it is headed in the near future. Of course, with the introduction of helical CT angiography, MRA is no longer the only cross-sectional angiographic method. It remains to be seen what role will be taken by each of these technologies in the angiographic practice of the future, but a book such as this one would have been incomplete without a chapter on this new technology.

Finally, introductory chapters have been included which cover the basic principles as well as more advanced concepts of time of flight and phase-contrast MRA written by pioneers in the field. My hope is that this text will encourage practicing MR radiologists, angiographers, and clinicians interested in vascular disease to begin incorporating some of these new techniques into their routine clinical practice for the benefit of both their patients and the health care system. This is an area where MRI, often derided as an overly expensive and unnecessary technology, can improve the safety, quality, and expense of the medical care we deliver. In closing, I would like to thank my current chairman, Dr. Joseph T. Ferrucci, for his support and encouragement as well as my former colleagues at the Massachusetts General Hospital—Fred Steinberg, Stuart Geller, John Kaufman, Arthur Waltman, and Christos Athanasoulis—who believed that MRA was possible even in the early days when their faith was not always supported by the images I showed them.

Chapter 1

Basic Principles of Magnetic Resonance Imaging and Magnetic Resonance Angiography

Michael S. Silver

This chapter on magnetic resonance (MR) pulse sequences is written to give the clinician or radiologist unfamiliar with MR angiography (MRA) insight into the appearance of MR angiograms and indications where particular MR techniques are appropriate.

The chapter is divided into three sections: first, a brief review of how the MR signal is generated and detected; second, a description of the pulse sequences and how the parameters affect the MR angiogram; and, third, a discussion of important advanced techniques that are quickly becoming standard components of commercial MRA packages.

THE MAGNETIC RESONANCE SYSTEM

The basic components of an MR system are the magnet, the radiofrequency (RF) chain, the magnetic field gradients, and a computer that controls the internal system communication. A pulse sequence is a series of instructions that controls the gradients and the RF chain. The main magnetic field is usually not controlled by the pulse sequence except for fine tuning of the magnetic field homogeneity. The magnetic field gradients are used to encode the spatial position of tissue with that tissue's MR frequency.

When the nuclear spins in the human body are subjected to a constant magnetic field, the spins will behave similarly to a top and precess about the constant magnetic field at a characteristic frequency called the *Larmor frequency* (ω_0). There is a fundamental relationship between the Larmor frequency and the strength of the static magnetic field produced by a large magnet:

$$\omega_0 = \gamma B_0 \qquad (1.1)$$

where ω_0 is the Larmor frequency, γ is the gyromagnetic ratio (a physical constant, having a different value for each element), and B_0 is the main magnetic field.

The MR pulse sequence is to an MR imaging (MRI) system what nerve impulses are to the human body; they "instruct" the spins or magnetization how, when, and where to move. This document is designed to take the mystery out of ideas of pulse sequence design and give the reader an appreciation for the steps leading up to the image display.

Frequency and Phase

The essence of the resonant effect in MRI is that the spins experience simultaneously a constant magnetic field, supplied by, for example, a superconducting magnet, and the RF magnetic field applied at the Larmor frequency using the RF synthesizer and amplifier. This relationship is key to understanding the pulse sequences. This basic principle is applied in concepts such as slice selection, pixel size, and flow effects.

PULSE SEQUENCES

The most basic pulse sequence is an RF pulse followed by turning on the receiver so that the MR signal can be collected and processed. In engineering, the concept of an electronic box is used to explain in simple terms how a system works without going into the details of that system. Thus, only the input and output of the system are used to determine the behavior or characteristics of that "black box." If we consider the MRI system as a *simple electronic box*, all we need in order to understand the characteristics of the MRI system

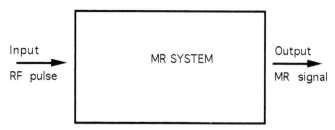

FIGURE 1-1 An electronic black box.

are the inputs, or RF pulses, and the outputs (responses), or the MR signal. This is shown in Fig. 1-1. The response of the MR system to an RF pulse is called a *free induction decay (FID)*. The duration, amplitude, and shape of the FID depend upon the characteristics of the tissue, which are, in turn, affected by chemical composition and pathology. The characteristics of the FID will also depend upon the performance of the gradients, RF synthesizer, and B_0 field homogeneity. Thus, the FID can be used to determine the characteristics or behavior of the MR system.

The term *free induction decay* refers to the signal generated by the movement of the nuclear spins and detected in an electronic coil placed around the sample. This means that the nuclear spins are precessing (like the motion of a spinning top) freely in the absence of an RF pulse. The spins will induce a voltage in the detection coils placed about the sample. This induced voltage will decay with a characteristic time, which is determined by the B_0 field inhomogeneity, other patient-induced (magnetic susceptibility) inhomogeneities, and the inherent physical properties of the tissue. This is shown in Fig. 1-2.

Contrast Behavior and Measurement

The two relaxation effects that are exploited in MRI are the longitudinal relaxation time, T_1, and the transverse relaxation

time, T_2. The differences in T_1 or in T_2 between the tissues provide contrast in the images. First, we turn to a description of T_1 relaxation, also called *longitudinal relaxation*, which occurs in the direction of the static magnetic field. The T_1 value is also dependent upon the main magnetic field strength, B_0. The pulse sequences used in MRI are designed to exploit differences in tissue T_1, making it possible to differentiate tumors, cysts, and other lesions.

The T_1 contrast is generated using pulse sequences in which either the repetition time, or TR, is short compared with the T_1 values in the tissue or in which the equilibrium magnetization along B_0 can be sampled. The first type of sequence is realized in the short TR spin echo. The second is the gradient echo sequences. A third type of sequence is called an *inversion recovery sequence* and refers to the act of inverting the equilibrium magnetization and subsequently measuring the magnetization at a given time, TI.

The other relaxation time is called the *transverse relaxation time*, T_2, and characterizes the spin relaxation in a direction perpendicular to T_1 relaxation. The T_2 measurement is sensitive to the water content of tissue, and the T_2 relaxation time is measured by applying a spin echo pulse sequence.

How Are Magnetic Resonance Images Made?

Once the MR signal is generated by applying an RF pulse, we must provide a means of distinguishing the MR signal from one region of the body to another. This is accomplished by applying the magnetic field gradients, which encode spatial position with the Larmor frequency. The gradients are applied to encode the Larmor frequency in all three directions, so that all spatial information is made available. The resulting data are then run through a mathematical process, called the *Fourier transform*, of decoding the Larmor frequency into spatial information. We now turn to a description of how MR images are created.

The magnetic field gradients applied during image acquisition provide a means of encoding the spatial information in the data. The gradients are applied at different amplitudes so that fine detail and the basic image contrast are obtained within a single acquisition. The mathematical representation of the MR data, called K space, is nothing more than the spatially encoded representation of the MR signal. This representation is placed in a form that makes it understandable by the Fourier transform. In other words, the gradients encode the MR signal into spatial position, and K space is the way in which the encoded signal is stored. The Fourier transform then decodes the signal, which results in an MR image. The way in which the MR signal is stored in K space depends on what kind of pulse sequence method was used in the measurement. Virtually all of the MR systems in operation today collect the data essentially as described in the Fourier zeugmatography technique developed by Ernst and colleagues.[1]

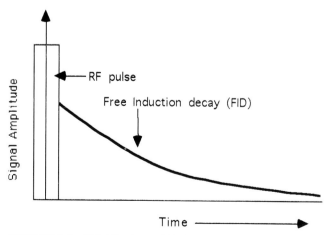

FIGURE 1-2 FID following an RF pulse.

After an RF pulse is applied and the FID has decayed completely, it is possible to recall a coherent (all spins in phase) MR signal or echo by causing a reversal of the dephasing processes due to static magnetic field inhomogeneity. This is accomplished in spin echo imaging by applying a 180° refocusing pulse. An alternative method for obtaining an echo is to reverse the magnetic field gradients. This is the basis for the methods used in MRA. Applying such magnetic field gradients and then reversing their amplitudes reverses the incoherence of the spins, causing the spins to refocus at a desired moment, the echo time, or TE. It also permits the spatial encoding of the information contained in the echo. This concept is shown in Fig. 1-3. This is discussed in more detail in the section that follows.

The Gradient Recalled Echo Sequence: The Building Block for MR Angiography

As mentioned above, it is possible to recover the MR signal by reversing the applied magnetic field gradient. This is called a *gradient recalled echo*, sometimes referred to as a *gradient echo* or *field echo*, and is different from the spin echo in that the gradient echo amplitude is dependent on the parameter T_2^*, not T_2. The T_2^* is referred to as *transverse relaxation* in the presence of magnetic field inhomogeneity. The true transverse relaxation time, T_2, represents relaxation that occurs in the plane transverse to the static magnetic field, excluding effects of static magnetic field inhomogeneity.

The advantage of using such sequences is that they are faster and permit shorter echo and repetition times than spin echo sequences. Disadvantages of gradient recalled sequences include a higher sensitivity to static magnetic field inhomogeneities and a lower signal-to-noise ratio.

Figure 1-4 shows a generic gradient echo sequence. Contrast in gradient echo sequences is controlled by the TR, TE, magnetization dephasing using the gradients, and the RF flip angle, α. Following the diagram, we can identify the important features of the gradient echo sequence. The first line is the RF pulse, typically an angle below 90°. Inversion or other RF preparation pulses may be applied before this low flip angle RF pulse to give the spins a greater T_1 weighting. This is discussed briefly in the discussion on turbo field echo.

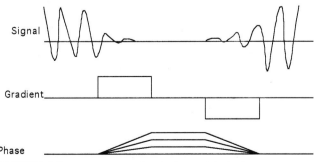

FIGURE 1-3 Gradient reversal rephasing, and dephasing.

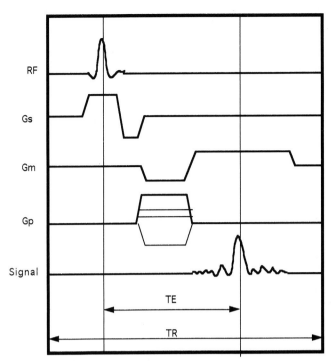

FIGURE 1-4 Gradient-recalled echo pulse sequence.

The next line is the timing for the slice-selection gradient. The measurement or readout gradient is below. The phase-encoding gradient, G_p, is shown with several phase encoding lines to indicate that the amplitude of this gradient is incremented per echo during the scan. The last line represents the echo, along with the definition of TE and TR. It should be clear from this diagram why manufacturers need short rise times on the gradients in order to achieve short TRs and TEs.

In addition to the basic gradient echo sequence described above, for T_1-weighted gradient echo images spoiler or spin dephasing gradients are applied to eliminate the formation of spin echoes from previous RF excitations.

ADVANCED MR ANGIOGRAPHY PULSE SEQUENCES AND BACKGROUND–SUPPRESSION METHODS

In this section several improvements to the basic MRA gradient recalled echo sequence are described. The common thread in all these methods is the optimization of contrast-to-noise between the stationary tissue and blood flow in vessels. The following techniques are divided into two categories: those sensitive to flow dynamics and those designed to remove stationary tissue signal.

Gated Inflow

One of the major problems with the inflow or time-of-flight technique is the loss of signal due to pulsatile flow. This is

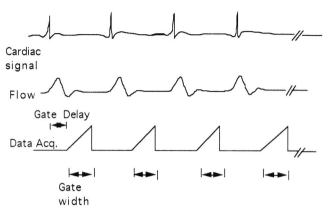

FIGURE 1-5   Principle of gated inflow.

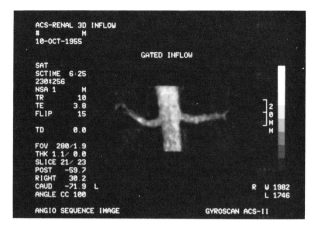

FIGURE 1-6   An example of gated inflow of the renal artery.

illustrated in Fig. 1-5, where a typical normal arterial flow pattern is shown with respect to the MR pulse-sequence data acquisition. The MR signal may be collected in a window centered about early diastole in the carotids to reduce the dephasing of spins due to turbulent flow,[2] or in mid systole in the extremities to maximize inflow effects and minimize retrograde flow.[3] One of the advantages of this technique is that as a cardiac *gating* technique, the acquisition continues without waiting for the R wave, as opposed to cardiac *triggering*, where the acquisition begins only when an R wave is detected.

The advantage of gated inflow over standard inflow is in the use of the cardiac cycle to reduce the influence of pulsatile flow. Consider a gradient recalled echo acquisition where the echoes are acquired only during a window 500 ms wide, and delayed 250 ms from the peak of the R wave. This corresponds to a point in the cardiac cycle where the acceleration of the blood is considerably less than that at peak systole and increased coherence of spin velocities is maintained. In order to collect the full matrix of data despite reducing the window over which data are acquired, the total imaging time must increase inversely with the size of the acquisition window. The advantage of reducing the window is acquiring signal from flowing blood which exhibits maximal laminarlike flow, with minimal retrograde or turbulent flow and more constant velocities throughout the scan. An example of gated inflow of the renal artery is shown in Fig. 1-6.

Turbo Field Echo Inflow

The term *turbo field echo* (TFE), or fast gradient echo, refers to the high-speed variety of the gradient echo sequence. The advantages of this method over the gradient echo method are the shorter acquisition time and the ability to obtain a greater contrast-to-noise ratio than with standard gradient echo due to the use of segments, or "shots." The TFE sequences differ from the standard gradient echo sequences with respect

to the application of prepulses, flip angle sweep, and, of course, the actual duration of the sequences.

There are major differences between gradient echo and TFE with respect to contrast behavior, due to the effect of acquiring data over a time comparable to T_1, rather than over a duration much longer than T_1, as is the case with standard gradient echo. In standard gradient echo sequences, a steady state magnetization is built up over the duration of the measurement, since the duration of a gradient echo sequence is at least five times T_1, the time necessary for the spins to return to equilibrium. The steady state condition exists when the difference between two consecutive MR signals (echoes) is zero. Thus, once the spins reach a steady state, the echo signal will essentially remain constant for the duration of the measurement. Under the conditions, each phase-encoded MRI signal is generated from the same "initial" conditions.

During a TFE measurement, a steady state is not reached

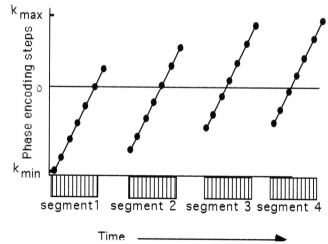

FIGURE 1-7   Segmented TFE sequence.

because the TFE sequence duration is on the order of T_1. This means that a steady state magnetization cannot be achieved with so short a sequence duration. Before the spins reach a steady state, they will generate echo signals with different intensities, which means echo amplitudes will be different for each phase-encoded line of data, and the specific phase-encoded amplitude is dependent upon its position relative to the start of the scan. This modulation imposed upon the echo can create serious ghosting artifacts and a general reduction in contrast.

The basis of spin echo (SE) and gradient echo sequences is that the signal amplitude remains constant during the scan, since the processing of the data assumes that the only spatial encoding is performed by the gradients. If another process modulates the amplitude of the signal, then the data processing, or fast Fourier transform, will interpret this change in amplitude as a change in spatial position, which is incorrect. This results in a misregistration of an object, better known as a *ghosting artifact*. A technique called the *flip-angle sweep* helps eliminate these ghosting artifacts by reducing the echo-to-echo intensity variations.

PREPULSES

When the imaging times are on the order of T_1, the contrast will tend to be more T_2-weighted, since the magnetization is not given ample time to reach a steady state condition. This is a problem if strong T_1 weighting is desired, as is the case in MRA, where the signal from stationary tissue must be saturated. Prepulses (PP) are used to enhance and control the contrast in TFE.[4]

T_1-weighting is accomplished by applying a single inversion pulse prior to the image acquisition. This gives an inversion-recovery type of contrast. Other variations in T_1 weighting can be applied by using a saturation pulse instead of an inversion pulse. This can be used to further control the contrast.

Since the beginning and end of the scan correspond to the echoes with the largest phase-encoding values (the periphery of K space), there will be little contribution to the image contrast from these signals; they will largely contribute to the image resolution. The small-amplitude phase-encoding steps (the center of K space) contribute primarily to the image contrast. Therefore, the selection of the timing of the prepulse should be made relative to the position in time of the zero-amplitude phase-encoding step.

For applications such as abdominal imaging, this type of acquisition provides a major improvement over gradient echo and SE methods. A quick calculation would reveal that, for example, a 128 × 256 matrix with TR/TE = 10/4 ms would result in a minimum acquisition time of 1.28. This seems impressive at first thought; however, the imaging requirements cannot be met with these imaging parameters for many clinical applications. The next section describes a method of

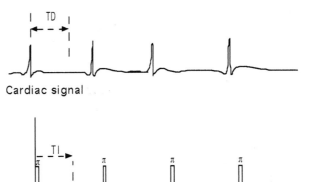

FIGURE 1-8   A segmented cardiac-triggered TFE acquisition.

reducing the acquisition time while maintaining high resolution and image quality.

SEGMENTED ACQUISITION

The turbo field echo sequences were developed to reduce scan time and motion artifacts while maintaining clinical image resolution and quality. However, the duration of the acquisition must be under 1s in order to freeze most physiological motion except cardiac, for which about 30 ms is required. Furthermore, short imaging times and high resolution are opposing requirements. What method can be employed that would meet all requirements? One solution would be to break up the entire acquisition into a set of smaller acquisitions, each subacquisition collecting fewer phase-encoded echoes but encompassing the full range of spatial frequencies over several acquisitions. This results in a final image that covers the full range of spatial frequencies, but the data are collected over a time of about 100 to 200 ms, freezing most physiological motion. This is called *segmented acquisition* and can be implemented with the turbo field echo sequence.

An example of a segmented acquisition is shown in Fig. 1-7, where an acquisition is subdivided into a number of segments, each with seven excitations, covering a time period dictated by the TR and number of excitations.

Figure 1-8 shows a further improvement in the segmented TFE sequence: the inclusion of cardiac triggering. Cardiac triggering can greatly improve the image quality of an MR angiogram by controlling when during the cardiac cycle the data acquisition occurs. Thus, by keeping the segment duration short with respect to the cardiac cycle, there is some freedom in selecting the timing of the data acquisition within the cardiac cycle. For example, data acquisition that avoids peak systole will reduce the probability of signal loss due to turbulence caused by pulsatile acceleration, and excluding end diastole will improve inflow contrast by eliminating the period of the cardiac cycle with the least flow (Fig. 1-9). In

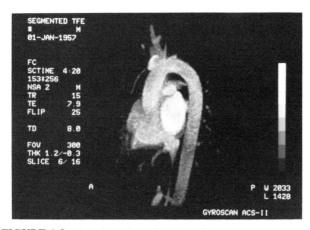

FIGURE 1-9   A cardiac-triggered TFE acquisition.

this example, an inversion prepulse was chosen as part of the acquisition parameters and is applied in every segment.

CONCLUSIONS

Magnetic resonance angiography is, relatively speaking, a newcomer in the realm of vascular diagnostic techniques. As such, it is the subject of much scrutiny. This chapter was written with the intent to acquaint the beginning reader with MRI and to provide the scientific basis for MRA as a clinically valuable technique in the diagnosis of vascular disease.

ACKNOWLEDGMENT

The author thanks Dr. H. E. Simon for his comments and suggestions in the preparation of this document.

REFERENCES

1. Kumar A, Welti D, Ernst RR: NMR Fourier zeugmatography. *J Magn Reson* 18:69, 1975.
2. Saloner D, Selby K, Anderson CM: MRA studies of arterial stenosis: improvements by diastolic acquisition. *Magn Reson Med* 31:196, 1994.
3. De Graaf RG, Groen JP: MR angiography with pulsatile flow. *Magn Reson Med* 10:25, 1992.
4. Edelman RR, Chien D, Atkinson DJ, Sanstrom J: Fast time-of-flight MR angiography with improved background suppression. *Radiology* 179:867, 1991.

Chapter 2

Time-of-Flight Magnetic Resonance Angiography

Dennis L. Parker

At the present time, methods used to image blood flow and other types of motion can generally be classified as time-of-flight (TOF) techniques or phase-contrast (PC) techniques. As a general rule, TOF techniques are those where the image contrast is obtained from motion-related modulation of the longitudinal (z) component of the magnetization, while PC techniques derive signal from the motion-dependent phase shift of the transverse (x or y) components of the magnetization.

Time-of-flight imaging methods in magnetic resonance imaging (MRI) are those techniques where spins are tagged, then given time to move, and finally imaged in such a manner that the tagged spins appear different than the stationary spins. The first demonstration of the TOF effect in the detection and study of blood flow was that of Singer in 1959.[1] These early experiments were examples of the excitation of magnetization in one location and the detection of the magnetization at a later time in a second location.[2] Various types of tagging have been used in the process of blood vessel imaging, including selective inversion of the magnetization,[3–5] striped excitation and/or striped presaturation,[6] and simple passive tagging where spins with unsaturated magnetic moments flow into a region where the stationary spins are highly saturated by the imaging sequence.[7] In many applications, spins are tagged outside of the region to be imaged and then allowed time to flow into the region.

Most currently used TOF magnetic resonance angiography (MRA) techniques, which generate high-resolution images of blood vessels, are based on passive saturation, where blood contrast arises from the inflow of fresh (completely magnetized), unsaturated spins into a region in which the signal from stationary tissue is suppressed by rapid repeated excitation.[7–15] The imaging gradient waveforms are usually designed to minimize signal loss from moving spins due to motion-caused phase dispersion. Subtraction techniques have also been studied to suppress the signal from stationary tissue,[16] but this suppression is obtained at the expense of a significant increase in imaging time over the rapid repeated excitation techniques.[17]

In this chapter we review the basic principles and define the terminology of some common TOF MRA techniques. We begin with a description of the various image acquisition formats, review the sources of blood vessel contrast and the concept of signal saturation, and then discuss the relative advantages of the various formats. We end with a discussion of the properties of the commonly used display algorithms.

VESSEL VISIBILITY

The goal of MRA in general is portrayal of all vascular lumen anatomy for all blood vessels of interest. Currently, x-ray imaging techniques can display vascular detail down to dimensions on the order of 0.1 to 0.3 mm. For many diagnostic applications it is useful to see blood vessel detail down to such small sizes. At the present time, MRA techniques are limited by gradient strength, sampling times, and noise limits to the visualization of vessels on the order of 0.4 to 0.6 mm minimum. Further, all MRA techniques are severely limited in sensitivity when the flow rates are reduced as might occur in various disease states.

IMAGE ACQUISITION FORMATS

There is a great diversity in TOF MRA techniques. The successful development and clinical application of MRA techniques results in large measure from the flexible methods of image acquisition and complementary display algorithms. Line (one-dimensional), plane (two-dimensional), and volume (three-dimensional) acquisition techniques have been successfully applied to MRA. The type of image acquisition

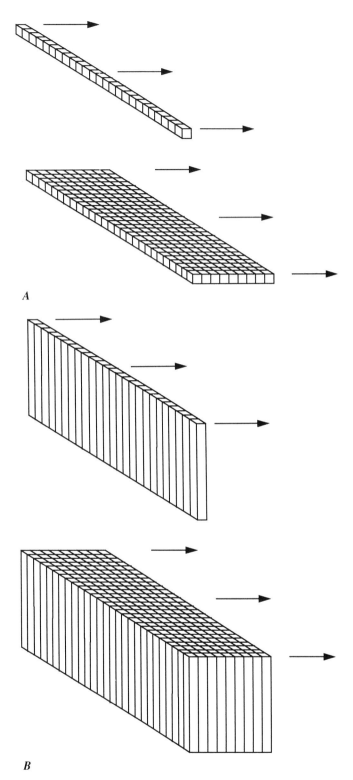

A

B

FIGURE 2-1 *A*. Example of a shaft excitation for a line scan, and how the line can be swept through the magnetization. *B*. Geometry of line projection imaging.

is defined in terms of each object region that is excited or can be reconstructed independently from a set of acquired data.

Line acquisition techniques, as illustrated in Fig. 2-1, acquire image data only along a single line of points, and the measurements can be obtained from a single excitation. Special selective gradient and radio frequency (RF) pulses can be used to excite the magnetization only along a single shaft[18] without significantly affecting the magnetization external to the shaft. By changing the excitation to elongate the width of the shaft in one direction, the set of line measurements can become a set of projection measurements through the object as shown in Fig. 2-1B. Line techniques have the advantage of rapid acquisition with relative insensitivity to motion artifacts. There are two major disadvantages with line scan techniques. First, the thin dimension, or width, of the line excited is, in general, inversely proportional to the strength of the gradient applied during the excitation pulse. Due to gradient strength limitations, it is difficult to excite a region of less than a few millimeters. Second, the noise efficiency of the technique is significantly lower than in two- or three-dimensional acquisition techniques.

In two-dimensional (2D) acquisitiuon techniques[8–12] (Fig. 2-2), a plane (or volume if a thick plane is excited) of magnetization is excited, and imaging gradients (readout and phase encoding) are used to encode the plane into an image or two-dimensional array of pixels.[19,20] If a thick plane is excited (Fig. 2-2B), the 2D image obtained appears to be a set of projections through the object. Again, the slice thickness is inversely proportional to the gradient strength; therefore there are limitations on how thin a plane can be excited.

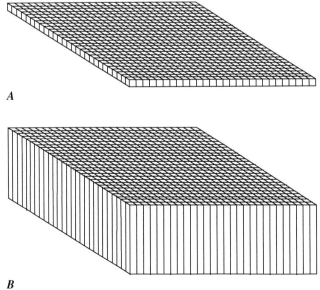

A

B

FIGURE 2-2 Example of 2D image (*A*) from a thin plane and (*B*) when the plane is sufficiently thick that a projection image is obtained.

Unless echo planar techniques are used, the signal measurements for 2D acquisition must be obtained from multiple excitations.

Three-dimensional (3D) acquisition techniques[13–15] can be used to excite and obtain signal measurements from an entire volume of the object (Fig. 2-3). In general, 3D MRA techniques acquire vascular image data in a three-dimensional matrix[13–15] of approximately isotropic voxels which can be viewed in arbitrary cross-sectional orientation or from which projection images can be formed in arbitrary directions. Imaging gradients must be applied along all three imaging directions, and the signal measurements must be obtained from multiple excitations.[21] These three-dimensional techniques have the advantage of being very noise-efficient, but at the same time they are susceptible to significant signal loss due to inflow saturation.

A great deal of experience has been gained in applications of the various types and formats of MRA to various disease states and diagnostic processes. Although vessel visibility is a complicated function of many properties of the human visual system, it is convenient and instructive to consider issues of vessel contrast and image noise, which are properties which can be measured and subjected to quantitative comparative analysis.

SIGNAL

The concept of signal in MRA as well as in all types of MRI is very basic. Each element of an image (referred to as a pixel, for picture element, or a voxel, for volume element) represents a small volume of the object, and the signal strength in each voxel is related to the total transverse component of magnetization within the voxel at the moment the sampling is performed. Because the total transverse component is the vector sum of all of the magnetization elements within the voxel, the signal will be greatest when all of the transverse components are pointing in the same direction (in phase). Because of (1) small inhomogeneities in the local magnetic fields due to microscopic tissue structure as well as (2) molecular structure (chemical shift), the small magnetic moments do not all precess at the same rate and lose phase coherence relatively rapidly.

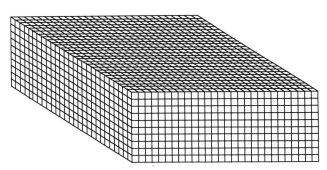

FIGURE 2-3   Example format of 3D image acquisition.

IMAGE CONTRAST

Contrast is defined as the difference in signal intensity between two regions. In the case of MRA, contrast is defined as the signal difference between flowing blood and the adjacent stationary tissue (e.g., muscle, gray, or white matter, or fat). The contrast between various tissue types will depend on the tissue's spin density and relaxation rates and upon the imaging parameters of the sequence used.[22,23] Factors which affect vessel contrast include the size and shape of the region imaged, the geometry of the blood flow, and the rate and tip angle of the excitation pulse.

IMAGE NOISE

Noise in nuclear magnetic resonance (NMR) experiments and in MR images has been studied extensively over the years.[24–33] Random image variations occur because of random variations (i.e., noise voltage) in the received signal. The noise voltage is due to random thermal electrical currents (noise) in the patient or object being scanned as well as random thermal electrical currents (noise) in the receive electronics. Unwanted structured image variations typically arise from actual patient or object structure.

The primary source of noise in MR imaging is of a thermal nature (e.g., Johnson noise from the effective coil resistance, black-body radiation from the patient, etc.) rather than the quantum noise obtained in x-ray or other forms of imaging that are limited by the number of photons "counted." Noise can therefore be reduced by any process that reduces the physical source of the noise. Such processes include reducing coil dimensions and careful impedance matching. Reducing coil dimensions also reduces the sensitive field of view as well as the RF homogeneity of the coil and must be balanced with other imaging considerations.

For noise which is uncorrelated in the original measurements, the noise in the reconstructed image will cover the entire image and also appear uncorrelated. It is therefore possible to estimate the magnitude of such noise from measurements of the image variance in a region of interest external to the object. Such measurements will then be free of any contribution to the variance due to object structure variation but must be corrected for the magnitude operation.[34]

TRADE-OFFS IN TOF MRA—FACTORS THAT AFFECT VESSEL CNR

Given the above discussion of signal, contrast, and noise, it is possible to discuss vessel visibility in terms of the ratio of vessel contrast to noise (CNR). From the large amount of experience gained to the present time, it would appear that vessel CNR in TOF MRA is a strong function of many factors, including vascular geometry, imaging parameters, and imaging formats. In the following, we discuss some of these dependencies, and we refer the reader to other excellent chapters and articles on this subject.[35,36]

TRADE-OFFS BETWEEN SPATIAL RESOLUTION, CONTRAST RESOLUTION, AND TIME

Efficiency

When multiple contiguous image slices are to be obtained, it is generally true that either two- or three-dimensional acquisition techniques can be used. The choice of which imaging technique is "best" cannot be made based on signal-to-noise ratios (SNRs) alone, as either technique could be improved by simply acquiring multiple sets of measurements and averaging these measurements or equivalently averaging the images obtained from these measurements. Uncorrelated noise will decrease and hence the SNR will increase in proportion to the square root of the number of measurements averaged. Because imaging time is proportional to the number of measurements averaged, it is convenient to define an imaging efficiency figure or merit as the SNR divided by the square root of the imaging time[33]:

$$\eta = SNR/time^{1/2}$$

The efficiency of the various data acquisition formats can be compared based upon the relative efficiency of each for specific imaging situations. From a consideration of noise alone, the CNR is proportional to voxel volume multiplied by the square root of the number of measurements included in the reconstruction process. Thus, with all other factors equal (slice thickness, repetition time, echo time, etc.), a 3D acquisition with N slices will be more efficient by the square root of N. Thus, where possible, 3D sequences are more efficient than 2D sequences, which, in turn, are more efficient than line scan techniques. Although thick-voxel projection techniques have larger voxels, the vessel signal is only proportional to the vessel dimensions, thus increasing voxel dimensions beyond the size of the vessel does not increase the vessel signal in the image.

IMAGING PARAMETER TRADE-OFFS

Echo Time versus Field Echo Time

Once the magnetization has been tipped into the transverse plane, the transverse component of the magnetization, from which the signal is derived, begins to decay due to various factors. A principal source of signal loss is the randomization of magnetization phase, which occurs due to fluctuations in the local magnetic field experienced by each magnetic moment. Because the signal is the vector sum of the magnetization over the dimensions of the voxel, any process which causes a spread in the phase of the magnetic moments, either

over microscopic dimensions or over dimensions the size of the voxel, will cause the signal to decrease, as illustrated in Fig. 2-4. If the spread in phase is due to static field inhomogeneities, the signal can be retrieved by a refocusing RF pulse (a 180° pulse). If the signal loss is due to a randomization of the magnetic moments, then phase memory is lost and the signal cannot be regained by a refocusing RF pulse.

The total relaxation rate can be considered to be the sum of the rates due to each of the processes that contribute to the loss in phase memory. These processes include (1) random thermal motions of local magnetic moments, (2) very slowly varying local magnetic fields, (3) motion of the magnetic moments in external applied gradients, (4) motion of the magnetic moments in internal susceptibility-induced magnetic field gradients.

Because tissue will, in general, exhibit different transverse relaxation rates than blood, the tissue/blood contrast will depend upon the echo time. Further, because the fluctuations in the local field experienced by the blood can also depend upon the motion of the blood during the imaging gradients or through local internal field inhomogeneities, significantly greater amounts of signal loss can occur in regions of blood vessel curvature or disordered/nonuniform flow. Because this signal loss is much more a function of the duration than of the amplitude of the imaging gradients, it can be minimized by increasing the amplitudes and decreasing the durations of the imaging gradients. If the motion-induced signal loss is due to the externally applied imaging gradients, then the only time the magnetization is dephasing is during the application of the gradients. In this case it is possible to increase the echo time by simply delaying the start of the imaging gradients. In this manner, no motion-induced dephasing will occur, and if the blood T2 is longer than the tissue T2, it is possible that the contrast between muscle and blood will increase. In regions where flow occurs through internal field inhomogeneities, increasing the echo time will result in a significant decrease in blood signal and a potential loss in muscle/blood contrast.

Spatial Resolution versus Echo Time

One of the most direct trade-offs to affect vessel CNR is that between voxel dimensions (spatial resolution) and echo time. The signal loss is caused by the distribution of the magnetic moments over the dimensions of the imaging voxel. For some situations, as shown in Fig. 2-4, the signal loss is related to a macroscopic dispersion in the phase of the magnetization such as incomplete spin rephasing due to imperfections in the imaging gradients, due to noncompensated motion during the gradients or due to motion in local field gradients. In these cases, merely reducing the voxel dimensions can reduce the region over which the dephasing occurs and thereby reduce the total signal loss due to dephasing. However, if the signal loss is due to dephasing over microscopic dimensions, then reducing voxel dimensions will have

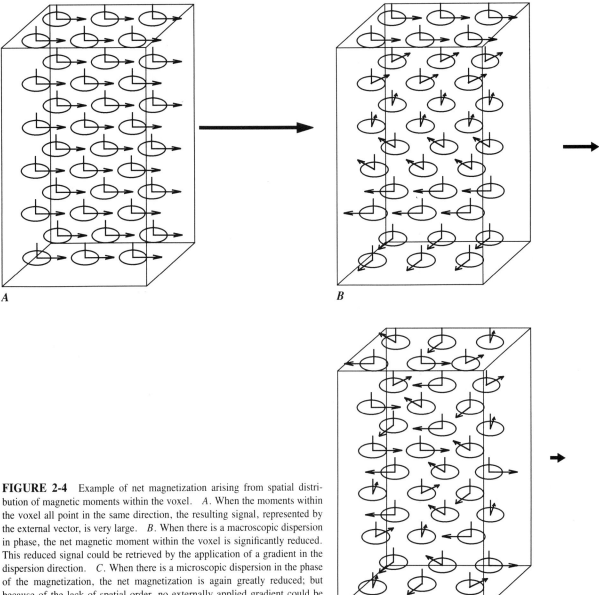

FIGURE 2-4 Example of net magnetization arising from spatial distribution of magnetic moments within the voxel. *A.* When the moments within the voxel all point in the same direction, the resulting signal, represented by the external vector, is very large. *B.* When there is a macroscopic dispersion in phase, the net magnetic moment within the voxel is significantly reduced. This reduced signal could be retrieved by the application of a gradient in the dispersion direction. *C.* When there is a microscopic dispersion in the phase of the magnetization, the net magnetization is again greatly reduced; but because of the lack of spatial order, no externally applied gradient could be used to reduce the phase dispersion or retrieve the signal.

no impact on the lost signal. Further, because of the technical limitations of gradient strength, decreasing voxel dimensions will result in an increase in the minimum achievable echo time, as shown in Fig. 2-5. Thus, reducing voxel dimensions will increase the time that the imaging gradients must be applied and thereby result in an increase in gradient- and motion-related dephasing and signal loss. Thus there is a clear trade-off between spatial resolution and echo time, and the optimum vessel CNR will occur for some compromise between the available combinations. It is likely that improvements in gradient technology, which increase allowable amplitudes and decrease required rise times, will result in further optimization in this trade-off and an improvement in attainable vessel CNR.

Repetition Time versus Flip Angle

In nearly every TOF angiography technique, the source of blood flow contrast depends on the relatively long longitudinal relaxation time (T1) of soft tissues and blood. The process of excitation (see Fig. 2-6) consists of using an RF magnetic field at the resonant frequency of the desired region to tip the magnetization in the region by a small angle (usually from 10 to 90°). The transverse (*x* and *y*) component of the magnetization precesses around the main magnetic field and is used to obtain the received signal from which the image is made. This component undergoes rapid exponential decay, with a time constant known as T2. The longitudinal component of the magnetization relaxes exponen-

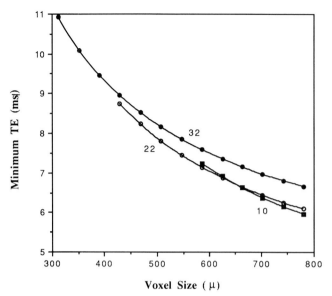

FIGURE 2-5 Trade-off between echo time and voxel size using a standard 3D time-of-flight pulse sequence. The top line represents the trade-off for the standard sampling rate of 32 μs per sample. As the voxel size is decreased, the readout gradient amplitude increases, increasing the length of time required for the gradient compensation waveforms that precede the readout time. When the sampling time is reduced to 22 μs, there is a further increase in readout gradient amplitude, but the required increase in gradient compensation time is more than balanced by the decrease in echo time, yielding a net reduction in echo time. If the sampling time is further decreased to 10 μs per sample, the echo time does not decrease due to the finite gradient rise times.

tially back to the full equilibrium value with a time constant known as T1. For physical reasons, T1 is always longer than T2; in tissue at a field strength of 1.5 tesla, the ratio of T1 to T2 is between 5 and 10.

If sufficient time is allowed between excitations, the magnetization will return exponentially to the full equilibrium value. However, if the excitations are repeated rapidly, as illustrated in Fig. 2-6, the magnetization decreases to a significantly lower equilibrium value. This process of signal decrease by repeated excitations is referred to as *saturation*. Blood that then enters the region imaged will be fully magnetized (unsaturated) and generate a significantly larger signal than tissue that remains in the region imaged. Figure 2-6 illustrates graphically how the signal approaches a steady-state value as a function of the number of pulses experienced and of the tip angle of each pulse. Assuming that there is no residual transverse magnetization before each pulse, a tip angle of 90° will result in the full *z* component of the magnetization being tipped into the transverse plane. As shown in Fig. 2-6A, when the repetition time is long, there is time for the magnetization to return to the fully magnetized state. When the repetition time is short, the magnetization returns to a much lower value. Note that for a tip angle of 90°, the signal from the first pulse is strong, while all subsequent signals are of the same reduced value. If a tip angle of less

than 90° is used, then the first signal is the largest; the subsequent signals reduce exponentially in magnitude to a steady-state value that is greater than the steady-state value obtained for the 90° pulses, as shown in Fig. 2-6B. Note that the curve for each relaxation period is the same as the corresponding segment from the full relaxation curve. Thus the signal decreases exponentially until it reaches the point where the decrease due to the tip angle is just matched by the increase due to the relaxation that occurs in the time interval between excitation pulses.

The actual value of the steady-state magnetization magnitude depends on the repetition time, (TR), the tip angle, and the nature of spoiling and/or rephasing of the transverse magnetization just prior to each subsequent RF pulse. Generally, the primary contribution to the transverse magnetization for each pulse is the steady-state longitudinal (*z*) component magnetization. The shorter the repetition time and TR and the larger the tip angle, the smaller will be the equilibrium longitudinal magnetization. For techniques which spoil the transverse magnetization after each echo is acquired (e.g., "FLASH"), little if any residual transverse magnetization remains to contribute to the transverse magnetization on subsequent pulses. Further, if spoiling is not performed and care is not taken to control the phase encoding experienced, the residual magnetization will have experienced an incorrect phase encoding and will not contribute image detail to the final image. The "ROAST" (nearly equivalent to spoiled "GRASS") technique is similar to FLASH, but the phase encoding gradient is reversed after echo readout to remove the phase encoding from any residual magnetization. The FISP technique carefully rephases all gradients before subsequent RF pulses and therefore retains contributions from previous transverse magnetization for all RF pulses.

Maximum image contrast would be obtained for blood which has just entered the region being imaged. The signal strength from the first excitation will be directly proportional to the sine of the tip angle and will increase as the angle increases up to 90°. However, if the blood remains in the imaged region for multiple excitation pulses, the signal received for subsequent excitations will decrease as the excitation angle is increased up to 90°. The contrast between blood and soft tissue will thus be a complicated function of the tip angle and the number of pulses experienced by the blood (assuming that the soft tissue has achieved a steady state). Maximum blood/tissue contrast would be obtained if it were possible to configure the imaging region such that blood entering the region is exposed to only one excitation pulse and then exits the region.

Contrast agents such as Gd-DTPA will change the muscle/blood contrast dramatically by reducing T1 from 1200 ms to between 300 to 600 ms. To the extent that the contrast remains intravascular, the blood signal will be greatly enhanced over the signal from stationary tissue.

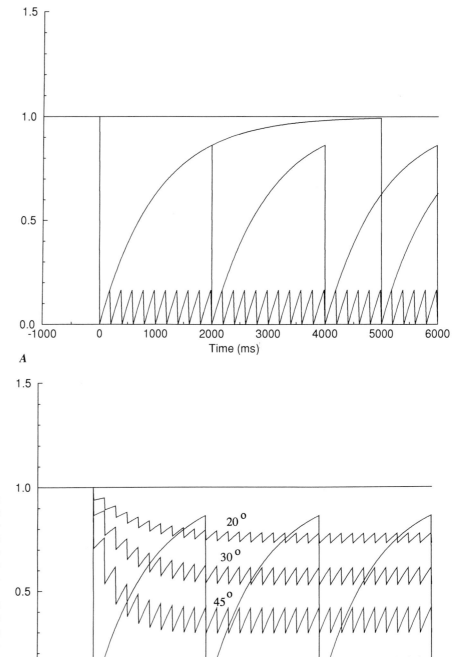

FIGURE 2-6 Excitation and relaxation curves. *A.* The longitudinal component of the magnetization is plotted for the case of an imaging sequence with 90° pulses. A steady-state situation is reached immediately with significantly lower values achieved for the shorter repetition rates. The assumed T1 is 1 s and repetition rates of 5 s, 2 s, and 0.2 s are plotted. *B.* The longitudinal magnetization for tip angles of 20, 30, and 45° are plotted for repetition rates of 0.2 s and a T1 of 1 s. Note that the relaxation segment of each curve matches the corresponding curve of the 90° pulse for that same amplitude. For these tip angles, the signal decreases exponentially toward a value where the increase in longitudinal magnetization due to relaxation is matched by the decrease in magnetization due to the small tip angle.

IMAGE ACQUISITION FORMAT TRADE-OFFS

Multiplanar 2D Techniques

As discussed above, in 2D imaging, a thin slice is excited and imaging is usually performed by freqeuency encoding one dimension (*x*) during readout and phase encoding the other dimension (*y*) during the time between excitation and readout. The slice can be made arbitrarily thin by increasing gradient amplitude during the excitation pulse or decreasing the bandwidth of the pulse, which is equivalent to increasing the duration of the excitation RF pulse. Thus decreasing the slice width will, in general, increase the minimum achievable echo time. Echo time is reduced by using an asymmetrical

RF pulse and an asymmetrical echo readout gradient. With current gradient limitations, these techniques yield slice thicknesses on the order 2 mm and echo times on the order of 8 ms with first-order flow compensation.

Because of the thin slice, the blood usually passes quickly through the slice, and the number of pulses experienced by the blood as it passes through the slice is usually very small. It is therefore convenient to use a very large flip angle in order to maximize the signal obtained from the blood while also achieving maximum saturation of signal from the stationary tissue. Thus 2D TOF techniques achieve a very large contrast enhancement. However, because of the thick slice dimensions and/or the long echo time, there is significant signal loss from regions of nonuniform flow, as occurs near vessel curvature and vessel disease.

Direct 3D Techniques

The signal loss due to the moderately large echo time and the moderately large voxel dimensions of 2D imaging can be reduced by performing a 3D acquisition of the slab of interest. The imaging format of 3D TOF techniques is very similar to that of 2D techniques except that a thick slab is excited and phase encoding is used in the slab selection direction in order to segment the slab into very thin slices. Again, using an asymmetrical RF pulse and an asymmetrical echo readout, the large-slice selective dimension allows the reduction of echo time to just over 5 ms with first-order gradient moment nulling and around 4 ms with only zero-order nulling, depending on the slab dimensions and the slice dimensions obtained from the z-phase encoding.

Because of the increased number of phase encodings, 3D image acquisition formats are in general much more noise-efficient than 2D acquisition formats, which, in turn, are more efficient than line-scan formats. Because the slab excited is very thick, the RF excitation duration can be very short and the slab-selection-phase encoding can occur during the other phase encoding time, making the echo time very short. The small voxel dimensions and short echo times greatly reduce signal loss due to disordered blood flow, and the portrayal of disease is much more accurate. However, due to the slab thickness, blood will spend a lot of time and experience many pulses in the slab and thus 3D techniques are much more sensitive to signal loss due to saturation of the inflowing blood. This decrease in signal is especially true for small vessels with slow flow.[37,38] The loss in vessel detail due to the time blood spends in the slab as well as to phase dispersion across the voxel dimensions can be reduced with the use of a thinner slab (and thus fewer or smaller voxels) in the acquisition. Decreased slab thickness—which results in a thinner field of view—also limits the diagnostic utility of the tecnique. The saturation can also be reduced by reducing the flip angle of the excitation pulse, but this also reduces the signal from blood and the saturation of stationary tissue and thus reduces the contrast between tissue and blood.

Recently, a significant improvement in vascular detail has been achieved by the use of excitation pulses with a small tip angle where the blood enters the slab and a large angle where the blood exits the slab. Further improvement is achieved by the use of magnetization transfer where a large, off-resonance excitation pulse is used to saturate the bound water component which exists primarily in tissue. The exchange of free protons with the bound protons results in a large signal loss or saturation of stationary tissues, while blood signal is affected very minimally. By using variable tip angle RF pulses and magnetization transfer, it is possible to image regions up to 10 cm thick. Larger slab thickness will still experience significant loss in vascular detail.

Using these techniques, high-quality images of normal individuals with high vascular flow can be obtained on a routine basis. Image quality is still significantly compromised in the presence of slow flow subsequent to vascular disease.

2D versus 3D versus Multiple Overlapping Thin-Slab 3D Acquisition (MOTSA)

As discussed above, both 2D and 3D TOF MRA techniques have advantages and disadvantages. For example, 2D techniques allow maximum inflow enhancement while requiring long echo times and thick-slice dimensions; these also suffer greater signal loss due to phase dispersion. On the other hand, 3D TOF MRA techniques minimize both the echo time and voxel volume, but they suffer significant contrast loss due to the saturation of inflowing blood and less saturation of stationary tissue background. The three-dimensinal techniques are therefore limited in the total slab thickness that can be imaged.

A significant improvement in vessel visibility has been observed by acquiring multiple, overlapping thin 3D regions.[39,40] Keeping the regions thin maintains the advantages of 2D imaging with fresh inflow enhancement, while using a 3D technique allows very small voxels, very short echo times, and reduced noise due to signal averaging. The primary disadvantage of multiple slab techniques is the periodic variation in vessel intensity and vascular detail that occurs at slab boundaries due to the profile of the excitation pulse and saturation effects. This artifact, often referred to as the *venetian blind* artifact, has been greatly reduced by attention to the slab profile shape and careful combining of the detail from the overlapping slices.

Projection Techniques

The projection techniques of MRI provide the most direct method to maximally shorten the echo time and thereby recover the signal from complex motion. These techniques are relatively fast because they acquire only a single projection image through the object. Further acquisitions must be used to obtain additional views. The echo time can be made arbitrarily short by clever design of the RF pulse and by clever gradient modulation during signal readout. Usually image reconstruction requires some form of resampling before the inverse Fourier transform.

The most serious problem with techniques that directly project a volume onto a plane is the saturation of blood signal that remains in the moderately large volume imaged. Although this is a significant problem in TOF imaging, it is also a problem in PC, where, for noise elimination, the image is a product of the image phase and signal magnitude.

Significantly, all projection techniques (both phase and magnitude contrast) are very sensitive to any remaining phase dispersion along the projection direction, and there can be significant signal loss due to this phase dispersion. The short echo time minimizes the phase dispersion over the dimensions of a single vessel, and typically a vessel segment would appear bright in the image. However, even though the phase may change very little over the vessel dimensions, it is likely that a large phase change will occur between two separated vessels and there will be significant signal loss when the two vessels appear overlapped in the image. Finally, the signal-to-noise ratio is further reduced because the fraction of the projection voxel that passes through signal-generating vessels is very small relative to the length of the voxel covering signal-generating stationary tissue. The signal of stationary tissue can be reduced by actually adding a small phase dispersion in the projection direction, further ensuring a loss of signal for overlapping vessels.

The effect of phase dispersion along the long projection direction as well as the loss in signal from saturation can be minimized by using a slice-selective pulse to limit the extent of the projection dimension. Full projections through the body can then be obtained by acquiring and adding together multiple adjacent projection slabs.

ARTIFACTS IN TOF MRA

There are many sources of interpretation error in MRA. The most serious problem concerns signal dropout where vessels that are truly patent and would be visible on an x-ray angiogram simply do not appear on the MR angiogram. The type and extent of signal loss depends on the type of blood flow imaged and the imaging technique used (2D TOF versus 3D TOF). Other problems include signal loss at edges of vessels, which results in misinterpretation of vascular disease; also effects of pulsatile blood flow and respiratory motion and image distortions due to motion of the blood in the time between the effective application of the imaging gradients (e.g., slice selection, phase encoding, and frequency encoding).

Signal Loss at Vessel Edges

There are two independent yet coupled effects that cause signal loss at vessel edges in MRA. The first is simply the increased saturation that occurs because of the slow flow and the increased length of time that blood at the vessel edges remains in the region being excited. Because of the finite viscosity of blood, the fluid at the vessel boundary must be stationary, and the velocity increases parabolically to a maximum at the vessel center. Thus the greatest signal enhancement will occur at the vessel center, with very little enhancement at the edges of the vessel.

The second source of signal loss at vessel edges results because of the MIP (maximum intensity projection) algorithm used to display the MR angiograms. Because the signal from blood near the vessel edges is much lower than that near the center, this signal is often much lower than the intensity from the surrounding tissue. Further, random variations in the surrounding soft tissue will occur and the MIP algorithm will often pick an intensity from the background, thus masking the lower intensity from the edges of the vessel lumen.

Signal Loss Due to Variations (Spatial and Temporal) in Flow

There are at least two ways in which disordered flow can result in signal loss. First, if the flow is not the same from one RF pulse to the next, the received signal will have different TOF enhancement and/or phase direction and be different in each echo. This signal variation results in an inconsistency that causes the signal from the blood in the reconstructed image to be spread external to the voxel from which it originates.[41] This artifact can be reduced by a technique similar to that used to reduce respiratory artifacts where the order of phase encodings is modified in synchrony with blood pulsation.

Second, even if the motion is the same for all echo signals, the presence of spatially dependent changes in velocity (velocity shear, acceleration, etc.) can result in spatially dependent phase dispersion within the voxel. The net magnetization is thus reduced. This phenomenon is significant, is a strong function of the structure of the imaging gradients, and plays a major role in the determination of vessel contrast.[42] Motion is described mathematically by the derivatives of the fluid position with time. Higher-order motions are represented by higher-order derivatives of the position. The phase change for *n*th derivative position is proportional to the *n*th gradient moment and thus to the *n*th power of the duration of the gradient. Thus, signal loss due to the higher-order-motion terms such as *acceleration, jerk* and so on is greatly exacerbated for long echo times.

When only low orders of motion occur, it is possible to design gradient waveforms with zero low-order moments such that no signal loss occurs for the corresponding velocity terms. Because waveforms that are designed to null low-order moments result in increases in higher moments, it is generally true that such waveforms result in an increase in signal loss in the presence of complex flow. In the presence of complex flow, it has been found that a much greater increase in signal is obtained when the echo is made as short as possible rather than lengthened by attempting to null even the low-order gradient moments.

From the above discussion it would appear that there might be a trade-off in vessel detail between nulling gradient moments up to some specific moment order. The process of imaging requires that the zero-order moment step through the appropriate set of values. Experience now indicates that nulling the first moment of the imaging gradients results in an increase in signal from regions of constant flow. However, attempting to null second-order or higher gradient moments actually increases echo time and results in a decrease in signal from regions of complex flow.

Phase-Frequency Artifact

The motion of blood between the applications of the phase encoding and readout gradients can result in an apparent shift of the blood vessel.[43] This is illustrated in Fig. 2-7. This can result in subtle changes in the shape of blood vessels in regions of curved flow and can lead to misdiagnosis of aneurysms or other anatomic anomalies. This artifact can be reduced by flow compensating the phase-encoding gradient around the center of the readout gradient, but this correction technique also greatly increases the duration of the phase-encoding gradient and related phase-dispersion signal loss.

An excellent discussion of motion-related artifacts and compensation is given by Duerk and Wendt.[42]

CONCLUSION

Time-of-flight MRA has achieved clinical utility in a few important applications. Although many challenges still remain, many new developments are occurring and it should be expected that current technical limitations will continue to be reduced. It is evident that significant improvement in vessel detail must occur before MRA procedures can replace conventional x-ray angiography. Some improvements will be made by developing optimal imaging techniques in accordance with the vascular anatomy to be imaged. Other improvements can be expected with the development of gradient systems with faster rise times and larger gradient magnitudes. Such improvements will allow significant shortening in echo times and improved visualization of the disordered flow that occurs in regions of vascular disease.

REFERENCES

1. Singer JR: Blood flow rates by nuclear magnetic resonance measurements. *Science* 130:1652, 1959.
2. Bowman RL, Kudravcev V: *IEEE Trans Med Eng ME* 6:267, 1959.

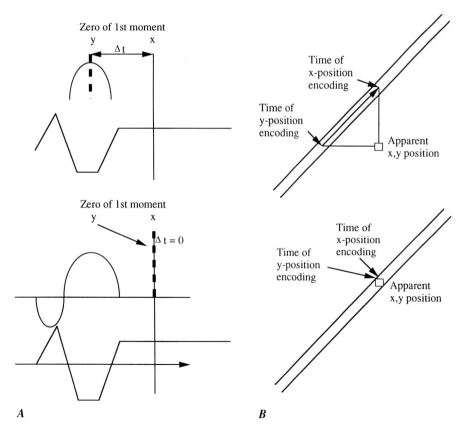

FIGURE 2-7 Phase frequency artifact. *A.* Uncompensated waveforms demonstrate that spatial encoding for the phase direction occurs before spatial encoding for the frequency direction, resulting in an apparent shift in vessel position. *B.* First moment gradient compensation for the phase encoding gradient can be used to move the position of phase encoding to the time of spatial encoding by the frequency encoding gradient, resulting in the correct image placement of the vessel.

3. Nishimura DG, Macovski A, Pauly JM, Conolly SM: MR angiography by selective inversion recovery. *Mag Res Med* 4:193,1987.

4. Nishimura DG, Macovski A, Pauly JM: Considerations of magnetic resonance angiography by selective inversion recovery. *Mag Res Med* 7:472, 1988.

5. Nishimura DG, Macovski A, Jackson JI, et al: Magnetic resonance angiography by selective inversion recovery using a compact gradient echo sequence. *Mag Res Med* 8:96, 1988.

6. Axel A, Dougherty L: MR imaging of motion with spatial modulation of magnetization. *Radiology* 172:349, 1989.

7. Keller PJ, Saloner D: "Time-of-flight flow imaging," in Potchen EJ, Siebert JE, Haacke EM, et al (eds): *Magnetic Resonance Angiography. Concepts and Applications.* St. Louis, Mosby, pp. 146–159, 1993.

8. Gullberg GT, Wehrli FW, Shimakawa A, Simons MA: MR vascular imaging with a fast gradient refocusing pulse sequence and reformatted images from transaxial sections. *Radiology* 165:241, 1987.

9. Wehrli FW, Shimakawa A, Gullberg GT, MacFall JR; Time-of-flight MR flow imaging: Selective saturation recovery with gradient refocusing. *Radiology* 160:781, 1986.

10. Keller PJ, Drayer BP, Fram EK et al: 2D Magnetic resonance arteriography of the neck. *Mag Res Imag* 7 (suppl 1):186, 1989.

11. Keller PJ, Drayer BP, Fram EK, et al: MR Angiography via 2D-acquisition yielding a 3D-display: A work in progress. *Radiology* 173:527, 1989.

12. Laub GW, Kaiser WA: MR angiography with gradient motion refocusing. *J Comp Assist Tomog* 12:377, 1988.

13. Wagle WA, Dumoulin CL, Souza SP, Kleine HE: 3DFT MR angiography of carotid and basilar arteries. *AJNR* 10:911, 1989.

14. Dumoulin CL, Cline HE, Souza SP, et al: Three-dimensional time-of-flight magnetic resonance angiography using spin saturation. *Mag Res Med* 11:35, 1989.

15. Ruggieri PM, Laub GA, Masaryk TJ, Modic MT: Intracranial circulation: Pulse-sequence considerations in three-dimensional (volume) MR angiography. *Radiology* 171:785, 1989.

16. Wedeen VJ, Reto AM, Edelman RR, et al: Projective imaging of pulsatile blood flow with magnetic resonance. *Science* 230:946, 1985.

17. Axel L, Morton D: MR flow imaging by velocity-compensated/uncompensated difference images, *J Comput Assist Tomog* 11:31, 1987.

18. Frahm J, Merboldt KD, Hanicke W, et al: Rapid line scan NMR angiography. *Mag Res Med* 7;79, 1988.

19. Kumar A, Welti D, Ernst RR: NMR Fourier zeugmatography. *J Mag Res* 18;69, 1975.

20. Edelstein W A, Hutchison JMS, Johnson G, Redpath T: Spin warp NMR imaging and applications to human whole-body imaging. *Phys Med Biol* 25:751, 1980.

21. den Boef JH, van Uigen CMJ, Holzscherer CD: Multiple-slice NMR imaging by three-dimensional Fourier zeugmatography. *Phys Med Biol* 29:857, 1984.

22. Tkach JA, Haacke EM: A comparison of fast spin echo and gradient echo sequences. *Mag Res Imaging* 4:359, 1986.

23. Haacke EM, Masaryk TJ, Wielopolski PA, et al: Optimizing blood vessel contrast in fast three-diemsnional MRI. *Mag Res Med* 14:202, 1990.

24. Wagner RF, Brown DG, Pastel MS: Application of information theory to the assessment of computed toography. *Med Phys* 6:83, 1979.

25. Karis JP, Johnson GA, Glover GH: Signal-to-noise improvements in three-dimensional NMR microscopy using limited-angle excitation. *J Mag Res* 71:24, 1987.

26. Brunner P, Ernst RR: "Sensitivity and performance time in NMR imaging. *J Mag Res* 33:83, 1979.

27. Edelstein WA, Bottomley PA, Hart HR, Smith LS: Signal noise, and contrast in nuclear magnetic resonance (NMR) imaging. *J Comp Assist Tomog* 7:391, 1983.

28. Ortendahl DA, Hylton NM, Kaufman L, Crooks LE: Signal to noise in derived NMR images. *Mag Res Med* 1:316, 1984.

29. Wagner RF, Brown DG: Unified SNR analysis of medical imaging systems. *Phys Med Biol* 30:489, 1985.

30. Callaghan PT, Eccles CD: Sensitivity and resolution in NMR imaging. *J Mag Res* 71:426, 1987.

31. Vinitski S, Griffey R, Fuka M, Matwiyoff N, Prost R: Effect of the sampling rate on magnetic resonance imaging. *Mag Res Med* 5:278, 1987.

32. Carlson J, Crooks L, Ortendahl D, et al: Signal to noise ratio and section thickness in two-dimensional versus three-dimensional Fourier transform MR imaging. *Radiology* 166;266, 1988.

33. Parker DL, Gullberg GT: Signal to noise efficiency in magnetic resonance imaging. *Med Phys* 17:250, 1990.

34. Henkleman RM: Measurement of signal intensities in the presence of noise in MR images. *Med Phys* 12:232, 1985.

35. Parker DL, Haacke EM: Signal-to-noise, contrast-to-noise and resolution, in Potchen EJ, Haacke EM, Siebert JE, et al (eds): *Magnetic Resonance Angiography, Concepts and Applications.* St. Louis, Mosby, pp. 56–79, 1993.

36. Haacke EM, Masaryk TJ, Wielopolski PA, et al: Optimizing blood vessel contrast in fast three-dimensinal MRI. *Mag Res Med* 14:202, 1990.

37. Chao PW, Goldberg H, Dumoulin CL, Wehrli FW: Comparison of time of flight versus phase contrast techniques: Visualization of the intra- and extracerebral carotid artery. *Proc Soc Mag Med* August 1989.

38. Masaryk TJ, Modic MT, Ross JS, et al: Intracranial circulation: Preliminary clinical results with three-dimensional (volume) MR angiography. *Radiology* 171:793, 1989.

39. Parker DL, Yuan C, Blatter DD: MR angiography by multiple thin slab 3D acquisition. *Mag Res Med* 17:434, 1991.

40. Blatter DD, Parker DL, Robinson RO: Cerebral MR angiography with multiple overlapping thin slab acquisition. *Radiology* 179:805, 1991.

41. Wood ML, Henkelman RM: MR image artifacts from periodic motion. *Med Phys* 12:143, 1985.

42. Duerk JL, Wendt RE: Motion artifacts and motion compensation, in Potchen EJ, Haacke EM, Siebert JE, et al (eds): *Magnetic Resonance Angiography, Concepts and Applications.* St. Louis, Mosby, pp. 80–133, 1993.

43. Firmin DN, Nayler GL, Kilner PJ, Longmore DB: The application of phase shifts in NMR for flow measurements. *Mag Res Med* 14:230, 1990.

Chapter 3

Phase-Contrast Magnetic Resonance Angiography

Charles L. Dumoulin

Perhaps the most important reason for the success of magnetic resonance (MR) imaging is the relatively large number of intrinsic parameters which contribute to contrast in an image. Whereas x-ray methods are sensitive to a single intrinsic parameter (electron density) and ultrasound methods are sensitive to two (tissue reflectivity and motion), MR methods can make use of many intrinsic parameters. These parameters include the concentration of the nuclei which generate the MR signal (proton density), the chemical environment of the nuclei (chemical shift), motion on a molecular scale (T1, T2), motion on a microscopic scale (diffusion and perfusion), and motion on a macroscopic scale (blood flow).

Of these parameters, macroscopic motion has proven to be most useful in magnetic resonance angiography (MRA). The term *magnetic resonance angiography* describes a variety of magnetic resonance imaging (MRI) methods in which blood vessel images are created by the selective detection of macroscopic blood motion. There are two general classes of MRA procedures which are defined by the two fundamental flow effects in MR: time-of-flight phenomena and phase-shift phenomena. Each of these classes contains a variety of implementations having a variety of clinical uses, and it appears that different clinical problems are best served by different MRA methods. Both classes of MRA have properties which make them fundamentally different from x-ray angiography (and each other), and it is essential that these differences be recognized whenever MRA is used. This chapter focuses on the class of MRA methods which exploits the phenomena of flow-induced phase shifts.

HISTORY OF PHASE-CONTRAST METHODS

Flow measurement with MR was demonstrated long before the development of magnetic resonance imaging (MRI).

Early work by Singer[1] and Hahn[2] explored the relationships of flow phenomena in nonimaging applications using both time-of-flight and phase-sensitive methods. In 1982, Moran[3] published a theoretical analysis of velocity-induced phase shifts in the context of MR imaging. It was not until 1985, however, that the first MR angiograms were demonstrated by Wedeen et al.[4] In Wedeen's technique, cardiac-grated spin-echo images were obtained at systole and diastole. Difference images were then calculated to highlight arterial flow. Arterial structures were visualized because the distribution of blood velocity within the imaged volume caused phase cancellation and hence loss of signal at systole but not at diastole. Due to the duration of the exam and its insensitivity to smaller vessels, particularly those with only slightly pulsatile or steady flow, the technique has not seen much clinical use.

Wedeen's method was able to selectively image blood vessels because the characteristics of the imaged blood varied during the cardiac cycle. To overcome some of the limitations of Wedeen's method, several researchers proposed an alternative strategy in which the flow sensitivity of the pulse sequence was varied. With the new method, data were acquired with and without flow compensation gradient pulses.[5–7] Complex differences between compensated and uncompensated images were computed to highlight vessels containing a distribution of blood velocity. Although these difference images have proven to be superior to systolic/diastolic difference images, compensated/uncompensated MRA is not heavily used today.

Concurrently with Wedeen's work, Dumoulin and Hart[8] developed a gradient echo technique that relied on additional gradient pulses to create discrete velocity-induced phase shifts rather than signal cancellation. Their technique, called phase-contrast MRA, reduced the imaging time to only a few minutes and allowed more precise detection of blood flow, even in the presence of steady flow. Subsequent developments in phase-contrast MRA have included time-resolved[9-10] and three-dimensional imaging procedures.[11] Two- and three-dimensional phase-contrast methods have come into wide clinical use. They are fundamentally different than other forms of MRA (particularly time-of-flight MRA). Consequently, it is important that the unique characteristics of phase-contrast methods be understood.

Velocity-Induced Phase Shifts

There are two basic flow phenomena in MR which alter the appearance of moving blood. The first phenomenon, frequently referred to as the *time-of-flight effect*, arises from the movement of blood during a relatively long period of time. This phenomenon occurs when blood in one region of the body has an amount of longitudinal magnetization which is different from that found within the field of view of the image. As this blood moves into the imaged region, its longitudinal spin magnetization causes the blood signal to have a different intensity than that of the surrounding tissue. In most time-of-flight angiography methods, blood enters the imaged region fully relaxed (i.e., with a substantial amount of longitudinal magnetization) and appears bright because the signal from stationary tissue within the imaged region is suppressed by saturation effects. In other time-of-flight procedures, known as "black blood" methods, the blood is intentionally saturated and appears dark within the imaged region.

The second MR flow phenomenon occurs whenever transverse magnetization is created in blood and the blood moves in the direction of a magnetic field gradient. When this gradient has a time dependency such as the one shown in Fig. 3-1, the phase of transverse spin magnetization in the blood is shifted by an amount directly proportional to velocity. Since conventional MRI sequences generate transverse magnetization and since most have bipolar gradient pulses,

this effect is a common source of image artifacts. Fortunately, the same physical processes can be exploited to form angiographic images.

When a magnetic field gradient is applied in an MRI system, the magnetic field is made to vary with position across the region of interest. Transverse magnetization at different locations along such a gradient resonates at different frequencies. Nuclei experiencing a stronger magnetic field resonate at a higher frequency than those experiencing a lower field. As different nuclei resonate at different frequencies, they acquire phase shifts with respect to each other which are directly proportional to the position of each nucleus. These phase shifts grow with the duration of the magnetic field gradient but at the same time are proportional to position (and thus encode position).

The position-dependent phase shifts generated by a magnetic field gradient can be undone by applying a second magnetic field gradient of equal duration but opposite polarity. This is illustrated in Fig. 3-2 by the phase shifts Φ_{S1} and Φ_{S2}. If the nuclei move during the interval between the first and second gradient pulses, however, the phase shift induced by the first pulse, Φ_{M1}, will not be exactly canceled by that of the second pulse, Φ_{M2}. The residual phase shift will be directly proportional to the distance that the nuclei traveled in the interval between the gradient pulses, and thus it will also be proportional to the flow velocity. This phase change, illustrated in Fig. 3-3, is the key to phase-sensitive flow-imaging procedures such as phase-sensitive flow quantification and phase-contrast MRA.

The most common flow-encoding gradient waveform is the simple bipolar gradient pulse described above and shown in Fig. 3-1. This waveform induces a phase shift that is independent of position but is proportional to velocity and higher-order terms of motion such as acceleration. More complicated gradient waveforms can be used to create motion-induced phase shifts which are proportional to any com-

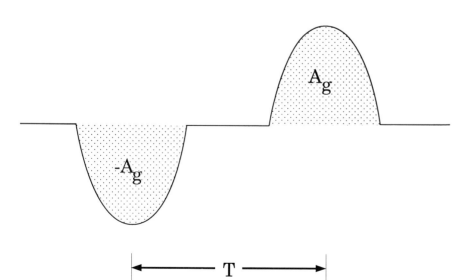

FIGURE 3-1 The bipolar flow-encoding gradient pulse. The first lobe dephases transverse magnetization by an amount proportional to position. The second lobe rephases the magnetization. If the magnetization moves in the interval between the pulses, however, the cancellation of the induced phase shift is incomplete. The residual phase shift is proportional to velocity.

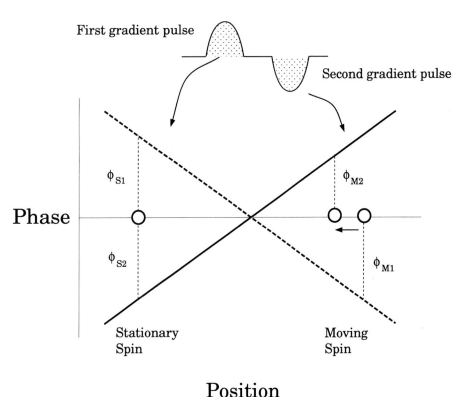

FIGURE 3-2 The effect of a bipolar gradient pulse on the phase of stationary and moving spin magnetization. The first magnetic field gradient lobe of the bipolar pulse induces a phase shift which is proportional to position. The second lobe also induces a phase shift, but this phase shift has an opposite sign. The phase shifts induced in stationary nuceli by the first and second lobes, Φ_{S1} and Φ_{S2}, cancel upon subtraction. The phase shifts for moving nuclei, Φ_{M1} and Φ_{M2}, on the other hand, are not equal and thus do not entirely cancel. The residual phase shift is proportional to the nuclei's velocity.

bination of these terms. Spin-echo versions of flow-encoding gradient pulses are also possible if a refocusing rf pulse is placed between the gradient lobes and if both lobes have the same polarity. Spin-echo flow-encoding pulses are rarely used for angiography, however, because they create larger eddy currents than bipolar flow-encoding pulses in addition to increasing the echo time (TE).

CHARACTERISTICS OF PHASE-CONTRAST MRA

Flow Specificity

In phase-contrast MRA procedures, the source of image contrast is blood motion. Flow-encoding gradient pulses are used to induce signal phase shifts which are proportional to velocity. These phase-shifted signals are detected in the presence of non-phase-shifted signals from stationary tissue. All of the signals are then stored as complex numbers (i.e., numbers which have both magnitude and phase) inside the imaging system. Unless the phases of the signals are displayed, however, the phase-shifted signals from flowing blood are not readily distinguished from the nonshifted signals arising from stationary tissue.

To suppress unwanted stationary tissue in the angiogram, phase-contrast methods collect data twice. The first data set is obtained with flow-encoding gradients of a given polarity. The second data set is acquired under identical conditions except that the flow-encoding gradients are given the oppo-

site polarity. The difference between the two acquired data sets is then computed. Signals from stationary tissue have no velocity-induced phase shifts and thus cancel upon subtraction. If the velocity is the same for each measurement, however, the velocity-induced phase shift of the second data set has an opposite mathematical sign than that of the first. Consequently, signals from moving nuclei combine additively and are preserved as illustrated in Fig. 3-4. The intensity of each pixel in the final image is usually generated by determining either (a) the magnitude of the complex difference of the two data sets or (b) the difference between the phase shifts in each data set.

Velocity Aliasing and Sensitivity

The velocity sensitivity of a phase-contrast angiogram is determined by the amplitude and duration of the flow-encoding gradient pulses. These gradient pulses induce a phase shift in the acquired data which is proportional to velocity. Very strong gradient pulses (or, conversely, very fast velocities) can result in phase shifts in excess of $+/- \pi$ radians. When this happens, the detected phase shifts are indistinguishable from those obtained from blood traveling at a lower velocity. This "aliasing" of information can lead to severe image artifacts. Fortunately, velocity aliasing in phase-contrast angiograms can be avoided by selecting a flow-encoding gradient which will not induce more that a 90° phase shift for all moving blood in the image. The velocity giving a 90° phase shift for a selected flow-encoding gradient is often

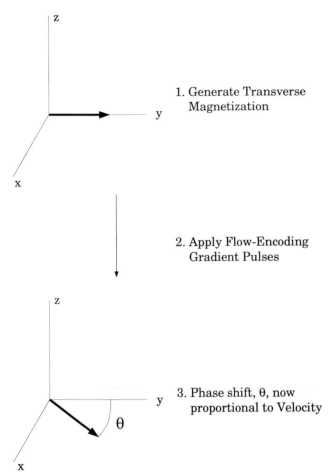

FIGURE 3-3   Velocity-induced phase shifts in transverse spin magnetization. In the first step, transverse spin magnetization is created by nutating longitudinal spin magnetization with an rf pulse. This transverse magnetization is represented as a vector in the *xy* plane. Then a flow-encoding gradient pulse is applied. This flow-encoding pulse induces a phase shift which is independent of the location of the nuclei within the magnet but is proportional to velocity. The phase shift, denoted as θ in step 3, is the angle of rotation that has been induced in the vector representing the transverse magnetization. It can be expressed as either radians (i.e., a number between $-\pi$ and π) or as degrees (-180 to $180°$). Note that this effect is the fundamental phenomenon of phase-sensitive MRA methods.

used to characterize the strength of the flow-encoding gradient and is frequently referred to as V_{enc}.

When the magnitude of the complex difference is displayed in an angiogram, the pixel intensity is approximately proportional to velocity only if the velocity induces a phase shift less than about 1 radian (i.e., 57.29°). When the phase of the complex difference is displayed, however, the pixel intensity is directly proportional to velocity over a greater dynamic range. The relationship between pixel intensity and velocity for both display strategies, are shown in Fig. 3-5. Both display strategies work well for most applications, although the appearance of pixel intensity discontinuities due to velocity aliasing is more striking in phase-difference images. In addition, suppression of stationary tissue in phase-

difference displays is sometimes incomplete due to small phase errors introduced into the data by instrument imperfections. This effect is frequently minimized by scaling each pixel in the phase difference display by its magnitude.

The ability to select the flow-encoding strength gives the operator a great deal of power in determining the final appearance of the angiogram. Very slow flow or very high flow velocities can be detected by adjusting the strength of the flow encoding. The detected phase shifts also carry directional information which frequently proves to be diagnostically useful. Phase-contrast methods are equally sensitive to flow in all directions and rarely suffer from signal loss due to spin saturation as the blood penetrates the imaged volume.

The sensitivity of phase-contrast angiograms to velocity is related to the signal-to-noise ratio of the image. If the signal-to-noise ratio is high, the range of velocities which can be detected without aliasing is also high. This relationship arises because the maximum velocity detectable without aliasing is determined by the strength of the flow-encoding gradient pulses, while the minimum detectable velocity is determined by both the strength of the flow-encoding gradient and the level of the random noise in the image. When the sigal-to-noise ratio is low, random variations in amplitude and phase obscure smaller velocity-induced phase shifts. Fortunately, several strategies can be employed to maximize the signal-to-noise ratio. These include the use of high field magnets, optimum receiver coil design, longer acquisition times, and the use of larger image voxels.

Vector Addition of Flow Components

In phase-contrast angiography, only the component of flow parallel to the flow-encoding gradient contributes to the velocity-induced phase shift. If the blood vessels are aligned primarily in a single direction, detection of a single component of flow may be sufficient. If tortuous vessels are imaged, however, flowing blood will have components in all directions and a single component image may be inadequate. To obtain a total flow image, the individual flow components must be detected by the application of discrete flow-encoding gradient pulses. These components can then be mathematically combined using the Pythagorean relationship:

$$I = \sqrt{x^2 + y^2 + z^2}$$

where I is the pixel intensity of the resultant image and x, y, and z are the pixel intensities of the individual flow components. Note that simultaneous application of flow-encoding gradient pulses in multiple directions simply creates a flow-encoding gradient in an oblique direction.

Background Suppression

One of the most important technical attributes of a phase-contrast angiogram is the suppression of background signals

Stationary spins:

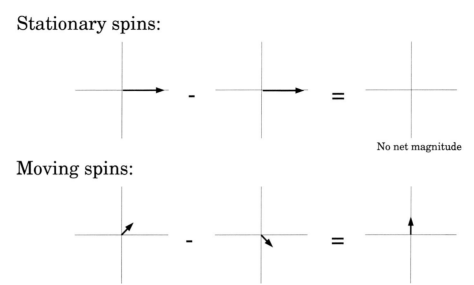

No net magnitude

Moving spins:

FIGURE 3-4 Vector representation of the suppression of stationary tissue and the preservation of moving blood in phase-contrast angiography. In a phase-contrast procedure, two sets of data are collected. The first data set is collected with a bipolar gradient pulse (e.g., a positive lobe followed by a negative lobe), which induces a phase shift proportional to velocity. The second data set is collected in an identical fashion except that the polarity of the bipolar gradient is reversed (e.g., a negative lobe followed by a positive lobe). The difference between these two data sets is then calculated. Stationary tissue is not affected, since the flow-encoding pulses induce a phase shift proportional to velocity and the velocity of stationary tissue is zero. Consequently, the signals from stationary tissue are canceled upon subtraction of the detected signals, as illustrated in the top row of the figure. Signals from moving blood, on the other hand, undergo a phase shift proportional to the blood's velocity and has a mathematical sign controlled by the gradient polarity. Consequently, when the difference is calculated, the signals from moving blood add constructively and appear in the angiogram.

arising from stationary tissue. If the stationary tissue signal component is substantially larger than the signals from flowing blood, small fluctuations in stationary tissue signals may lead to inaccuracies in subtraction. These inaccuracies will in turn leave residual stationary tissue pixels which are comparable in amplitude to the pixels containing flow information. Poor suppression due to subtraction of large background signals is rarely a problem in many MRA procedures, but it can present a problem for those protocols in which the volume of the acquired voxel is relatively large (e.g., projective two-dimensional methods).

To overcome the problem of poor stationary tissue suppression caused by large stationary tissue signals, a small magnetic field inhomogeneity can be introduced into the volume of interest. This is easily accomplished by the application of a magnetic field gradient along the direction of the projection, as shown in Fig. 3-6. In this illustration, an observer (the eye) uses MR to look at an object having uniform density. In the presence of a uniform magnetic field (right), signals from each part of the object occur at the same frequency and phase. Consequently, when the signals are detected, they add constructively and give a relatively large signal intensity. If the object is detected in the presence of a magnetic field gradient (left), however, nuclei at different

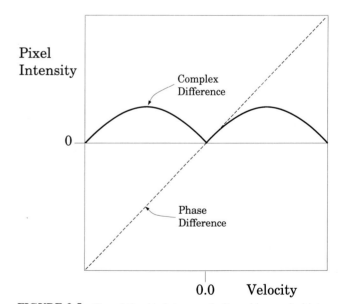

FIGURE 3-5 The relationship between velocity and image pixel intensity in phase-contrast angiography. The data can be displayed as either the magnitude of the complex difference or as the difference of the phases. In both cases, if the phase shift is too large, it becomes indistinguishable from a smaller phase shift (an effect called *aliasing*). Note that phase difference displays produce a more linear response than magnitude displays but can have more severe discontinuities in the event of velocity aliasing.

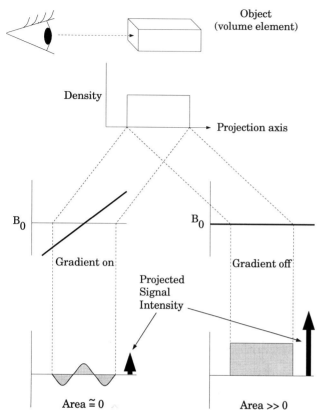

FIGURE 3-6 The effect of projection dephasing on a large object. In this figure an observer (the eye) is using MR to look at an object. The density of the object is uniform and is examined in the absence of a magnetic field gradient (*right*) or in the presence of a magnetic field gradient (*left*). Without the gradient, all the detected signals occur at the same frequency and phase and thus add constructively to give a relatively large signal intensity. If the object is detected in the presence of a magnetic field gradient applied in the direction of the projection, however, nuclei at different locations resonate at different frequencies and have different phase shifts. This results in destructive interference of signals from the various parts of the object and a much weaker signal intensity. Signals from small objects, such as blood vessels, are unaffected, since the strength of the dephasing gradient is chosen so that small objects have only a small frequency distribution along the projection direction.

locations along the gradient resonate at different frequencies and develop different phase shifts. This results in destructive interference of signals from the various parts of the object and a much weaker signal intensity. Signals from small objects, such as blood vessels, are unaffected, since the strength of the dephasing gradient is chosen so that small objects have only a small frequency distribution in the projection direction.

Quantitative Measurements

Although quantitative flow information exists in the magnitude of the complex difference data presented in many phase-contrast angiograms,[12] it may be difficult to extract reliably. Phase-difference presentations, on the other hand, are easily analyzed and readily provide quantitative velocity informa-

tion. Quantitative phase information can also be extracted with nonangiographic techniques. Several methods create velocity-induced phase shifts in cross-sectional images of selected vessels.[13–15] Other methods display velocity as an image dimension rather than as a pixel phase shift.[16–19] In these methods, the phase-encoding dimension of the image is detected with bipolar velocity-encoding gradient pulses rather than unipolar spatial-encoding pulses. When velocity is acquired as an image dimension, artifacts arising from distributions of phase shifts within an imaged voxel are greatly reduced. Both peak and mean velocities are easily measured in a display format similar to that of Doppler ultrasound.

Multiplexed Flow Encoding

Phase-contrast angiograms are sensitive only to the component of flow that is parallel to the direction of the applied flow-encoding gradient pulse. Consequently, data from three orthogonal flow-sensitive directions must be collected to construct a complete flow angiogram. Since the MR signal is detected twice in a phase angiogram for each of these flow directions, a total of six acquisitions are required for each point in the data matrix.

The inherent information contained in a six-excitation phase-contrast acquisition has only four components: stationary-tissue information and flow information in three orthogonal directions. Two multiplexing schemes have been proposed to obtain these four components more efficiently. The first scheme employs a four-excitation phase-contrast sequence in which one data set is acquired in the absence of flow encoding, and the remaining three data sets are acquired with three mutually orthogonal flow-encoding gradient pulses. Complex differences are then computed between the nonencoded data and the individual flow components. The total flow image is created by combining the three flow-component images using the Pythagorean relationship.

A second approach to multiplexed detection of multiple flow components uses a Hadamard transform.[20–22] With Hadamard encoding, it is possible to acquire the same information more efficiently in a four-excitation phase-contrast acquisition. In this method, four excitations are performed for each point in the data matrix. Flow encoding occurs on all gradient axes for each excitation, but each excitation has a unique combination of flow-encoding gradient pulse polarities. For example, the flow-encoding gradient pulses in the *x, y,* and *z* directions for the four excitations of a multiplexed acquisition can take form:

| | | Gradient axis | | |
		x	*y*	*z*
Excitation	1	−	−	−
	2	+	+	−
	3	+	−	+
	4	−	+	+

Where − and + denote flow-encoding gradients of opposite polarity. The stationary tissue component and three orthogonal flow components can then be extracted by taking the following linear combinations of the acquired data to give data sets:

$$\text{Stationary tissue} = \text{Ex}_1 + \text{Ex}_2 + \text{Ex}_3 + \text{Ex}_4$$
$$x \text{ flow component} = -\text{Ex}_1 + \text{Ex}_2 + \text{Ex}_3 - \text{Ex}_4$$
$$y \text{ flow component} = -\text{Ex}_1 + \text{Ex}_2 - \text{Ex}_3 + \text{Ex}_4$$
$$z \text{ flow component} = -\text{Ex}_1 - \text{Ex}_2 + \text{Ex}_3 + \text{Ex}_4$$

where Ex_i represents the data from the ith excitation.

PHASE-CONTRAST MRA TECHNIQUES

The term *phase-contrast MRA* describes a certian type of imaging procedure, but in reality there are many phase-contrast methods, each having some unique features and limitations. Because of the relative strengths and weaknesses of each method and the complicated nature of flow in the body, different clinical applications are best served by different imaging protocols. Various phase-contrast methods have been used for peripheral,[23] abdominal,[24–26] neck,[27] and cranial vessels.[28–30]

Two-Dimensional Phase-Contrast Angiography

Phase-contrast MRA pulse sequences are created by incorporating flow-encoding gradient pulses into conventional gradient recalled imaging sequences. Scan orientation, slice thickness, and field of view are not affected by the presence of a flow-encoding pulse and retain their normal function. Two-dimensional (2D) phase-contrast angiograms can easily be obtained in thin slices (e.g., 3 to 5 mm). Since the phase-contrast mechanism efficiently suppresses signals from stationary tissue, however, it is frequently possible to obtain images from relatively thick sections (e.g., 2 to 10 cm). Thick slices are particularly useful in minimizing scan times, since a projection angiogram, even one taken with a slice thickness which encompasses the entire body, can be obtained in the same scan time as a conventional thin-slice image.

The speed of 2D phase-contrast procedures can be advantageously used in a number of ways. For example, speed can be used to shorten the overall patient exam time. Quite often, however, it is useful to acquire additional data to provide more diagnostic information. With 2D phase-contrast MRA, this might include additional view angles or slice locations. Alternatively, certain types of artifacts can be minimized by acquiring additional data. For example, phase-encoding artifacts arising from changes in blood velocity during the cardiac cycle can be minimized by detecting the average velocity-induced phase shift rather than one detected at an arbitrary instant in time. This can be done by acquiring data with a relatively large number of excitations (NEX).

For example, with a repetition time (TR) of 50 ms and a heart rate of 60 beats per minute, choosing NEX to be about 20 will cause velocity variations during the cardiac cycle to be averaged.

One limitation of projective MR methods is that the image voxel is highly anisotropic. The in-plane resolution of the image may be high, but each voxel has a depth that can be as large as the thickness of the anatomy being imaged. Overlapping vessels in a projection angiogram can share image voxels yet be physically in regions having different magnetic field strengths, particularly if a projection dephasing magnetic field gradient is used. If this happens, signals from each vessel may have different absolute phases, and destructive interference of signals in the overlapping region is possible. Similarly, if overlapping vessels have very different flow or if a vessel is large enough to have a substantial variation of flow velocities in its projection, anomalous loss of signal is possible.

Two-dimensional phase-contrast MRA has been used for a number of clinical applications. One of the earliest was in the evaluation of carotid artery disease. The method has also proven useful for imaging the sagittal sinus, renal arteries, and vessels of the hand. Figure 3-7 is an example of a two-dimensional phase-contrast angiogram of the hand. The orthogonal flow-component images illustrate the selective nature of the flow sensitivity. The total flow image was generated by combining the individual flow-component images using the Pythagorean relationship described above.

Cine Phase-Contrast Angiography

Cine phase-contrast MRA is a variant of 2D phase-contrast angiography in which images from many points in the cardiac cycle are obtained. Data acquisition can be performed using retrospective gating methods such as those used in cardiac MRI[31,32] or simple cardiac triggering, as illustrated in Fig. 3-8. Both forms of cine phase-contrast MRA have proven particularly useful for applications in the pelvis and extremities, where blood flow is highly dynamic.

Blood flow in the extremities of healthy individuals has a triphasic pattern during the cardiac cycle. During systole, the blood moves with a rapid forward velocity. At the beginning of a diastole, however, the flow reverses. This period of reverse flow is followed by a period of either no flow or slow forward flow for the duration of diastole. Consequently, in nongated techniques, apoproximately two-thirds of the data acquisition occurs when there is no significant flow.

To overcome problems created by changing velocity, cardiac-gated cine angiograms acquire images at multiple points during the cardiac cycle. While the images acquired during periods of slow or no flow may contain little useful information, some images are guaranteed to be acquired during periods of high flow. Because dynamic flow is found primarily in arteries rather than veins, cardiac-gated angiograms can also be used to differentiate arteries from veins.

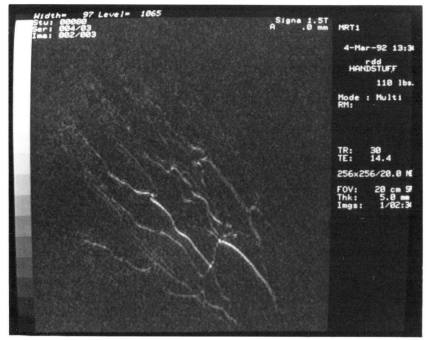

A

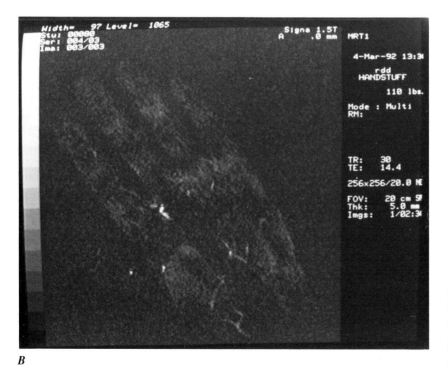

B

FIGURE 3-7 Two-dimensional phase-contrast angiogram of the hand of a healthy volunteer. Three orthogonal flow component images were acquired in the (*A*) *x*, (*B*) *y*, and (*C*) *z* direction. The total flow image (*D*) was generated by using the Pythagorean relationship.

Several strategies for the acquisition of cine phase-contrast angiograms are possible. The earliest methods acquired data in an order which caused data from sequential heartbeats to be subtracted.[9] While this strategy worked well in the head and lower extremity, it was less successful in regions where physiological motion such as breathing and peristalsis cause significant motion of nominally stationary tissue between heartbeats. Artifacts due to these physiological motions are minimized with an alternative strategy,[33,34] in which data from adjacent TR intervals within the same heartbeat are subtracted. Although this method halves the temporal resolution, differences are calculated on pairs of data acquired

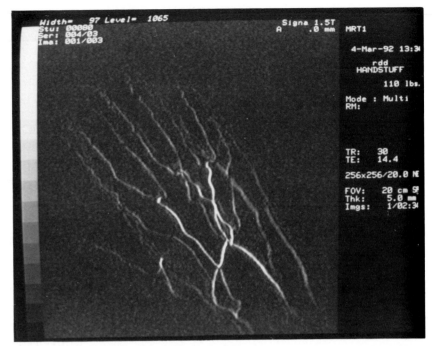

C

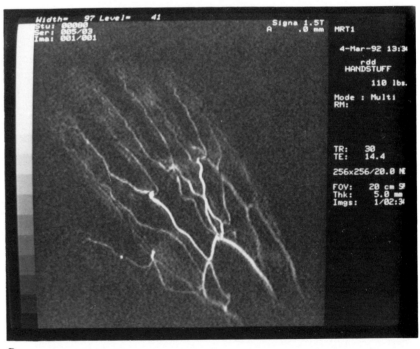

FIGURE 3-7 *(Continued)*   D

within a relatively short period (i.e., TR) during which physiological motion is negligible.

Cine phase-contrast MRA has proven to be useful in a number of clinical applications, including those in the head, neck, and abdomen. The method is particularly well suited to imaging arteries carrying highly pulsatile flow. Figure 3-9 is an example of a cine angiogram taken of the aortic arch of a healthy individual using the acquisition strategy which minimizes artifacts due to physiological motion. This image is a composite image in which three flow-sensitive directions are combined using the Pythagorean relationship for each time frame, and all time frames are combined using a stan-

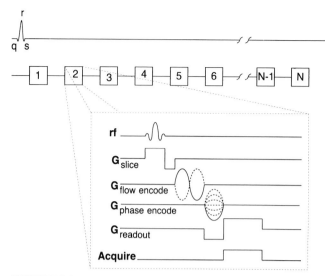

FIGURE 3-8   Time-resolved or cine two-dimensional phase-contrast angiography pulse sequence. The pulse sequence includes an rf excitation pulse and gradient pulse for slice selection, flow encoding, and image formation. The sequence is repeated N times for each cardiac cycle.

dard deviation calculation to highlight the dynamic blood flow.

Three-Dimensional Phase-Contrast MRA

Two-dimensional phase-contrast angiograms have several limitations which can be overcome by the collection of the data in three dimensions. Unlike a projection angiogram, a typical 3D angiogram has approximately isotropic voxels. Phase variations across a voxel are minimized because the voxel dimensions are small. Perhaps the most significant advantage, however, is that the data can be analyzed retrospectively in a number of ways. Subsets of the acquired data can be extracted to remove features which interfere with the presentation of features of interest. Also, two-dimensional projections can easily be generated for any view angle and cross-sections of vessels are readily generated.

Three-dimensional phase-contrast MRA is now widely used for neurovascular and abdominal applications, including the diagnosis of aneurysms, arteriovenous malformations, venous angiomas, and occlusive disease. Figure 3-10 shows three selected stationary tissue images from a Hadamard flow-encoded three-dimensional phase-contrast acquisition of the head of a healthy volunteer. These data were obtained with a voxel resolution of 256 × 256 × 128 and a field of view of 24 cm in all three dimensions. Figure 3-11 shows three selected total-flow projection angiograms obtained from the same data set as in Fig. 3-10. Each projection was obtained with a maximum-pixel algorithm.

Strategies for Vessel Selectivity

With x-ray angiography, vessels are selectively imaged by placing a catheter in the chosen vessel. Veins are distinguished from arteries by virtue of the time delay as the contrast medium passes from the arterial to the venous system. Selective MRA is more difficult, however, since vascular structures are detected by virtue of blood motion rather than the selective replacement of a bolus of blood. Nevertheless, several strategies to isolate selected structures in MR angiograms exist. Some of these strategies are applied during data acquisition and others are applied during postpro-

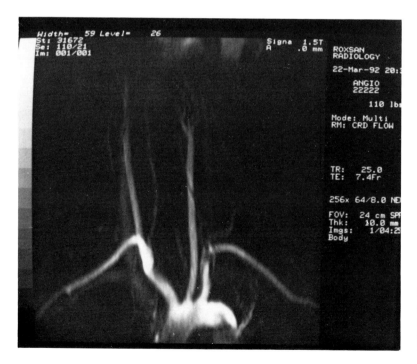

FIGURE 3-9   Cine phase-contrast angiogram of the aortic arch of a healthy volunteer. This image is a composite of data acquired in all three orthogonal flow-sensitive directions and over multiple time frames during the cardiac cycle. (From Dumoulin et al.[34] Reproduced by permission.)

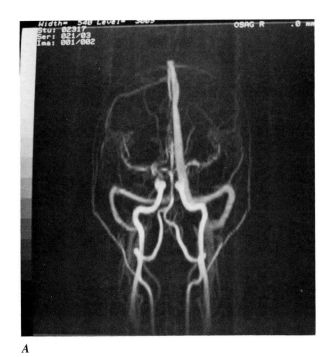

A

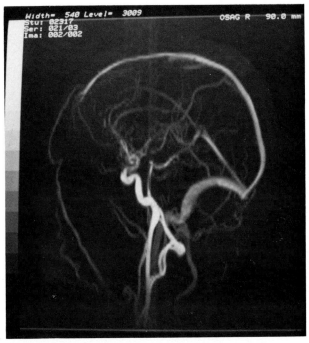

B

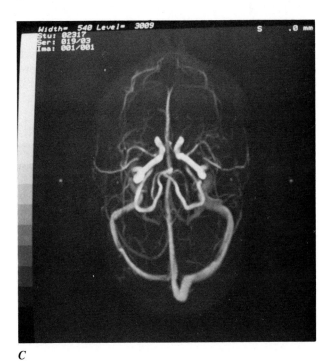

C

FIGURE 3-10   Three stationary tissue images extracted from a Hada-mard flow-encoded three-dimensional MR angiogram of the head. (From Dumoulin et al.[20] Reproduced by permission.)

cessing. These techniques can be used to select vessels by virtue of location, flow direction, mean velocity, and flow dynamics.

SATURATION

Saturation of longitudinal magnetization is a widely used method of selectively removing signals in some vessels. With this method, extra rf pulses are applied in a zone adjacent to the imaged volume. These rf pulses typically have a flip angle between 90 and 135° and are applied in each TR interval. Since these saturation pulses are applied frequently, longitudinal spin magnetization in the saturation zone does not have time to recover and becomes greatly reduced in magnitude. Loss of longitudinal magnetization, in turn, causes a decrease in the amount of transverse magnetization

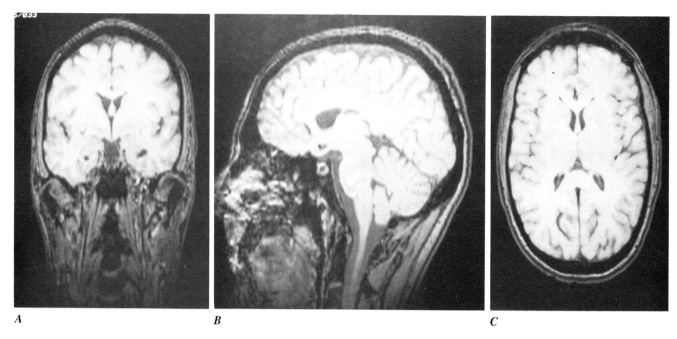

A   *B*   *C*

FIGURE 3-11   Three-phase contrast angiograms extracted from the same data set used in Fig. 3-10. (From Dumoulin et al.[20] Reproduced by permission.)

which can be generated. As blood moves through the saturation zone, it too becomes saturated and loses longitudinal magnetization. Blood entering the imaged region from the opposite direction, however, does not traverse the saturation zone and is imaged with full intensity.

USE OF PHASE INFORMATION

Phase-contrast MRA procedures collect data which contain information about the direction as well as speed of blood flow. Although speed is typically displayed as pixel intensity, alternate displays in which the phase of the moving blood is displayed are usually available. Such a presentation makes the direction of flow in a vessel immediately obvious. Placement of saturation bands solely for the purpose of determining the direction of blood flow is rarely necessary with phase-contrast methods.

RELAXATION CONTRAST AGENTS

Intravenous injections of relaxation agents, such as Gd-DTPA, are widely used to alter the T1 of selected tissues. In neurological applications, for example, Gd-DTPA injections highlight breakdown of the blood-brain barrier, making many neoplasms (and other pathology) more visible.

Contrast agents are also beginning to find use in MRA. Contrast agents make blood more difficult to saturate and thus increases the penetration of relaxed blood into the imaged volume. While helpful in phase-contrast methods, this effect is most dramatic for slowly moving blood (such as

that found in veins) in time-of-flight procedures. With time-of-flight MRA, however, tissues such as mucous membranes, neoplasms, and regions of edema are also highlighted and become more readily visible. Since the source of image information in phase-contrast procedures is motion, however, changes in the T1 of blood and other tissues are a secondary issue. Consequently, the primary benefit of a contrast injection in phase-contrast procedures is an increase in the signal-to-noise ratio (particularly if the flip angle is increased to maximize the available signal). In general, contrast agents make certain vascular structures easier to image but are of limited use in selectively highlighting a given vascular feature.

DIFFERENCES BETWEEN TIME-OF-FLIGHT AND PHASE-CONTRAST MRA

Information Content

Time-of-flight and phase-contrast angiographic procedures contain fundamentally different types of information. Contrast in a time-of-flight angiogram is determined by the relative amounts of spin saturation in the blood and the surrounding tissue. While the degree of saturation in the blood is influenced by velocity, it is also a function of the blood's T1, the geometry of the blood flow, and the pulse repetition time, TR. Stationary tissue signals are suppressed by spin saturation, but the need to visualize vessels in the same region of anatomy limits the strength of the saturation. Suppression of stationary tissue becomes even more difficult when the tissues surrounding the vessel of interest have relatively short relaxation times. This is particularly true for mucosal tissues and certain neoplasms, particularly after an injection of Gd-DPTA.

Image contrast in phase-contrast angiographic procedures, on the other hand, comes only from blood motion. Consequently, total suppression of stationary tissue is possible regardless of its T1. Blood and surrounding stationary tissue can still become saturated during the procedure, but saturation results in a decrease in the signal-to-noise ratio of the moving blood without changing the suppression of the stationary tissue signals.

Complete suppression of stationary tissue in a phase-contrast angiogram makes the visualization of slow flow in smaller vessels easier. It is even possible to visualize flow in vessels smaller than the image voxel, since phase detection of the flowing signal component can occur in the presence of a larger but phase-invariant stationary tissue signal component.

In a time-of-flight angiogram, signals from stationary tissue are suppressed before the acquisition of data. With phase-contrast procedures, however, stationary tissue images can readily be extracted by changing the mathematical combination of the acquired data (i.e., adding instead of subtracting). These stationary tissue images are fully registered with the angiogram and typically have a T1-weighted appearance.

Limitations

Unlike most time-of-flight methods, phase-contrast procedures are independent of the size and placement of the field of view. Two- and three-dimensional protocols using very large fields of view encompassing the abdomen and small fields of view over the hand are possible. This is a consequence of the direct detection of blood motion rather than the detection of an MR parameter such as spin saturation, which is influenced by motion (and other phenomena). Because phase-contrast methods rely only on velocity for contrast, phase-contrast procedures are relatively insensitive to partial saturation effects caused by slow and/or tortuous flow within the volume of interest.

Phase-contrast angiography methods are more demanding on the quality of an MR instrument than almost all other imaging techniques including time-of-flight methods. This is particularly true with respect to system phase stability, since small changes in signal phases have a profound effect on the image. Sources of phase instabilities can include phase and/or gain instability in the receiver, transmitter, and gradient subsystems. Another common source of instability is the creation of eddy currents in metallic structures of the magnet. These eddy currents are created whenever the metallic structures are subjected to a changing magnetic field such as those generated by the imager's gradient subsystem. Fortunately, most modern MR scanners are capable of obtaining high quality phase-contrast angiograms.

Use of Saturation

Saturation can be used to selectively eliminate vessels in both time-of-flight and phase-contrast MRA procedures. The suppression of blood vessels by saturation, however, is intrinsically a time-of-flight method. As the saturated blood moves into the imaged volume, it is no longer subjected to the saturation rf pulses and may eventually reach a new steady state determined by the rf pulses in the imaging volume. In a time-of-flight procedure, this new steady state is similar to that of the surrounding stationary tissue and the blood remains poorly visualized. With phase-contrast procedures, however, the image contrast mechanism is motion rather than saturation, and when the saturated blood reaches its new steady state, enough magnetization may exist to make the vessel visible.

Artifacts

Both time-of-flight and phase-contrast MRA methods tend to suffer from signal loss when the flow is complex or turbulent. This is most often seen in regions of moderate to severe stenosis. Consequently, it is easy to overestimate the degree of stenosis with both time-of-flight and phase-contrast methods. For example in severely stenotic lesions an apparent discontinuity, or occlusion, of the vessel can occur. This occurs when there is a distribution of velocities (and thus velocity-induced phase shifts) within the imaged voxel. Stenoses can be differentiated from occlusions, however, by the reappearance of undisturbed flow distal to the stenosis. Ths use of smaller voxel size and shorter echo times helps to minimize this effect for both time-of-flight and phase-contrast angiography.

Complex and turbulent flow are not the only potential sources of signal loss in magnetic resonance angiography. Both time-of-flight and phase-contrast methods will show signal voids in regions surrounding most surgical clips. This loss of signal is caused by magnetic field susceptibility gradients between the clip and the surrounding tissue. As with complex flow signal loss, signal loss due to susceptibility gradients becomes less severe with shorter echo times.

In two-dimensional time-of-flight angiography, signal loss in regions of vessel stenoses need not arise from complex or turbulent flow effects.[35] Since the nuclei are excited using a thin (typically 2-mm) slice, it is possible for fast-moving blood to traverse the excitation slice in a time which is shorter than the duration of the rf pulse. When this happens, the blood is not excited and does not give an MR signal. If the blood flow is nonturbulent, the same vessel imaged with a phase-contrast or three-dimensional time-of-flight procedure, does not suffer from the loss of signal.

By necessity, phase-contrast angiograms are not flow-compensated in the flow-encoding direction. Consequently, pulsatile flow can cause ghosting artifacts in the phase-encoding direction if the scan is not cardiac-gated. While these artifacts are usually inconsequential, they tend to be more apparent in phase-contrast angiograms than in time-of-flight angiograms because of better suppression of stationary tissue with phase-contrast angiography.

Acquisition Times

Phase-contrast methods can acquire as many as four unique pieces of information for each pixel. Consequently, angiograms in which all three orthogonal flow components are imaged require a minimum of four excitations for each point in the acquired data matrix. Time-of-flight angiograms, on the other hand, require a single excitation. A phase-contrast acquisition is not necessarily four times longer than a comparable time-of-flight angiogram, however. This is because phase-contrast methods typically use the shortest possible TR (e.g., 10 to 16 ms), but time-of-flight methods require a longer TR (e.g., 40 to 50 ms) to maximize the penetration of unsaturated blood into the imaged volume.

CONCLUSIONS

Magnetic resonance angiography is an imaging modality encompassing a number of methods. Two classes of MRA exist; those based on time-of-flight effects or those based on velocity-induced phase shifts. While no single method has been demonstrated to be clearly superior to the others in all situations, it is becoming apparent that different clinical applications are best served by different MRA techniques.

Phase-contrast methods have unique features which make them the method of choice in a number of clinical situations. Although demanding on instrument requirements, phase-contrast methods are sensitive to a wide range of blood velocities and are independent of the field-of-view and vessel geometry. Furthermore, the source of image contrast in phase-contrast angiography is motion. Consequently, complete suppression of stationary tissue is usually possible, and the only features that appear in these images arise from blood flow.

Much progress in this field has been made since the first MR angiograms were obtained. Magnetic resonance angiography has already replaced x-ray angiography in several clinical applications and is used as an adjunct in others. Some clinical applications are still best served by x-ray methods and perhaps will always be. Nevertheless, the prospects for future developments in techniques and instrumentation are excellent, and advancements in the clinical utility of MRA are certain to occur.

REFERENCES

1. Singer JR: Blood flow rates by nuclear magnetic resonance. *Science* 130:1652, 1959.
2. Hahn EL: Detection of sea-water motion by nuclear precession. *J Geophys Res* 65:776, 1960.
3. Moran PR: A flow velocity zeugmatographic interlace for NMR imaging in humans. *Mag Res Imaging* 1:197, 1982.
4. Wedeen VJ, Meuli RA, Edelman RR, et al: Projective imaging of pulsatile flow with magnetic resonance. *Science* 230:946, 1985.
5. Wedeen VJ, Rosen BR, Buston R, et al: Projective MRI angiography and quantitative flow-volume densitometry. *Mag Res Med* 3:226, 1986.
6. Axel L, Morton D: MR flow imaging by velocity-compensated/uncompensated difference images. *J Comput Assist Tomogr* 11:31, 1987.
7. Laub GA, Kaiser WA: MR angiography with gradient motion refocusing. *J Comput Assist Tomogr* 12:377, 1988.
8. Dumoulin CL, Hart HR: Magnetic resonance angiography. *Radiology* 161:717, 1986.
9. Dumoulin CL, Souza SP, Walker MF, et al: Time-resolved magnetic resonance angiography. *Mag Res Med* 6:275, 1988.
10. Souza SP, Dumoulin CL: Dynamic magnetic resonance angiography. *Dynam Cardiovasc Imaging* 1:126, 1987.
11. Dumoulin CL, Souza SP, Walker MF, et al: Three-dimensional phase contrast angiography. *Mag Res Med* 9:139, 1989.
12. Walker MF, Souza SP, Dumoulin CL: Quantitative flow measurement in phase contrast MR angiography. *J Comput Assist Tomogr* 12:304, 1988.
13. van Dijk P: Direct cardiac NMR imaging of heart wall and blood flow velocity. *J Comput Assist Tomogr* 8:429, 1984.
14. Bryant DJ, Payne JA, Firmin DN, et al: Measurement of flow with NMR imaging using gradient pulse and phase difference technique. *J Comput Assist Tomogr* 8:588, 1984.
15. Young IR, Bydder GM, Payne JA: Flow measurement by the development of phase differences during slice formation in MR imaging. *Mag Res Med* 2:555, 1985.
16. Feinberg DA, Crooks LE, Sheldon P, et al: Magnetic resonance imaging of the velocity vector components of fluid flow. *Mag Res Med* 2:555, 1985.
17. Henning J, Muri M, Brunner P, et al: Quantitative flow measurement with the fast Fourier flow technique, *Radiology* 166:237, 1988.
18. Souza SP, Steinberg FL, Caro C, et al: Velocity- and cardiac phase-resolved MR flow imaging, in Proceedings, 8th Annual Meeting of the Society of Magnetic Resonance in Medicine, Amsterdam, 1989, p. 102.
19. Dumoulin CL, Souza SP, Hardy CJ, et al: Quantitative measurement of blood flow using cylindrically localized Fourier velocity encoding. *Mag Res Med* 21:242, 1991.
20. Dumoulin CL, Souza SP, Darrow RD, et al: Simultaneous acquisition of phase-contrast angiograms and stationary tissue images with Hadamard encoding of flow-induced phase shifts. *J Mag Res Imaging* 1:399, 1991.
21. Pelc NJ, Bernstein MA, Shimakawa A, et al: Encoding strategies for three-direction phase-contrast MR imaging of flow. *J Mag Res Imaging* 1:405, 1991.
22. Hausmann R, Lewin JS, Laub G: Phase-contrast MR angiography with reduced acquisition time: New concepts in sequence design. *J Mag Res Imaging* 1:415, 1991.
23. Steinberg FL, Yucel EK, Dumoulin CL, et al: Peripheral vascular and abdominal applications of MR flow imaging, *Mag Res Med* 14:315, 1990.
24. Yuasa Y, Endo M, Tanimoto A, et al: Abdominal two dimensional phase contrast angiography, in Proceedings, 8th Annual Meeting of the Society of Magnetic Resonance in Medicine, Amsterdam, 1989, p. 233.
25. Dumoulin CL, Yucel EK, Vock P, et al: Two- and three-dimensional phase contrast MR angiography of the abdomen. *J Comput Assist Tomogr* 14:779, 1990.

26. Vock P, Terrier F, Wegmuller H, et al: Magnetic resonance angiography of abdominal vessels: Early experiences using the three-dimensional phase-contrast technique. *Br J Radiol* 64:10, 1991.

27. Kido DK, Barsotti JB, Rice LZ, et al: Evaluation of the carotid artery bifurcation: Comparison of magnetic resonance angiography and digital subtraction arch aortography. *Neuroradiology* 33:48, 1991.

28. Pernicone JR, Siebert JE, Potchen EJ, et al: Three-dimensional phase-contrast MR angiography in the head and neck: Preliminary report. *Am J Radiol* 155:167, 1990.

29. Huston J, Rufenacht DA, Ehman RL, et al: Intracranial aneurysms and vascular malformations: Comparisons of time-of-flight and phase-contrast MR angiography. *Radiology* 181:721, 1991.

30. Nussel F, Wegmuller H, Huber P: Comparison of magnetic resonance angiography, magnetic resonance imaging and conventional angiography in cerebral arteriovenous malformation. *Neuroradiology*, 33:56, 1991.

31. Glover GH, Pelc NJ: A rapid-gated cine MRI technique, in Kressel HY (ed): *Magnetic Resonance Annual 1988*. New York, Raven Press, 1988.

32. Pelc NH, Herfkens RJ, Pelc LR: Phase-contrast MR imaging measurement of myocardial motion. *J Mag Res Imaging* 1:181, 1991.

33. Lanzer P, Bohning D, Groen J, et al: Aortoiliac and femoropopliteal phase-based NMR angiography: A comparison between FLAG and RSE. *Mag Res Med* 15:372, 1990.

34. Dumoulin CL, Steinberg FL, Yucel EK: Reduction of peristalsis and breathing artifacts in phase-contrast magnetic resonance angiography of the chest and abdomen. *J Comput Assist Tomogr* 17:328, 1993.

35. Cousins JP, Wagle WA, Zirinsky K, et al: High-velocity flow detected with phase-contrast MR angiography but not with time-of-flight MR angiography. *Radiology* 185:203, 1992.

Chapter 4

Intracranial Magnetic Resonance Angiography

Richard L. Robertson, Jr. / Philip A. Blaustein
R. Gil Gonzalez

Intracranial magnetic resonance angiographs (MRA) has advanced rapidly in recent years and is the subject of continued technical refinements. The development of intracranial MRA is driven by the need to image small tortuous vessels in a wide variety of pathological states. This chapter will present the general principles of intracranial MRA as well as specific sequences which can be performed in various clinical settings.

Two MRA bright-blood techniques, time-of-flight (TOF) and phase-contrast (PC) MRA, are currently in widespread use. The physical principles underlying these techniques have been previously described in detail.[1,2] Time-of-flight imaging uses repetitive radio frequency (RF) pulses to suppress stationary tissues. The unsuppressed spins of inflowing blood are then used to create a vascular image. Phase contrast imaging utilizes a subtraction technique in which moving protons acquire a phase shift proportional to their velocity during the application of a biopolar gradient. The net phase shift of stationary protons is zero. Both TOF and PC sequences have unique advantages and disadvantages which must be considered when establishing imaging protocols.

Time-of-flight imaging is more widely available and requires a shorter acquisition time for a given spatial resolution than PC study. Time-of-flight techniques have the additional advantage of being sensitive to the wide range of flow velocities encountered in the intracranial circulation, where vessel caliber varies considerably. The major disadvantage of TOF is that background tissue suppression is less effective than with PC. The poorer background suppression of TOF results from the dependency of these sequences on repetitive RF pulses to effect stationary tissue suppression. Tissues having a short T1, such as fat or methemoglobin, recover significant longitudinal magnetization between RF pulses and can demonstrate high signal intensity mimicking flow.

Phase-contrast imaging is an alternative imaging strategy to TOF. It is less dependent on T1 effects than TOF and therefore provides superior background tissue suppression without interference from fat or blood products. Phase-constrast studies are also capable of yielding velocity-of-flow information which is not readily obtainable with TOF. The major deterrants to the routine use of PC techniques are their relatively long acquisition and postprocessing times as well as their sensitivity to a restricted velocity range, which must be specified prior to the initiation of the scan. Velocities greater than the chosen velocity-encoding gradient value will be aliased, resulting in signal loss. The problem of aliasing is of particular importance in evaluating regions of stenosis where high velocities are encountered.

Intracranial MRA can be performed with either two-dimensional (2D) (multislice) or three-dimensional (3D) (volume) Fourier transform acquisition. In a multislice sequence, an individual slice thickness is obtained by alterations in the strength of the gradient orthogonal to the plane of the slice.[3] Due to technical demands on this gradient, slices are generally limited to a minimum thickness of 1.5 mm. In a volume acquisition, a 3D Fourier transform is performed on a slab of tissue, with slice selection obtained by the application of a second phase-encoding step rather than by changes in the orthogonal gradient.[4] As the demands on the z gradient are lessened, slices can be made as thin as 0.7 mm in a volume sequence.

In general, 3D sequences are preferred for intracranial MRA because of their increased spatial resolution and improved signal-to-noise ratio compared to 2D techniques. Volume studies are also less susceptible to in-plane signal loss than multislice sequences. Volume techniques do, however, suffer from progressive saturation of spins through the volume[5] and are less sensitive to slow flow than is multislice imaging.[3] Therefore, in studying regions of slow arterial or venous flow, a 2D sequence may be preferable to a 3D acquisition.

The most common method for presenting MRA data is by use of a maximum-intensity projection (MIP) technique. The MIP technique is a ray-tracing algorithm in which multiple rays are sent through an imaging volume with recording of the maximum-intensity pixel encountered.[6] These data are then used to construct projections of the vascular anatomy, which can be rotated about an axis to allow inspection of the vessels from multiple angles.

NORMAL ANATOMY OF THE INTRACRANIAL VASCULATURE

An understanding of the normal vascular anatomy of the brain is essential in the interpretation of intracranial MR angiograms. Arterial blood flow to the brain can be divided into the caroticoopthalmic (anterior) and vertebrobasilar (posterior) circulations.

The circle of Willis provides important anastamoses between the anterior and posterior circulaton (Fig. 4-1). Anteriorly, the circle consistes of the precommunicating (A1) segment of the paired anterior cerebral arteries and the anterior communicating artery. Posteriorly, the circle comprises the posterior communicating arteries bilaterally and the pre-

communicating (P1) segments of the posterior cerebral arteries.

The intracranial internal carotid artery (ICA; Fig. 4-2) can be subdivided on the basis of location into petrous, presellar, juxtasellar and supraclinoid segments. The petrous segment of the ICA has both vertical and horizontal components. Initially, upon reaching the skull base, the ICA ascends vertically within the petrous bone for approximately 1 cm. The vessel then turns anteromedially into the horizontally oriented carotid canal. At the petrous apex, the ICA passes sharply upward, slightly medially, and anteriorly above the foramen lacerum to form the proximal portion of the presellar segment. The distal presellar ICA bends slightly posteriorly and superiorly before making another sharp anterior turn to become the juxtasellar ICA. The juxtasellar ICA proceeds anteriorly, inferiorly, and laterally within the cavernous sinus before making an acute turn to pass superiorly, medial to the anterior clinoid process. The presellar and juxtasellar ICA gives rise to meningohypophyseal and lateral main-stem branches, which are sources of important external to internal carotid collateral pathways but are too small to be imaged routinely with MRA.

The supraclinoid segment begins as the internal carotid artery pierces the dura at the anterior clinoid process. In 89 percent of cases,[7] the ophthalmic artery arises as the ICA exits the cavernous sinus and forms the first intradural branch of the ICA. The ophthalmic artery enters the orbit via the optic canal in close apposition to the inferior margin of the optic nerve.

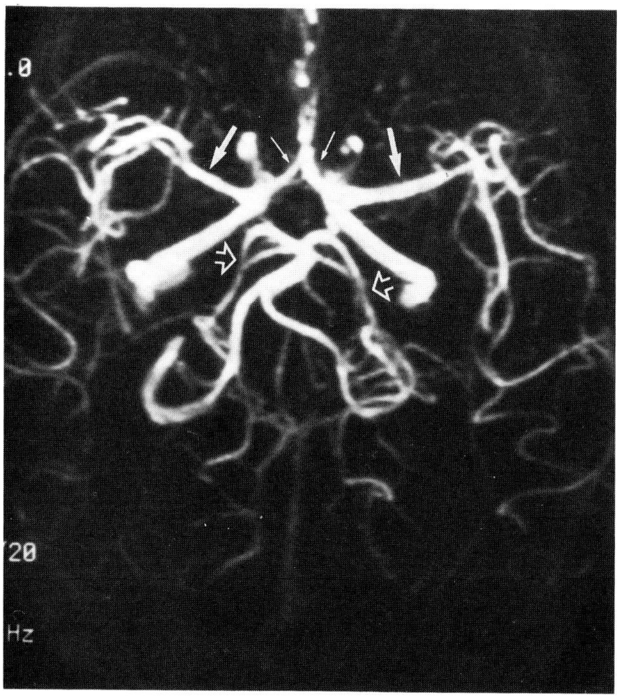

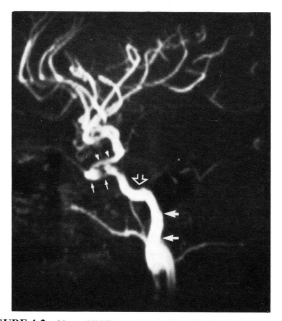

FIGURE 4-1 Normal TOF collapse view of the circle of Willis showing flow-related enhancement in the anterior cerebral arteries (*small arrows*), middle cerebral arteries (*large arrows*), and posterior cerebral arteries (*outlined arrows*).

FIGURE 4-2 Normal TOF lateral projection of the internal carotid artery in which the distal cervical (*large arrows*), petrous (*outlined arrows*), cavernous (*small arrows*), and supraclinoid (*arrowheads*) segments can be identified.

The next major branch which takes its origin from the supraclinoid ICA is the posterior communicating artery, which extends posteromedially above cranial nerve III to the posterior cerebral artery, forming a portion of the circle of Willis.

The last major branch to arise from the supraclinoid ICA prior to its terminal bifurcation is the anterior choroidal artery (AchA). The AchA is a small-caliber vessel with an average external diameter of 0.6 to 1.0 mm.[8] Due to its small size, the AchA is not normally demonstrated on MRA.

The supraclinoid ICA bifurcates under the anterior perforated substance into its two terminal branches, the anterior and middle cerebral arteries.

The smaller of the two branches, the anterior cerebral artery (ACA), courses anteromedially above the optic nerve and chiasm to reach the interhemispheric fissure. The precommunicating (A1) segment of the ACA gives rise to the medial lenticulostriate vessels. Within the interhemispheric fissure, the ACA anastamoses with the contralateral ACA via the anterior communicating artery (ACoA). The postcommunicating (A2) segment courses within the interhemispheric fissure adjacent to the lamina terminalis. The two terminal branches of the ACA, the callosal marginal and pericallosal arteries, arise near the genu of the corpus callosum. The callosal marginal artery runs within the cingulate sulcus and ramifies over the medial surface of the frontal lobes. The pericallosal artery lies within the callosal cistern and supplies the paracentral and internal parietal regions. The continuation of the pericallosal artery anastamoses with the splenial branch of the posterior cerebral artery.

The middle cerebral artery is the larger of the two terminal branches of the internal carotid artery. The proximal stem (M1 segment) courses laterally from the ICA bifurcation to the sylvian fissure. The M1 segment gives rise to the lateral lenticulostriate vessels, which supply the basal ganglia and portions of the internal capsule. The anterior temporal branch also typically originates from the M1 segment and supplies the anterior temporal lobe. Laterally within the sylvian fissure, the middle cerebral artery bifurcates into anterior and posterior divisions. These branch vessels intially course superiorly over the insula and then make a sharp turn inferiorly to run along the medial surface of the frontal and parietal opercula. The MCA branches then exit laterally from the sylvian fissure and ramify over the lateral convexity of the cerebral hemispheres.

The anterior division of the MCA supplies the lateral surface of the frontal lobe and motor region, with variable supply to the primary sensory cortex. The posterior division supplies the remainder of the lateral portion of the parietal lobe as well as the lateral occipital lobe and posterior temporal region.

Vascular supply to the posterior fossa and posterior portions of the cerebral hemispheres is derived from the vertebrobasilar system. The paired vertebral arteries enter the cranium through the foramen magnum.

The first major intracranial branch of the vertebral artery is the posterior inferior cerebellar artery (PICA), which courses posteriorly around the lower medulla and frequently has a prominent caudal loop called the *lateral medullary segment.* The PICA then ascend superiorly (posterior medullary segment) and gives rise to choroidal branches before turning posteriorly to end in inferior vermian and cerebellar hemispheric branches.

Small paired vessels originate from the last centimeter of the vertebral arteries and unite in the midline to form the anterior spinal artery. This artery continues inferiorly in the anterior median sulcus of the spinal cord, with tributaries from the cervical and thoracolumbar regions.

The vertebral arteries unite at the pontomedullary junction to form the basilar artery (Fig. 4-3). The basilar artery courses along the ventral margin of the pons to terminate at the pontomesencephalic junction in the paired posterior cerebral arteries. Branches of the basilar artery include the anterior inferior cerebellar arteries (AICA), pontine perforators, and the superior cerebellar arteries (SCA).

The AICA takes its origin from the proximal basilar artery. The caliber of the AICA and its vascular territory are inversely proportional to the size and distribution of the

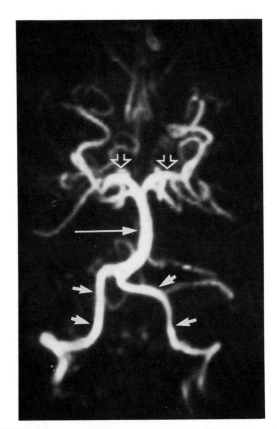

FIGURE 4-3 Normal TOF, frontal projection, of the posterior circulation showing the distal vertebral arteries (*short arrows*), basilar artery (*long arrow*), and posterior cerebral arteries (*outlined arrows*).

PICA. Typically, the AICA gives off a labyrinthine branch which supplies the inner ear before turning to supply portions of the middle cerebellar peduncle, flocculus, and superior and inferior semilunar lobules.

Multiple pontine branches arise from the mid portion of the basilar artery to supply the pons. At the upper border of the pons, the basilar artery gives rise to the paired superior cerebellar arteries. These arteries are relatively constant in vascular territory, as opposed to the PICA and AICA. The SCAs course laterally around the brainstem, inferior to the third nerve and tentorium. The vessels approach each other posteriorly in the midline and continue inferiorly along the superior margin of the cerebellar vermis, providing vascular supply to this structure. Hemispheric branches of the SCA supply the superior portions of the cerebellar hemispheres, with vascular supply also to the superior cerebellar peduncles, dentate nuclei, and part of the middle cerebellar peduncles.

As the basilar artery becomes supratentorial, it bifurcates into its terminal branches, the paired posterior cerebral arteries (PCAs). The precommunicating (P1) segment of the PCA lies within the interpeduncular cistern just above the third cranial nerve. This segment gives off multiple small perforating branches, the posterior thalamoperforators and branches to the nuclei of cranial nerves III and IV. After anastamosing with the posterior communicating artery (PCoA), the P2 segment of the PCA continues around the mesencephalon with branches to the optic tract, geniculate body, thalamus, and corticospinal tract. The PCAs approach each other in the quadrigeminal cistern and then proceed posteriorly in the midline as the P3 segment to the anterior margin of the calcarine sulcus with terminal branches supplying the medial occipital, parietal, and inferior temporal lobes. Additional branches from the P3 segment supply the choroid plexus in the atria of the lateral ventricles and the third ventricle as the lateral and medial posterior choroidal branches, respectively. Splenial branches also arise from the P3 segment and anastamose with the pericallosal artery of the ACA.

In addition to the arterial vasculature, the venous structures of the brain can also be evaluated with MRA. The venous drainage of the brain can be subdivided into superficial and deep structures, which drain into the venous sinuses.

The superficial cortical veins course along the lateral and medial surfaces of the brain and terminate in the venous sinuses. A majority of the superficial cortical veins are unnamed and vary in size and location. The veins of Trolard and Labbe are large veins which drain into the superior sagittal and transverse sinuses respectively. The superficial middle cerebral vein parallels the sylvian fissure and empties into the sphenoparietal sinus. The basal vein of Rosenthal provides drainage for the medial temporal lobe and runs posteromedially to drain the medial temporal lobe. This vein unites posteromedially and superiorly with the internal cerebral vein to form the great vein of Galen.

The deep veins are more constant in location than the superficial veins. Small septal veins unite with the thalamostriate veins at the foramen of Monroe to form the internal cerebral veins. The paired internal cerebral veins (ICVs) course posteriorly along the roof of the third ventricle within the cistern of the velum interpositum to join with the basal vein of Rosenthal to form the vein of Galen. The vein of Galen turns sharply upward to meet the inferior sagittal sinus, which runs in the inferior free edge of the falx. Together, the vein of Galen and the inferior sagittal sinus drain into the straight sinus, which courses posteroinferiorly to the internal occipital protuberance.

Venous sinus drainage is provided along the convexity by the superior sagittal sinus (SSS). The SSS lies within the dural reflection of the falx in the midline over the convexity of the cerebral hemispheres. The SSS is frequently incomplete in its anterior third and increases in caliber posteriorly as it receives cortical venous tributaries. The SSS and straight sinus meet at the torcular Herophili. At the torcular, the SSS and straight sinus are joined by a small midline sinus, the occipital sinus, which drains a portion of the posterior fossa. Venous blood then drains laterally into the right and left transverse sinuses. These sinuses are frequently asymmetrical in size, the right commonly being larger than the left. The transverse sinuses are contiguous with the sigmoid sinuses, which are in turn contiguous with the internal jugular veins.

Anteriorly, the superficial middle cerebral vein and meningeal veins drain into the sphenoparietal sinus, which courses along the lesser sphenoid wing to empty into the paired cavernous sinuses, which lie along the lateral walls of the sphenoid sinuses. The cavernous sinuses also receive blood from the superior and inferior ophthalmic veins. Intercavernous connections permit communication between the cavernous sinuses. The cavernous sinuses also connect with the clival plexus posteriorly and pterygoid plexus inferolaterally. A portion of the blood from the cavernous sinuses also drains through the inferior petrosal sinus to the jugular bulb on either side.

ANATOMIC VARIANTS

Magnetic resonance angiography provides an accurate, noninvasive modality for evaluating variations of normal anatomy.[9] Confirming that a structure is an anatomical variant is important in limiting patient exposure to invasive tests. Additionally, identification of vascular anatomical variants may aide in planning the neurosurgical approach to some lesions.

A number of anatomical variants may be demonstrated with MRA. The most commonly seen variations are in the circle of Willis. An incomplete circle of Willis is present in 80 percent of cases with frequent hypoplasia or aplasia of one or more of the posterior communicating arteries, the anterior communicating artery, or the proximal anterior cerebral arteries (Fig. 4.4).[10,11] Another frequently seen anom-

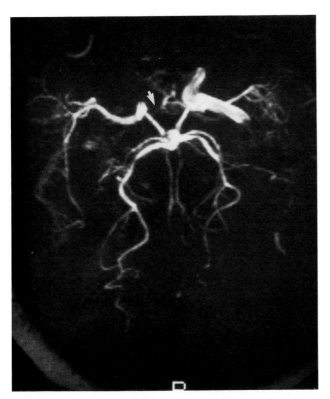

FIGURE 4-4 Patient with right internal carotid artery occlusion with a hypoplastic right A1 segment (*arrow*). Note the large posterior communicating arteries bilaterally.

aly of the circle of Willis is the fetal-type posterior cerebral artery in which the P1 segment is absent, with the result that the ipsilateral PCA territory is supplied from the ICA via the posterior communicating artery.

Developmentally, several anastomoses exist between the carotid and vertebrobasilar systems. These connections usually regress during fetal life. Failure of regression of these arteries results in persistent carotid-to-vertebrobasilar communications. The most common of these connections is a persistent trigeminal artery which connects the cavernous carotid to the basilar artery (Fig. 4-5). Less frequently encountered persistent communications occur via the otic artery, which connects the petrous ICA to the ipsilateral anterior inferior cerebellar artery, the hypoglossal artery which links the cervical ICA to the proximal basilar artery through the anterior condyloid foramen, and the proatlantal intersegmental artery which connects the distal cervical ICA or external carotid artery (ECA) to the ipsilateral vertebral artery.[7]

Anomalies of the ICA and its terminal branches can be imaged with MRA. An aberrant internal carotid artery can be identified on intracranial MRA by its unusual lateral course within the petrous bone (Fig. 4-6A and B). The ICA enters the skull base posterior to the external auditory canal between the facial canal and jugular foramen and then turns anteriorly and runs through the middle ear. Imaging of the cervical carotid in these cases reveals a single vessel supplying ECA as well as intracranial ICA branches. The cervical carotid bifurcation is not present.[7] An azygous type of ACA may occasionally be demonstrated on MRA. In this anomaly, a single vascular pedicle supplying both ACA territories is seen in the interhemispheric fissure (Fig. 4-7).

ARTERIAL OCCLUSIVE DISEASE

Cerebrovascular disease is a major cause of disability and death, with an estimated prevalence of 794 per 100,000. In the United States alone, there are approximately 400,000 cases of stroke per year.[12] By far, most of these neurological events are related to vascular occlusive disease.

Among the causes of cerebrovascular occlusive disease, atherosclerosis is the most common. Other intrinsic vascular abnormalities—such as vasculitis, vasospasm, and amyloid deposition—represent a smaller but important percentage of occlusive disorders. Ischemic changes of the brain may also be the result of emboli from remote sites such as the heart or the internal carotid artery. Decreased perfusion related to diminished cardiac output or severe proximal vascular disease is also implicated in certain ischemic brain lesions.[12]

The high prevalence of cerebrovascular occlusive disease

FIGURE 4-5 TOF MRA demonstrating a persistent trigeminal artery (*arrow*). Also note absence of the right P1 segment (*arrowhead*). A "fetal" type posterior cerebral artery is frequently found ipsilateral to a persistent trigeminal artery.

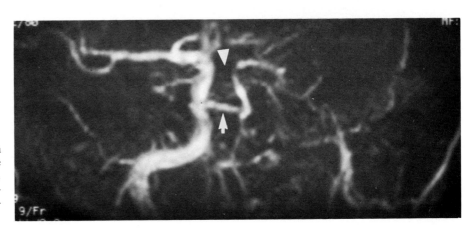

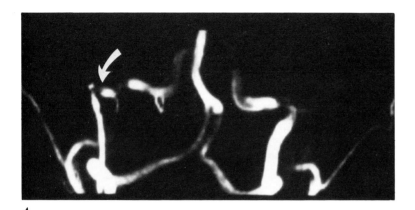

A

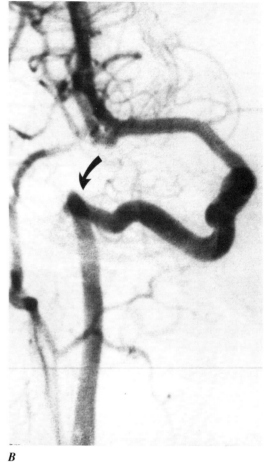

FIGURE 4-6 *A.* MRA of an aberrant right trigeminal carotid artery as diagnosed by the lateral course of the vessel in the petrous bone (*arrow*). *B.* A conventional contrast angiogram in the same patient confirming the typical configuration of an aberrant ICA (*arrow*).

B

has led to a desire to image the intracranial vasculature noninvasively. While conventional contrast x-ray angiography remains the gold standard, noninvasive tests such as MRA and transcranial Doppler are receiving increasing attention. Due to the small caliber of the intracranial vessels, MRA is generally restricted to the evaluation of the larger vessels at the skull base, including the ICA and the proximal branch vessels of the circle of Willis. In the following section, we outline our approach to intracranial imaging in the setting of vascular occlusive disease and discuss some of the limitations and potential pitfalls of the current techniques.

For routine evaluation of intracranial vascular stenosis or

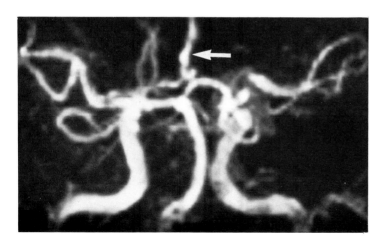

FIGURE 4-7 Azygous anterior cerebral artery (ACA) as seen by TOF MRA (*arrow*). A single anterior cerebral vessel supplies ACA territory bilaterally.

occlusion, we employ a 3D TOF gradient echo sequence with interpulse RF spoiling (Fig. 4-8A and B). An imaging volume is obtained which includes the vertebrobasilar junction inferiorly and the circle of Willis superiorly. Centering the volume at the midclivus will usually accomplish this objective. Current sequence parameters on our system include TR = 49 ms, TE = 6.9 ms, and flip angle = 20°, with a 256 × 192 × 60 matrix. A 1.2-mm partition thickness and a 72-mm-thick volume is routinely obtained. A superior saturation band is placed outside the field of view to eliminate venous signal. Image acquisition time for this sequence is 10 min, 16 s.

As in all TOF sequences, vessel conspicuity is dependent on background tissue suppression. In theory, one way to achieve better background suppression is with increased flip angles; however, increasing the flip angle results in progressive saturation of spins, with unacceptable signal loss at the top of the imaging volume. We have found a flip angle of 20° to be an acceptable compromise between the need for background suppression and the limitations imposed by saturation effects. Recently, a variable ramped flip-angle sequence has been designed in which the flip angle is progressively increased throughout the imaging volume.[13] This

sequence does result in less saturation toward the top of the volume as compared with conventional 3D volumes, but is not widely available at present. Another newly developed technique utilizes magnetization transfer contrast methods to improve background tissue suppression. This pulse sequence uses an off-resonance RF pulse to saturate stationary tissues while flowing blood is relatively unaffected.[14] A combination of these techniques may further improve vessel delineation.[15] Another approach used to improve TOF imaging is to acquire multiple thin volumes with a small amount of overlap between volumes. The individual slices are then reordered to eliminate the overlap and produce a continuous vascular representation. This technique, termed *multiple overlapping thin slab acqusition* (MOTSA), improves the detection of small vessels and allows coverage of larger areas with less saturation effects than single-volume techniques.[16]

Signal from fat, due to its short T1, poses particular difficulties in intracranial TOF imaging. Several strategies have been devised to limit the interference of fat on the images. One technique is to use anterior, posterior, right, and left saturation bands positioned within the field of view to decrease the signal from scalp and orbital fat. This technique has the advantage of rendering the initial reprojection

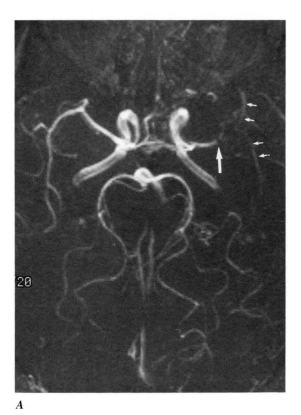

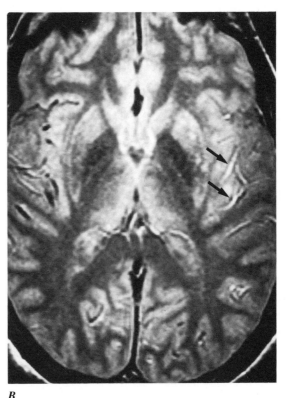

A *B*

FIGURE 4-8 *A*. TOF MRA showing a stenosis of the distal M1 segment on the left (*large arrow*) as well as diminished flow related enhancement in middle cerebral artery (MCA) branch vessels (*small arrows*). *B*. Slow flow in the sylvian branches of the MCA is confirmed on cross-sectional spin-echo imaging by increased intravascular signal (*arrows*).

images interpretable, in most cases without requiring additional postprocessing. The major disadvantage of this technique is the saturation of retrograde flow through the ophthalmic artery in cases of internal carotid artery stenosis. Additionally, if placed too close to the circle of Willis, the saturation bands will eliminate inflow signal from the internal carotid artery in the neck and produce a pseudo-occlusion of the intracranial ICA (Fig. 4-9A and B). An alternative method to remove peripheral fat signal is to acquire the data without saturation bands in the field of view and to perform a restricted maximum intensity (MIP) after the data acquisition (Fig. 4-10A and B). This technique requires additional postprocessing time and software to create the restricted MIPs.

Neither saturation bands nor restricted MIPs can eliminate centrally located fat within the petrous apex and cavernous sinuses. However, one way to diminish from central fat is to chose a TE at which fat and water are out of phase. The time at which fat and water are out of phase can be determined by the equation $t = \frac{1}{2} (f \text{ water} - f \text{ fat})$, where f is the Larmor frequencies for water and fat, which vary linearly with field strength. On a 1.5-tesla system, fat and water spins are in phase and out of phase approximately every 2.3 ms. Maximizing water to fat signal may, therefore, be obtained by utilizing a TE of 6.9 ms when fat and water are out of phase rather than choosing a minimum TE value of around 4.7 ms when they are in phase. The longer TE does allow for more intravoxel phase dispersion, but in our experience it provides superior images in most patients due to better fat suppression. Recent work has suggested, however, that in the pediatric population, where higher velocities are routinely present, use of a TE = 5 ms may improve overall image quality.[17]

As an alternative to TOF, PC imaging may be performed. Phase-contrast techniques are unaffected by the presence of fat, as the signal obtained is proportional to flow velocity and not directly dependent on the T1 of the tissue being imaged. The relative independence of PC techniques from tissue T1 also makes these sequences useful in evaluating the vasculature in areas of hemorrhage where the short T1 of methemoglobin renders TOF sequences inadequate. Our current sequence parameters for a 3D PC sequence are TR = 24 ms, TE = 7.1 ms, 256 × 128 × 60 matrix, flip angle = 20°, velocity encoding = 40 cm/s, 6.0 = cm volume with 1-mm slice thickness, and acquisition time 12 min, 51 s.

Phase-contrast studies are also used to obtain directional information at the circle of Willis (Fig. 4-11A, B, and C). Ross et al.[18] found that by using a 3D PC method with a velocity encoding value (VENC) of 80 cm/s, collateral circulation through the circle of Willis could be evaluated without significant aliasing. They were also able to identify the posterior communicating artery in 78 percent of cases. The difficulty with performing a 3D PC sequence with this VENC is that smaller vessels with slower velocities are less well

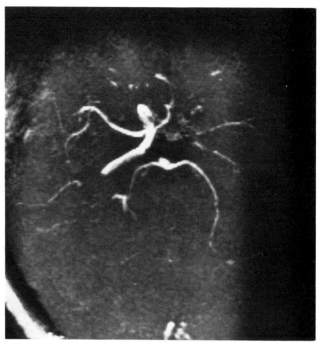

A

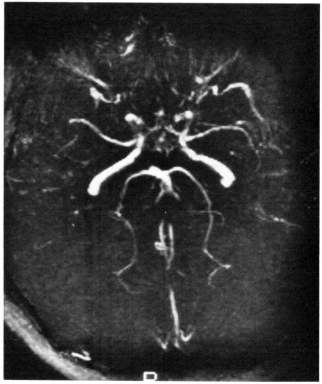

B

FIGURE 4-9 *A.* TOF MRA with the left peripheral saturation band too far into the field of view, producing the appearance of markedly decreased flow in the left internal carotid artery (ICA) and middle cerebral artery (MCA). *B.* Repeat study of the same patient with the saturation band appropriately placed, showing normal ICA and MCA flow.

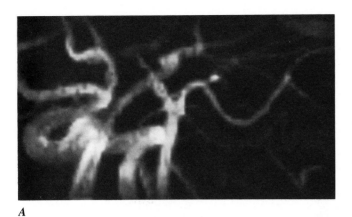

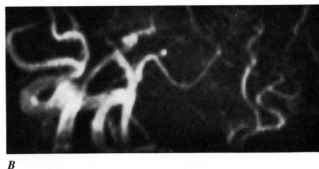

A   *B*

FIGURE 4-10 *A.* Maximum-intensity projection (MIP) image of an entire data set of a TOF MRA. *B.* "Restricted" MIP with the scalp and orbital fat excluded from the projection. Vessel conspicuity is improved on the projection images with this postprocessing manipulation.

demonstrated than with VENCs in the range of 30 to 45 cm/s. The relatively long acquisition time of approximately 13 min per sequence prohibits performing multiple sequences with different velocity encodings. An alternative to a 3D acquisition is to perform a 2D PC study with the following parameters: 1-cm slice thickness, 256 × 192 matrix, 20° flip angle, TR = 33 ms, TE = 8.4 ms, 8 NEX, and velocity encoding = 80 cm/s, with encoding in all flow directions. This series requires approximately 6 min 51 s to acquire and can be added to the 3D TOF sequence outlined above in cases where directional information is desirable. When more rapid imaging is required, use of 4 NEX will produce diagnostic images and necessitates only half the acquisition time. Use of first-order gradient moment nulling (flow compensation) is essential in this as in all MRA sequences to avoid signal loss from dephasing. The directional information is displayed as velocity-phase images in which the vector of flow in the direction of encoding is indicated as bright and flow in the opposite direction is black. Review of the source data images is necessary to optimize the detection of small vessels.

Interpretation of intracranial MRA is facilitated by familiarity with common artifacts and an appreciation for the limitations of the available techniques. The vertical segment of the petrous ICA is the site of frequent artifactual signal loss on MRA, which produces a "pseudostenosis" in this location. The signal loss is related to susceptibility effects caused by air within the petrous bone and mastoid air cells. Another area which is the site of frequent artifactual signal loss is the carotid siphon. The signal loss in the siphon is likely the result of the complex flow patterns and acceleration of spins around the tight turns of the siphon.[1] This signal loss appears to be less prominent on 3D PC sequences; when significant siphon disease is suspected, a phase contrast study may be the exam of choice.

In cases where an intracranial stenosis is present, MRA

may produce an appearance of vessel occlusion. In these circumstances, a 2D TOF sequence may be preferable to a 3D technique due to the greater sensitivity of the 2D sequence to slow flow (Fig. 4-12A and B). Additionally, one should inspect the spin-echo sequences, particularly the T2-weighted images, for signal voids, as these are more sensitive than the gradient-echo flow images to the presence of slow flow. Consideration should also be given to the administration of gadolinium in cases of vessel occlusion versus slow flow, as the T1 shortening effect of the contrast will improve flow detection.[19] At present, only conventional contrast angiography can confirm vessel occlusion.

Evaluation of the intracranial arterial anatomy is also difficult in the setting of severe proximal carotid occlusive disease. The slow flow distal to a tight stenosis results in marked saturation of inflowing spins and makes the detection of tandem lesions difficult. Caution should be exercised in evaluating the vasculature distal to a significant stenosis. Correlation with transcranial Doppler may be useful in this setting, and conventional contrast angiography may be warranted to clarify the MRA findings.

VENOOCCLUSIVE DISEASE

In addition to arterial occlusive disease, venous thromboses can also be imaged with MRA. Magnetic resonance angiography is most useful in the evaluation of large venous structures such as the dural sinuses (Fig. 4-13A and B). Sinus occlusions may be precipitated by infection, trauma, dehydration, and encasement by tumor. Since sinus occlusion is typically accompanied by high intravascular signal, PC imaging is preferred over TOF sequences. Sagittal 2D PC imaging using five 1-cm-thick slices and velocity encoding values of 15 cm/s are usually adequate to evaluate the superior and inferior sagittal sinuses, the internal cerebral

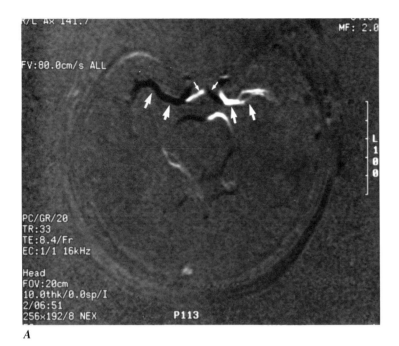

A

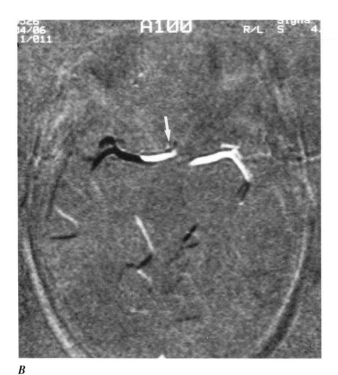

B

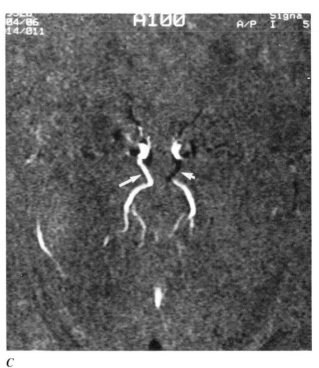

C

FIGURE 4-11   *A*. 2D PC angiogram velocity image with right to left flow encoding (flow toward the right is white, flow toward the left is black) with normal flow direction in the anterior (*small arrows*) and middle cerebral arteries (*large arrows*).   *B*. Right-to-left directional study in a patient with a hypoplastic left A1 segment with the right A1 supplying both A2 segments (*arrow*).   *C*. Directional study with anteroposterior flow encoding in a patient with a severe left internal carotid artery stenosis, showing a normal direction of flow in the right posterior communicating artery (*long arrow*) with reversed (*posterior to anterior*) flow in the left posterior communicating artery.

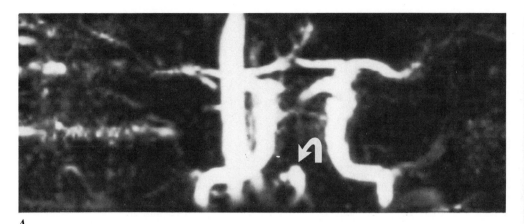

A

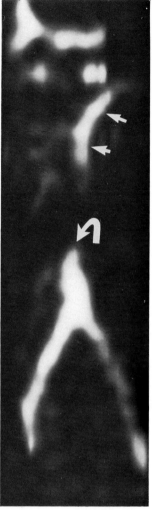

B

FIGURE 4-12 *A.* 3D PC angiogram with a VENC = 40 cm/s, suggesting occlusion of the basilar artery (*curved arrow*). *B.* 2D TOF angiogram on the same patient showing antegrade flow distally (*arrow*) within the basilar, consistent with a nonocclusive stenosis (*curved arrow*).

veins, the vein of Galen, and the straight sinus in a single acquisition. An axially or coronally oriented sequence is useful in inspecting the transverse sinuses.

ANEURYSMS

The incidence of intracranial aneurysms is difficult to estimate accurately. Recent studies indicate the prevalence of aneurysms within the general population to be approximately 5 percent.[19-24] The ratio of ruptured aneurysms, presenting as acute subarachnoid hemorrhage, to unruptured aneurysms is approximately 1:1. Therefore, nearly 50 percent of all aneurysms rupture.[20] An estimated 28,000 aneurysm ruptures occur each year in North America. The detection and treatment of aneurysms merits consideration, as the outcome following rupture with subarachnoid hemorrhage is poor. The mortality from the first subarachnoid hemorrhage approaches 65 percent. Even in patients with no focal neurological deficit

after aneurysm rupture, less than 50 percent are able to recover fully and return to their previous employment. Although the true risk of rupture of incidentally discovered aneurysms is unknown, the annual rupture rate is now estimated as 1 percent per year. Of those reaching neurosurgical care, the mortality and serious morbidity rates from hemorrhage-induced vasospasm are approximately 7 percent each.[21]

From 90 to 95 percent of all intracranial aneurysms occur in the carotid system, with the most common locations including

anterior communicating	30 percent
posterior communicating	25 percent
middle cerebral artery fiburcation	20 percent

Posterior circulation aneurysms account for 5 to 15 percent, including

basilar tip	10 percent
vertebral artery/PICA	5 percent

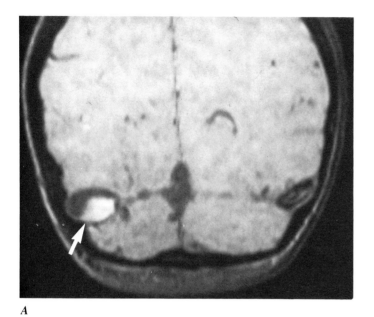

A

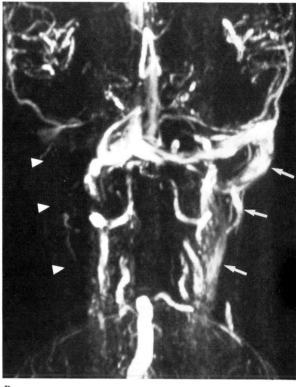

B

FIGURE 4-13   *A*. Coronal T1-weighted image of a patient with high signal intensity clot in the right transverse sinus (*arrow*).   *B*. Use of a TOF sequence in this setting would potentially suggest patency of this vessel. A phase-contrast exam shows absence of flow in the distal transverse sinus, sigmoid sinus, and jugular vein on the right (*arrowheads*) with normal flow on the left (*arrows*).

In addition, 20 to 30 percent of aneurysm patients have multiple aneurysms.[22]

Aneurysms may be congenital, atherosclerotic, mycotic, marantic, or associated with other medical disorders. These include autosomal dominant polycystic kidney disease, fibromuscular disease, arteriovenous malformations, connective tissue disorders, coarctation of the aorta, and Osler-Weber-Rendu syndrome. An increased incidence of intracranial aneurysms is also noted in patients whose families include several members with aneurysms.[23] Aneurysms are found in approximately 10 percent of patients with intracranial arteriovenous malformations.

The risk of bleeding appears to be related to the size of the aneurysm; the estimated annual risk of rupture for aneurysms less than 1 cm in diameter is below 4 percent. The risk of rupture of aneurysms less than 5 mm in diameter is close to zero.[24] Several reports in the radiology literature have claimed that the size limit for detection of intracranial aneurysms by MRA is 3 mm.[25–27] The morbidity and mortality from acute subarachnoid hemorrhage far exceeds the surgical risk of treatment of unruptured aneurysms.[28,29]

Therefore, the detection and characterization of unruptured aneurysms is of great clinical significance. Magnetic resonance imaging (MRI) and/or MRA represents a promising imaging technique for this diagnostic problem.

The principal indication for performing MRA is the detection of unruptured aneurysms. This includes the evaluation of incidental findings on CT or MRI. Screening of patients with a family history of aneurysms or those patients with any of the aforementioned predisposing medical conditions is also performed.

The most common presentation of an intracranial aneurysm is with the sudden onset of headache and neurological findings related to aneurysm rupture. Currently, MRA has no proven role in this acute setting, where conventional contrast angiography is the study of choice. However, MRI/MRA is useful in the evaluation of those patients with aneurysms who present with symptoms other than those of subarachnoid hemorrhage (Fig. 4-14A and B). Aneurysms occasionally produce symptoms related to mass effect. This phenomenon is particularly prevalent in posterior communicating artery aneurysms, which often result in an ipsilateral

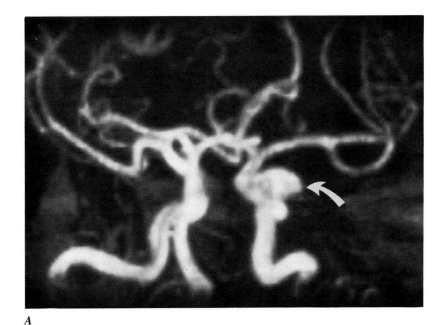

A

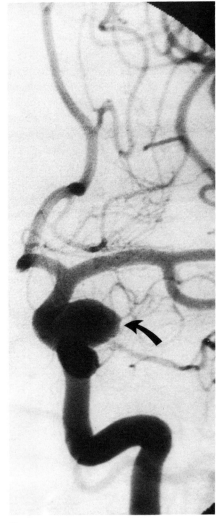

B

FIGURE 4-14 *A.* 3D TOF of a left internal carotid artery aneurysm (*curved arrow*), with (*B*) conventional angiographic correlation (*curved arrow*).

third-nerve palsy. Giant aneurysms, those greater than 2.5 cm in diameter, also commonly come to medical attention due to symptoms related to mass effect rather than acute subarachnoid hemorrhage. Infarctions due to distal embolization of aneurysm thrombus are infrequently seen. Aneurysms may rarely present with seizures or headace.

In addition to the detection of aneurysms, MRA permits the noninvasive workup of these lesions to help determine the best type of therapy. Surgery, endovascular obliteration, or conservative management may be considered optimal in any given patient, and MRI/MRA can provide useful anatomical information that is not as easily appreciated with other imaging modalities to aid in this treatment decision. In addition, MRA permits noninvasive follow-up of untreated aneurysms. The use of MRA as a routine procedure in patients who have undergone aneurysm clipping is controversial. The ''MR compatibility'' of even the most recently manufactured aneurysm clips cannot be guaranteeed at this

time.[30] Also, significant artifacts arise at the site of the clip. Further evaluation will be required to determine definitively when MRI is safe in patients with aneurysm clips.

Of the currently available MRA techniques, aneurysm evaluation is most frequently accomplished using either 3D TOF or 3D PC imaging. We prefer the use of time-of-flight (TOF) sequences for the detection of small aneurysms and phase contrast imaging for the study of larger aneurysms where intraaneurysmal thrombus may be present. With the 3D-TOF technique, the radiologist can obtain the smallest possible voxel size while maintaining a satisfactory signal-to-noise ratio and a reasonably short scan time. Selection of a small voxel size serves to minimize signal loss due to intravoxel phase dispersion. Phase dispersion results from the complex flow patterns encountered within aneurysms, leading to incoherence of spins within a given voxel. Choosing the shortest possible echo time will also lessen the effects of intravoxel spin dephasing. Our current ''aneurysm search'' protocal is an axial 3D TOF sequence using a 256 × 256 × 60 matrix, TR/TE = 40/4.7, flip angle = 20°, 18-cm field of view, and a volume of 4.2 cm (0.7-mm partition thickness) centered at the circle of Willis (Fig. 4-15). Targeted reconstructions (''restricted MIPs'') may also be of benefit in the study of an individual lesion. Use of 1-mm-thick partitions (60-mm slab thickness) allows inclusion of less common locations for aneurysms such as the PICA of AICA orgins within a single imaging volume, but at the expense of increased voxel size. Alternatively, one may employ an additional axially or coronally oriented slab to more fully interrogate the posterior fossa vascular anatomy.

Potential pitfalls of TOF imaging include the misdiagnosis of clot as flow due to the short T1 of methemoglobin, although frequently clot is less intense than flow signal on MIP reconstructions. In fact, any lesion which is bright on T1-weighted images may mimic or obsure an aneurysm.[25] Careful scrutiny of routine cross-sectional spin-echo images will readily solve this problem in most cases.

In cases where artifacts related to tissues with a short T1 remain problematic phase contrast imaging should be performed. We attempt aneurysm screening in these patients with a 3D PC technique (TR/TE = 24/6.9, flip angle 20°, 1-mm partition thickness, 256 × 128 × 60 matrix, 18-cm field of view, 6-cm slab thickness, velocity encoding = 45 cm/s, acquisition time-13 min). Since phase contrast techniques are independent of T1 effects, only flow will be displayed as high signal intensity.[31] Also, 3D PC has the additional advantage of better background suppression than TOF techniques. The larger voxel size and longer TE used in phase contrast imaging does, however, render this technique more susceptible to signal loss due to intravoxel phase dispersion, which theoretically would make phase contrast less sensitive for the detection of small aneurysms than TOF. Another difficulty in using phase contrast techniques is the requirement of choosing a velocity sensitivity or encoding range prior to the initiation of the scan. Since the velocity within the aneurysm is not known, selection of the appropriate velocity encoding value to maximize flow detection is difficult. Scan and reconstruction times of 3D PC angiograms also tend to be greater than 3D TOF studies of comparable resolution.[31]

The MRA evaluation of giant aneurysms (>2.5 cm) creates different problems for the diagnostic radiologist. Giant aneurysms typically have very slow, swirling flow. This pattern of flow results in significant signal loss on TOF studies and, therefore, underestimation of aneurysm diameter. Additionally, intramural thrombus is commonly present in giant aneurysms and may be confused with flow on TOF MRA. Phase-contrast imaging allows greater and perhaps more accurate visualization of the entire aneurysmal lumen in large lesions.[25,27,32] In the evaluation of large aneurysms, we currently collect a series of 2D phase contrast images employing different velocity encoding values (multi-VENC 2D PC

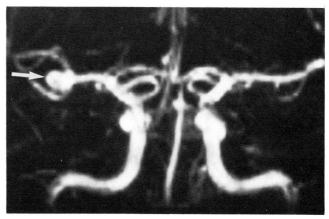

FIGURE 4-15   Routine ''aneurysm search'' 3D TOF demonstrating a left middle cerebral artery bifurcation aneurysm (*arrow*). Use of small voxel size and short TE will help to maximize aneurysm detection.

MRA; Fig. 4-16A and B). The primary advantage of using a 2D PC study is the rapid acquisition time. This allows the selection of several different velocity encoding values (VENC) which separate out various properties of flow within an aneurysm. For example, selecting a low VENC will tend to accentuate the slow intraaneurysmal flow, while selecting a higher velocity may allow visualization of the ''jet'' of inflow to and outflow from the aneurysm. The use of high-velocity encoding values may also be helpful in defining the aneurysm neck.[25] Demonstration of these flow properties has proved useful in planning treatment options for certain lesions.

The noninvasive detection and evaluation of intracranial aneurysms, clearly an important clinical problem, has taken a major step forward with the advent of current MRA techniques. While contrast angiography remains the gold standard for aneurysm study, it is believed that continued advances in MR technology will allow noninvasive evaluation of these lesions to assume an even greater role in the future.

VASCULAR MALFORMATIONS

The term *vascular malformation* describes a number of non-neoplastic vascular lesions of the central nervous system. These include arteriovenous malformations (AVMs), cavernous angiomas (cavernous hemangiomas), venous anomalies (venous angiomas), and capillary telangiectasias.

As with conventional contrast angiography, MRA angiography is limited to the study of AVMs and venous anomalies. Flow within cavernous angiomas and capillary telangiectasias is too slow to be imaged with MRA techniques, although nonangiographic MR sequences are frequently useful in detecting and characterizing these lesions.

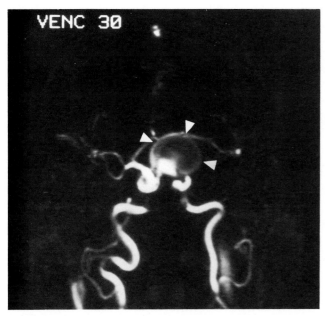

A

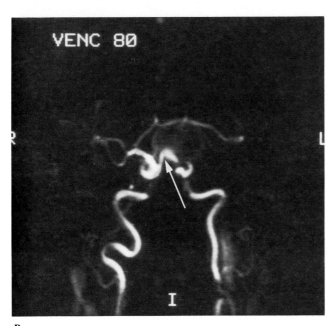

B

FIGURE 4-16 *A.* 2D PC angiogram of a giant right internal carotid artery aneurysm with velocity encoding of 30 cm/s. At this low velocity sensitivity, the luminal diameter of the aneurysm is clearly seen (*arrowheads*). *B.* At a velocity encoding of 80 cm/s, a jet of inflow is appreciated at the site of the aneurysm neck (*arrow*).

ond most common cause of spontaneous subarachnoid hemorrhage in the adult population.[33] Cerebral AVMs may present with intracranial hemorrhage (subarachnoid, intraparenchymal, or intraventricular), seizures, progressive ischemia due to arterial steal, local mass effect, regional venous hypertension, hydrocephalus, an audible bruit, or severe headaches.[34] The indicence of a clinically recognizable hemorrhage from an AVM ranges between 2 to 4 percent per year with the exception that within the first year after the initial hemorrhage, the risk of rebleeding exceeds 6 percent. Each episode of hemorrhage has a 10 to 15 percent mortality rate, with a 1 percent death rate per year after that hemorrhage.[35] When AVMs present as seizures or are accidentally diagnosed, they have a decreased risk of hemorrhage.[36]

Most AVMs are readily diagnosed with routine cross-sectional MRI methods. Spin-echo techniques display the relationship of the AVM nidus to the surrounding brain parenchyma. The proximity of the lesion to the eloquent areas of brain such as the sensorimotor cortex, language and visual centers, the diencephalon, and brainstem can be determined. This anatomical information is critically important in the determination of therapeutic risk. The utility of MRA in the evaluation of AVMs has not been clearly established; however, we have used MRA information to supplement conventional MRI in the noninvasive evaluation of AVMs.

Currently, we examine patients with a questioned or known AVM with routine spin-echo sequences and a gradient

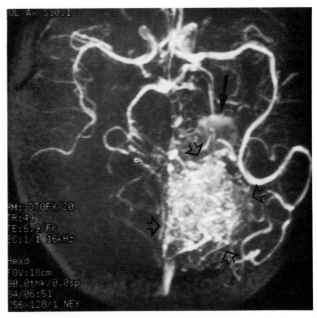

FIGURE 4-17 Postgadolinium DTPA TOF angiogram of a large left parietal arteriovenous malformation. With the use of an IV T1-shortening contrast agent, the nidus of the lesion is clearly demonstrated (*outlined arrows*). A venous varix is also identified (*arrow*).

High-flow brain AVMs are developmental vascular lesions in which abnormal communications between arteries and veins are present. Such AVMs are the most common symptomatic type of vascular malformation and they are the sec-

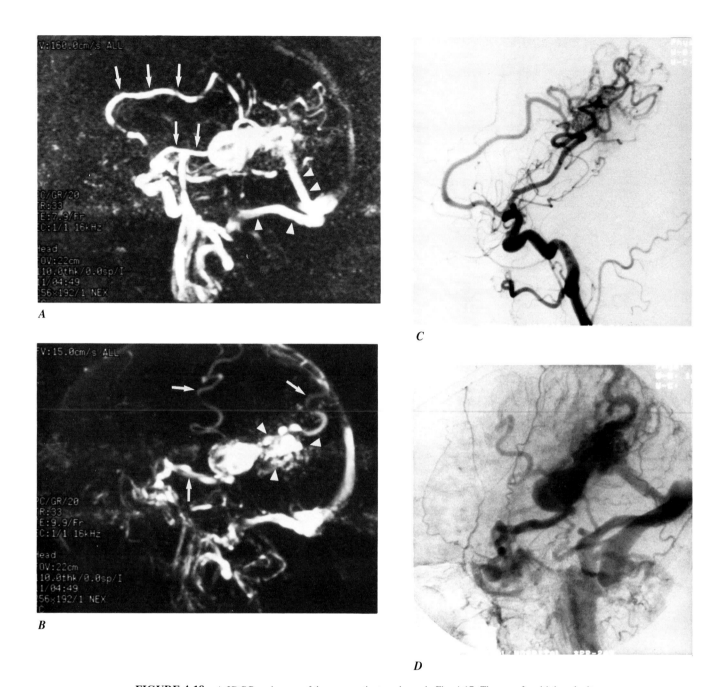

FIGURE 4-18   A 2D PC angiogram of the same patient as shown in Fig. 4-17. The use of multiple velocity encoding values can highlight arterial and venous structures.   *A*. A velocity encoding of 160 cm/s emphasizes arterial structures (*arrows*), although fast flow in draining veins results in some venous sinus visualization (*arrowheads*).   *B*. Use velocity encoding of 15 cm/s results in increased signal in the nidus (*arrowheads*) and slower draining veins (*arrows*), with less emphasis on the arterial inflow and higher-velocity draining veins. Arterial (*C*) and venous (*D*) phases of a conventional contrast angiogram are shown for comparison.

echo susceptibility sequence to define the anatomic relationships of the suspected lesion and to identify the presence of blood breakdown products from previous episodes of hemorrhage.

Once the AVM is identified, we evaluate the intracranial circulation with 3D TOF, with an adequate scan volume to encompass the entire lesion or as much of the lesion as possible without unduly compromising spatial resolution or unacceptably lengthening scan time. When there has been significant recent hemorrhage, the TOF sequence may be untenable because of the presence of high signal from methemoglobin. In these cases, a phase contrast study is usually preferable.

Due to the turbulent flow as well as the effects of saturation on flow detection within an AVM nidus and draining veins, signal loss frequently occurs distal to the arterial feeders. Much of the anatomy of the AVM may then be lost on unenhanced MRA. When saturation effects are particularly problematic, the administration of an intravascular T1 shortening contrast agent such as gadolinium DTPA will improve nidal and draining vein visualization (Fig. 4-17). With this technique, the vasculature of the AVM is usually well demonstrated. Additionally, one may detect lesions such as aneurysms of feeding arteries or venous stenoses, which increase the risk of hemorrhage. Unfortunately, many other structures such as the cavernous sinuses, normal cortical veins and dural sinuses, the pituitary gland and stalk, and the nasopharyngeal mucosa will also demonstrate enhancement. The enhancement of these other structures often renders the reprojection images cluttered and difficult to interpret, although restricted MIPs are often helpful in evaluating lesion morphology. After contrast administration, use of the source images frequently provides complementary data to the cross-sectional spin-echo images.

Multi-VENC 2D PC is a useful technique to identify and characterize the venous drainage of AVMs without the contrast cost and imaging disadvantages of intravenously enhanced 3D TOF. We generally perform this sequence in the sagittal plane, being careful to encompass the nidus in its entirety and also as much of the feeding arteries and draining veins as possible. Our current sequence parameters are TR = 33 ms, TE = 9.9 ms, flip angle = 20°, 256 × 192 matrix, 10-mm slice thickness. These imaging parameters are kept constant for a series of three scans (each scan takes from 2 to 3.5 min, depending on the number of slices needed) with the exception that we select a different VENC for each series. Velocity encoding values selected are typically 180 cm/s, 80 cm/s, and 15 cm/s (Fig. 4-18A, B, C, and D). At the higher VENC settings, the feeding arteries and portions of the nidus will be displayed. As the VENC is decreased, the venous signal will become more prominent, thus providing selective arterial and venous examinations. We advise against the use of paramagnetic contrast with this technique because—although greater intravascular signal will be obtained—persistent arterial signal will be seen even at slow

velocity encoding values, thereby complicating the "selective" venous portion of the study by decreasing the relative conspicuity of the draining veins.

As stated earlier, the diagnosis of intracranial vascular malformations is readily made with routine cross-sectional MRI. The additional vascular anatomical information obtained with MRA provides further useful data with which to make appropriate management decisions. In particular, the neurosurgeons at our institution have found the three-dimensional quality of the rotating projectional images to be supplementary to the two-dimensional appearance of conventional contrast angiography in operative planning.

Venous anomalies are congenital abnormalities of venous drainage which are almost always asymptomatic and usually come to attention only as incidental findings on cranial computed tomography (CT) or MRI. These "lesions" are variants of venous anatomy in which numerous dilated medullary veins converge into a single transparenchymal vein which extends to the superficial or deep venous system ("medusa head" configuration). The intervening brain parenchyma is usually normal. Hemorrhage related to venous anomalies is exceedingly rare but may be present when a venous anomaly is associated with a cavernous angioma. Common sites of venous anomalies are the frontal lobes and cerebellum.

The classic "medusa head" appearance of venous anomalies is usually diagnostic on routine cross-sectional imaging, but occasionally the radiologist is called upon to further characterize these lesions with MRA. The 3D TOF sequence described earlier in this chapter is usually sufficient for the demonstration of venous anomalies, although—due to the slow blood flow in the draining veins—use of a T1 shortening intravenous contrast agent may be necessary. If the drainage of the anomaly is predominantly in a superior-to-inferior direction, use of an inferior rather than superior saturation band outside the field of view will improve the venous visualization.

Clearly, the definitive anatomical and physiological detail provided by standard x-ray angiography make conventional angiography the "gold standard" in the evaluation of intracranial vascular malformations; however, the combination of MRI and MRA can be expected to provide ancillary information which is of value in contemplating treatment options and surgical approaches to these lesions.

REFERENCES

1. Ruggieri PM, Laub GA, Masaryk TJ, Modic MT: Intracranial circulation: Pulse-sequence considerations in three-dimensional (volume) MR angiography. *Radiology* 171:785, 1989.
2. Dumoulin CL, Souza SP, Walker MF, Wagle W: Three dimensional phase contrast angiography. *Mag Res Imaging* 9:139, 1989.
3. Keller, PJ, Drayer BP, Fram EK, et al: MR Angiography with two-dimensional acquisition and three-dimensional display. *Radiology* 173:527, 1989.

4. Edelman RR, Mattle HP, Atkinson DJ, Hoogewould HM: MR angiography. *AJR* 154:937, 1990.

5. Marchal G, Bosmans H, Van Fraeyenhoven L, et al: Intracranial vascular lesions: Optimization and clinical evaluation of three-dimensional time-of-flight MR angiography. *Radiology* 175:443, 1990.

6. Anderson CM, Saloner D, Tsuruda JS, et al: Artifacts in maximum-intensity-projection display of MR angiograms. *AJR* 154:623, 1990.

7. Osborn AG: *Introduction to Cerebral Angiography.* Philadelphia, Harper & Row, 1980, p. 114.

8. Newton TH, Potts GD: *Radiology of the Skull and Brain: Angiography,* vol. 2. Great Neck, NY, MediBooks, 1974, p. 1628.

9. Perl J, Ross JS, Smith AL, et al: 3D time-of-flight magnetic resonance angiography of congenital malformations, presented at the annual meeting of the ASNR. Vancouver, BC, May 16–20, 1993, p. 90.

10. Riggs HE, Rupp C: Variations in form of the circle of Willis. *Arch Neurol* 8:24, 1963.

11. Alpers BJ, Beery RG, Raddison RM: Anatomical studies of the circle of Willis in normal brain. *Arch Neurol Psychiatry* 81:409, 1959.

12. Kistler JP, Ropper AA, Martin JB: Cerebrovascular diseases, in *Harrison's Principles of Internal Medicine,* 12th ed. New York, NY, McGraw-Hill, 1991, pp. 1977–2002.

13. Purdy D, Cadena G, Laub G: Ramped excitation variable flip angle TOF. Proceedings of the 11th annual meeting of the Society of Magnetic Resonance in Medicine. Berlin, August 8, 1992, p. 882.

14. Edelman RR, Ahn SS, Chien D, et al: Improved time-of-flight MR angiography of the brain with magnetization transfer contrast. *Radiology* 184:395, 1992.

15. Dagirmanjian A, Ross JS, Lewin JS, et al: Use of high-resolution, variable flip angle, time-of-flight MR angiography in the detection of intracranial vascular stenoses. Presented at the annual meeting of the ASNR. Vancouver, BC, May 16–20, 1993, p. 92.

16. Blatter DD, Parker DL, Robison RO: Cerebral MR angiography with multiple overlapping thin slab acquisition: Part I. Quantitative analysis of vessel visibility. *Radiology* 179:805, 1991.

17. Smith AS, Haacke EM, Weili Lin MS, et al: TE 5 vs TE 8: Utility of short TE, 3D TOF intracranial MRA in children compared to adults. Presented at the annual meeting of the ASNR. Vancouver, BC, May 16–20, 1993, p. 97.

18. Ross MR, Pelc NJ, Enzmann DR: Qualitative phase contrast MRA in the normal and abnormal circle of Willis. *AJNR* 14:19, 1993.

19. Murakami DM, Bradley WG, Bucciarelli NR, et al: Gadodiamide enhanced 3D TOF magnetic resonance angiograhy: Slow flow versus vascular occlusion. Presented at the annual meeting of the ASNR. Vancouver, BC, May 16–20, 1993, p. 93.

20. Fox JL: The incidence of intracranial aneurysms, in Fox JL (ed): *Intracranial Aneurysms,* vol. 1. New York, Springer-Verlag, 1983, p. 15.

21. Kassell NF, Sasaki T, Colohan ART, Nazar G: Cerebral vasospasm following aneurysmal subarachnoid hemorrhage. *Stroke* 16:562, 1985.

22. Nehls DG, Flom RA, Carter LP, Spetzler RF: Multiple intracranial aneurysms: Determining the site of rupture. *J Neurosurg* 63:342, 1985.

23. Bigelow NH: The association of polycystic kidneys with intracranial aneurysms and other related disorders. *Am J Med Sci* 225:485, 1953.

24. Wiebers DO, Whisnant JP, Sundt TM, O'Fallon JM: The significance of unruptured intracranial saccular aneurysms. *J Neurosurg* 66:23, 1987.

25. Huston J, Rufenaht DA, Ehman RL, Wiebers DO: Intracranial aneurysms and vascular malformations: Comparison of time-of-flight and phase-contrast MR angiography. *Radiology* 181:721, 1991.

26. Pernicone JR, Sieber JE, Potchen EJ, et al: Three-dimensional MR angiography of the head and neck: Preliminary report. *AJNR* 11:457, 1990.

27. Ross, JS, Masaryk TJ, Modic MT, et al: Intracranial aneurysms: Evaluation by MR angiography. AJR 155:159, 1990.

28. Drake CG: Management of cerebral aneurysms. *Stroke* 12:273, 1981.

29. Wirth FP: Surgical treatment of incidental intracranial aneurysms. *Clin Neurosurg* 33:123, 1986.

30. *On MR and Aneurysm Clips.* U.S. Food and Drug Administration Medical Bulletin. June 1993, Rockville, MD.

31. Dumoulin CL: Phase-contrast magnetic resonance angiography. *Neuroimaging Clin North Am* 2:656, 1992.

32. Sevick RJ, Tsuruda JS, Schmalbrock P: Three-dimensional time-of-flight MR angiography in the evaluation of cerebral aneurysms. *JCAT* 14:874, 1990.

33. Jellinger K: Vascular malformations of the central nervous system: A morphologic overview. *Neurosurg Rev* 9:177, 1986.

34. Wilkins RH: Natural history of intracranial vascular malformations: A review. *Neurosurgery* 16:421, 1985.

35. Wilkins RH: *Natural History of Arteriovenous Malformations of the Brain,* in Barrow DL (ed): *Intracranial Vascular Malformations.* Park Ridge, IL, AANS Publications Committee, American Association of Neurosurgical Surgeons, 1989.

36. Crawfrd PM, West CR, Shaw MDM, Chadwick DW: Cerebral arteriovenous malformations and epilepsy: Factors in the development of epilepsy. *Epilepsia* 27:270, 1986.

Chapter 5

Carotid Magnetic Resonance Angiography

Georg M. Bongartz

Magnetic resonance imaging (MRI) demonstrated its capabilities for the diagnosis of disease in neuroradiology prior to being applied to other organ systems throughout the human body. Aside from the clinical need for a highly detailed imaging modality of the brain, with improved contrast over computed tomography (CT), the technical and anatomical requirements for a circumscribed and relatively motionless region were the main reasons for the initial successful application of MRI to this field. The development of dedicated coils to investigate the head and neck resulted in improved signal-to-noise ratios (SNR), enabling the detection of small structures with high confidence. The relatively easy access to the organs of the head and neck and the limited motion in this part of the body supported the application and testing of innovative techniques and sequences. Therefore, as with MRI, so with the development of magnetic resonance angiography (MRA): the first clinically useful results were achieved in the carotid and intracranial arteries.[1-4]

Anatomical Considerations

The carotid system consists of the common carotid artery (CCA), the internal carotid artery (ICA), and the external carotid artery (ECA). Originating from the aortic arch, the left CCA is approximately 1 to 2 cm longer than the right, which derives from the brachiocephalic trunk close to the right vertebral artery. The distance between the aortic arch and the skull base (carotid siphon) varies from 17 to 19 cm in the normal Western population. The carotid bifurcation usually lies at the level of the third cervical vertebral body, but a variation of 4 cm caudad or cephalad is possible. The lumen of the CCA widens at the bifurcation, forming the carotid bulb, which continues predominantly into the ICA. Rarely, a second bulb at the ECA origin or a single ECA bulb can be found. The bifurcation is usually rotated 10 to 30° from the sagittal plane, with the ICA lying posteriorly and laterally to the ECA. In up to 35 percent of the population, a variation in the orientation of the bifurcation can be found. Identification of the orientation of the carotid bifurcation is essential for the selection of the proper projection in conventional x-ray angiography.

The jugular veins run dorsal and lateral to the carotids on both sides and overlie the arteries in a nonselective MRA display. The vertebral arteries can readily be separated from the carotids in frontal projection, due to their more central position; in the lateral projection, the carotid and vertebral arteries may superimpose.

The vessels of the neck are surrounded by several muscle bundles which are themselves separated by fat planes. These fat layers are concentrated laterally and posteriorly and are displayed with relatively high signal intensity in T1-weighted sequences and in many MRA sequences.

Motion artifacts in carotid artery MRA usually originate from swallowing motion, which causes a complex up-and-down displacement of the hyoid and thyroid structures. In the case of large thyroid glands, the carotids may be displaced laterally during the swallowing process.

Flow Characteristics

Peak systolic velocities in the carotid system may exceed 100 cm/s, with an average velocity of 20 to 40 cm/s. The centrifugal blood flow in the aortic arch is oriented directly toward the origins of the brachiocephalic trunk and left CCA, giving rise to only minor flow eddies in the proximal CCAs. The straight course of the CCAs and the ICAs enable a laminar flow pattern to be maintained throughout the carotid arteries. However, at the bifurcation, vortical flow patterns with reversed flow may be present in the carotid bulb. Possibly related to the disturbances in laminar flow at the bifurcation, this site is most commonly affected by atherosclerosis, with resulting stenosis or occlusion.[5] Atherosclerotic plaques in the vessel wall produce irregularities in the flow pattern, or turbulence. The further stages of turbulence include vortical flow and flow eddies, in which a multitude of velocities and flow directions can be found simultaneously.[6]

In stenotic vessels, as the velocity of blood increases, turbulence is created. The degree of turbulence is related to the degree of stenosis.

TECHNIQUES OF CAROTID MRA

Optimal MRA techniques must respect the geometry and physiology of flow in the relevant vessels. Imaging of straight vessels with fast flow requires a different sequence design than that of curved vessels with slow flow. In the carotid system, the relatively fast laminar flow and the unidirectional course of the vessels make the application of inflow MRA techniques relatively straightforward (Fig. 5-1).[7,8]

Inflow MRA (Time of Flight)

PRINCIPLES AND LIMITATIONS

In time-of-flight sequences, the differences in longitudinal magnetization between static background and moving spins

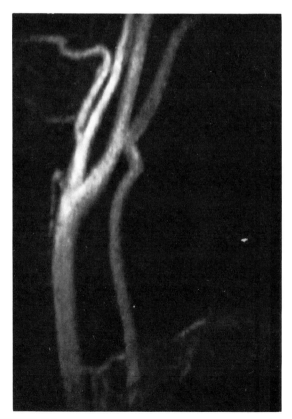

FIGURE 5-1 Time-of-flight MRA of a normal volunteer. Display of the right carotid artery in sagittal projective reconstruction (MIP) from a 128-partition axial volume acquisition. Note the signal decay at the periphery of the carotid arteries.

are highlighted. The achievable contrast depends on the repetition time (TR), the flip angle (FA), the longitudinal relaxation time (T1), and the velocity (v) of the blood in relation to the length of the investigated vessel (d). Under fast-flow conditions, the TR can be reduced to a minimum because strong inflow preserves the signal of the blood at a high level while the background signal is suppressed due to the frequent transmission of radiofrequency (rf) power. At the same time, the measurement time is minimized.[9] The flow velocity also affects the persistence of the signal of blood within an excited slice or volume: saturation effects are reduced in fast-flow conditions, allowing one to increase the length of the vessel investigated. Slow flow becomes saturated under such conditions (Fig. 5-1).[9,10]

SELECTIVITY

In carotid artery imaging, venous signal is suppressed by the inherent tendency of slow flow to become saturated in time-of-flight sequences. In addition, saturation pulses are added. These are usually placed transversely cephalad to the visualized portion of the carotid arteries. Alternatively, a coronal saturation slab to cover dural sinus inflow can also help remove signal from the jugular veins (Fig. 5-2). By saturation of the venous signal, a selective arterial MRA including both carotids and vertebrals can be created. For selective display of a single carotid artery, the maximum-intensity projection (MIP) reconstruction may be restricted to either the left or right side. Most of the time, vertebral signal cannot be removed completely and some overlap of arterial signals may occur.[11-13]

TWO-DIMENSIONAL ACQUISITION

In two-dimensional thin-slice imaging, a slice perpendicular to the vessel will experience replacement of the entire blood volume within that slice from one excitation to the next, even with relatively slow flow. In other words, each slice in a two-dimensional sequential MRA acquisition is an entry slice with unsaturated magnetization of the inflowing blood. Therefore, two-dimensional acquisitions are sensitive to flow even when flow in a vessel is reduced locally (for example, distal to high-grade stenoses) or by systemic conditions (for example, low-cardiac-output syndromes). Ideally, two-dimensional images should be acquired sequentially in order to prevent signal saturation from one slice to the next. As each slice takes only a few seconds, imaging of the entire carotid system requires only minutes. Slice thickness in sequential two-dimensional MRA varies between 3 and 5 mm, while in-plane resolution usually approximates 1 mm in both directions. This relatively large voxel size may cause increased signal dephasing in turbulent flow states, as in poststenotic segments or at the region of the bifurcation.[14,15]

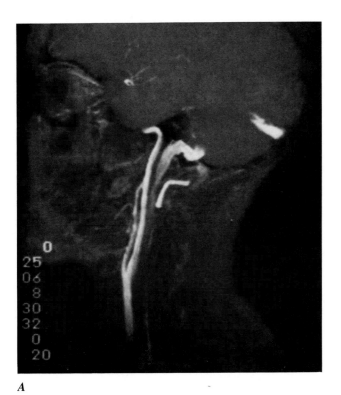
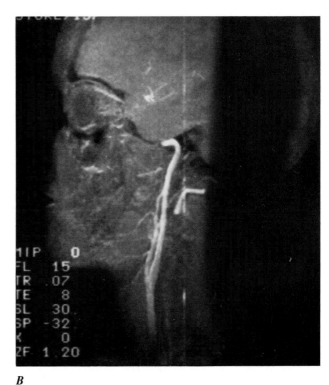

A *B*

FIGURE 5-2 Sagittal time-of-flight MRA of the left carotid artery. In (*A*), no presaturation pulses are applied, while in (*B*) a coronal presaturation pulse placed on the posterior venous drainage system of the brain eliminates the signal from the jugular vein.

In-plane saturation effects can be problematic in two-dimensional MRA with high flip angles, which are commonly used for imaging. In carotid artery MRA, this artifactual signal loss due to saturation occurs in the presence of elongated vessels which run horizontally as well as in the intracranial carotid. Overlap of 30 to 40° of the slice thickness is mandatory in two-dimensional MRA to avoid signal inhomogeneities between adjacent slices. Nevertheless, MIP reconstructions of the carotid vasculature are fairly coarse due to the relatively large slice thickness. Gross patient motion between each slice acquisition causes a shift of the blood vessel signal with a stair-step appearance, which may cause considerable image degradation (Fig. 5-3).

THREE-DIMENSIONAL ACQUISITION

In three-dimensional imaging, a volume of data is excited by a single broad rf pulse. A second phase-encoding gradient in the slice selection axis allows separation of thin, sharply defined partitions. With respect to the signal from inflowing spins, a volume acquisition enlarges the imaging volume in which the blood must flow and in which it experiences rf pulses. In other words, for the same velocity and imaging parameters, progressive signal saturation will occur as the vessel proceeds through the imaging slab.[16–18]

For a given acquisition time, the SNR in three-dimensional techniques is superior to that in two-dimensional MRA. This allows a reduction in voxel size, improving resolution.

EFFECTS OF VOXEL SIZE IN TIME-OF-FLIGHT MRA

With a field of view (FOV) of 200 to 250 mm in a matrix of 256 × 256, the in-plane resolution of a three-dimensional data set is less than 1 mm. In contrast to the two-dimensional technique, the partition thickness can readily be reduced to 1 mm or less, resulting in isotropic resolution. As the voxel size becomes smaller, the MIP reconstructions become more reliable diagnostically and show finer detail. Besides this improvement in image reconstruction in high-resolution three-dimensional MRA, the amount of incompletely rephased spins is repetitious—for example, at sites of turbulent flow, they are reduced with the smaller voxel sizes. Of course, the decrease in voxel size is limited by SNR considerations (due to the reduction of the total number of spins in each voxel).[2,19]

The vortical flow in the normal carotid bifurcation causes flow eddies, which may not be completely rephased with reduction in the apparent diameter of the bulb. The reduction in intravoxel phase dispersion by high-resolution three-

FIGURE 5-3 Comparison of a two-dimensional (*left*) and a three-dimensional (*right*) MRA in a patient with a moderate stenosis of the internal carotid artery. The "venetian blind" artifact raises a diagnostic problem at the carotid bulb, where the gross motion affected one particular slice such that the signal is missing completely. (Inverted gray scale for improved detection of small details and suppression of background noise.)

dimensional imaging helps maintain high vascular signal, with improvement in the imaging of vessel branches and stenotic areas. Further improvements in resolution can be obtained by the application of a 512 matrix. However, doubling the number of phase-encoding steps doubles the imaging time; therefore asymmetrical matrices (for example, 512 pixels in the readout axis and 256 or less in the phase-encoding axis) are more practical. Another approach is the use of rectangular FOVs, which maintain high spatial resolution in the phase-encoding axis while minimizing imaging time.

EFFECTS OF SLICE ORIENTATION

The orientation of the volume acquired in three-dimensional MRA affects the size of the volume which can be investigated, saturation effects, and the imaging parameters that should be used. From the anatomical point of view, a coronal or sagittal volume may be preferable because it allows the carotid system to be covered from the aortic arch to the siphon. However, there is a trade-off in the relatively pronounced saturation effects on the inflowing spins within the carotid arteries, which run parallel to the slice orientation. Imaging parameters must therefore be adjusted to reduce saturation effects. One approach is to utilize longer TRs, which allows the blood to recover magnetization between consecutive rf pulses. In addition, lower FAs, which also reduce saturation effects, are helpful in coronal and sagittal acquisitions.

Sagittal three-dimensional MRA can be performed efficiently using two excitation slabs, each of which covers one carotid artery. Both slabs can be acquired simultaneously, with alternating excitation of each volume (Fig. 5-4). By reducing the number of partitions within each slab to half of a standard single-volume three-dimensional acquisition, the acquisition time can be kept constant even though the TR is doubled. The increased TR in sagittal double-slab acquisition helps maintain high signal even in poststenotic areas of diminished flow.[21,22]

The application of coronal or sagittal three-dimensional volumes requires skillful operation positioning, because the narrow coverage in the slice-selection direction leave only a small window for the carotid arteries. Elongated, tortuous vessels may course out of the volume and can be misinterpreted as stenotic or occluded. Appropriate planning of the study requires not only a correct estimation of the location of the carotid bifurcation but also rapid scout views which can demonstrate the entire posterior and lateral extent of the carotid arteries.[1,17,19]

There is one important hardware issue that must be considered when utilizing coronal or sagittal acquisition. In receive-only neck coils, the rf pulse is transmitted by the body coil. Coronal or sagittal pulses of the body coil are not limited to the neck area and therefore the blood in the aortic arch is affected by the rf power, which may produce saturation effects and reduce vascular signal from inflow into the carotid arteries.[22] The orientation of the imaged volume can be tilted slightly in order to avoid the aortic arch and heart, but the degree of obliquity obtainable is restricted by the need to cover the entire length of the carotid artery. Optimally, coronal or sagittal MRA acquisitions should be performed in transmit-receive coils, which restrict the rf power to the investigated volume and preserve maximum inflow effect.[22,23]

For axial three-dimensional MRA studies, this hardware issue is less important, since axial acquisitions limit the rf power to the neck or head. Axial three-dimensional inflow techniques are most often utilized for carotid MRA. The advantages of this approach are high in-plane resolution, flexibility in coil design, strong sensitivity to inflowing blood, and reduced saturation effects. The disadvantage to this approach is limited coverage of the carotid in the ce-

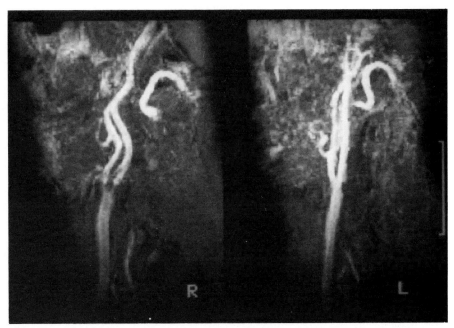

A

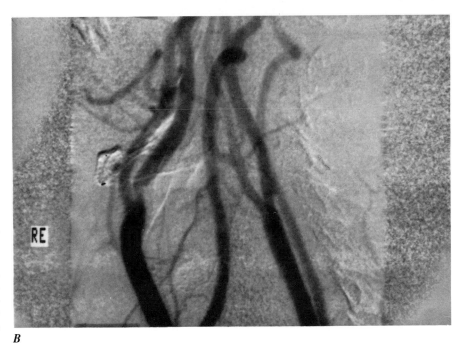

FIGURE 5-4 *A*. Sagittal double-slab three-dimensional acquisition in a patient with bilateral bifurcational stenoses, as confirmed by the nonselective digital subtraction arteriograhy, or DSA. *B*. Note a minor overestimation of the stenotic degree in MRA. Relatively strong signal from the background due to the long repetition time (TR = 80 ms, TE = 8 ms). The distal parts of the vertebral arteries are demonstrated with high signal intensity because they enter the two slabs without being affected by rf pulses earlier.

B

phalocaudad direction. Using standard protocols, the length of the carotid which can be covered varies between 6 and 8 cm centered at the carotid bifurcation. As resolution increases, smaller ECA branches and subtle irregularities of the vessel wall can be displayed. A reasonable set of imaging parameters for us to study would be a rectangular 200 mm × 150 mm FOV, 512 × 200 matrix, and 1-mm partition thickness, which combines high resolution with a resonable measuring time (Fig. 5-5).

Comparison of Two- and Three-Dimensional Acquisitions: Benfits and Trade-offs

The data published to date on carotid artery MRA do not allow a final assessment as to which of the above techniques is optimal for all clinical uses. With two-dimensional MRA, the strong inflow signal and unlimited number of slices obtainable are balanced by relatively low resolution and greater in-plane saturation. Conversely, three-dimensional acquisi-

FIGURE 5-5 Axial high-resolution time-of-flight MRA of a patient with an atherosclerotic plaque at the bifurcation, leading to a flattening of the bulb. Improved detail of the carotid system, including the branches of the external carotid artery, is seen when compared to a sagittal or coronal acquisition technique (Fig. 5-4).

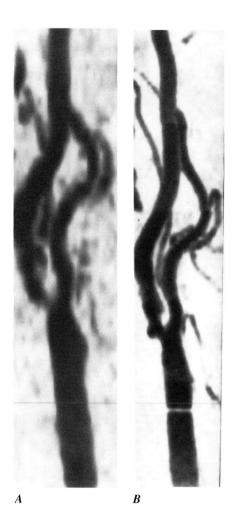

A   *B*

FIGURE 5-6 Two- and three-dimensional axial inflow MRA of the same patient in lateral projection. The two-dimensional MRA (*A*) shows much inferior resolution due to a slice thickness of 3 mm. The partition thickness of 1 mm in the three-dimensional approach (*B*) enables detection of the centrally ulcerated plaque formation at the carotid bulb. In-plane resolution is identical.

tions exhibit opposite features: signal saturation as the vessel penetrates the imaged volume (this increases with volume size), a restricted slab thickness, but high resolution and reduced variation of flow signal between in-plane and through-plane vessels.[15,17,24,25]

For clinical carotid artery MRA, the most important information to be obtained is the presence of atherosclerotic plaque, the degree of stenosis, and the presence of complicated lesions such as ulcerated plaques. For detection of carotid stenosis, either method is capable of achieving diagnostic results. Exact grading of a stenosis and morphological evaluation requires the highest resolution possible; therefore, three-dimensional MRA is preferable. With the thicker slices obtainable with two-dimensional MRA, small details will be smoothed out and subtle morphological features may be missed completely (Fig. 5-6).[26,27]

The relatively large voxel sizes in two-dimensional MRA also produce stronger sensitivity to intravoxel phase dispersion, both in regions of poststenotic turbulent flow and in the vortical flow in the carotid bulb. Signal loss at the origin of the internal carotid artery may therefore be pronounced

and may artifactually increase the apparent degree of stenosis.[28]

The main disadvantage of the three-dimensional technique is the saturation effect, which is most pronounced in slow-flow conditions. The reduction in flow in a vessel with a tight stenosis can lead to complete signal loss in three-dimensional techniques. Sequential two-dimensional MRA is extremely sensitive to slow flow and may display improved vascular signal in such cases. An example of such a "pseudoocclusion" in three-dimensional MRA is shown in Fig. 5-7. Elongated and tortuous internal carotid arteries are demonstrated better with three-dimensional than with two-dimensional MRA provided that they are contained within the three-dimensional volume. A signal void due to in-plane saturation of tortuous vertebral and carotid arteries can de-

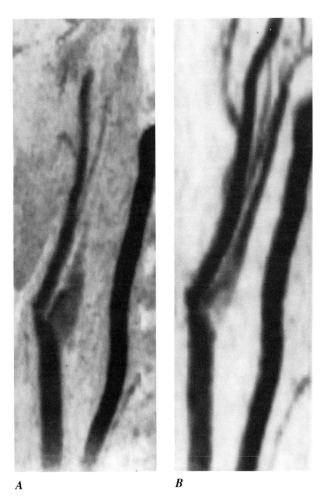

A   *B*

FIGURE 5-7 *A.* Carotid dissection with "pseudoocclusion" in three-dimensional MRA. The signal in the internal carotid artery decays, forming a "tail," suspicious for residual flow. *B.* The two-dimensional MRA demonstrates the persistent flow in the peripheral internal carotid artery correctly.

grade two-dimensional MRA images such that correct interpretation may be impossible (Fig. 5-8).

Gross patient motion in sequential two-dimensional techniques creates artifacts which complicate clinical interpretation (Fig. 5-3). Shifting of a slice in one direction or another may give a steplike appearance to the vessel, which may be difficult to distinguish from pathological alterations in the wall.[29] With three-dimensionl MRA, motion does not produce actual vessel misregistration but rather generalized blurring, which decreases the contrast-to-noise ratio (CNR) and may also seriously degrade the image quality. In summary, the effects of patient motion tend to be more noticeable and harmful in sequential two-dimensional than in three-dimensional acquisitions.

The optimal technique for carotid artery MRA depends on the pathology to be detected. Since the diagnoses is not usually known prior to the study, a compromise has to be made or both methods must be combined to meet all clinical requirements.[22]

Multiple Overlaping Thin Slab Angiography (MOTSA)

The MOTSA technique combines the advantages of three-dimensional MRA with the benefits of sequential two-dimensional MRA and produces a sequentially acquired three-dimensional data set. In acquiring multiple three-dimensional slabs, the thickness of each slab is reduced, which helps prevent saturation within the volume. While a single slab would not allow adequate coverage, multiple thin slabs of 8 to 32 partitions each can be produced to provide a sufficiently long data set for clinical use.[22,35]

The contour of a three-dimensional volume in the slice-select direction is rather poorly defined with broad rf shoulders. This makes considerable overlap of the adjacent three-dimensional slabs necessary for clinical applications, and overlap of at least 33 percent is required to provide homogeneous signal along the vessel.

Up to 10 or 15 of such separate axial slabs can be acquired sequentially to cover the carotid arteries from the aortic arch to the skull base. The signal persistence within the volume exceeds that in a standard single-volume three-dimensional acquisition. As in the sequential two-dimensional technique, patient motion between adjacent acquisitions can create artifactual step artifacts. Especially at the carotid bifurcation, this effect can mimic atheromatous plaque or stenosis (Fig. 5-9).[36] Within each slab, saturation can occur depending on the actual flow or velocity present. The TR and FA must be adjusted to produce consistent signal throughout the slab. In practical terms, the FA can be subtly increased compared to single-volume three-dimensional acquisitions due to the smaller distance through which the vessel is liable to become saturated. However, in reduced-flow conditions, a low FA is more appropriate to prevent saturation effects from diminishing flow signal. The TR should be kept as short as possible, because measurement time is longer in the MOTSA technique due to the requirement for overlapping the individual slabs.

Tilted Optimized Nonsaturation Excitation (TONE)

Another way to reduce saturation effects in three-dimensional TOF MRA is to reduce the rf power. Either increasing TR or decreasing FA results in a reduction in the rf power to which the excited slab is exposed. However, prolongation of the TR increases background signal and prolongs imaging time, neither which is acceptable in clinical imaging. Low FAs, in addition to reducing saturation effects, also diminish

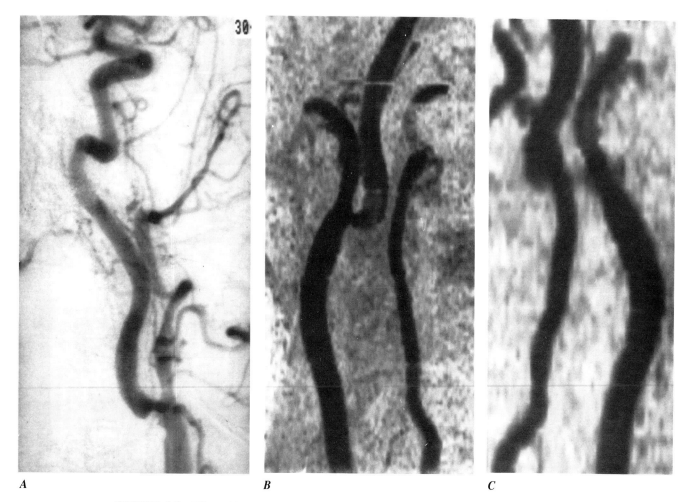

A   *B*   *C*

FIGURE 5-8 Effect of in-plane saturation in two-dimensional acquisition: comparison of the selective DSA (*A*), the multivolume (*B*), and the sequential two-dimensional MRA (*C*) of a patient with a prominent atheroma at the bifurcation. The horizontal course of the proximal internal carotid artery creates strong in-plane saturation in (*C*) which hides the stenosis completely.

the vessel-to-background contrast in the MRA slices. The high flow in the carotid arteries and their straight course have allowed the implementation of another technique to help resolve the problem of saturation in three-dimensional MRA. At the origin of the carotid arteries, the strong inflow of unsaturated spins requires only small FAs for the identification of flow signal. In addition, low FAs result in less rf power deposition and greater persistence of signal over a longer distance. The applied FA can then be increased along the course of the carotid artery, with stronger rf power implemented in the distal portion of the vessel. This results in increased recovery of the progressively decaying signal due to saturation effects.[37] The relationship between the entry and exit FAs must be optimized for the flow velocity: in the normal carotids, this relationship is 1 to 2. The most sophisticated technique for implementing this method is to use nonrectangular (tilt) rf profiles, which demonstrate a steady increase along the volume and the slope of which can be adjusted to different flow conditions (Fig. 5-9).

Background Suppression

In contrast to phase-contrast (PC) MRA, the background signal in TOF MRA is not completely eliminated but only relatively suppressed. Depending on the precise parameters used for the MRA sequence, the background signal can sometimes produce considerable problems by superimposition on important arterial structures. Structures with very short T1 relaxation times, like fat or hematoma, are most likely to be mistaken for vascular signal.

For the reduction of background signal, short TRs and low FAs are used. The echo time (TE) plays an additional important role in decreasing signal from fatty tissues. In general, the TEs should be as short as possible to minimizing

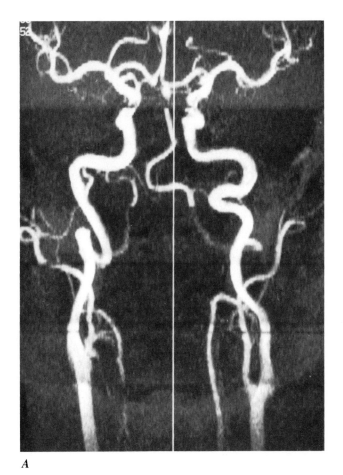

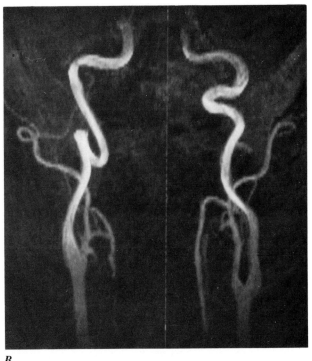

A   *B*

FIGURE 5-9   Direct comparison of a combined MOTSA study (*A*) to a TONE-optimized three-dimensional data set (*B*) of the carotid system. The extension of the FOV to the intracranial part in (*A*) clearly demonstrates the advantages of the MOTSA procedure. Minor signal inhomogeneities at the edges of each single slab in (*A*) can lead to misinterpretations, especially at the carotid bulb.

the dephasing effects. However, the TE selected should not be shorter than that which allows fat and water protons to be in opposed phase, as this helps reduce signal from fatty tissue. The optimal TEs are approximately 7 ms for 1.5 T and 10 ms for 1T systems.[22]

Another tool to reduce background signal in MRA is the use of magnetization transfer saturation (MTS).[38] However, MTS pulses are ineffective in suppressing fat signal. In the neck, the widespread distribution and perivascular location of the fatty tissue prevents MTS from being very useful here.

A reduction of fat signal by chemical-selective fat-suppression rf pulses has also not proven to be very effective in carotid MRA. The extra time required for fat suppression pulses requires longer TE times, with consequent increased loss of phase coherence and intravoxel phase dispersion. Moreover, most available fat-suppression pulses are unable to suppress fat signal efficiently and homogeneously within the FOV.[39]

Careful reconstruction of a subvolume of the data set restricted to the vasculature of interest (targeted MIP) helps to eliminate the majority of confusing signal from overlying soft tissue. Further developments in postprocessing will enable improved background suppression through thresholding and tissue-segmentation algorithms.

Phase-Contrast MRA

PRINCIPLES AND LIMITATIONS

The application of PC MRA to the carotids has proven less useful than TOF techniques. The flow-encoding gradients in three directions require longer measurement times and longer TEs. The long TEs produce greater phase incoherency in conditions of turbulent flow, which in turn lead to increased signal voids. Laminar flow in normal vessels can readily be depicted, but in stenotic vessels the results are inferior to TOF acquisitions.

For proper application of PC MRA, the velocity encoding

(VENC) must be adjusted correctly to the peak systolic flow velocity. If too high a velocity encoding is chosen, the flow sensitivity of the sequence is reduced; if too low an encoding is chosen, phase aliasing occurs.[30–33] In pathological conditions, the flow of velocity in the carotid system may vary considerably (e.g., between a normal CCA and a severely stenotic ICA). In such cases, PC MRA can be extremely problematic to implement.

A single thick-slab acquisition using the two-dimensional PC technique can be performed with low resolution in a relatively short time. The resulting projective angiogram can be helpful in planning and positioning a dedicated TOF MRA sequence.[7,34]

CLINICAL IMPLEMENTATION OF MRA

Clinical Requirements and Indications

Cerebrovascular disease is a common cause of death in western populations, directly after cancer and heart disease. Stroke and stroke-related impairments have a tremendous impact on health care costs in the United States and Europe. Atherosclerosis of the carotid arteries is an important contributor to the incidence of cerebral infarction. The risk of stroke is related to the degree of atherosclerotic narrowing of the vessel lumen. Carotid endarterectomy has proven to be a valuable tool for the treatment of atherosclerotic stenoses. The NASCET study demonstrated the efficacy of surgical therapy in symptomatic patients with greater than 70 percent stenosis. Severe stenoses in asymptomatic patients and ulcerated plaques in symptomatic patients may require endarterectomy in some, although these issues have yet to be resolved.[40–45]

Because of the importance of available therapeutic interventions, precise imaging of atherosclerotic stenosis is required for clinical management. X-ray angiography has been the most reliable method for the documentation of stenoses. However, the inherent risks from emboli or contrast media interactions during the procedure must be considered. The accuracy of angiography improves with selectivity of catheterization, but the invasiveness and consequently the risk also increase.[46,47] Duplex Doppler ultrasound has been applied to carotid artery disease. The diagnosis is based on the evaluation of flow velocities in stenotic vessels. This noninvasive and inexpensive method has had limited acceptance as a definitive examination. Calcified plaques limit access by ultrasonographic methods, and the investigation requires an experienced and knowledgeable operator. Most of the time, ultrasound is used as a screening technique and x-ray angiography is used prior to endarterectomy.[48–52] Magnetic resonance imaging may combine the benefits of a noninvasive diagnostic technique with the comprehensive documentation of atherosclerotic disease reproduced by digital sub-traction arteriography (DSA). Requirements for a successful MRA study are adequate resolution, sufficient coverage of the carotid artery, and reproducibility. The MRA examination focuses on the carotid bifurcation, since most manifestations of atherosclerosis are found there. The combination of a carotid MRA and an MRI of the brain in a single investigation reduces overall imaging costs and helps MRA to compete with the combination of x-ray angiography and CT.

Until recently, MRA of the carotid arteries has been limited to a research tool. As confidence in the technique has grown, MRA has been and will progressively be used as a primary clinical diagnostic method. Staging of atherosclerotic stenosis is the most common indication for carotid MRA. Anatomical variants and tumor staging are less frequent indications. Small tumor vessels cannot be reliably demonstrated due to insufficient resolution and saturation effects. In subclavian steal syndrome, acquisition of axial gradient slices with saturation placed alternately cephalad and caudad provides adequate information about the direction of vertebral artery flow in only a few seconds. MRA of the subclavian artery may be added to directly visualize the cause of the flow reversal.[53]

Based on the results of the NASCET trial, carotid imaging must be able to identify stenoses above the critical 70 percent threshold. Occlusions must be identified and differentiated from high-grade stenoses. Also, degrees of plaque and plaque ulceration must be detected.[54–56]

Interpretation

The technique of MRA is based on the flow dynamics in vessels rather than on the distribution of an injected bolus of contrast medium. This difference from x-ray angiography must be kept in mind for correct interpretation of the images, which are dependent on physiological and pathological flow conditions. Furthermore, the MRA technique that is used also affects the final image, since different techniques demonstrate different sensitivity to various kinds of flow disturbances.

When compared to an intraarterial DSA, MRA of a normal carotid artery displays a slightly flattened carotid bulb. This effect is explained by flow effects resulting from eddy currents at the bifurcation. The flow direction in the outer layer of the carotid bulb is inverted compared to the central carotid flow, and this so-called vortical flow causes spin dephasing and saturation, with resultant low signal in TOF MRA.[19,20,22]

As the wall becomes increasingly irregular due to atherosclerotic plaques, the laminar flow state is progressively more disturbed. Residual phase dispersion of the transverse magnetization remains in spite of applied rephasing gradients. This lack of phase coherence due to turbulence leads to focal signal voids in the MRA projection images. These flow-induced signal voids add to the luminal defect caused by the atherosclerotic plaque itself; therefore, stenoses in MRA tend to be overstaged compared to x-ray angiography.[1,14,57]

In MRA, the apparent length of the stenosis is also affected by poststenotic flow disturbances. Flow separation leads to differences in flow velocities and direction distal to the stenosis, with stagnant flow in the "shadow" behind a large plaque. This stagnant blood is readily saturated, mimicking a longer segment of stenosis on MRA than on conventional angiography (Fig. 5-5).

Medium-grade stenoses (50 to 70 percent) may resemble high-grade stenoses. High-grade stenoses may manifest as complete, focal signal voids on MRA with reappearance of the signal a few millimeters distally. In many cases, the critical limit of 70 percent stenosis may be marked on MRA by a short signal increase in the poststenotic portion of the vessel (Fig. 5-10). This effect (positive poststenotic jet) represents plug flow conditions in narrow stenoses and can be explained by improved rephasing when all flow vectors show identical length and orientation. In contrast, in laminar flow conditions, the outer layers of flow vectors (adjacent to the vessel wall) are shorter than the central ones due to slower flow velocities.[22,58]

Vascular occlusion in MRA gives the same appearance as in DSA: complete interruption of the vascular signal without reconstitution up to the intracranial portion of the carotid artery. For therapeutic decision making, the differentiation between occlusion and high-grade stenosis is of major importance. While in true occlusion further therapeutic maneuvers are contraindicated, severe stenoses are amenable to surgical treatment. This differentiation can become important in both atherosclerotic stenosis as well as dissections of the carotid arteries. Even in conventional angiography, the differentiation between severe stenoses and occlusion can sometimes be problematic. With severe stenosis, marked flow reduction can result in a so-called pseudoocclusion, in which the blood flow through the carotid artery is so slow as to be undetectable.[59] In both MRA and conventional angiography, one hint for residual flow in the distal carotid is provided by the shape of the signal drop-off: in a pseudoocclusion, the residual flow creates a slowly narrowing lumen with a relatively long "tail" of signal or contrast medium, whereas a true occlusion demonstrates abrupt interruption of the vessel lumen. Magnetic resonance angiography may have a theoretical advantage over DSA when applied in a sequential two-dimensional mode: the sensitivity to inflow in each slice of the data set can visualize extremely slow residual flow with high confidence and confirm the diagnosis of patency (Fig. 5-7). However, the relative sensitivity of MRA and DSA in the diagnosis of pseudoocclusion has yet to be determined.

The effects of turbulence in MRA mentioned above tend to produce an overestimation of the extent and severity of stenoses. The signal voids behind atherosclerotic plaque or in turbulent flow states are related to intravoxel phase dispersion and therefore depend directly on the voxel size, as discussed previously (Fig. 5-10). Improving resolution in MRA decreases the signal void effect and improves the ability to estimate the degree of stenosis. As MRA evolves with newer generations of sequences, interpretations also have to adapt to the lesser degree of overestimation that may occur. Meanwhile, three-dimensional MRA techniques are able to demonstrate a detailed wall morphology, such as ulcerations.

For correct interpretation, one must be aware of the saturation effects occurring with different types of MRA. In three-dimensional MRA, the inflow effect is influenced strongly by the choice of sequence parameters (TR, FA, or TONE). Furthermore, the patient's clinical condition must be taken into account, since a reduced cardiac output may strongly affect the degree of inflow enhancement on three-dimensional MRA. In low-output syndromes, two-dimensional or multislab three-dimensional methods are highly recommended. Two-dimensional MRA has shortcomings in patients with tortuous and kinked vessels. Under these conditions, in-plane saturation effects must be considered for proper interpretation (Fig. 5-8). Multiple views of the MIP reconstruction are helpful to detect this artifact. Viewing such an apparently interrupted vessel in only one or two projections is likely to lead to misinterpretation. Similarly, review of the original slices and highly restricted MIP projections may be required to diagnose such tortuous segments correctly.

As the interpreter gains experience in the clinical use of MRA, he or she will adjust to the effects of overestimation of stenosis with different MRA techniques. As imaging methods improve, the opposite problem may occur: the previously adapted mental correction of the MRA images to a slightly lower degree of stenosis may persist and cause underestimation of the degree of stenosis. This demonstrates the inherent potential for interpretational errors in MRA. Consequently, stable protocols are necessary to avoid such misinterpretations and to make MRA a clinically accepted modality.[60]

As for all clinical MRA procedures, viewing of the slices from the original data set provides additional information about vascular pathology. Areas of decreased signal in poststenotic segments and actual contours are better evaluated than on the MIP reconstructions. In the future, it may be possible to differentiate various types of atheroma based on their MRA appearance, and this may have implications with regard to phrmacological and surgical therapy.[55,61]

PROTOCOLS

Due to the larger number of MRA sequences available and the nonuniform types of MRA provided by difference man-

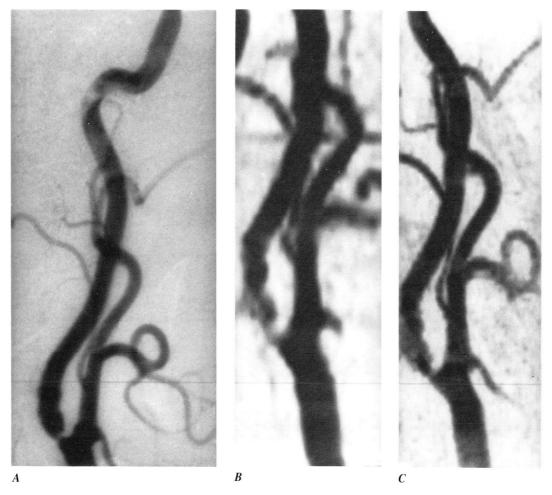

A   *B*   *C*

FIGURE 5-10   Patient with severe stenosis at the origin of the internal carotid artery. Identical projection of (*A*) a selective DSA, (*B*) a sequential two-dimensional MRA, and (*C*) a three-dimensional MRA. The degree and the extent of the stenosis is overestimated in (*B*), but correctly demonstrated in (*C*), the highly resolved MOTSA technique. Note the small increase of signal intensity behind the stenosis in the three-dimensional image, indicating a severe stenosis and plug-flow conditions.

ufacturers, fixed recommendations for clinical carotid artery MRA cannot be given. However, parameter selection should respect some general principles:

1. Three-dimensional TOF sequences offer the best resolution and represent the first choice for carotid artery MRA.

2. For covering a sufficient length of artery, either TONE or multislab three-dimensional MRA is recommended. If these are not available, two-dimensional MRA may be a substitute.

3. In slow-flow conditions (for example, severe stenosis or cardiac failure), multislab three-dimensional or two-dimensional MRA will provide improved images.

4. Sequential two-dimensional techniques are required for the recognition of pseudoocclusions.

5. Shortest TE, no less than that which will provide opposed fat and water phase, should be chosen to minimize intravoxel phase dispersion and maintain vessel-to-background contrast.

6. In three-dimensional MRA, short TRs and low FAs are recommended to minimize imaging time and maintain signal persistence for a longer distance.

7. First-order motion compensation should be routinely applied in slice-select and readout direction. Higher-order motion compensation lengthens TE time and gives worse results.

8. A combination of a three-dimensional and a sequential two-dimensional MRA sequence may be optimal for routine clinical imaging, as the actual flow conditions are unknown prior to the investigation (Fig. 5-11).

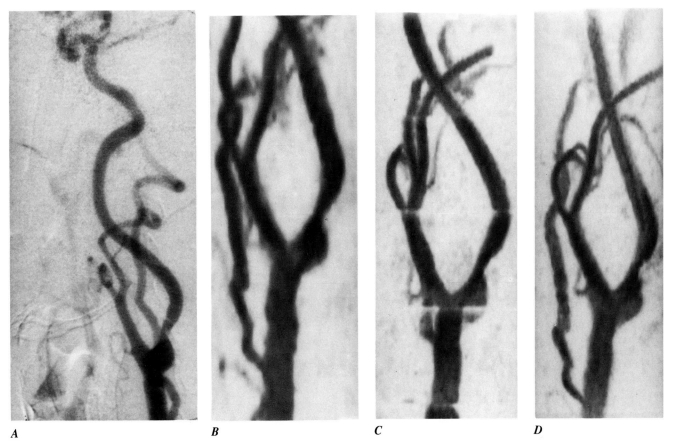

A   *B*   *C*   *D*

FIGURE 5-11   Three different techniques of inflow MRA in direct correlation to the gold standard, DSA (*A*). Sequential two-dimensional MRA (*B*) exaggerates the length of the stenosis. Multi-three-dimensional acquisition (*C*) demonstrates the atherosclerotic lesion exactly with persistent signal throughout the FOV. In this case, the volume overlap is insufficient, resulting in stripe artifacts across the vessel and in signal inhomogeneities at the carotid bulb. The rf-pulse-optimized (TONE) three-dimensional MRA (*D*) gives even better detail and sufficiently stable signal.

CLINICAL RESULTS

A multicenter trial utilizing the range of available software and hardware conditions is still lacking. In addition, a major problem in properly evaluating the reliability of MRA is the requirement to establish a gold standard for the grading of stenosis. No single method exists which is acknowledged to exhibit the true degree of area stenosis; x-ray angiography and Doppler methods as well as intraoperative assessment of residual lumen are prone to interpretive errors and demonstrate a considerable range of interobserver variability.[62] Interarterial selective DSA of the common carotid artery in at least two planes must be regarded as in the single best available gold standard.

The available data demonstrate a range of 75 to 94 percent agreement between MRA and DSA for carotid bifurcational stenoses. In most studies, overstaging of stenosis by one grade (normal, mild, moderate, severe, or occluded) is the commonest error of interpretation. When compared to ultrasound, MRA demonstrates similar accuracy with the advantage of better coverage of the length of the carotid artery. Compared with conventional angiography, both techniques suffer from a restricted FOV and the inability to detect ulcerations. Calcifications cannot be seen on MRA, while in ultrasound they may obscure portions of the vessel.[29,63,64]

The fact that MRA is highly complementary to routine MRI of the brain—and the potential for refinements such as flow quantification and direct analysis of the plaque composition—encourages the hope that this may become a standard for the clinical evaluation of carotid disease in the near future. A major need remains that of being able to visualize the entire length of the carotid artery from the aorta to the intracranial portion. As MR systems become more available, the role of MRA as a noninvasive and accurate modality for visualizing the carotid artery should increase.

REFERENCES

1. Peters PE, Bongartz G, Drews CI: Magnetresonanztomographie der hirnversorgenden Arterien. *Fortschr Röntgenstr* 152:528, 1990.
2. Ross JS, Masaryk TJ, Modic MT, et al: Magnetic resonance angiography of the extracranial carotid arteries and intracranial vessels: A review. *Neurology* 39:1369, 1989.
3. Russell EJ: Detection of significant extracranial carotid stenosis with routine cerebral MR imaging. *Radiology* 170:623, 1989.
4. Gullberg GT, Wehrli FW, Shimakawa A, Simons MA: MR vascular imaging with a fast gradient refocusing pulse sequence and reformatted images from transaxial sections. *Radiology* 165:241, 1987.
5. Kishore PR, Chase NE, Kricheff II: Carotid stenosis and intracranial emboli. *Radiology* 100:351, 1971.
6. Blackshear WM, Phillips DJ, Chikos PM: Carotid artery velocity patterns in normal and stenotic vessels. *Stroke* 11:67, 1980.
7. Chao PW, Goldberg H, Dumoulin CL, Wehrli FW: Comparison of time-of-flight versus phase contrast techniques: Visualization of the intra- and extracerebral carotid artery. *SMRM Book of Abstracts* 1:165, 1989.
8. Edelman RR, Mattle HP, Atkinson DJ, Hoogewoud HM: MR angiography. *AJR* 154:937, 1990.
9. Laub GA, Kaiser WA: MR angiography with gradient motion refocussing. *J Comput Assist Tomogr* 12:377, 1988.
10. Masaryk TJ, Ross JS, Modic MT, et al: Carotid bifurcation: MR imaging. *Radiology* 166:461, 1988.
11. Masaryk TJ: MR angiography, in *Syllabus of MR Imaging*. RSNA 1990, pp. 57–62.
12. Felmlee JP, Ehman RL: Spatial presaturation: A method for suppressing flow artifacts and improving depiction of vascular anatomy in MRI. *Radiology* 164:559, 1987.
13. König HA, Laub G: The processing and display of three-dimensional data in magnetic resonance imaging. *electromedica* 56:42, 1988.
14. Litt AW, Eidelman EM, Pinto RS, et al: Diagnosis of carotid artery stenosis: Comparison of 2DFT time-of-flight MR angiography with contrast angiography in 50 patients. *AJNR* 12:149, 1991.
15. Heiserman JE, Drayer BP, Fram EK, et al: Carotid artery stenosis: Clinical efficacy of two-dimensional time-of-flight MR angiography. *Radiology* 182:761, 1992.
16. Bongartz GM, Vestring Th, Fahrendorf G, Peters PE: Einsatz schneller Sequenzen bei der kraniozerebralen MR-Diagnostik. *Fortschr Röntgenstr* 153:669, 1990.
17. Masaryk AM, Ross JS, DiCello MC, et al: 3DFT MR angiography of the carotid bifurcation: Potential and limitations as a screening examination. *Radiology* 179:797, 1991.
18. Masaryk TJ, Modic MT, Ruggieri PM, et al: Three-dimensional (volume) gradient-echo imaging of the carotid bifurcation: Preliminary clinical experience. *Radiology* 171:801, 1989.
19. Bongartz GM, Vestring Th, Drews CI, et al: Effect of slice orientation in 3D magnetic resonance angiography of the supraaortic arteries. *Eur Radiol* 1:158, 1991.
20. Lin W, Haacke EM, Smith AS: Lumen definition in MR angiography. *J Mag Res Imaging* 1:327, 1991.
21. Li D, Kramer J, Kleefield J, Edelman RR: MR angiography of the extracranial carotid arteries using a two slab oblique 3-D acquisition. *AJNR* 13:1423, 1992.
22. Anderson CM, Haacke EM: Approaches to diagnostic magnetic resonance carotid angiography. *Semin Ultrasound CT MRI* 13:246, 1992.
23. Daniels DL, Kneeland JB, Foley WD, et al: Cardiac-gated local coil MR imaging of the carotid neck bifurcation. *AJNR* 7:1036, 1986.
24. Pernicone JR, Siebert JE, Potchen EJ, et al: Three-dimensional phase-contrast MR angiography in the head and neck: Preliminary report. *AJR* 155:167, 1990.

25. Keller PJ, Drayer BP, Fram EK, et al: MR-angiography with two-dimensional-acquisition and three-dimensional-display. *Radiology* 173:527, 1989.
26. Bongartz GM, Laub G, Peters PE: Imaging of atherosclerosis with MRI, in Strano A, Novo S (eds): *Advances in Vascular Pathology*. Amsterdam-NewYork-Oxford, Elsevier Science Publishers B.V. (Excerpta Medica), 1990, pp. 121–126.
27. Laub GA: Displays for MR angiography. *Mag Res Med* 14:222, 1990.
28. Lewin JS, Laub G: Intracranial MR angiography: A comparison of three different time-of-flight techniques. *AJNR* 12:1133, 1991.
29. Huston J, Lewis BD, Wiebers DO et al: Carotid artery: Prospected blinded comparison of two-dimensional time-of-flight MR angiography with conventional angiography and duplex US. *Radiology* 186:339, 1993.
30. Dumoulin CL, Hart HR: Magnetic resonance angiography. *Radiology* 161:717, 1986.
31. Dumoulin CL, Souza SP, Walker MF, Wagle W: Three-dimensional phase contrast angiography. *Mag Res Med* 9:139, 1989.
32. Wagle WA, Cousins JP, Dumoulin CL, Souza SP: Magnetic resonance angiography of the cervical and intracranial vasculature. *SMRM Book of Abstracts*, 1989, p. 157.
33. Pernicone JR, Siebert JE, Laird TA, Potchen EJ: Determination of blood flow direction using velocity-phase image display with 3-D phase-contrast MR angiography. *AJNR* 13:1435, 1992.
34. Kido DK, Barsotti JB, Rice LZ, et al: Evaluation of the carotid artery bifurcation: Comparison of magnetic resonance angiography and digital subtraction arch aortography. *Neuroradiology* 33:48, 1991.
35. Blatter DD, Parker DL, Robinson RO: Cerebral MR angiography with multiple overlapping thin slab acquisition. *Radiology* 179:805, 1991.
36. Masaryk TJ, Obuchowski NAS: Noninvasive carotid imaging: Caveat emptor. *Radiology* 186:325, 1993.
37. Ruggieri PR, Tkach JA, Ding X, et al: Three-dimensional time-of-flight MR angiography with stacked volumes, special RF pulses, and background suppression. *Radiology* 189:106, 19??.
38. Edelman RR, Ahn SS, Chien D, et al: Improved time of flight MR angiography of the brain with magnetization transfer contrast. *Radiology* 184:395, 1992.
39. Robinson RO, Blatter DD, Parker DL, et al: Fat suppression in combination with multiple overlapping thin-slab 3-D acquisition MR angiography. *AJNR* 13:1429, 1992.
40. Moneta GL, Taylor DC, Nicholls SC, et al: Operative versus nonoperative management of asymptomatic high-grade internal carotid artery stenosis: Improved results with endarterectomy. *Stroke* 18:1005, 1987.
41. Nobbe F: Prognose beim akuten Karotisverschluß. *Versicherungsmedizin* 6:157, 1988.
42. Raithel D: Diagnostik und Therapie der zerebro-vaskulären Insuffizienz. *Versicherungsmedizin* 41:165, 1989.
43. Towne JB, Weiss DG, Hobson RW: First phase report of cooperative Veterans Administration asymptomatic carotid stenosis study: Operative morbidity and mortality. *J Vasc Surg* 11:252, 1990.
44. North American Symptomatic Carotid Endarterectomy Trial Collaborators: Beneficial effect of carotid endarterectomy in symptomatic patients with high grade stenosis. *N Engl J Med* 325:445, 1991.
45. Warlow C: European Carotid Surgery Trialists' Collaborative Group: MRC European carotid surgery trial: Interim results for symptomatic patients with severe carotid stenosis and with mild carotid stenosis. *Lancet* 337:1235, 1991.
46. Gryska U, Fritag J, Zeumer H: Selective cerebral intraarterial DSA: Complication rate and control of risk factors. *Neuroradiology* 32:296, 1990.

47. Olivecrona H: Complications of cerebral angiography. *Neuroradiology* 14:175, 1977.
48. Zierler RE, Phillips DJ, Beach KW, et al: Noninvasive assessment of normal carotid bifurcation hemodynamics with color-flow ultrasound imaging. *Ultrasound Med Biol* 13:471, 1987.
49. Taylor KJW, Holland S: Doppler US: Part I. Basic principles, instrumentation, and pitfalls. *Radiology* 174:297, 1990.
50. Steinke W, Kloetzsch C, Hennerici M: Carotid artery disease assessed by color Doppler flow imaging: Correlation with standard Doppler sonography and angiography. *AJR* 154:1061, 1990.
51. Scoutt LM, Zawin ML, Taylor KJW: Doppler US: Part II. Clinical applications. *Radiology* 174:309, 1990.
52. Mendel HJ, Olbert F, Schlegl A, Nebosis M: Duplex sonography, intravenous digital subtraction angiography, intraarterial digital subtraction angiography and conventional angiography in assessing carotid atherosclerosis. *Ann Radiol* 2:115, 1987.
53. Turjman F, Tournut P, Baldy-Porcher C, et al: Demonstration of subclavian steal by MR angiography. *JCAT* 16:756, 1992.
54. Renz J, Merritt CRB, Bluth EI: Sonographic evaluation of carotid plaque. *Appl Radiol* 8:29, 1990.
55. Polak JF, Kalina P, Donaldson MC, et al: Carotid endarterectomy: Preoperative evaluation of candidates with combined Doppler sonography and MR angiography. Work in progress. *Radiology* 186:333, 1993.
56. Polak JF: Noninvasive carotid evaluation: Carpe diem. *Radiology* 186:329, 1993.
57. Wilkerson DK, Keller I, Mezrich R: The comparative evaluation of three-dimensional magnetic resonance for carotid artery disease. *J Vasc Surg* 14:803, 1991.
58. Urchuk SM, Plewes DB: Mechanisms of flow-induced signal loss in MR angiography. *J Mag Res Imaging* 2:453, 1992.
59. O'Leary DH, Mattle H, Potter JE: Atheromatous pseudo-occlusion of the internal carotid artery: A review of 34 patients. *Stroke* 20:1168, 1989.
60. Wesby GE, Bergran JJ, Moreland SI, et al: Cerebrovascular magnetic resonance angiography: A critical verification. *J Vasc Surg* 16:619, 1992.
61. Anderson CM, Saloner D, Tsuruda JS, et al: Artifacts in maximum intensity projection display of MR angiograms. *AJR* 154:623, 1990.
62. Fox AJ: How to measure a carotid stenosis. *Radiology* 186:316, 1993.
63. Anderson CM, Saloner D, Lee RE, et al: Assessment of carotid artery stenosis by MR angiography: Comparison with x-ray angiography and color-encoded ultrasound. *AJNR* 13:989, 1992.
64. Mitchell DG: Color-Doppler imaging: Principles, limitations, and artifacts. *Radiology* 177:1, 1990.

Chapter 6

Magnetic Resonance Angiography: A Clinical Neurological Perspective

Daryl R. Gress

The clinician dealing with cerebrovascular disease often requires precise information of vascular anatomy. Traditional contrast angiography has been refined over the last forty years from direct carotid puncture to superselective digital subtraction angiography. Conventional contrast angiography currently is considered the standard to which all other vascular imaging modalities are compared. Precise anatomical features are detailed and hemodynamic information is inferred in conventional angiography. All decisions concerning diagnostic studies must, however, balance risk and benefit. The risks of conventional angiography depend not only on operator experience but also on the extent of vascular disease. Extensive atheromatous disease associated with diabetes and hypertension provides for significantly higher risk of embolization of either cholesterol or thrombotic fragments than when the same procedure is carried out in a normal vasculature. In this sense conventional angiography to study vasoocclusive disease is most needed in settings of highest risk. The risks of permanent morbidity and mortality have been reported as low as 0.5 percent or less,[1,2] although in elderly patients with severe, diffuse atherosclerotic disease the risks may well be several fold higher.

There is a clear need for a precise noninvasive technique for vascular imaging. Ultrasound and Doppler examination provides for reliable detection of significant stenosis of the carotid artery at the bifurcation. Transcranial Doppler can detect intracranial stenoses, although with less reliability. These studies combined can provide valuable information regarding hemodynamic consequences associated with severe stenoses. However, ultrasound provides only limited imaging detail and cannot adequately assess much of the cerebral circulation.

Magnetic resonance angiography (MRA) is a noninvasive imaging modality that utilizes properties of moving protons in an applied magnetic field to provide a representation of blood flow. The technique is rapidly emerging as a valuable tool in the evaluation of both extracranial and intracranial vasculature, and it is most useful when focused upon a particular clinical cerebrovascular problem.

CAROTID SYSTEM—EXTRACRANIAL

Stroke related to stenosis of the extracranial carotid accounts for a significant portion of stroke related morbidity and mortality. It has been clearly demonstrated that carotid endarterectomy reduces stroke risk in the setting of symptomatic severe stenosis.[3] The efficacy of surgical intervention in the setting of asymptomatic stenosis remains to be demonstrated. The vast majority of the vascular lesions are localized to the cervical carotid bifurcation.

Magnetic resonance angiography has been used to image the extracranial carotid. Current imaging sequences most often involve two-dimensional (2D) time-of-flight technique and have achieved good reliability. Series with a sensitivity of over 90 percent and a specificity of 80 to 90 percent for detection of severe stenoses have been reported.[4,5]

Signal dropout in severe stenoses leads to a "skip sign," and overestimation of the severity of stenosis can occur. It is therefore not possible to distinguish critical stenosis from total occlusion reliably. Conventional angiography is necessary to confirm total occlusion when that information is clinically necessary. Magnetic resonance angiography does not provide information concerning the hemodynamic consequences of the stenosis. High-quality ultrasound and Doppler studies can provide hemodynamic information, and correlation with MRA can provide reliable noninvasive imaging. It is possible, under circumstances where the clinical features and noninvasive data are consistent, to proceed to surgical endarterectomy without conventional angiography. This approach helps minimize both morbidity and expense.

Spontaneous or posttraumatic carotid dissection is a common cause of stroke in young adults. Diagnosis of dissection of the internal carotid has been made from standard magnetic resonance imaging (MRI) and MRA. Narrowing of the vessel lumen as visualized on MRA and evidence of subintimal thrombus on MRI provide the diagnostic findings. However, the sensitivity of MRA for this vascular lesion is sufficiently low that MRA currently should not be used to exclude dissection as a diagnostic possibility.

CAROTID SYSTEM—INTRACRANIAL

The technique of MRA has afforded the clinician the first practical noninvasive technology for imaging intracerebral vessels. A 3D time-of-flight technique is most often used for visualization of the intracranial vessels. It is possible to visualize the intracranial carotid through the siphon as well as the interior and middle cerebral arteries. Divisions and small branches remain difficult to visualize and cannot be done with sufficient reliability to be clinically useful. Occlusive vascular disease affecting the intracranial carotid, proximal anterior cerebral artery, or middle cerebral stem, however, can be reliably evaluated with MRA. For many patients with ischemic stroke symptoms, MRA can provide the diagnosis and eliminate the need for conventional angiography.

As with MRA of the cervical carotid, the intracranial examination does not give significant information concerning the hemodynamic consequences of vascular lesions. It may be necessary to combine MRA with information derived from transcranial Doppler in order to understand the cerebrovascular dynamics more fully.

VERTEBROBASILAR SYSTEM

A major advance for the clinician faced with the need for evaluation of the posterior circulation is provided by MRA. While noninvasive Doppler information has been available for the assessment of vertebrobasilar disease, it is difficult to evaluate the full extent of the vessels. Transcranial Doppler can provide some information about stenotic lesions, although segments of the vertebrobasilar system are not routinely examined. However, MRA can visualize the intracranial vertebrobasilar system and provide reliable diagnosis of occlusive lesions. Perforators and basilar branches are not well visualized, but the main vessels are reliably seen. For many clinical problems, it is now possible to avoid invasive conventional angiography.

ANEURYSMS AND VASCULAR MALFORMATIONS

An increasingly common indication for vascular imaging relates to intracranial vascular malformations, and MRA has been used to provide information for a variety of clinical questions surrounding cerebrovascular malformations.

Aneurysms involving the vessels around the base of the brain may occur in 1 to 3 percent of the population and are felt to be the most common cause of nontraumatic subarachnoid hemorrhage. In patients with known subarachnoid hemorrhage, conventional angiography remains the study of choice for the evaluation of possible aneurysms or other vascular lesions. However, many clinical situations may not clearly demand the risk of conventional angiography, and MRA may be the most appropriate study for screening of asymptomatic individuals felt to be at risk for aneurysm. This would include patients with a history of several direct family members with intracranial aneurysm as well as patients with polycystic kidney disease. Current technology allows reliable diagnosis of aneurysms as small as 3 to 4 mm. It is also possible to follow with serial examinations to document aneurysmal growth.

The vascular detail of arteriovenous malformations is best visualized with conventional angiography. Standard MRI of brain parenchyma in axial, coronal, and sagittal sections is of extreme importance to the clinician when working out the anatomical relationships between neurological function, brain parenchyma, and vascular malformation. Currently, MRA cannot replace conventional angiography and often has little to add to the evaluation of arteriovenous malformations.

Standard MRI has expanded and helped to define the clinical concept of cavernous angioma. These vascular malformations are small parenchymal-based vascular lesions with no clear arterial input or venous drainage; MRA can be used to demonstrate the absence of feeding or draining vessels and provide support for the diagnosis of cavernous angioma. In many cases this can replace the need for invasive angiography.

Deep venous anomalies can be readily visualized by MRA. These vascular anomalies are classically described by conventional angiography, although the MRA appearance is quite distinct. These lesions are considered quite benign in their natural history. A cavernous angioma is often seen in the neighborhood of a deep venous angioma, and MRI has helped establish the cooccurence of these lesions. The occasional hemorrhage attributed to a deep venous anomaly now appears most likely to have been the result of an associated cavernous angioma. In many clinical settings, a high-quality MRA can reliably identify the deep venous anomaly and conventional angiography can be avoided.

VENOUS SINUS

Venous sinus disease is a challenging diagnosis for the clinician, and MR technology has proven extremely beneficial. Standard MRI can often provide at least clues to sinus disease, if not definitive diagnosis, and MRA can allow a definitive diagnosis in cases where the standard MR imaging is equivocal. Thrombosis of the sagittal or transverse sinus can be readily demonstrated. Phase-contrast sequences allow both directional information and flow velocity to be incorporated in the imaging process.

CONCLUSIONS

Today, MRA offers the clinician advances in cerebrovascular imaging comparable to what computed tomography (CT) provided for parenchymal imaging. The ability to have non-invasive imaging has truly revolutionized the approach to cerebrovascular disease, with clear benefits to the patient in terms of the increased application and decreased morbidity involved in the diagnostic technology.

REFERENCES

1. Hankey GJ, Worlow CP, Selar RJ: Cerebral angiographic risk in mild cerebrovascular disease. *Stroke* 21:209, 1990.

2. Hankey GJ, Worlow CP: Symptomatic carotid ischemic events: Safest and most cost effective way of selecting patients for angiography before carotid endarterectomy. *Br Med J* 300:1485, 1990.

3. NASCET Collaborators: Beneficial effects of carotid endarterectomy in symptomatic patients with high-grade carotid stenosis. *N Engl J Med* 325:445, 1991.

4. Huston J, Bradley LD, Wieberg DO, et al: Carotid artery: Prospective blinded comparison of two-dimensional time-of-flight MR angiography with conventional angiography and duplex US. *Radiology* 186:339, 1993.

5. Mattle HP, Kent, KG, Edelman RR, et al: Evaluation of the extracranial carotid arteries: Correlation of magnetic resonance angiography, duplex ultrasonography, and conventional angiography. *J Vasc Surg* 13:838, 1991.

Chapter 7

Magnetic Resonance Imaging of the Heart and Great Vessels: A Text Atlas

George J. Hunter / Eléonore Paquet

Diseases of the heart account for approximately 50 percent of all causes of mortality and morbidity worldwide. It is not surprising, therefore, that a large research effort has been expended in developing imaging methods for the diagnosis of cardiovascular disease. In order to provide clinically applicable results, the investigation of cardiac diseases revolves around two distinct needs: to define (1) cardiac anatomy and (2) cardiac function. Magnetic resonance imaging (MRI) efficiently fulfills these requriements by allowing *simultaneous* assessment of cardiac function and anatomy.[1-3]

CARDIOVASCULAR DISEASE

Cardiac diseases fall into three broad categories: diseases affecting (1) the conduction system, (2) the valvular and paravalvular structures, and (3) the myocardium and pericardium. At present, MRI is not usually used to investigate conduction abnormalities, although recent advances in rapid imaging may make feasible the demonstration of regional disturbances of contraction secondary to altered conduction patterns.[4]

While valvular diseases secondary to childhood rheumatic fever have become less common as the incidence of this condition has declined,[5,6] bacterial endocarditis as a cause of valvular disease has increased with the rising incidence of intravenous drug abuse and immunosuppression.[7,8] These factors cancel each other and result in a relatively stable incidence of valvular disease, which is quite low in comparison with disorders related to the myocardium. Magnetic resonance imaging has an important role in the investigation of valvular disease, both in terms of anatomical imaging and

in the imaging of valvular and paravalvular function. In particular, MRI is capable of demonstrating altered flow patterns as the blood passes through a valve, such as due to a regurgitant jet. From such images both the regurgitant flow and any pressure changes across the valve may be determined.[9]

The pathology of the myocardium may be divided into that stemming from congenital and acquired causes. Magnetic resonance imaging has become *the* method of choice for the investigation of complex congenital heart disease.[10-13] While not completely supplanting ultrasound in this regard, MRI allows anatomical images to be produced in planes which closely match those seen by the pathologist and which can be more easily interpreted than those produced by ultrasound. Congenital heart disease is now seldom investigated by means of arteriography because both ultrasound and particularly MRI offer superior three-dimensional visualization of abnormal anatomy.[13] Functional imaging is not often an issue in the assessment of congenital heart disease, as high-resolution anatomical images usually provide the information necessary to manage the treatment of these patients.

Acquired diseases of the myocardium and pericardium may be separated into (1) ischemic heart disease, by far the largest grouping, which includes angina and myocardial infarction, and (2) a set of heterogeneous disorders, such as viral myocarditis, sarcoidosis, and tumor infiltration. In addition, both hypertrophic cardiomyopathy and pericardial disease may be conveniently considered as part of the nonischemic group of acquired cardiac disorders. The principal imaging requirement of the nonischemic group of cardiac diseases is the demonstration of normal and altered anatomy. In other words, while functional imaging in these disease states may be useful to show contractility or perfusion, it is not usually the primary reason for performing an MRI study.

Ischemic heart disease forms the largest group of cardiac disorders for which MRI has an important role to play. This is a diagnosis which encompasses several disparate conditions unified by a common pathophysiological state, that is, reduction of blood supply to the myocardium. Exertional angina, congestive cardiac failure, and myocardial infarction are all examples of ischemic heart disease. With MRI, both the primary pathology (that is, reduction in myocardial perfusion) and the secondary effects of this perfusion deficit (for example, wall motion abnormalities and wall thinning) may be elegantly demonstrated.[14–16] In short, MRI offers the unique capability of demonstrating both cardiac anatomy and function simultaneously and could form the basis of a comprehensive, single examination of the cardiovascular state.[17]

CARDIOVASCULAR MAGNETIC RESONANCE IMAGING

Reduction of Motion Artifacts

Imaging the heart poses additional challenges when compared with the imaging of other parts of the body. Simply put, the heart moves in a complex fashion during the course of image acquisition: this motion must be recognized and taken into account. An MR image of any given slice is created, one phase-encoding step at a time, over many repetition times. Clearly, unless the structure being imaged is in the same place in three-dimensional space for each individual repetition, anatomical images of good quality cannot be obtained. The two principal causes of cardiac motion are the heart's intrinsic contraction and the effects of respiration on the thoracic contents; strategies for MRI are available which can compensate for each of these. Acquisition triggered by an electrocardiogram (ECG) takes direct cardiac contraction into account, while a pneumatic pressure-sensitive cuff around the thorax allows breathing to be monitored and image acquisition to be gated to a specific phase of respiration. The most recent MRI technique, echo-planar imaging (EPI), permits a complete image to be obtained in as little as 40 ms; this effectively freezes both cardiac and respiratory motion. Nevertheless, in order to obtain the same anatomical slice position on successive EPI acquisitions and to control the point in the cardiac cycle at which these images are obtained, ECG gating is still essential. As a complete study of the heart may be obtained in as little as 15 s using EPI, the patient may be asked to suspend respiration during acquisition, thus obviating the need for external respiratory gating. The effects of respiration should not be overemphasized: the most significant contribution to the reduction of motion artifact in cardiac MRI has been the use of ECG gating, and in many instances respiratory gating has not proved necessary for the production of high-quality images.

Standard Sequences and Techniques

Specific applications of different MRI sequences depend on the requirements of the study. The most common sequence used is a T1-weighted spin-echo acquisition with a typical repetition time (TR) of 700 ms and an echo time (TE) of 20 ms. This provides very good anatomical delineation of cardiac and great vessel structures, with excellent contrast between blood and myocardium or vessel endothelium. With the T1-weighted sequences, moving blood returns very little signal following excitation and appears almost black, while effectively stationary structures, such as the myocardium, appear bright, depending on their intrinsic longitudinal relaxation rates. Most, if not all, cardiac MRI examinations use a T1-weighted sequence to define the final planes to be imaged. The conventional spin-echo T1-weighted acquisition produces static images at points in the cardiac cycle determined by the ECG trigger and a delay time from that trigger. Usually muliple slices are acquired, staggered through the cardiac cycle, in order to demonstrate the entire heart in one study. This results in an image stack of the heart where each anatomical level is shown at a distinct phase of the cardiac cycle. The other common sequence used is a rapid gradient echo acquisition. This has a typical TR of 25 ms, a TE of 10 ms, and a flip angle of 30°. This fast gradient echo sequence results in blood which is bright in comparison with myocardium and slightly reduced contrast between myocardium and blood. The principal use of this sequence is to produce, in one plane, a series of images, typically eight, whereby a complete cardiac cycle may be demonstrated in cine mode. This sequence allows assessment of regional wall motion and contractility. Global and regional cardiac wall motion may be assessed using standard sequences. However, one penalty of these is that a typical multislice cine acquisition, for instance, may take over 10 min to obtain. Recent advances in technology, described below, have allowed this burden to be reduced.

As MR images are reconstructed using Fourier transformation in two dimensions, both phase and amplitude information is available for review. Usually only the amplitude images are displayed. However, images of the phase component can provide important information about blood movement. Phase images are particularly useful in demonstrating regurgitation jets with valvular incompetence and in differentiating between static blood (e.g., in a thrombus) and moving blood.[9]

Echo-Planar Imaging and Perfusion Techniques

Since the earliest days of MRI, a significant research effort has been ongoing to provide truly fast imaging. Gradient echo methods achieve a significant measure of time reduction but still generate images using one excitation for each phase-encoding step at a time. Echo-planar imaging while first described by Mansfield in 1977,[18] has only recently become available in the clinical arena. With EPI, a complete image is obtained from a single excitation, and images take as little as 40 ms to acquire. The potential for repeated, rapid acquisition has made possible dynamic perfusion imaging of the myocardium. By injecting paramagnetic contrast material peripherally, with rapid imaging over the heart, the hemodynamics of the myocardium may be demonstrated. It should be stressed that while each individual image may be acquired in a short time, the rate at which a series of images may be acquired is still governed by the ECG trigger. Other factors, such as relaxation rates, also constrain the time between individual images. While it is still necessary to use ECG gating in order to define accurately the point in the cardiac cycle at which a particular image is obtained, the state of the myocardium at that point is captured within 40 ms. This is a time frame during which little change in paramagnetic contrast in the myocardium has occurred, making accurate assessment of contrast dynamics possible.[19,20] Observation of these dynamic changes is based on T1 relaxivity altering with time due to the movement of paramagnetic contrast between intra- and extravascular spaces. At present such studies are still being evaluated; much work will be required to bring them into routine clinical use. Nevertheless, echoplanar imaging has the potential to bring to reality the integrated examination of cardiac anatomy and physiology.[17] An alternative to measurements based on T1 relaxivity is the assessment of purely intravascular hemodynamics resulting from susceptibility contrast imaging. This is predicated on a paramagnetic contrast agent remaining in the intravascular space at sufficient concentration to increase T2* relaxivity substantially. This leads to a measurable signal drop, which may be converted into units related to contrast concentration. From such a suceptibility curve, blood volume, and possibly blood flow, may be calculated. To date, very promising results have been obtained in animal models[21] using nanoparticulate ferrite as the contrast agent. Once such agents become available for clinical use, the potential for detailed perfusion imaging becomes almost limitless.

CLINICAL APPLICABILITY

In summary, cardiac MRI is beginning to fulfill its promise. As a method for gross anatomical imaging it is unsurpassed, except perhaps by the pathologist—hardly a clinical aim! For assessment of regional and global myocardial function, it offers superior temporal and spatial resolution comparable to nuclear medicine techniques at about the same cost. For the quantification of myocardial perfusion, it holds the promise of superb spatial resolution (1.5 mm) together with minimal invasiveness, making MRI, and especially EPI, a logical choice for repeated examinations. Patient compliance is good and, with the introduction of intravascular MRI agents, there will be no logical reason to avoid MRI for complete cardiac evaluation.

Case Studies

There follows a selection of case studies which exemplify and expand on the points mentioned in the body of the text. These studies contain information which is not duplicated elsewhere and should be read with frequent reference to the figures and figure legends.

Case A

Figure 7-1 illustrates the case of a young woman 16 years of age with ventricular inversion and transposition of the great arteries. There is left atrioventricular valve atresia with a single left ventricle and a rudimentary subaortic right ventricular outflow chamber with a large ventricular septal defect acting as the ventricular outlet foramen. There is a large atrial septal defect. A left-sided aortic arch is present with a dilated ascending aorta and pulmonary valve stenosis. In order to permit oxygenation of blood, a Fontan procedure (right atrial to main pulmonary artery conduit) was performed. The patient is stable, and MRI has provided a straightforward, repeatable method for the monitoring of her very complex cardiac anatomy.

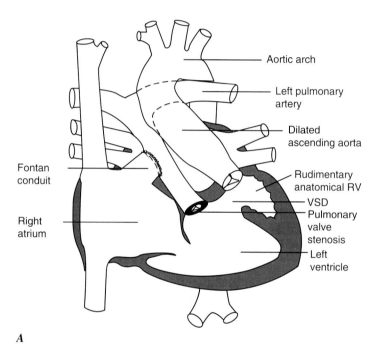

A

FIGURE 7-1 Stylized diagram (*A*) provided for comparison with the MR image. Two coronal slices (*B* and *C*) through the midportion of the heart are shown. These are spin-echo T1-weighted images acquired with ECG gating (TR/TE 690/20 ms). Note the rudimentary right ventricle and the Fontan conduit. The ability of MRI to demonstrate the heart in any plane makes it invaluable for demonstrating complex anatomy such as this.

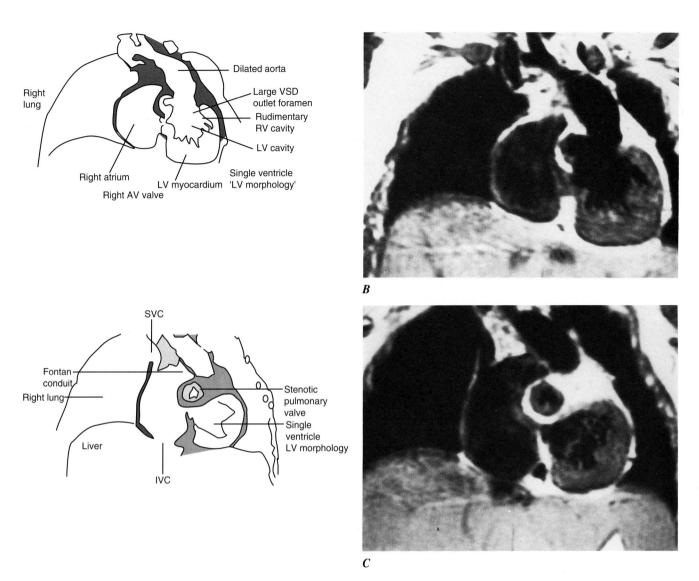

FIGURE 7-1 (*Continued*)

Case B

Figure 7-2 illustrates the case of a 70-year-old woman suffering from dyspnea and pulmonary arterial hypertension. Following investigation, it was found that she had a large patent ductus arteriosus. Here, the coronal, sagittal, and axial slices demonstrate the relationships between normal and abnormal anatomy very clearly. In this instance, MRI provided the information required for a complete diagnosis, without radiation and with a minimum of discomfort to the patient.

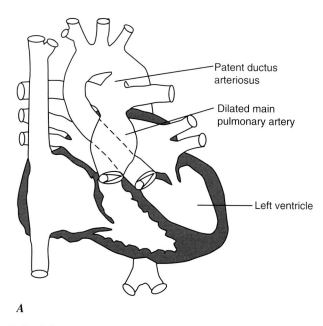

A

FIGURE 7-2   Stylized diagram (*A*) provided for comparison with the MR image. (*B, C,* and *D*) Coronal, Sagittal, and Axial slices respectively, demonstrate the anatomy of the heart. They are all T1-weighted spin-echo acquisitions. In each instance, ECG gating was used, with an effective TR of one cardiac cycle, which translated into a TR of 632 ms. The TE was 20 ms. The T1-weighted image series provided good anatomical delineation at the expense of increased scan time.

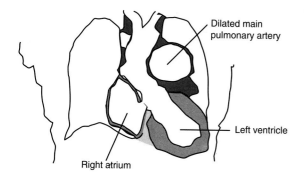

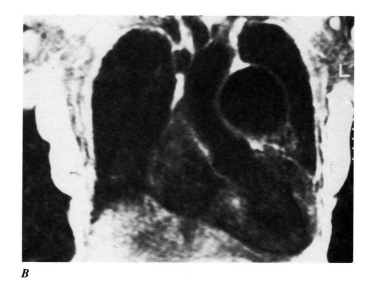

B

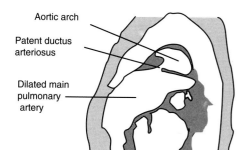

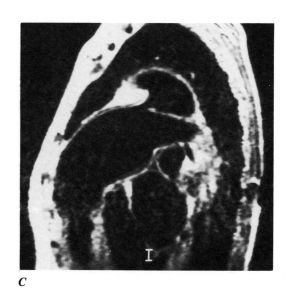

C

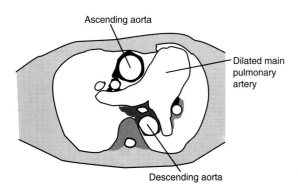

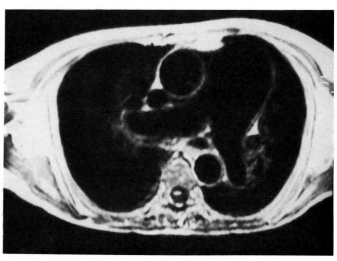

D

FIGURE 7-2 (*Continued*)

Case C

Figure 7-3 illustrates a very complicated case of treated congenital heart disease. The patient is a 23-year-old man with situs solitus, an L-loop ventricular transposition, and severe pulmonary stenosis. This is a variant of uncorrected transposition of the great vessels, marked by atrioventricular discordance with concurrent atriovascular concordance. In this instance, survival was assured by the Fontan conduit fashioned between the right atrium and main pulmonary artery. The morphological right ventricle is the systemic pumping chamber and shows marked myocardial hypertrophy. The morphological left ventricle should have been the main pulmonary pumping chamber; however, the pulmonary valve atresia results in a small left ventricle. The Fontan conduit connects the right side of the circulation with the lungs, allowing oxygenation to occur.

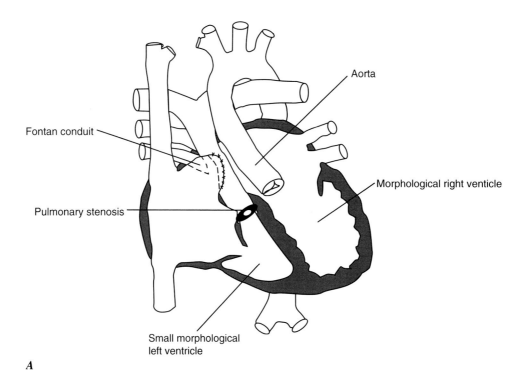

A

FIGURE 7-3 Stylized diagram (*A*) provided for comparison with the MR image. Adjacent slices (*B* and *C*) are in the coronal plane through the morphological right ventricle (functional systemic ventricle). These were acquired with a T1-weighted ECG-gated spin-echo sequence with an effective TR of one cardiac cycle, approximately 652 ms, and a TE of 20 ms. Note the Fontan conduit between the right atrium and the main pulmonary artery.

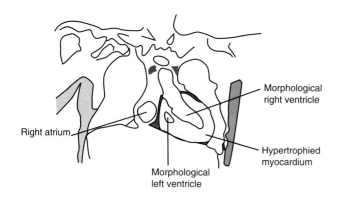

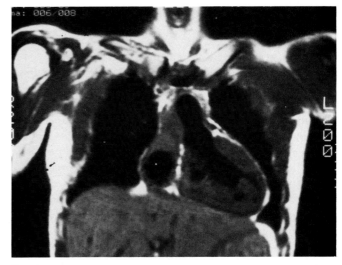

B

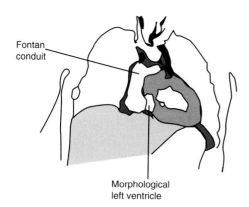

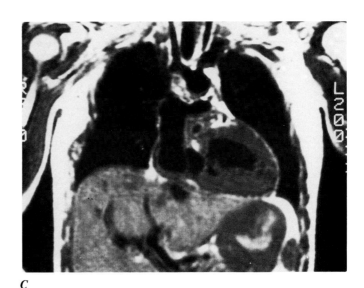

C

FIGURE 7-3 (*Continued*)

Case D

This 50-year-old man (Fig. 7-4) had long-standing, mild cyanotic heart disease. As an infant, he was only mildly and rarely cyanotic; there had been no squatting episodes. On examination, there was a murmur of pulmonary regurgitation, and MRI revealed the classic features of Fallot's tetralogy. In addition, there was main and left pulmonary artery dilatation and absent normal pulmonary valve leaflets. This constellation is a very rare variant of classic Fallot's tetralogy. Because of the pulmonary regurgitation, there is relatively little pulmonary stenosis, and these patients do remarkably well without correction, as evidenced by the age of this patient. This man did not develop significant respiratory symptoms and thus his prognosis is good.

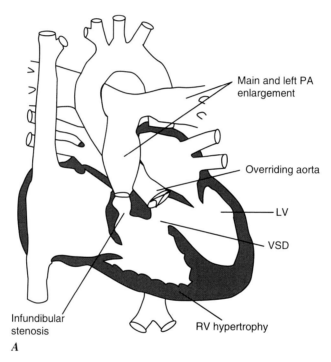

FIGURE 7-4   Stylized diagram (*A*) of the classic tetralogy of Fallot, consisting of overriding aorta, membranous ventricular septal defect, infundibular stenosis, and right ventricular hypertrophy, provided for comparison with the MR image. In addition, the absent pulmonary valve is recorded. Axial, T1-weighted scans (*B, C,* and *D*) through three levels of the heart are seen. Due to the heart's orientation, the images present a slightly rotated view of the four chambers. Note the large ventricular septal defect, overriding aorta, and right ventricular hypertrophy. In addition, the enlarged left pulmonary artery is visualized.

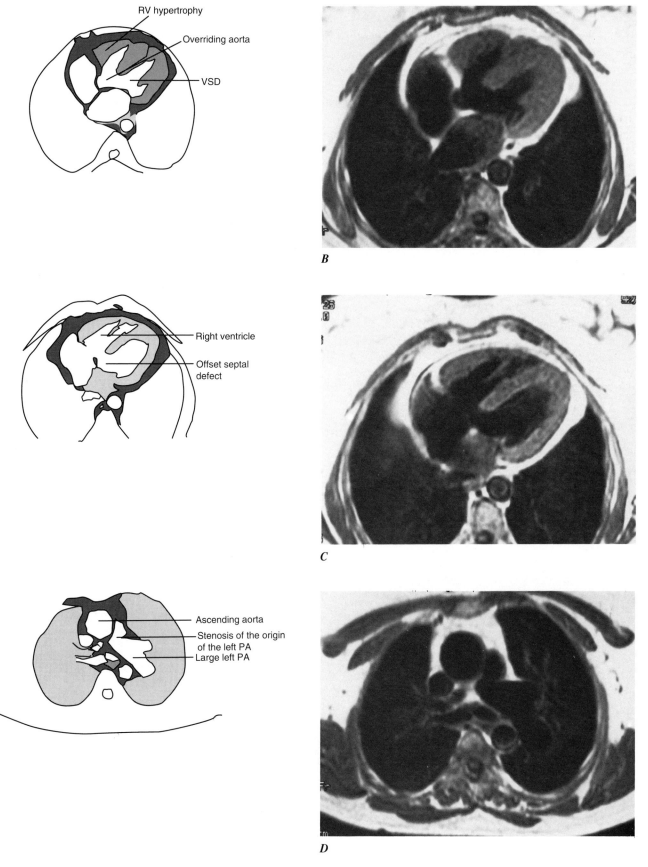

FIGURE 7-4 (*Continued*)

Case E

This is a 42-year-old man (Fig. 7-5) with transposition of the great arteries. There is a very large ventricular septal defect, which effectively makes for a single ventricular cavity, with both great arteries arising from it. There is also an atrial septal defect. In complex cases such as this, the multiple anomalies lead to sufficient oxygenation and systemic perfusion to prevent early diagnosis. The MRI is invaluable in correctly identifying the relationships of the aorta and pulmonary artery with respect to the atria and ventricles. In this case, the aorta is anterior to the pulmonary artery and slightly to the right of the infundibulum, a classic transposition.

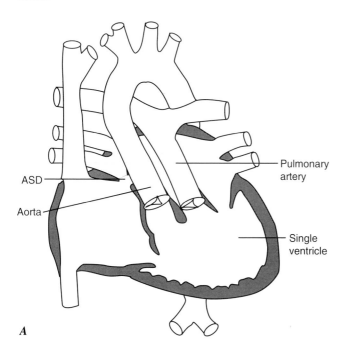

A

FIGURE 7-5 Stylized diagram (*A*) provided for comparison with the MR image. An axial T1-weighted spin-echo scan (*B*). It clearly demonstrates the atrial septal defect and large ventricular septal defect leading to the appearance of a single ventricle. Contiguous slices (*C, D,* and *E*) from below upward are seen. The orientation is a steep, double oblique four-chamber view. Note the relationships of the aortic root and infundibulum as well as the origins of both aorta and pulmonary artery from the right and left sides of the single ventricle, respectively. Both studies were T1-weighted spin-echo scans with ECG gating, a TR of 697 ms, and a TE of 11 ms.

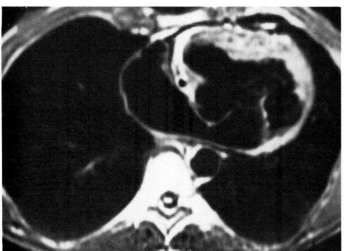

B

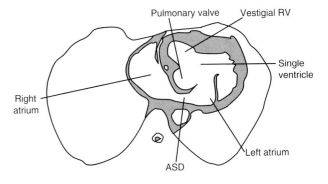

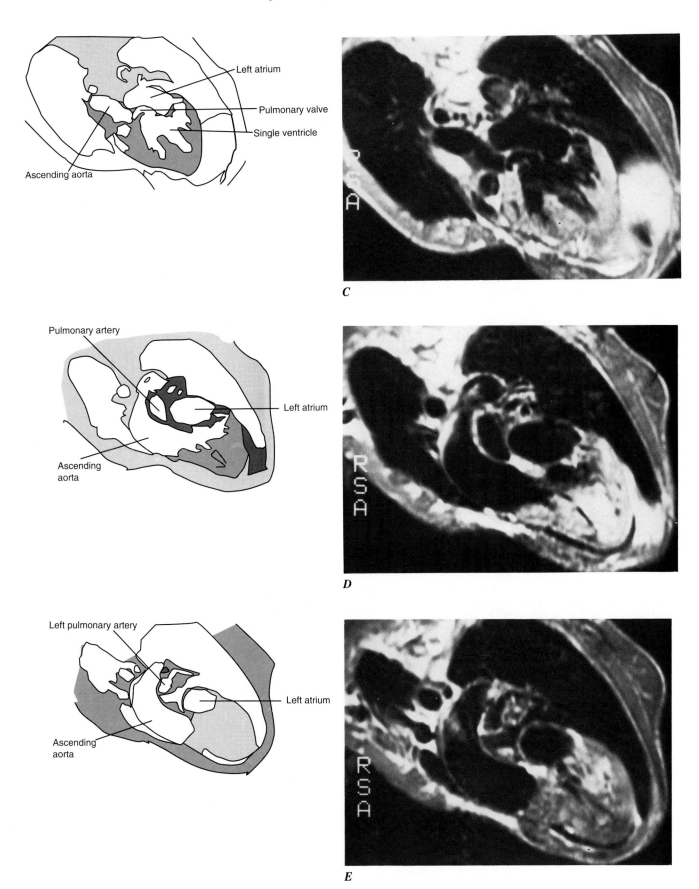

FIGURE 7-5 (*Continued*)

Case F

These studies were obtained from a 38-year-old man with increasing hypertension in both arms and normotension in the legs. Clinically the patient exhibited the signs of radio-femoral delay. These are the classic features of aortic coarctation of the postductal type. Comprehensive assessment of the case included anatomical definition of the area of coarctation and a functional estimate of flow velocities in the affected region. Anatomical imaging was acquired in the sagittal plane with a T1-weighted spin-echo sequence gated to the ECG. An effective TR of 895 ms was obtained by using a single cardiac cycle as the repetition time. The TE was 20 ms. Two distinct acquisitions were required to determine the correct plane for demonstration of the coarctation tissue. Figure 7-6A shows the coarctation tissue quite clearly. The technique of velocity mapping by using phase information is useful in cases such as this to identify the functional impact of a stenosis or coarctation. By using a gradient echo sequence with a TR of 22 ms, TE of 6.9 ms, and a flip angle of 30°, the data necessary to construct the amplitude (Fig. 7-6B) and phase (Fig. 7-6C) images could be obtained. Note the bright blood on the amplitude image; this is characteristic of this type of gradient echo imaging. The phase map shows high velocity in the ascending aorta and immediately distal to the coarctation. Postsurgical mapping of blood velocities can monitor the success of correction without the need for arterial intervention. The gradient echo technique can also be used to produce pseudocine loops of cardiac contraction.

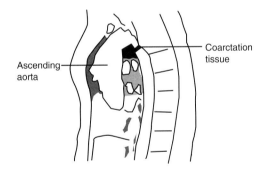

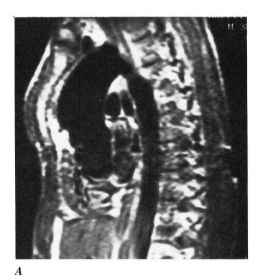

A

FIGURE 7-6   A spin-echo image (*A*) defining the area of coarctation in the sagittal plane. The amplitude and phase images (*B* and *C*), respectively, are from a gradient echo acquisition. Note the high velocities, seen as bright signal, distal to the coarctation and in the ascending aorta.

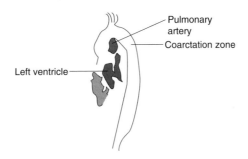

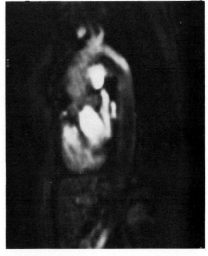

B

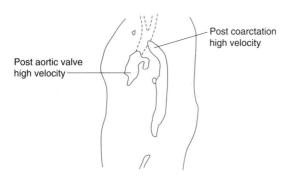

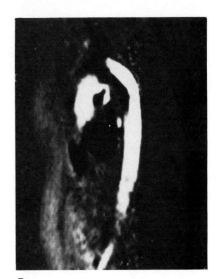

C

FIGURE 7-6 (*Continued*)

Case G

This 27-year-old man (Fig. 7-7) had a family history of sudden death. On several occasions, he noticed a fluttering in his chest which resolved spontaneously and was associated with some mild substernal pain. Upon MRI examination, asymmetric septal hypertrophy (ASH) was revealed. The picture was not entirely that of pure ASH; rather, there was also some diffuse left ventricular myocardial hypertrophy (ASH is part of a heterogenous spectrum of hypertrophic cardiomyopathy). In this patient, MRI also revealed some right ventricular hypertrophy.

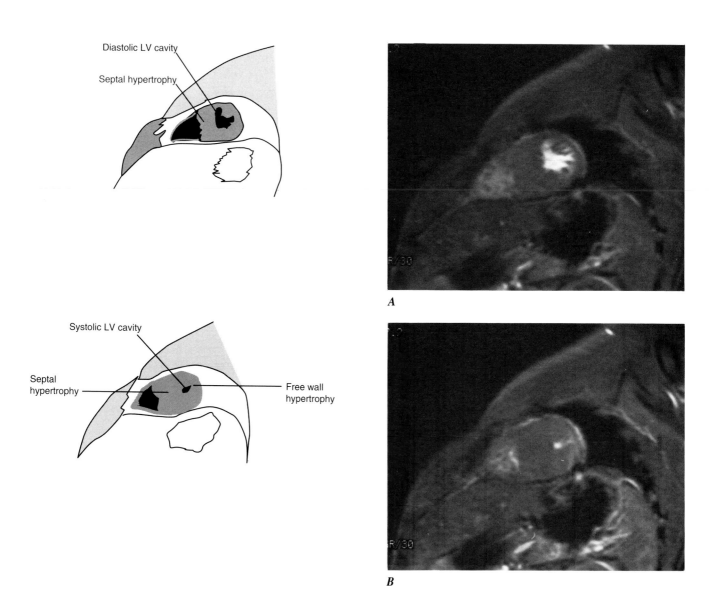

A

B

FIGURE 7-7 Sagittal, oblique diastolic and systolic images (*A* and *B*), respectively, obtained from a gradient echo cine acquisition with a TR of 50 ms, TE of 12 ms, and 30° flip angle. Note the overall increase in myocardium with disproportionate increase in septal myocardium (*C*). A four-chamber view at end diastole; a cine acquisition with identical factors to those in the previous images (*A* and *B*). Note the clearly defined bulge of the interventricular septum. These are findings consistent with asymmetric septal hypertrophy.

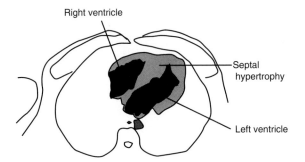

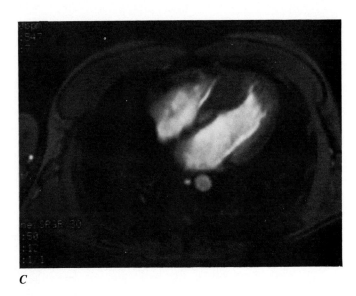

C

FIGURE 7-7 (*Continued*)

Case H

This study (Fig. 7-8) was obtained from a 20-year-old woman with a history of slowly increasing dyspnea. T1-weighted MRI showed a very large secundum atrial septal defect. The sequelae of this defect are well demonstrated—namely, a large right atrium and a very large pulmonary artery. The enlargement of the pulmonary artery is secondary to volume overload and functional stenosis of the pulmonary valve. The patient remains well and symptom-free after surgical intervention.

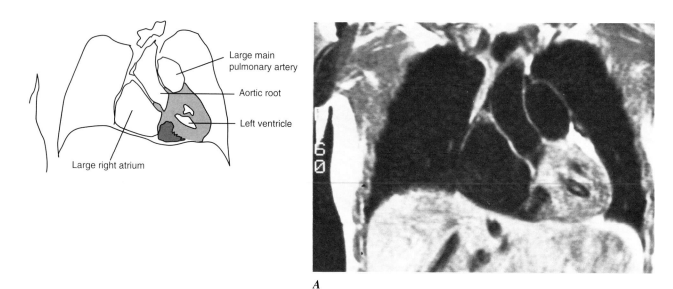

A

FIGURE 7-8 Three spin-echo images are presented here. In each case, ECG gating with a TR of one cardiac cycle gave an effective TR of approximately 857 ms. The TE was 20 ms. The coronal image (*A*) shows the grossly dilated main pulmonary artery and dilated right atrium. The axial view (*B*) through the left ventricular vestibule clearly shows the large atrial septal defect. The atrial septum (*C*) is seen to be restored following surgery.

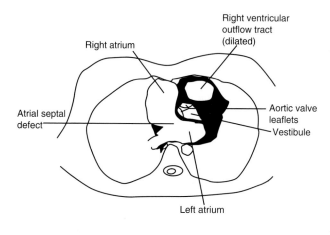

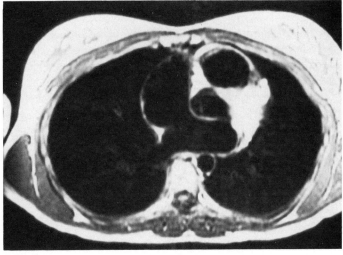

B

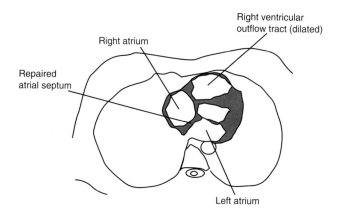

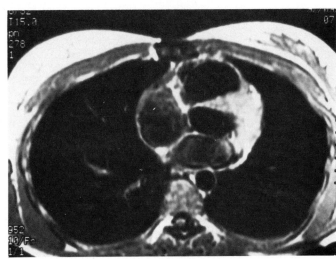

C

FIGURE 7-8 (*Continued*)

Case I

This 61-year-old man (Fig. 7-9) also complained of increasing dyspnea. On MRI, a large, membranous ventricular septal defect was revealed, with secondary dilatation of the right ventricle and some right venticular hypertrophy. The right atrium was of normal size. Following surgical repair, the patient did well.

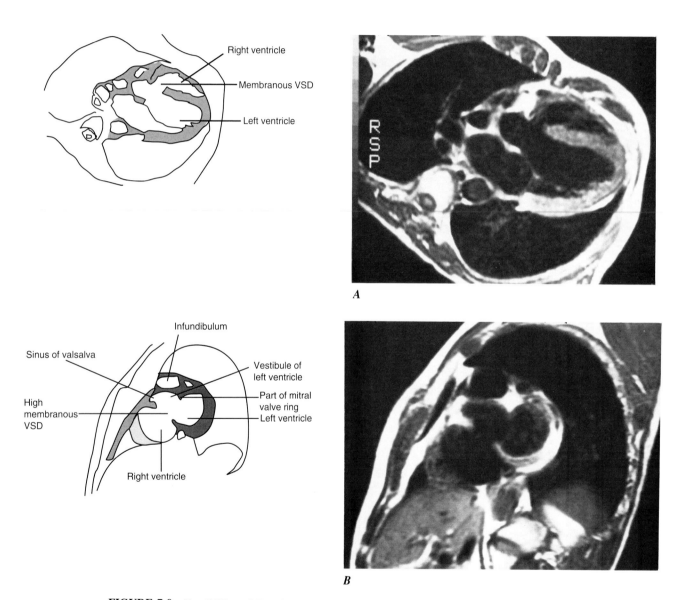

FIGURE 7-9   Two ECG-gated T1-weighted spin-echo sequences are shown. The TR was 750 ms, with a TE of 20 ms in both instances.   *A.* A slightly rotated, four chamber view shows some exuberance of the right ventricular myocardium secondary to the large septal defect. Virtually all the membranous portion of the septum is absent.   *B.* A double oblique view in a parasagittal orientation close to the mitral valve ring. The large ventricular septal defect is clearly seen, together with right ventricular hypertrophy and a dilated infundibulum.

Case J

This 52-year-old man (Fig. 7-10) suffered a recent myocardial infarction involving right coronary territory and resulting in a posteroinferior area of avascular myocardium. After an initially good recovery, he complained of increasing dyspnea without chest pain. The MRI shows a well-defined aneurysm arising from the scar tissue of his healed infarction. Management of such cases depends on the severity of the symptoms; resection of the acontractile tissue may prove curative.

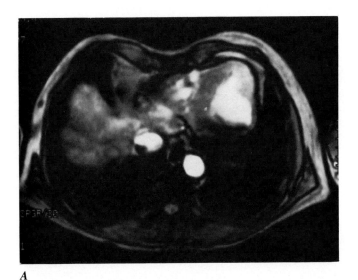

A

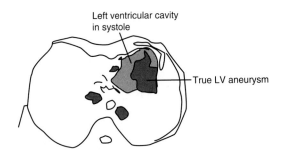

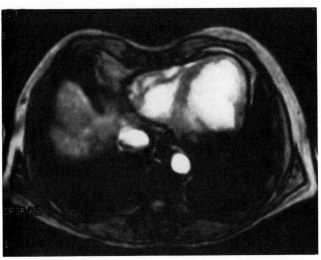

B

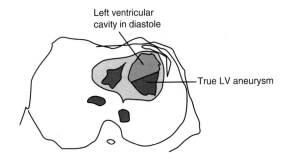

FIGURE 7-10   These are a pair of images from a cine series. The series was acquired in a true axial plane using a gradient echo sequence with a TR of 50 ms, TE of 12 ms, and a 30° flip angle. This type of acquisition results in bright blood and an intermediate myocardial signal.   *A.* The image at end systole.   *B.* The image at end diastole. Note that as the ventricle contracts, there is a thickening of the myocardium except over the aneurysm. The end-systolic ventricular volume is substantially less than the end-diastolic volume, but the volume of the aneurysm remains constant throughout the cardiac cycle. Indeed, it may even increase slightly during systole, so-called paradoxical filling.

Case K

This 51-year-old woman (Fig. 7-11) had an inferoposterior myocardial infarction. In the recovery phase, she developed increasingly severe dyspnea. The presence of a large aneurysm was confirmed by MRI. There was no rim of thinned myocardium surrounding the aneurysm. This was a false aneurysm, secondary to rupture of acutely ischemic myocardium. Adjacent to the apex of the dilatation is an area of reactive inflammatory pulmonary atelectasis. Following emergency repair of the left ventricular defect, the patient did well.

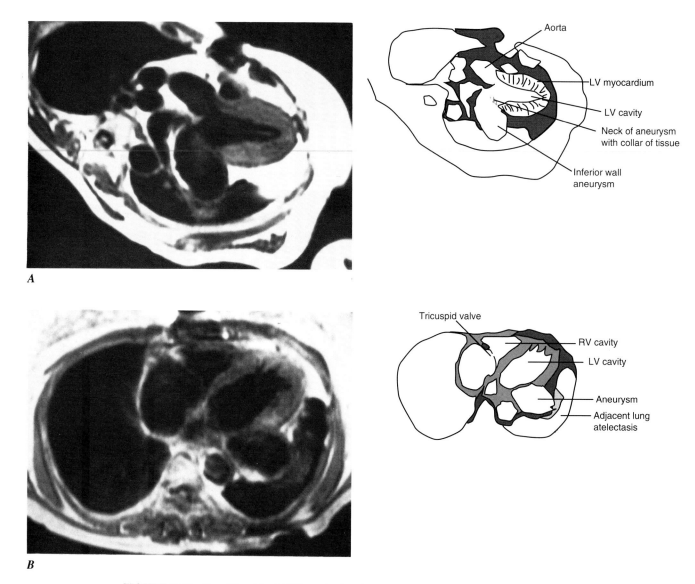

FIGURE 7-11   Two T1-weighted ECG-gated spin-echo acquisitions. The TR was 732 ms and the TE 20 ms.   *A*. A steeply obliqued slice, demonstrating the neck of the false aneurysm. *B*. A conventional anatomical axial slice, demonstrating the lateral extent of the dilatation with adjacent pulmonary inflammatory change and atelectasis.

Case L

This 62-year-old man (Fig. 7-12) complained of having had night sweats and intermittent dyspnea for several months. He was suspected of having tuberculosis, lymphoma, or bacterial endocarditis. No evidence confirming any of these conditions was forthcoming, so he underwent a cardiac MRI looking for vegetations secondary to fungal endocarditis. This figure reveals a mobile mass in the left atrium, the more common side for an atrial myxoma. This condition can mimic tuberculosis or lymphoma in its presentation. Weight loss may even occur, suggesting malignancy. Successful removal alleviated the man's symptoms completely.

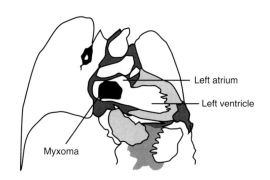

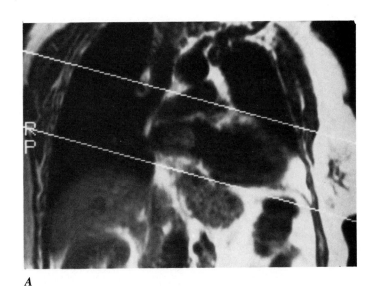

A

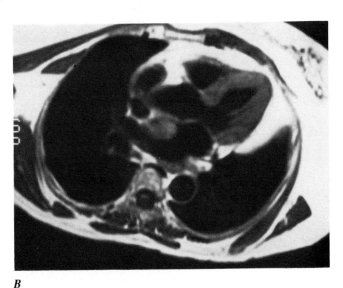

B

FIGURE 7-12   Coronal (*A*) and axial (*B*) T1-weighted ECG-gated scans that show abnormal signal return from within the left atrium. This proved to be a benign atrial myxoma. Note the thin stalk seen close to the right pulmonary vein inflow. Myxoma is often pedunculated and can move surprisingly large distances on its stalk; prolapse through the mitral valve is well described. Sudden death due to left ventricular outflow obstruction is also well described.

Case M

This 56-year-old man (Fig. 7-13) underwent an aortic valve replacement. The postoperative course was stormy. When persistent fever and positive blood cultures were compounded by first-degree heart block, an aortic root abscess was suspected. MRI revealed a large collection adjacent to the infundibulum, extending superiorly and laterally. Immediate surgery drained an infected hematoma that arose from one of the sutures fixing the aortic valve. Fortunately, the patient recovered without long-term complications. In such cases, MRI is particularly useful as it allows excellent definition of the anatomy without disturbing the infected tissue. Often, the only way to diagnose such complications in the past was to perform arteriography and run the risk of dislodging infected tissue into the circulation, possibly causing mycotic aneurysm, for instance, in the brain or kidney.

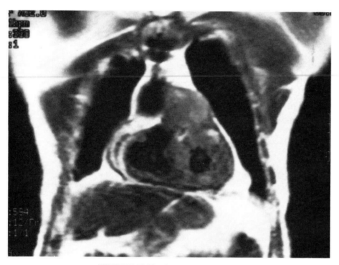
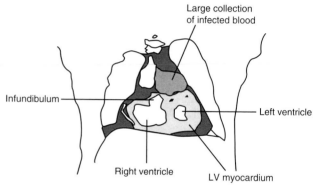

FIGURE 7-13   This is a single coronal T1-weighted spin-echo image acquired with ECG gating. The TR was 594 ms, with a 12-ms TE. Note the large, heterogeneous collection adjacent to the right ventricular outflow tract, which represents an infected hematoma.

Case N

This 47-year-old man (Fig. 7-14) presented to the emergency room with a history of sudden onset of dyspnea and a vague, diffuse, right-sided chest pain. His ECG showed a right heart strain pattern. Chest radiograph was unremarkable. He was suspected of having a pulmonary embolus and MRI was performed. This figure shows a well-defined filling defect totally obstructing the right pulmonary artery. The unequivocal diagnosis of pulmonary embolism was made and he was successfully treated with thrombolytic therapy.

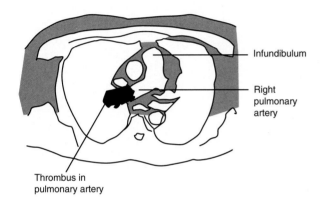

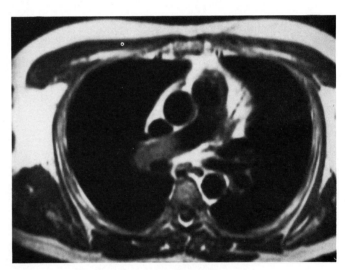

FIGURE 7-14 A T1-weighted axial spin-echo image obtained with ECG gating, a TR of 882 ms, and a TE of 20 ms shows an abrupt transition between flowing blood and thrombus at the origin of the right pulmonary artery. The appearances are unequivocally diagnostic in this instance.

Case O

This 44-year-old man (Fig. 7-15) suffering from low back pain underwent a conventional myelogram. Some weeks later, he complained of increasing weight loss with palpitations. An ECG revealed first-degree heart block. Blood cultures grew *Staphylococcus aureus*. Bacterial endocarditis with an aortic root abscess was suspected. The presence of a collection in the aortic root, arising from the tissue between the vestibule and infundibulum was confirmed by MRI. The collection extended posterolaterally into the aortopulmonary window. Surgical drainage and valve salvage together with triple antibiotic therapy was curative.

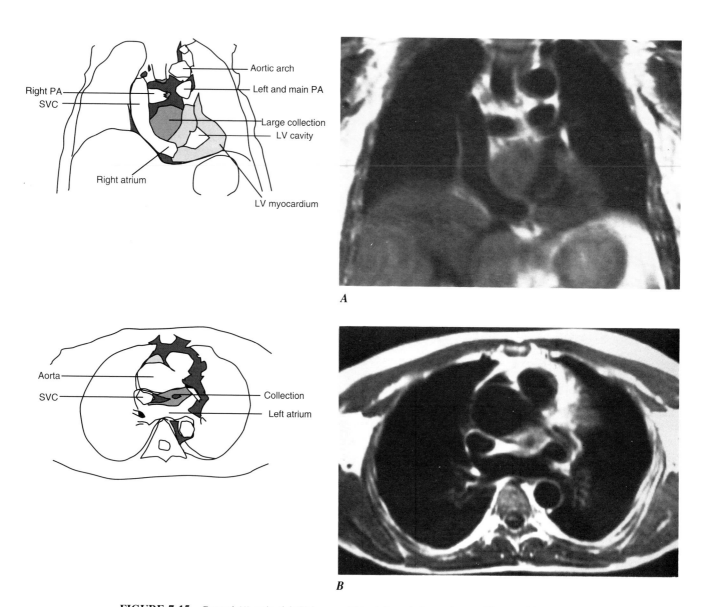

A

B

FIGURE 7-15   Coronal (*A*) and axial (*B*) images obtained through the aortic root. These are T1-weighted ECG-gated acquisitions with a TR of 632 ms and TE of 20 ms. The coronal slice, particularly, demonstrates the distorted anatomy, resulting from the large aortic root collection, which extends into the aortopulmonary window and distorts the ascending aorta and main pulmonary artery.

Case P

This is a 22-year-old man (Fig. 7-16) with pulmonary atresia, aortic malposition, and atrial septal defect. He was diagnosed shortly after birth and underwent a Fontan procedure to relieve cyanosis. Examination by MRI is useful in such cases as it allows routine monitoring of the anatomy without the need for angiography. This patient's early survival is due to an atrial septal defect with right-to-left shunting; this provided enough oxygenation to sustain life long enough for diagnosis and treatment.

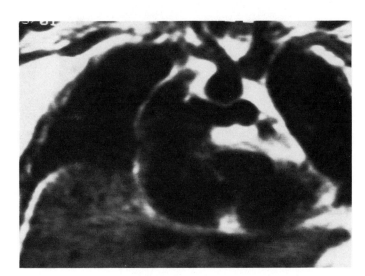

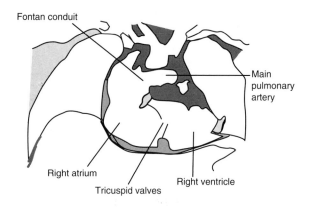

FIGURE 7-16 A single coronal slice. This image demonstrates the absence of right ventricular connection with the pulmonary artery and a connection from the right atrium to the main pulmonary artery (i.e., a Fontan conduit). The image is a T1-weighted spin-echo scan, ECG-gated with a TR of 882 ms and a TE of 20 ms.

Case Q

This is a 39-year-old male (Fig. 7-17) with upper body hypertension. Coarctation of the aorta was suspected. The MRI scan revealed not only a circumferential narrowing just distal to the left subclavian artery origin (postductal type) but also an intraaortic membrane partially obstructing the lumen. The MRI scan provided all the necessary workup for successful planning and treatment.

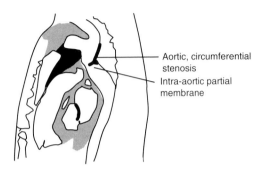

Aortic, circumferential stenosis
Intra-aortic partial membrane

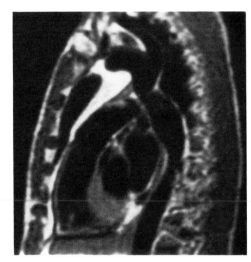

FIGURE 7-17   A sagittal T1-weighted nongated, spin-echo scan of the aorta shows postductal narrowing with a thin intraaortic membrane compounding the obstruction. The TR was 1000 ms and the TE 20 ms. The average of four consecutive excitations was used to improve image quality at the expense of scan time.

REFERENCES

1. Buchalter MB, Sims C, Dixon AK, et al: Measurement of regional left ventricular function using labelled magnetic resonance imaging. *Br J Radiol* 64:953, 1991.
2. Sectem U, Pfugfelder PW, Gould RG, et al: Measurement of right and left ventricular volumes in healthy individuals with cine MR imaging. *Radiology* 163:697, 1987.
3. Edelman RR, Thompson R, Kantor H, Brady TJ: Cardiac function: Evaluation with fast-echo MR imaging. *Radiology* 162:611, 1987.
4. Axel L, Goncalves RC, Bloomgarden D: Regional wall motion analyses and functional imaging with MR imaging. *Radiology* 183:745, 1992.
5. Markowitz M: The changing picture of rheumatic fever. *Arthritis Rheum* 20:369, 1977.
6. Sievers J, Hall P: Incidence of acute rheumatic fever. *Br Heart J* 33:833, 1971.
7. Banks T, Fletcher R, Ali N: Infective endocarditis in heroin addicts. *Am J Med* 55:44, 1973.
8. Hofflin JM, Potasman I, Baldwin JC: Infectious complications in heart transplant recipients receiving cyclosporin and corticosteroids. *Ann Intern Med* 106:209, 1987.
9. Søndergaard L, Thomsen C, Sthålberg F, et al: Mitral and aortic valvular flow: Quantitation with MR phase mapping. *J Mag Res Imaging* 2:295, 1992.
10. Fellows KE, Weinberg PM, Baffa JM, et al: Evaluation of congenital heart disease with MR imaging: Current and coming attractions. *AJR* 159:925, 1992.
11. Schlesinger AE, Hernandez RJ: Congenital heart disease: Applications of computed tomography and magnetic resonance imaging. *Semin US CT MR* 12:11, 1991.
12. Bisset GS III: Magnetic resonance imaging of congenital heart disease in the pediatric patient. *Radiol Clin North Am* 29:279, 1991.
13. Bank ER: Magnetic resonance of congenital heart cardiovascular disease: Update. *Radio Clin North Am* 31:553, 1993.
14. Akins EW, Hill AJ, Sievers KW, et al: Assessment of left ventricular wall thickness in healed myocardial infarction by magnetic resonance imaging. *Radiology* 164:884, 1987.
15. Pipe JG, Boes JL, Chenevert TL: Method for measuring three-dimensional motion with tagged MR imaging. *Radiology* 181:591, 1991.
16. van Rugge FP, Boreel JJ, van der Wall EE: Cardiac first-pass and myocardial perfusion in normal subjects assessed by subsecond Gd-DTPA enhanced MR imaging. *J Comput Assist Tomogr* 15:959, 1991.
17. Wolf GL: Contrast agents for cardiac MRI in cardiac imaging, in Marcus ML, Schelbert HR, Skorton DJ, Wolf GL (eds): *Cardiac Imaging: A Companion to Braunwald's Heart Disease.* Philadelphia, Saunders, 1991, pp. 808–809.
18. Mansfield P: Multiplanar image formation using NMR spin-echoes. *J Phys C Solid State Phys* 13:77, 1977.
19. Wendland MF, Saeed M, Masui T, et al: Echo-planar MR imaging of normal and ischemic myocardium with gadodiamide injection. *Radiology* 186:535, 1993.
20. Saeed M, Wendland MF, Higgins CB: Characterization of reperfused myocardial infarctions with T1-enhancing and magnetic susceptibility-enhancing contrast media. *Invest Radiol* 26:S239, 1991.
21. Weissleder R, Reimer P: Superparamagnetic oxides for MRI. *Eur Radiol* 33:198, 1993.

Chapter 8

Magnetic Resonance Angiography of the Coronary Arteries

Bettina Siewert / Robert R. Edelman / Warren J. Manning

Conventional angiography is regarded as the procedure of choice in the diagnosis of coronary artery disease. Over 500,000 diagnostic cardiac catheterizations are performed annually in the United States, resulting in annual costs of over $1.8 billion for cardiac catheterizations.[1] The planning of medical therapy—as well as mechanical interventions such as coronary artery bypass graft surgery or percutaneous transluminal coronary angioplasty—is based upon the results of such studies. Up to 20 percent of coronary angiograms reveal no significant coronary artery disease.[1] This observation suggests a role for noninvasive evaluation in screening for myocardial ischemia, particularly since coronary angiography may be complicated by death (0.12 to 0.20 percent), cerebrovascular accident (0.03 to 0.20 percent), or myocardial infarction (0.0 to 0.25 percent). Minor complications related to its invasiveness are vascular complication and local infection (0.57 to 1.6 percent) or arrhythmias (0.30 to 0.63 percent).[2–4]

AVAILABLE NONINVASIVE IMAGING MODALITIES

The noninvasive imaging of coronary arteries may provide diagnostic information with minimal risk and is an important tool for patients who are not suitable for angiography.[4] It may be useful for following patients who have had therapeutic procedures.

Two-Dimensional Echocardiography

Transthoracic echocardiography has had variable results in visualizing the coronary arteries. The extent to which the vessels can be reliably imaged depends on their location: > 80 percent for the left main, 53 percent for the proximal left anterior descending, 34 percent for the left circumflex, and 56 percent for the right coronary arteries.[4–6] The limitations of this technique relate to interference by the chest wall and intervening pulmonary parenchyma and have led to the application of transesophageal ultrasound in the evaluation of coronary artery stenosis.

Transesophageal Two-Dimensional Echocardiography

Transesophageal echocardiography (TEE) requires esophageal intubation with risk of its attendant though rare complications, such as esophageal perforation and laceration, aspiration pneumonia, arrhythmia, and death.[7] Encouraging results have been reported for TEE in the evaluation of left main coronary artery stenoses.[4] However, the overall percentage of patients with this condition is relatively small; only 5 to 10 percent of those with angina undergoing cardiac catheterization are found to have left main coronary artery stenoses.[8] In addition, TEE generally visualizes only the proximal vessel. The more distal portion of the vessel is usually not visible.

Magnetic Resonance Imaging

With its outstanding soft-tissue contrast multiplanar imaging capability (including the acquisition of double-oblique images), magnetic resonance (MR) imaging is an excellent method for the evaluation of cardiac disease. It has been demonstrated to give reliable information about complex cardiac anatomy and systolic function.[9,10] Magnetic resonance angiography (MRA) is currently being applied in screening for intracranial aneurysms as well as in the detection of stenoses of the extracranial carotid arteries, the vertebrobasilar system, and the renal arteries.[11–13]

MAGNETIC RESONANCE CORONARY ANGIOGRAPHY

Magnetic resonance techniques that are capable of demonstrating blood flow in small vessels and of measuring flow velocity within a small lumen are now available.[14] High-resolution MRA can successfully image arteries of a caliber similar to that of epicardial coronary vessels, such as the renal artery and branches of the circle of Willis; however, reproducible coronary angiography has remained elusive because of several specific problems that arise with coronary imaging.

Special Technical Considerations for the Imaging of Coronary Arteries

Techniques suitable for the imaging of the coronary arteries must be able to deal with the following problems:

1. *Small vessel size:* The diameter of the coronary arteries varies from 4 to 6 mm (left main coronary artery) to 3 to 4 mm (right coronary artery, left anterior descending and left circumflex coronary arteries). The small vessel size requires a sequence with high spatial resolution and high signal-to-noise to produce adequate images of the coronary tree.

2. *Cardiac motion:* There is significant cardiac motion during systole and diastole, including translation, rigid body rotation, regional twist, and change in long-axis dimension.[15] Rapid movements occur during ventricular systole and to some extent during rapid ventricular filling in early diastole, following atrial systole. There is a period of relative diastasis between these two events, when there is little intracavitary blood flow and cardiac motion but coronary artery flow remains high. This interval in late diastole is therefore the ideal acquisition time for coronary imaging.

3. *Respiratory motion:* During respiratory excursion, the heart moves several centimeters, creating potentially problematic respiratory motion artifacts. Thus, image acquisition should occur within a single breath-hold. To surmount this problem, ultrafast imaging techniques can be used.

Techniques

Electrocardiogram (ECG)-gated spin-echo and gradient-echo cine images only occasionally show portions of the coronary arteries, and these images are not adequate for detailed evaluation.[16] Three-dimensional MR acquisition methods have been used for coronary MRA but have suffered from saturation artifacts[17] which are more prominent than with two-dimensional acquisitions and may cause problems with low flow velocities. Other approaches involve subtraction methods[18] or the simultaneous oscillation of two gradients (spiral scan)[19] and have shown promising results in healthy volunteers.

For coronary MRA we use a 1.5-Tesla Magnetom SP whole-body imaging system (Siemens Medical Systems, Inc., Iselin, NJ) with a circularly polarized planar elliptical spine coil as radiofrequency receiver. The patient is in the prone position, with the heart directly above the surface coil.

Imaging parameters for the segmented turboFLASH sequence[20,21] consist of a repetition time of 13 ms and an echo time of 8 ms resulting in an effective temporal resolution of 78 to 104 ms. An incremented flip-angle series and k-space segmentation are used with 6 to 8 phase-encoding steps acquired in rapid sequence constituting one segment. In order to complete various matrix sizes (120 × 256, 128 × 256, or 160 × 256), 16 to 20 interleaved segments are acquired. Fat saturation is employed using a chemical shift-selective pulse with a 140° flip angle prior to each segment to maximally suppress fat signal at the central phase-encoding step of each segment. Slice thickness varies between 3 and 5 mm. The smallest field of view used was 18 × 21 cm (in-plane resolution of 1.1 × 0.9 mm for a 160 × 256 matrix). The examinations are performed within a single end-expiratory breath-hold using cardiac gating for image acquisition in mid diastole.

The examination begins with transverse images, starting at the aortic sinus level and covering a 2- to 3-cm vertical distance sequentially. Once flow through the proximal portion of the left main and right coronary arteries is identified, oblique views are acquired along an axis defined by the origins of the right (Fig. 8-1) and left (Fig. 8-2) coronary arteries. In our patient series, typical scan times for a single breath-hold image varies from 12 to 18 s due to differences in heart rates (from 54 to 90 beats per min), and total imaging time averages less than 45 min. After correction of misalignment and deletion of signals due to overlapping chambers and pericardial fluid, a maximum intensity projection (MIP) algorithm may be applied to these sequential images to obtain a "projection angiogram." This provides an image of vessel anatomy similar to that of a conventional coronary angiogram. Cine studies may also be acquired with a temporal resolution <85 ms.

Echo-planar imaging (EPI) employs stronger and faster gradients than conventional MR with an acquisition time of 50 to 100 ms per slice.[22] A series of gradient echoes that are individually phase-encoded is generated by rapidly oscillating the readout gradient. To date, the image quality of single-shot EPI of the coronary arteries does not match segmented turboFLASH. Improvement in spatial resolution and reduc-

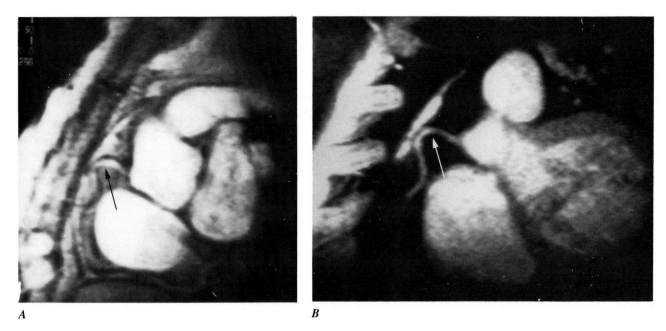

A   *B*

FIGURE 8-1   Oblique view of the right coronary artery. (Segmented turboFLASH sequence with TR/TE/ flip angle = 13 ms/8 ms/10-40° incremented flip angle, section thickness = 5 mm, field of view = 23 cm, 8 lines/segment, 128 × 256 matrix. *A*. No fat saturation. The right coronary artery (*black arrow*) is partially obscured by epicardial fat. *B*. With a fat saturation pulse (140° flip angle), there is a marked improvement in contrast between the right coronary artery (*arrow*) and epicardial fat.

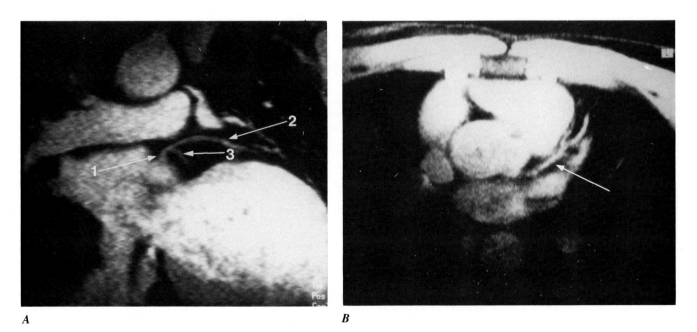

A   *B*

FIGURE 8-2   Coronary anatomy. (Segmented turboFLASH sequence; same parameters as in Fig. 8-1.) *A*. Oblique view of the left main (1), left anterior descending (2), and left circumflex (3) coronary arteries (*arrow*). *B*. Axial image shows the left anterior descending coronary artery (*arrow*).

tion of magnetic susceptibility artifacts will be necessary to achieve comparable image quality.

Preliminary Results

Thus far, we have performed coronary MRA in more than 60 subjects, including 39 patients who had undergone conventional coronary angiograms. These patients (35 men and 4 women, aged 33 to 84 years) were referred for evaluation of chest pain and had both examinations within 1 week. We used the technique described above to acquire overlapping transverse and oblique slices. Two independent observers (blinded to all clinical data) analyzed the cine loops and the results were correlated with angiographic data.

Conventional angiography demonstrated 29 patients to have significant coronary artery stenoses (where significant was defined as ≥ 50 percent diameter narrowing of a major epicardial vessel) with the following distribution: left main and three-vessel disease (n = 2), three-vessel disease (n = 4), two-vessel disease (n = 10), single-vessel disease (n = 13). No significant stenoses were found in the remaining 10 patients. The results of coronary MRA in this group are presented in Table 8-1[23] (Fig. 8-3).

Flow Measurements

In the past, intracoronary Doppler flow probes and TEE have been used to measure coronary blood flow.[24,25] Conventional angiography cannot quantitate coronary blood flow in order

TABLE 8-1   Sensitivity and Specificity of Coronary MRA[a]

	Number, (%) with Disease	Sensitivity, %	Specificity, %	PV (+)	PV (−)
Left main	2 (5)	100	100	1.00	1.00
LAD	23 (64)	87	92	0.95	0.80
LCX	7 (20)	71	90	0.63	0.93
RCA	20 (53)	100	78	0.83	1.00
Patient	29 (74)	97	70	0.90	0.88

[a] Sensitivity and specificity in classifying a vessel as having significant disease were 90 and 90 percent, respectively. Sensitivity and specificity for individual vessels are as listed.
Abbreviations: LAD = left anterior descending coronary artery; LCX = left circumflex coronary artery; RCA = right coronary artery; PV (+) = predictive value positive; PV (−) = predictive value negative.

to determine the functional significance of coronary artery stenosis.[26,27]

Magnetic resonance angiography has become well established for the evaluation of flow in other vessels.[28–31] With the phase contrast technique used for these purposes, flow across a magnetic field gradient induces a phase shift that is proportional to velocity.[28,30] Therefore, two images with different flow sensitivities are acquired and subtracted to eliminate stationary tissue. Flow measurement techniques are difficult to apply to small vessels in general and to coronary arteries in particular because of vessel movement through the imaging plane.

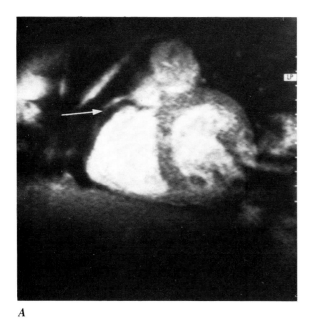
A

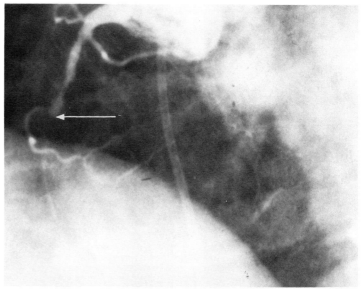
B

FIGURE 8-3   Severe stenosis of the right coronary artery. *A.* The MR angiogram shows the lesion (*arrow*). *B.* Selective right coronary injection at cardiac catheterization depicts subtotal occlusion (*arrow*) at position corresponding to MR signal void.

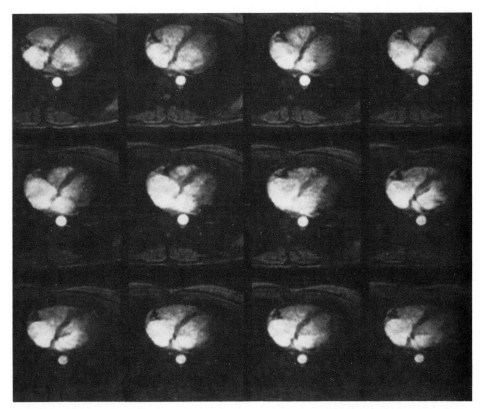

A

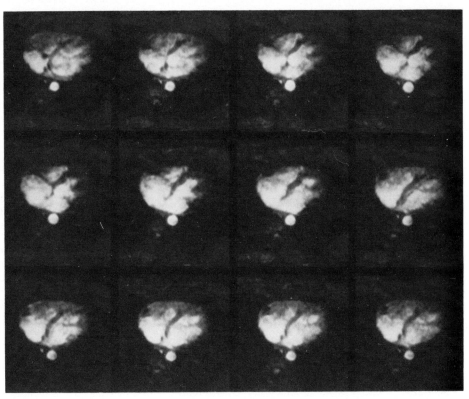

FIGURE 8-4 Cine MRA. *A*. Three-min standard cine. *B*. 15-s breath-hold cine.

B

We use a modification of a segmented turboFLASH sequence, in which two segmented turboFLASH images are acquired in a single breath-hold.[32] The first sequence, which is insensitive to flow, shows vessel anatomy. The second sequence is sensitive to the shift in the phase of the MR signal of flowing blood. Subtraction of these images produces a phase-difference image in which the phase shift is proportional to the flow velocity along the direction of slice selection. Image subtraction eliminates background phase shifts unrelated to blood flow.

We have tried this technique in flow phantoms and then in several subjects (12 subjects studied at rest and 4 studied before and during pharmacologic stress using intravenous adenosine). The flow velocities measured in the volunteers were in the mid portion of the right coronary artery, 9.9 ± 3.5 cm/s ($n = 12$), and in the proximal left anterior descending artery, 20.5 ± 5.2 cm/s ($n = 6$), at rest. Flow velocities typically increased at least fourfold with intravenous adenosine administration.

These results demonstrate that MRA can measure the velocity of coronary artery flow. It may be useful for determining the physiologic significance of coronary artery stenoses.

CONCLUSION

With the introduction of coronary MRA into clinical use, coronary artery anatomy can now be demonstrated entirely noninvasively. This technology can be regarded as a cost-effective, noninvasive alternative for the early detection of coronary artery disease and may be particularly useful in screening asymptomatic individuals with multiple risk factors for premature coronary artery disease or for evaluating patients with chest pain of unclear etiology. A comprehensive noninvasive cardiac evaluation of patients with suspected coronary artery disease—including evaluation of left and right ventricular systolic function, cardiac chamber volumes, wall thickness, and ventricular mass—is now possible.[33–35] Special advantages of coronary MRA include the ability to noninvasively quantify coronary artery blood flow, which may be used to measure the amount of myocardium perfused by a specific coronary vessel[36] or for the evaluation of effects of physiologic stress and/or cardioactive pharmacologic agents.

Persisting drawbacks of coronary MRA to date are its spatial resolution, which does not yet match that of contrast coronary angiography, as well as its dependence on a regular cardiac rhythm. In addition to the evaluation of the projection angiography, analysis of coronary MRA should still include a review of the individual slices either alone or in context with contiguous sections as a ''cine loop'' (Fig. 8-4) for more accurate diagnosis.

REFERENCES

1. Assessment of coronary artery disease, in Yang SS, Bentivolgio LG, Maranho V, Goldberg H (eds): *Cardiac Catheterization Data to Hemodynamic Parameters,* 3rd ed. Philadelphia, Davis, 1988, p. 256.
2. Davis K, Kennedy JW, Kemp HG, et al: Complications of coronary arteriography from the collaborative study of coronary artery surgery (CASS). *Circulation* 59:1105, 1979.
3. Kennedy JW and the Registry Committee of the Society for Cardiac Angiography: Complications associated with cardiac catheterization and angiography. *Cathet Cardiovasc Diagn* 8:5, 1982.
4. Wyman RM, Safian RD, Portway V, et al: Current complications of diagnostic and therapeutic cardiac catheterization. *J Am Coll Cardiol* 12:1400, 1988.
5. Gould KL: Detecting and assessing severity of coronary artery disease in humans. *Cardiovasc Intervent Radiol* 13:5, 1990.
6. Guidelines for coronary angiography: A report of the American College of Cardiology/American Heart Association Task Force on Assessment of Diagnostic and Therapeutic Cardiovascular Procedures (Subcommittee on Coronary Angiography). *Circulation* 76:963A, 1987.
7. Daniel WB, Erbel R, Kasper W, et al: Safety of transesophageal echocardiography: A multicenter survey of 10,419 examinations. *Circulation* 83:817, 1991.
8. Roberts KB, Califf RM, Harrell FE, et al: The prognosis for patients with new-onset angina who have undergone cardiac catheterization. *Circulation* 68:970, 1983.
9. Didier D, Higgins CB, Fischer MR, et al: Congenital heart disease: Gated MR imaging in 72 patients. *Radiology* 58:227, 1986.
10. Higgins CB, Holt W, Pflugfelder , Sechtem U: Functional evaluation of the heart with magnetic resonance imaging. *Mag Res Med* 6:121, 1988.
11. Ruggieri PM, Laub GA, Masaryk TJ, Modic MT: Intracranial circulation: Pulse-sequence considerations in three-dimensional (volume) MR angiography. *Radiology* 171:785, 1989.
12. Masaryk TJ, Modic MT, Ruggieri PM, et al: Three-dimensional (volume) gradient-echo imaging of the carotid bifurcation: Preliminary clinical experience. *Radiology* 171:801, 1989.
13. Kent KC, Edelman RR, Kim D, et al: Magnetic resonance imaging: A reliable test for the evaluation of proximal atherosclerotic renal arterial stenosis. *J Vasc Surg* 13:311, 1991.
14. Mattle H, Edelman RR, Reis MA, et al: Determination of flow velocities in the intracranial arteries by magnetic resonance angiography: Application to the middle cerebral artery. *Radiology* 181:527, 1991.
15. Rogers WJ, Shapiro EP, Weiss JL, et al: Quantification and correction for left ventricular systolic long-axis shortening by magnetic resonance tissue tagging and slice isolation. *Circulation* 84:721, 1991.
16. Paulin S, von Schulthess GK, Fossel E, Krayenbuehl HP: MR imaging of the aortic root and proximal coronary arteries. *Am J Roentgenol* 148:665, 1987.
17. Debiao L, Paschal CB, Haacke EM, Adler LP: Coronary arteries: Three-dimensional MR imaging with fat saturation and magnetization transfer contrast. *Radiology* 187:401, 1993.
18. Wang SJ, Hu BS, Macovski A, Nishimura DG: Coronary angiography using fast selective inversion recovery. *Mag Res Med* 18:417, 1991.
19. Meyer C, Hu B, Nishimura D, Macovski A: Fast spiral coronary artery imaging. *Mag Res Med* 28:202, 1992.
20. Edelman RR, Manning WJ, Burstein D, Paulin S: Coronary arteries: Breath-hold MR angiography. *Radiology* 181:641, 1991.
21. Manning WJ, Li W, Boyle NG, Edelman RR: Fat-suppressed

breath-hold magnetic resonance coronary angiography. *Circulation* 87:94, 1993.

22. Stehling MK, Turner R, Mansfield P: Echo-planar imaging: Magnetic resonance imaging in a fraction of a second. *Science* 254:43, 1991.

23. Manning WJ, Li W, Edelman RR: A preliminary report comparing magnetic resonance coronary angiography with conventional angiography. *N Engl J Med* 328:828, 1993.

24. Yamagishi M, Hotta D, Tamai J, et al: Validity of catheter-tip Doppler technique in assessment of coronary flow velocity and application of spectrum analysis method. *Am J Cardiol* 67:758, 1991.

25. Illiceto S, Marangelli V, Memmola C, Rizzon P: Transesophageal Doppler echocardiography evaluation of coronary blood flow velocity in baseline conditions and during dipyridamole-induced coronary vasodilatation. *Circulation* 83:61, 1991.

26. Gould KL: Detecting and assessing severity of coronary artery disease in humans. *Cardiovasc Intervent Radiol* 13:5, 1990.

27. Cusma JT, Toggart EJ, Folts JD, et al: Digital subtraction angiographic imaging of coronary flow reserve. Circulation 75:461, 1987.

28. van Dijk P: Direct cardiac NMR imaging of heart wall and blood flow velocity. *J Comput Assist Tomogr* 8:429, 1984.

29. Bryant DJ, Payne JA, Firmin DN, Longmore DB: Measurement of flow with NMR imaging using a gradient pulse and phase difference technique. *J Comput Assist Tomogr* 8:588, 1984.

30. Walker MF, Souza SP, Dumoulin CL: Quantitative flow measurement in phase contrast MR angiography. *J Comput Assist Tomogr* 12:304, 1988.

31. Mostbeck GH, Caputo GR, Higgins CB: MR measurement of blood flow in the cardiovascular system. *Am J Roentgenol* 159:453, 1992.

32. Edelman RR, Manning WJ, Gervino E, Li W: Flow velocity quantification in human coronary arteries with fast, breath-hold MR angiography. *J Mag Res Imaging* 3:699, 1993.

33. Spritzer CE, Herfkens RJ: Magnetic resonance of the heart, in Kressel HY (ed): *Magnetic Resonance Annual 1988*. New York, Raven Press, 1988, pp. 217–244.

34. Mazer MJ, Sandler MP, Kulkarni MV, et al: Gated MRI in congenital cardiac malformations. In Partain CL, Price RR, Patton JA, et al (eds): *Magnetic Resonance Imaging*. Philadelphia, Saunders, 1988, pp. 387–400.

35. Zerhouni EA, Parish DM, Rogers WJ, et al: Human heart: Tagging with MR imaging—a method for noninvasive assessment of myocardial motion. *Radiology* 169:59, 1988.

36. Kaul S, Glasheen WP, Oliner JD, et al: Relation between antegrade blood flow through a coronary artery and the size of the perfusion bed it supplies: Experimental and clinical implications. *J Am Coll Cardiol* 17:1403, 1991.

Chapter 9

Magnetic Resonance Angiography and Magnetic Resonance Imaging of the Pulmonary Vasculature

Pamela K. Woodard / H. Dirk Sostman / James R. MacFall

Magnetic resonance imaging (MRI) of the pulmonary arteries and the deep venous system of the lower extremity together in a single examination has recently become an attractive concept for the diagnosis of venous thromboembolism. Many patients with pulmonary embolism (PE) have detectable deep vein thrombosis (DVT). Therefore attention has been focused on the need to evaluate the deep venous system as an adjunct or alternative to evaluation of the pulmonary arteries in patients clinically suspected of have PE.[1] Advances in MRI of the deep venous system of the lower extremity have made MRI a clinically useful and highly accurate test for the detection of DVT,[2,3] but it is quite expensive. As well as being diagnostically valuable, it would improve the cost-benefit ratio of MRI if it were practical to perform pulmonary MR angiography (MRA) together with MRI of lower extremity veins[2,3] in patients with suspected PE. This would be a significant clinical advantage over other noninvasive techniques, which are limited to evaluation of either the legs (ultrasound) or the lungs (scintigraphy) and would more than compensate for the higher cost of MR.

Accepted techniques currently available to image suspected pulmonary emboli include ventilation-perfusion (V-Q) scintigraphy[4] and conventional angiography.[5] While ventilation-perfusion imaging is safe and can detect regions of decreased perfusion with great sensitivity, it does not give direct information about etiology. Conversely, while pulmonary angiography is highly sensitive and specific, it requires a skilled vascular interventionalist, is expensive and invasive, and is associated with a small degree of morbidity and mortality.[6]

In addition to the diagnosis of pulmonary embolism, other possible uses of noninvasive examination of the pulmonary arteries include evaluation of congenital vascular anomalies, arteriovenous malformations, and vascular tumors.

OVERVIEW OF IMAGING TECHNIQUES

Currently, most pulmonary MRA employs "white blood" techniques, in which pulmonary emboli are imaged as dark against the white background of the lung vasculature. The two principal white blood MRA imaging techniques are time of flight (TOF)[7,8] and phase contrast (PC).[9,10] Because many patients to be studied are critically ill, gradient echo sequences with very short repetition times (TR) and echo times (TE) are used in order to keep scan time at a minimum. Both two- and three-dimensional TOF imaging have been used extensively in pulmonary MRA. The longer TE and longer acquisition times associated with conventional PC implementations have limited their pulmonary applications.

"Black blood" techniques, in which pulmonary emboli are depicted as white against a black lung background, have also been described[11] and will be discussed below.

Time of Flight

Techniques for TOF pulmonary MRA use fast gradient recalled echo sequences, usually with radiofrequency (RF) spoiling (spoiled GRASS, FLASH, T1-FFE) or rephasing gradients (GRASS, FISP, FFE).

Several TOF methods exist, each with its own benefits and drawbacks. Recent research suggests that the most clinically useful technique will be single-breath-hold two-dimensional moderate thickness multislice imaging in which the signal-to-noise ratio (SNR) is improved by phased-array coils.[12] Other two-dimensional TOF techniques include (1) the thick-slice projection method and (2) moderate thickness multislice images without phased-array coils.

The simplest technique is the thick-slice projection method. Each lung is imaged separately in a sagittal slab 4 to 6 cm thick with a window to keep chest wall structures from obscuring pulmonary vasculature.[13] The sagittal approach avoids saturation of cardiac blood, especially if the slice is angled.[13] Typical parameters are TR = 13 ms; TE = 2.7 ms; 16-kHz bandwidth, 20-cm FOV, and number of excitations (NEX) = 12. The flip angles are low, usually on the order of 25°. While this low flip angle decreases the signal-to-noise ratio (SNR) to an extent, it also reduces pulsatility artifact.

Fairly good images can be obtained in a single 20-s breath-hold, and the quality of the image improves as time increases. This approach has both advantages and drawbacks. The acquisition time is short, which, as mentioned previously, is advantageous in imaging severely ill patients. Also, the thick slab provides relatively good venous suppression,[13] desirable when imaging is directed only to the pulmonary arteries, as in the detection of PE. Last, the thick-slice, single-breath-hold technique requires only an MRI system's standard body coil; postprocessing software is not necessary. The drawbacks include poor resolution of smaller vessels (which may hinder the diagnosis of thromboemboli) and saturation of slow-flowing pulmonary arterial blood (which may be falsely interpreted as arterial defects). Venous imaging is not possible, because the slower-flowing venous blood is completely saturated with this technique.

A better two-dimensional TOF alternative is moderate-thickness multislice imaging. Here, the angiogram is produced by using a projective algorithm such as the maximum-intensity pixel (MIP) method (Fig. 9-1). Parameters are similar to those of thick-slice projective imaging; however, the NEX and slice thickness are decreased and breath-holding is used. This thinner-slice technique improves resolution of the smaller, more peripheral arteries and prevents saturation of slow-flowing arterial blood (Fig. 9-2). The principal disadvantage of moderate-thickness multislice imaging is the long scan time. Acquiring 10 slices requires a breath-hold on the order of 70 s—an impossible feat for a patient whose respiration is compromised. Breath-holding for single slices or groups of slices is usually feasible, yet it is unlikely that a patient will be able to return to the same position with each breath-hold. The required breath-hold, however, may be reduced to the reasonable span of 10 to 20 s by using phased-array coils and a single excitation (NEX = 1). Venous suppression can be obtained using a thick saturation-excitation band on the side away from the heart. This band moves with the slice being imaged. Slices are scanned beginning farthest from the heart and moving centrally. Saturation bands, however, extend the acquisition time and are a disadvantage if image acquisition within a single breath-hold is required. Pulmonary venography may be obtained, if de-

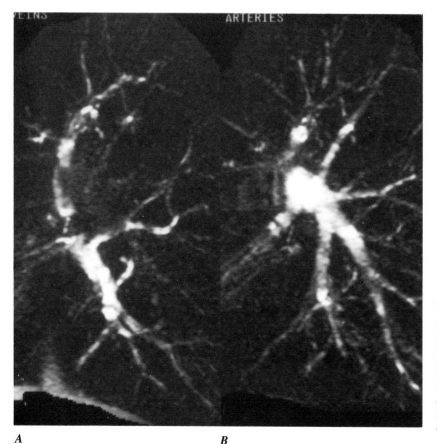

A   *B*

FIGURE 9-1 *A.* Multislice sagittal two-dimensional TOF pulmonary MRA (body coil) with arterial supression from a normal volunteer after MIP processing. Single-breath-hold scan, 1-min duration, 25° flip angle, TR = 13 ms, TE = 2.7 ms, 1-cm slice thickness, 10 slices, 4 NEX, 20-cm FOV. *B.* Multislice sagittal two-dimensional TOF pulmonary MRA (body coil) with venous suppression from a normal volunteer after MIP processing. Single-breath-hold scan, 1-min duration, 25° flip angle, TR = 13 ms, TE = 2.7 ms, 1-cm slice thickness, 10 slices, 4 NEX, 20-cm FOV.

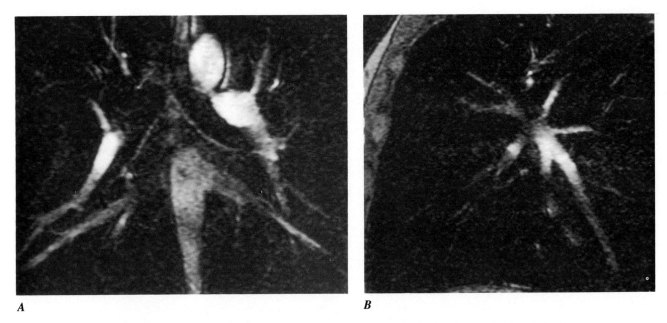

A   *B*

FIGURE 9-2 Coronal (*A*) and right sagittal (*B*) two-dimensional TOF pulmonary MRAs; single-slice images obtained from a subject with normal pulmonary arteries. Such images form the basis set for MIP processing to produce images such as those in Fig. 9-1. Parameters as above. (From Grist et al.[16] Reproduced by permission.)

sired, by placing the saturation band on the side toward the heart in order to saturate pulmonary arterial flow.

Angled sagittal imaging to avoid cardiac saturation is helpful. Imaging in two planes is desirable when searching for suspected PE. Additionally, reviewing original individual slices is important, especially in areas with findings suspicious for PE.

The use of phased-array surface coils to improve the SNR while maintaining a reasonably short breath-hold has been described.[12] Unlike surface coils, which do not provide adequate central body images, phased-array coils provide good central and peripheral imaging, maintain field homogeneity, and significantly improved SNR above that of the standard body coil (Fig. 9-3). Preliminary experiments used a specially designed phased-array receive-only coil to cover and image a single lung at a time.[12] Parameters were TR = 6.8 ms, TE = 2.2 ms, 32-kHz bandwidth, and flip angle = 20 to 25°. In order to obtain a single vascular MIP image, 10 to 14 sagittal images were acquired per study in a total of 10 to 15 s, each with a section thickness of 8 mm and a 3-mm overlap.[12] Peripheral vessels were well defined, the scanning time was short, images maintained a good SNR, and there were no pulsatility or respiratory motion artifacts. It is quite likely that this will be the most clinically applicable approach.

The three-dimensional TOF method for imaging pulmonary vasculature[14] is similar to the two-dimensional sequence; however, phase encoding in the slice-selection axis is added. This fast three-dimensional acquisition sequence improves the SNR, allows thinner slices to be obtained, and

reduces flow-related dephasing. However, the total acquisition time is on the order of 10 min, nearly 30 times as long as two-dimensional TOF imaging. Typical parameters are TR = 8 to 12 ms, TE = 2 to 3 ms, and a low flip angle of 7 to 20°.

Besides the clinical disadvantage of a long scan time, the prolonged volume imaging may saturate slow-flowing arterial blood, which may be falsely interpreted as arterial defects. On the other hand, when intrasequence delays are introduced to allow inflow of fresh spins, thrombi may not be effectively saturated, with the potential to reduce the contrast between thrombus and flowing blood. Moreover, intrasequence delays prolong the overall scanning time. Thrombus-blood contrast may also be strongly affected by the flip angle used in the sequence. Smaller flip angles decrease saturation effects, but reduce the conspicuity of thrombi.[15]

Other problems involve the visibility of peripheral vessels. Small peripheral vessels are poorly seen, as the blood which reaches the periphery of the volume is more saturated. Second, smaller, peripheral vessels are more susceptible to motion artifact and blurring with prolonged scanning times. While motion artifacts can be reduced with averaging, respiratory gating is required to improve blurring of peripheral vessels (Fig. 9-4). This blurring of peripheral vessels is most pronounced at the lung bases, in vessels closest to the diaphragm.

A final possible complicating factor is that in certain implementations of three-dimensional TOF imaging, both pulmonary arteries and veins are imaged together. While,

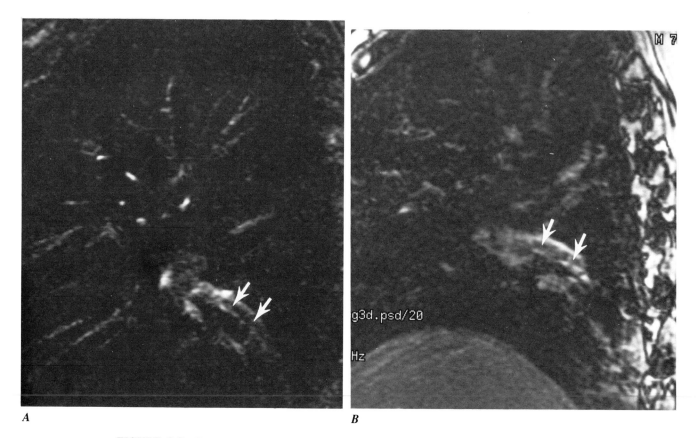

A   *B*

FIGURE 9-3 Single-slice TOF MR pulmonary MRAs in a patient with pulmonary artery embolism (*arrows*). *A.* Two-dimensional TOF with body coil and breath-holding at 4 NEX. *B.* Three-dimensional TOF with phased-array coil and respiratory gating at 1 NEX.

esthetically, three-dimensional TOF images can be pleasing because of the higher SNR, the added possible visual distraction of the pulmonary veins, along with low thrombus-blood contrast, may hinder the diagnostic usefulness of three-dimensional TOF imaging in the evaluation of PE (Fig. 9-5).

Phase Contrast

Phase-contrast angiography is another technique which may be useful in the imaging of main pulmonary arteries. It uses a gradient echo sequence sensitive to MR signal phase changes relative to a reference scan. Only flow in a single direction can be imaged with a single scan. If a scan sensitive to flow in three directions is desired, at least four scans are necessary, one scan sensitive to flow in each of the three directions and a fourth to serve as a phase reference. Accordingly, the main drawback of this method as it is conventionally implemented is the lengthy scan time associated with it as compared with TOF imaging. Respiratory-reordered phase-encoding algorithms are used to limit breathing motion artifact.

EXPERIENCE TO DATE WITH PULMONARY MRA

Pulmonary Embolism in Patients

There is currently little clinical application of pulmonary MRA. However, a body of clinical experience in the research setting is beginning to accumulate in addition to a considerable body of normal volunteer data. Several recent studies merit discussion.

Grist et al.[16] studied pulmonary MRA in 20 patients suspected clinically of having pulmonary embolism. Of these 20 patients, 13 also underwent MR venography of the lower extremity at the time of the pulmonary MRA. For pulmonary MRA, these authors used a multislice two-dimensional TOF technique. Patients were asked to hold their breath for 10 to 15 s or more and 1 to 10 sections were acquired per each breath-hold. In most cases only a body coil was used for signal excitation and reception. The quality of the pulmonary MRAs was graded: 11 were determined to be of good image quality and 9 as interpretable but of marginal quality. Problems hindering technique were "noise" secondary to the very short imaging times and dephasing or pulsatility artifact.[16]

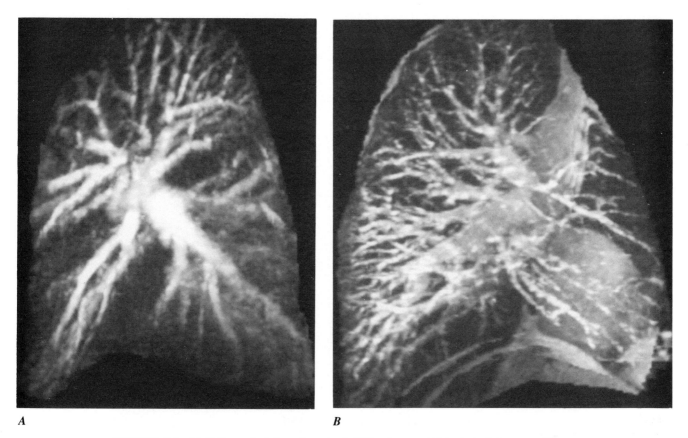

A   *B*

FIGURE 9-4 Multislice sagittal three-dimensional TOF pulmonary MRA obtained from two different normal subjects (*A*) without (8 NEX) and (*B*) with (1 NEX) respiratory gating. Note reduced blurring, especially of lower lobe arteries, with respiratory gating. Note also the reduced saturation of venous blood with respiratory gating due to prolonged interscan delays.

Of the 20 patients, 12 had acute PE (Fig. 9-6). Pulmonary MRA had a sensitivity of 92 to 100 percent and a specificity of 63 percent. Of the total of 6 false positives (3 for each of two blinded observers), 3 were associated with regions of atelectasis, 2 were in regions of prior PE, and 1 was a misinterpretation of normal anatomy. There was one false-negative examination. It occurred in a patient who had also undergone MR venography of the lower extremity, which demonstrated proximal deep venous thrombosis. Thus, sensitivity of the combined MR venography and pulmonary MRA examinations was 100 percent for detection of acute venous thromboembolic disease. No patient in this series would have been denied necessary anticoagulant therapy if MR had been used clinically as the only diagnostic study. However, 3 of the 20 patients would have received anticoagulant therapy inappropriately.[16]

In addition, Grist et al.[16] examined the feasibility of performing combined pulmonary MRA and lower extremity venography in a single examination (Fig. 9-7). The latter examination was performed in 13 of the 20 patients at the time of MRA. To acquire both studies during one examination typically required 1 hour (approximately 30 min for each study).

Several studies have addressed the use of phased-array coils in order to improve SNR in two-dimensional TOF imaging.[12,17] The main disadvantage, until recently, has been that if one wished to keep the acquisition time within the range of a single breath-hold (10 to 15 s), pulmonary venous flow suppression pulses could not be used. A spatially selective presaturation pulse applied before each radiofrequency pulse is quite effective yet adds nearly 8 s to the sequence TR.[17] This nearly doubles imaging time and thus increases the number of required breath-holds. Usually the patient cannot return to the same position on the repeat breath-holds and misregistration artifacts result.

Recent research by Foo et al.[17] has addressed this problem successfully. Rather than applying a spatially selective presaturation pulse prior to each RF excitation pulse, they applied the flow presaturation pulse once for multiple RF excitation pulses.[17] This technique does not increase sequence TR but instead adds several TR intervals to the total acquisition. These additional TR intervals only increase image

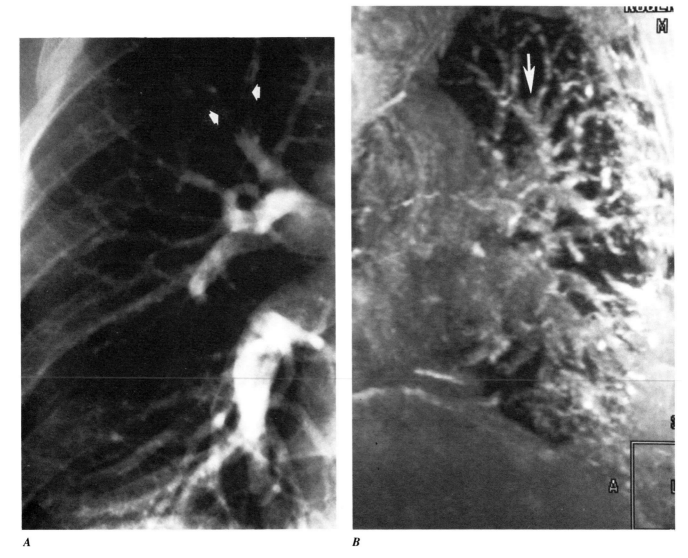

A   *B*

FIGURE 9-5   Patient with a pulmonary embolism of the right upper lobe as demonstrated by (*A*) conventional angiography, (*B*) three-dimensional TOF MR pulmonary angiographic projection (*arrow*), and progressively edited zoomed views (*C, D*). The presence of these emboli would be difficult to detect on three-dimensional TOF images without the conventional angiogram and the ability to focus image editing on the appropriate region.

acquisition time slightly. Foo et al.[16] demonstrated that the optimal presaturation frequency was once every 16 to 20 RF excitations. This provided the maximum venous flow suppression and the least artifact.

Other recent work has involved comparison of spin-echo imaging, saturation-tagged cine images, and two-dimensional TOF single-breath-hold images using a receive-only multicoil over the right lung.[18] A total of 15 patients were enrolled prospectively, of whom 12 had pulmonary embolic disease as demonstrated by angiographic findings, intraoperative findings, or high-probability ventilation-perfusion scan. Three patients demonstrated no disease with conventional

angiography. Breath-hold two-dimensional MRA was the most sensitive and specific of the three techniques, with a sensitivity of 83 percent and specificity of 100 percent.

Additional work has been done in three-dimensional TOF imaging in an attempt to overcome some of the problems caused by the long data collection times required.[11] Wielopolski et al.[11] have recently proposed a proton-density/inflow-weighted syncopated three-dimensional FLASH (white blood) sequence accompanied by an inversion recovery three-dimensional FLASH (black blood) sequence. The white-blood images define anatomy while the black-blood images demonstrate thromboemboli. The two sets of images

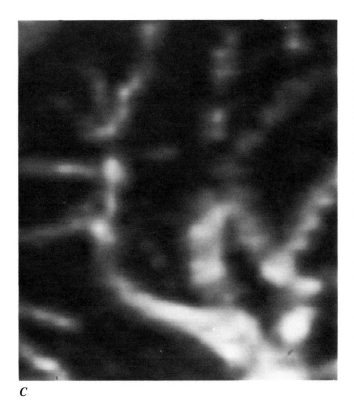

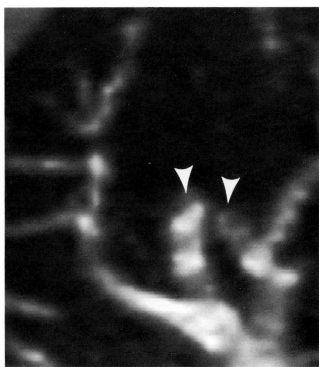

C

D

FIGURE 9-5 (*Continued*)

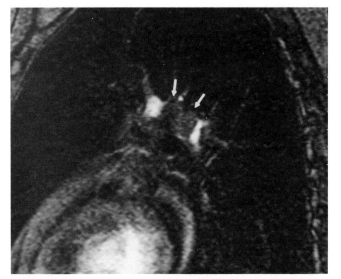

FIGURE 9-6 Positive two-dimensional TOF pulmonary MRA. The V-Q scan was categorized as "high probability for pulmonary embolism." Single-slice image of the left pulmonary artery shows a large filling defect (*arrows*) consistent with acute PE. (From Grist et al.[16] Reproduced by permission.)

are used in concert to localize thromboembolic disease. Breath-holding is not required, as the acquisition is syncopated and multiple acquisitions are averaged.

In the study by Wielopolski et al.,[11] the three-dimensional FLASH white-blood images obtained were of relatively good quality with the exception of blurring at the lung bases caused by diaphragmatic motion. Detection of pulmonary emboli on white-blood images, however, was a problem, likely secondary to saturation of slower-flowing blood despite the very low flip angles (7°). The black-blood three-dimensional suppressed (inversion recovery) angiogram was able to demonstrate bright thrombus. On the few subjects imaged, thrombus was consistently brighter than the suppressed blood. Clots, however, vary in signal intensity, and it is theoretically possible that some darker clots may not be as easily imaged as those which were demonstrated.[11]

Other Pulmonary Vascular Pathology in Patients

Recent studies have demonstrated that MRA may be useful in the assessment of diseases other than PE. Kauczor et al.[19] have shown that MRA in conjunction with MR tomography may be helpful in the preoperative evaluation of intrathoracic masses. In their studies, MRA demonstrated vessel displacement and stenosis (caused by tumor infiltration or compression) as well as poststenosis perfusion deficit or patency.[19] Evaluation of pulmonary arteriovenous malformations can be

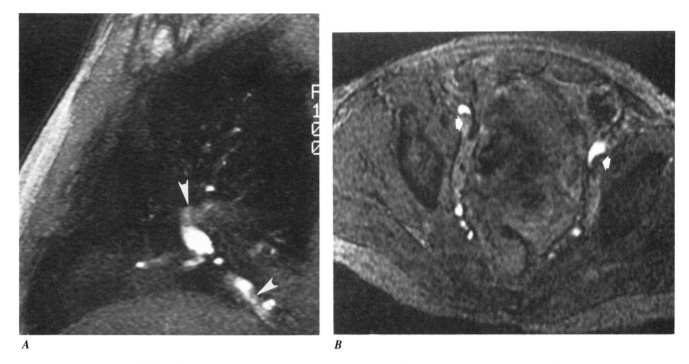

A   *B*

FIGURE 9-7   A patient with multiple right lung pulmonary emboli (*arrows*) demonstrated by two-dimensional TOF pulmonary MRA.   *B*. Bilateral femoral vein DVTs (*arrows*) demonstrated by lower extremity MR venography.

performed with TOF MRA (Fig. 9-8) or with a combination of spin-echo and cine-gradient echo sequences and phase-contrast imaging. The authors point out that cardiac-gated phase-contrast sequences are necessary to confirm the presence or absence of blood flow in these lesions.[20]

Experimental Studies

Dog models have also been used in researching the MR assessment of PE (Fig. 9-9). Early studies used tantalum-labeled autologous clot and barium-labeled 3-mm plastic spheres[21] or unlabeled clots.[22] Findings on cardiac-gated spin-echo images were compared to radiographic localization[21] or pathology.[22] Other early studies used boiled autologous clot and compared spin-echo MR images to conventional angiography.[23] These studies determined that MR might play a useful role in pulmonary thromboembolic imaging.

Most recently, dogs have been used in the evaluation of fast two- and three-dimensional TOF pulmonary MRA. In one study, MacFall et al.[24] approximated the T1 and T2 of thrombi in vivo. Clot was created from venous dog blood mixed with thrombin and ε-aminocaproic acid.[24] To confirm the location of the clots radiographically, barium-impregnated threads were included (confirmed by intraarterial digital subtraction angiography). These clots were inserted into the jugular veins of anesthetized mongrel dogs. Imaging with conventional radiography, digital subtraction angiography,

and two- and three-dimensional TOF imaging demonstrated hypointense areas within vessels on the white-blood images, which corresponded to known areas of thrombi seen on conventional radiography. In nine dogs, 23 lung zones were observed with two-dimensional TOF sequences and 21 of these zones were also imaged with three-dimensional TOF sequences. Review of these images by a single blinded observer gave results which appear to differ from those obtained in studies involving human subjects with two-dimensional TOF sequences. In the dogs, the two-dimensional sequence had a 65 percent sensitivity and an 80 percent specificity; three-dimensional imaging had a 62 percent sensitivity and an 85 percent specificity (*James MacFall, personal communication*). Given the small numbers of subjects involved in both the clinical studies and the experimental study, it is not clear that the results in the different settings are truly different. In addition, the emboli in the dog study were probably considerably smaller than most of those detected in the clinical work reported to date.

Current Limitations of Pulmonary MRA

The technical problems limiting widespread clinical application of pulmonary MRA include cardiac motion, respiratory motion, and motion caused by vascular pulsation. There are also MR susceptibility artifacts caused by air-tissue interfaces within the lung. Such artifacts reduce SNR and degrade spatial resolution. Still other problems include dif-

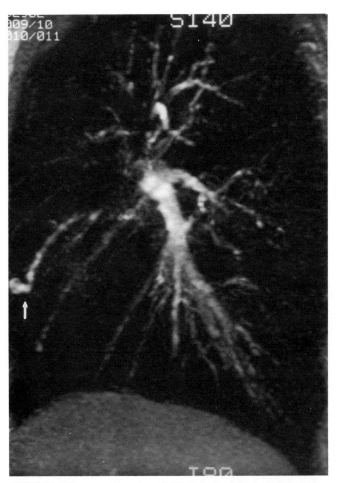

FIGURE 9-8 Two-dimensional TOF sagittal pulmonary MRA projection of AVM (*arrow*).

ferent directional orientation of vessels, overlap of pulmonary arteries and veins, and the need to simultaneously image large and small vessels with varied flow rates (Fig. 9-10).[16]

Since pulmonary MRA will be used mostly to image patients with suspected PE, researchers must implement methods to overcome PE-associated phenomena which do not occur in normal volunteers. Unlike conventional angiography, in which criteria for thromboemboli are established, little research has been done to determine specific or reliable criteria for the interpretation of pulmonary MRA. Conventional angiographic criteria for pulmonary emboli include (1) intraluminal filling defects or (2) occluded pulmonary arteries with "capping" of thromboemboli. However, with pulmonary MRA, demonstrating an intraluminal thrombus may be more difficult, since the appearance of thromboemboli varies with the age of the clot as chemical characteristics change. With pulmonary MRA, an occluded pulmonary artery should appear as intraarterial loss of flow-related enhancement. However, because of PE-associated slow-flow states and pulmonary parenchymal changes, or in the nonembolic case with hypoxic vasoconstriction, the appearance of surrounding unoccluded arteries may also be affected.

Frequently, poor visibility of subsegmental and segmental vessels limits immediate clinical application of pulmonary MRA. This has been attributed to many of the problems previously discussed. Respiratory motion artifacts have been implicated in patients unable to hold their breath during image acquisition. In addition, poor visibility of subsegmental vessels is thought to result from slow-flow states due to PE or nonembolic lung pathology. Subsegmental vessels have been only poorly visible even in normal volunteers secondary to limited SNR when imaging with the body coil alone. In this case, use of local coils or multicoil arrays can enhance SNR. Some observers feel that contrast material may be helpful in this regard; the effects of contrast agents are to some extent pulse sequence–dependent.

Finally, for pulmonary MRA to be clinically useful, all components of the examination time must be further reduced. Breath-hold time requirements must be minimized in order to acquire all slices of the lung together, eliminating misregistration in 2-dimensional approaches. In addition, the total MR pulmonary vascular imaging time must be minimized. This is especially important if the patient is to undergo imaging of the lower extremity for the detection of DVT in the same examination in which pulmonary MRA is to be done.

NONINVASIVE TECHNIQUES COMPETITIVE WITH MRA

Spin-Echo MRI

Spin-echo MRI is an alternative method of imaging the central cardiovascular system noninvasively; T1-weighted images demonstrate central anatomy well and are excellent for assessing congenital anomalies of the pulmonary arteries.[25–27]

Multiple studies have documented the usefulness of low- and medium-field-strength spin-echo MRI in the assessment of suspected central pulmonary emboli.[28–30] Indeed, spin-echo MRI might be the preferred choice subsequent to a ventilation-perfusion scan demonstrating large unilateral defects possibly caused by either a large central thrombus or an external compressing mass.

Spin-echo images differ from MRA TOF techniques in that flowing blood is black secondary to inflow saturation, spin dephasing, and outflow between the 90 and 180° pulses. Thus, flowing blood produces little or no signal and thrombus is usually bright (Fig. 9-11).[31] Spin-echo images are similar to MRA sequences in that normal lung is black. Electrocardiogram (ECG) gating to the R wave and respiratory gating are normally used to limit cardiac and respiratory motion artifact.

Although intraluminal signal may be seen in the diastolic cardiac phase of normal subjects, signal persisting into systole is usually indicative of slow-flowing blood (as in pul-

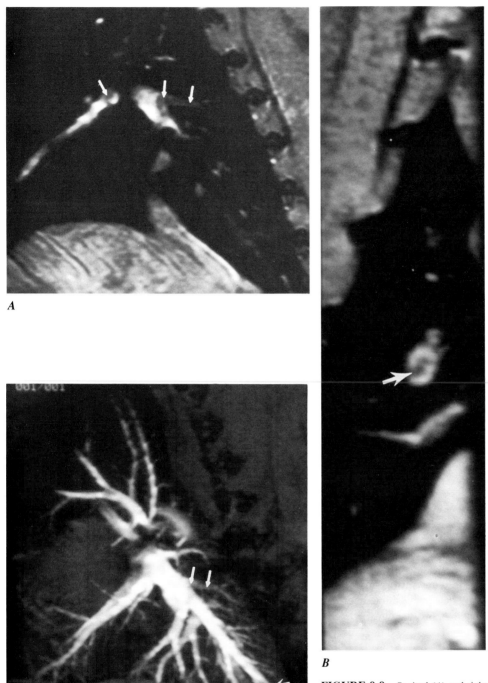

A

B

C

FIGURE 9-9   Sagittal (*A*) and right oblique (*B*) coronal single-slice images demonstrate PE (*arrows*) in a dog. Sagittal two-dimensional TOF pulmonary MRA projection shows clot in the right lower lobe arteries (*arrows*). Note that the emboli are more difficult to see on the projection image due to the properties of the MIP algorithm. The vessels are interrupted at the hilum because they are not included in the MIP basis set; this is another type of processing artifact, not pathology.

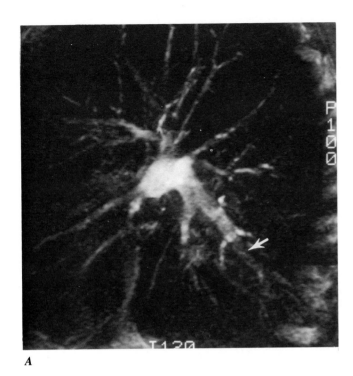

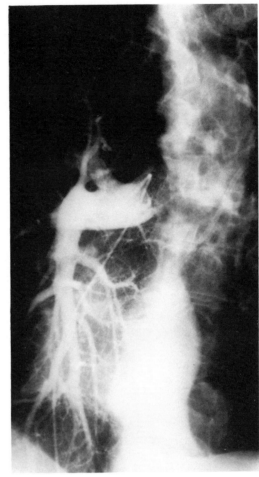

FIGURE 9-10 *A.* Region of slow flow (*arrow*) on two-dimensional TOF pulmonary MRA mimics embolus. *B.* It is, however, demonstrated to be normal by conventional angiography.

monary arterial hypertension)[32] or of thrombus.[33,34] While distinguishing between slow-flowing blood and thrombus may sometimes be problematic, White et al.[33] have shown that the two may be differentiated by (1) observing through the cardiac cycle and (2) using both first- and second-echo images ("even-echo rephasing"). Signal associated with slow-flowing blood disappears at some phase of the cardiac cycle, while thrombus-associated signal remains present throughout. Additionally, signal associated with thrombus shows little or no increase in relative intensity with change from first to second echo, whereas the signal intensity of slow-flowing blood increases. However, this even-echo rephasing technique of identifying thrombus works only when the pulse sequence produces gradient moment nulling. Actual signal changes seen with slow-flowing blood are variable, depending upon the details of the pulse sequence used. The use of saturation tagging[35] has also been successful in identifying thrombi in the presence of slow flow.

Further drawbacks include the inability to distinguish between chronic and acute PE, poor differentiation between thrombus and airless lung, and hyperintense signal from endobronchial mucous plugs, which, at times, may mimic pulmonary artery thrombus.

At least one case report suggests that the administration of Gd-DTPA could enhance vascularized tumor, thus differentiating it from a nonvascularized intraluminal thrombus.[36] Other than this, most paramagnetic contrast agents have yet to significantly improve the detection of PE in humans.[37] However, preliminary research on a ferric hydroxide sucrose complex as a negative contrast agent has shown some promise.[38]

The use of white-blood spin-echo techniques where saturated blood spins are refreshed has recently been described as a means of improving the definition of small vessles.[31]

Cine MRI

Cine-gradient echo-pulse sequences have also been used to image pulmonary vasculature and have demonstrated central PE[39] and vascular anomalies such as arteriovenous malformations (Fig. 9-12).[40]

The TR and TE are short, with a limited flip angle.

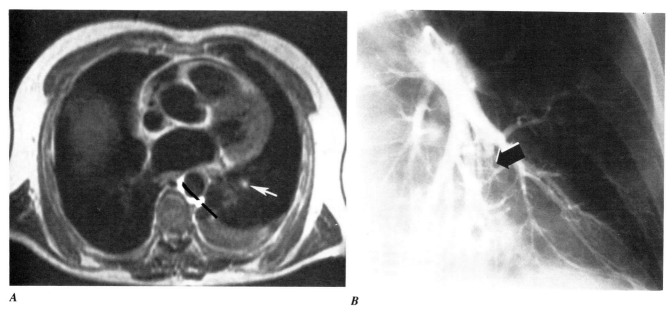

A

B

FIGURE 9-11   *A.* MR spin-echo transaxial image. A small bright focus (*arrow*) is seen in the left lower lobe, suggestive of thrombus. There is also a left pleural effusion.   *B.* A conventional angiogram confirms the findings of a thrombus in a basilar subsegmental artery (*arrow*).

Parameters include respiratory compensation and cardiac synchronization. Data are usually acquired in interleaved sets of three or four noncontiguous slices and are sorted temporally. Studies can then be viewed in a sequential play-back loop.[39]

Posteraro et al.[39] demonstrated in a group of 11 patients that cine-MRI was accurate in imaging central PE. No emboli, however, could be identified distal to lobar branches. The white-blood technique of cine-MRI offers some advantages over conventional spin-echo imaging of central emboli in that it eliminates the possibility of confusing bright atelectasis or mucous plugs with thrombus, since thrombus on cine-MRI is black. However, lengthy acquisition times and the possibility of saturating inflowing spins with multislice interleaved cine acquisitions are potential problems. Recent work[41] has demonstrated that the use of non–moment nulled fractional echo techniques to reduce TE significantly improves lung imaging in cine as well as static MRA acquisitions.

CT Angiography

Another modality which may play a role in direct (but still relatively noninvasive) pulmonary artery imaging is spiral volumetric computed tomography (CT). Recent studies demonstrate that spiral volumetric CT can nicely show PE in main (Fig. 9-13), lobar, and segmental arteries (Fig. 9-14).[42]

Conventional CT as a means of imaging thrombi in central pulmonary arteries was first described in 1978.[43] However,

visualization of more peripheral arteries, although reported,[44] was rare. Furthermore, the long breath-holds required for a technically adequate examination made routine imaging of PE by conventional CT impractical.

Spiral volumetric CT allows continuous scanning of the lungs during a single breath-hold while advancing the patient through the x-ray beam. Remy-Jardin et al.[42] showed that this could be accomplished during 24 s of scanning time. While a 24-s breath-hold may not be optimal for all patients, preliminary data suggest that breathing during scanning may cause motion artifacts on the lung windows, although not on the mediastinal images.

Vascular signs of PE on spiral CT were most frequently partial or complete vascular filling defects. Other findings were mural defects and floating intramural clot, causing "railway" or "tram-track" signs.

Besides the vascular signs, the parenchymal indications of infarct or emboli previously reported with conventional CT (such as wedge-shaped defects, focal oligemia, or pleural effusion[45]) are also demonstrated with helical technique.

Because of the ability to interpolate between gathered data points (in comparison to conventional CT), data between image slices is not lost. Thus three-dimensional angiography images can be reconstructed. While surface-rendered three-dimensional vascular images may be less than ideal for demonstrating intravascular filling defects, they have proven useful in the assessment of pulmonary arteriovenous malformations (Fig. 9-15).[46]

Ultrafast CT, as yet available in only a few major medical centers, also permits imaging of pulmonary emboli.[47]

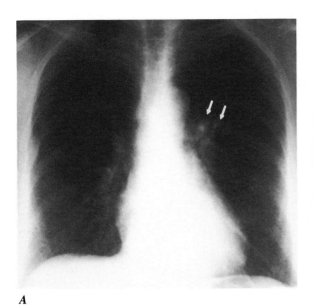

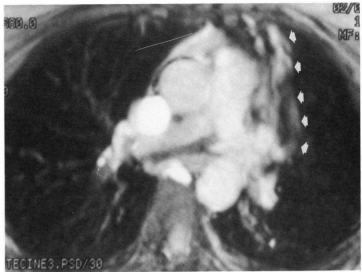

A

B

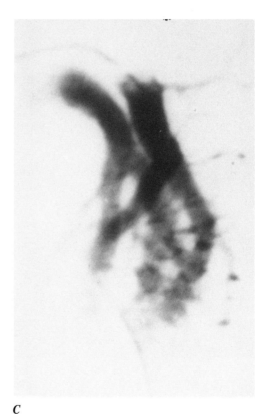

FIGURE 9-12   An arteriovenous malformation fed by a branch of the left pulmonary artery as seen on (*A*) plain radiograph (*arrows*) and (*B*) projection of three cine MR sections (*arrows*). Cine MR parameters: TR = 25 ms, TE = 6 ms, flip angle = 30°, 16-kHz bandwidth, 2 NEX, section thickness = 5 mm. The intraarterial digital subtraction angiogram is shown in (*C*).

C

Thrombus Scintigraphy

The idea of using a pharmaceutical agent which preferentially adheres to thrombi has been attractive for many years. The advantages of radiolabeled thrombus-detecting agent are that such an examination would likely be relatively inexpensive compared to CT or MRI, the entire body could be surveyed for thromboembolic disease in a single examination, nuclear medicine imaging equipment is widely available, and "active" and chronic thrombi could potentially be distinguished, aiding selection of treatment. A number of candidate agents have been investigated, including fibrin and fibrinolytic products, platelets, components of the fibrinolytic system, and a

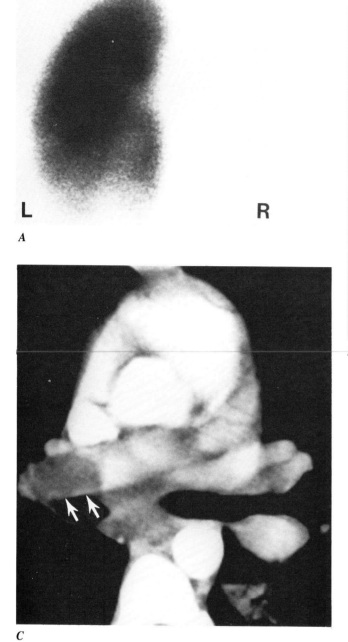

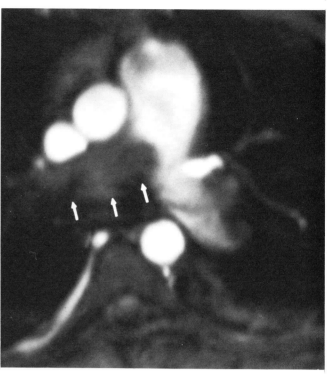

A

B

C

FIGURE 9-13   A 17-year-old female with sudden onset of dyspnea and history of oral contraceptive use.   *A*. A V-Q scan demonstrates complete absence of perfusion to the right lung.   *B*. Magnetic resonance cine trans-axial image (TR = 20 ms, TE = 7.6 ms, flip angle = 45°, 16-kHz bandwidth, FOV = 30 cm, 2 NEX, section thickness = 10 mm) shows a large, right pulmonary artery thrombus (*white arrows*).   *C*. Spiral volumetric CT image (10-mm interval) of the same patient. Large, completely obstructing right pulmonary artery thrombus (*white arrows*).

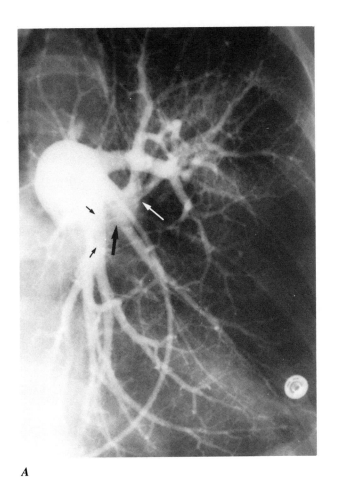

A

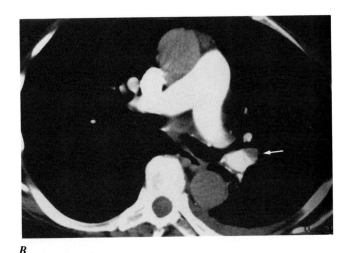

B

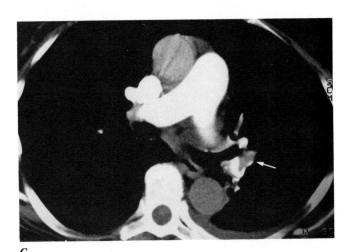

C

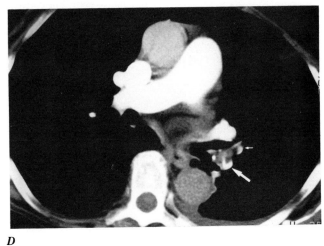

D

FIGURE 9-14   Images of a 62-year-old woman with left-side chest pain and hemoptysis. *A.* Left posterior oblique conventional angiogram shows intraluminal filling defects in the inferior lingular (*large black arrow*) and lower lobe (*small black arrows*) pulmonary arteries and suspected filling defects in the apicoposterior segmental artery (*white arrow*) that originates from a common trunk with the lingular artery. *B–D.* Spiral volumentric computed tomography scans, obtained at 3-mm intervals from the level of the left upper lobe bronchus (120 mL of 12% iodinated contrast material), show complete filling defects in the apicoposterior artery (*arrow in B*), slightly enlarged superior lingular artery (*arrow in C*), inferior lingular artery (*small arrow in D*), and initial part of the left lower lobe pulmonary artery (*large arrow in D*). (From Remy-Jardin et al.[42] Reproduced by permission.)

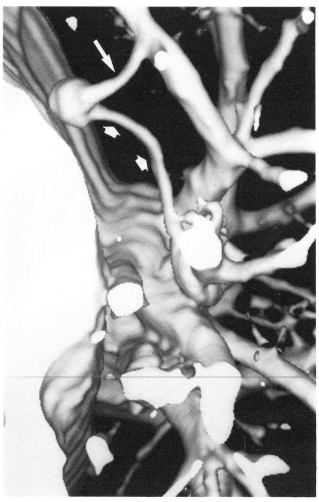

FIGURE 9-15 Young woman with a left upper lobe pulmonary arteriovenous malformation. Surface-rendered three-dimensional computed tomography image. A single artery (*two short arrows*) feeds the structure and a single artery (*long arrow*) drains it. The feeding artery originates from the anterior subsegmental artery of A1. (Courtesy of J. Remy and M. Remy-Jardin, Hôpital Calmette, Lille, France.)

variety of monoclonal antibodies and derivatives. To date, none of these agents has proven useful enough for widespread clinical use, but the powerful rationale for them has prompted continued investigations, which are yielding increasingly promising results. An excellent review of this topic has recently been published.[48]

CONCLUSIONS

There is great potential in the use of MR imaging of the pulmonary vasculature for the detection of thromboemboli and other less common disorders. A number of technical problems remain to be solved, but recent advances lead to considerable optimism about the ultimate outcome of this effort. Further improvements in scanner hardware will allow shorter scans and improved quality of both white-blood and black-blood techniques, which will probably have to be used together for greatest accuracy. Formal large-scale clinical trials which compare pulmonary MRA with other noninvasive approaches will soon be necessary. For evaluating suspected PE, it will be optimal to evaluate the lower extremity veins for DVT at the same time that the thorax is evaluated for PE.

ACKNOWLEDGMENTS

We are grateful for the collaboration of numerous colleagues who are now or were formerly in the Departments of Radiology and Medicine, Duke University Medical Center, and also at GE Medical Systems. We thank Dr. M. Remy-Jardin and Dr. J. Remy for their kind permission to reproduce illustrations of their work with CT of the pulmonary vasculature.

REFERENCES

1. Stein PD, Hull RD, Saltzman HA, Pineo G: Strategy for diagnosis of patients with suspected acute pulmonary embolism. *Chest* 103:1553, 1993.
2. Evans AJ, Sostman HD, Knelson MH, et al: Detection of deep venous thrombosis: Prospective comparison of MR imaging with contrast venography. *AJR* 161:131, 1993.
3. Spritzer CE, Sostman HD, Wilkes DC, Coleman RE: Deep venous thrombosis: Experience with gradient-echo MR imaging in 66 patients. *Radiology* 177:235, 1990.
4. Hanson M, Coleman RE: Pulmonary nuclear medicine evaluation of thromboembolic disease. *J Thorac Imaging* 4:40, 1989.
5. Dunnick NR, Sostman HD: Pulmonary thromboembolic disease, in Elliott LP (ed): *Cardiac Imaging in Infants, Children and Adults*. Philadelphia, Lippincott, pp. 891–905, 1991.
6. Stein PD, Athanasoulis C, Alavi A, et al: Complications and validity of pulmonary angiography in acute pulmonary embolism. *Circulation* 85:462, 1992.
7. Keller PJ, Drayer BP, Fram EK, et al: MR angiography with two-dimensional acquisition and three-dimensional display—Work in progress. *Radiology* 173:527, 1989.
8. Lenz GW, Haacke EM, Masaryk TJ, Laub G: In-plane vascular imaging: Pulse sequence design and strategy. *Radiology* 166:875, 1988.
9. Pernicone JR, Siebert JE, Potchen EJ, et al: Three-dimensional phase-contrast MR angiography in the head and neck: Preliminary report. *AJNR* 11:457, 1990.
10. Masaryk TJ, Modic MT, Ross JS, et al: Intra-cranial circulation: Preliminary results with three-dimensional (volume) MR angiography. *Radiology* 171:793, 1989.
11. Wielopolski PA, Haacke EM, Adler LP: Evaluation of the pulmonary vasculature with three-dimensional magnetic resonance imaging techniques. *Magma* 1:21, 1993.
12. Foo TKF, MacFall JR, Hayes CE, et al: Pulmonary vasculature: Single breath-hold MR imaging with phased-array coils. *Radiology* 183:473, 1992.
13. MacFall JR, Sostman HD, Foo TKF: Thick-section, single breath-hold magnetic resonance pulmonary angiography. *Invest Radiol* 27:318, 1992.

14. Wielopolski PA, Haacke EM, Adler LP: Three-dimensional MR imaging of the pulmonary vasculature: Preliminary experience. *Radiology* 183:465, 1992.
15. Wu JJ, MacFall JR, Sostman HD, Hedlund LW: Clot-blood contrast in fast gradient-echo magnetic resonance imaging. *Invest Radiol* 28:586, 1993.
16. Grist TM, Sostman HD, MacFall JR, et al: Pulmonary angiography using MRI: Initial clinical experience. *Radiology* 189:523, 1993.
17. Foo TKF, MacFall JR, Sostman HD, Hayes CE: Single-breath-hold venous or arterial flow-suppressed pulmonary vascular MR imaging with phased-array coils. *J Mag Res Imaging* 3:611, 1993.
18. Schiebler ML, Holland G, Listerud J, et al: Prospective evaluation of breath-hold pulmonary angiography (abstract). *J Mag Res Imaging* 3(P):43, 1993.
19. Kauczor HU, Layer G, Schad LR, et al: MR angiography complementing MR tomography in preoperative assessment of intrathoracic masses (abstract). *SMRI Annual Meeting Program Works in Progress Supplement* 1991; p. 8.
20. Silverman JM, Julien PJ: MR imaging evaluation of pulmonary vascular malformations (abstract). *Radiology* 181(P):156, 1991.
21. Stein MG, Crues JV, Bradley WG, et al: MR imaging of pulmonary emboli: An experimental study in dogs. *AJR* 147:1133, 1986.
22. Pope CF, Sostman HD, Carbo P, et al: The detection of pulmonary emboli by magnetic resonance imaging: Evaluation of imaging parameters. *Invest Radiol* 22:937, 1987.
23. Ovenfors CO, Batra P: Diagnosis of peripheral pulmonary emboli by MR imaging: An experimental study in dogs. *Mag Res Imaging* 6:487, 1988.
24. MacFall JR, Wu JJ, Sostman HD, et al: MR imaging detection of model pulmonary emboli in dogs (abstract). *Radiology* 185(P):217, 1992.
25. Julsrud PR: Magnetic resonance imaging of the pulmonary arteries and veins. *Semin Ultrasound CT MR* 11:184, 1990.
26. Lynch DA, Higgins CB: MR imaging of unilateral pulmonary artery anomalies. *JCAT* 14:187, 1990.
27. Gomes AS, Lois JF, Williams RG: Pulmonary arteries: MR imaging in patients with congenital obstruction of the right ventricular outflow tract. *Radiology* 174:51, 1990.
28. Gamsu G, Hirji M, Moore EH, et al: Experimental pulmonary emboli detected using magnetic resonance. *Radiology* 153:467, 1984.
29. Moore EH, Gamsu G, Webb WR, Stulbarg MS: Pulmonary embolus: Detection and follow-up using magnetic resonance. *Radiology* 153:471, 1984.
30. Thickman D, Kressel HY, Axel L: Demonstration of pulmonary embolism by magnetic resonance imaging. *AJR* 142:921, 1984.
31. Jung W-I, Sieverding L, Schick F, et al: Imaging of the human cardiovascular system using the rapid echo flow-rephased spin-echo technique. *Mag Res Imaging* 11:301, 1993.
32. Gefter WB, Hatabu H, Dinsmore BJ, et al: Pulmonary vascular cine MR imaging: A noninvasive approach to dynamic imaging of the pulmonary circulation. *Radiology* 176:761, 1990.
33. White RD, Winkler ML, Higgins CB: MR imaging of pulmonary arterial hypertension and pulmonary emboli. *AJR* 149:15, 1987.
34. Fisher MR, Higgins CB: Central thrombi in pulmonary arterial hypertension detected by MR imaging. *Radiology* 158:223, 1986.
35. Hatabu H, Gefter WB, Axel L, et al: MR imaging with spatial modulation of magnetization in the evaluation of central pulmonary thromboemboli (abstract). *Radiology* 177(P):139, 1990.
36. Weinreb JC, Davis SD, Berkmen HM, et al: Pulmonary artery sarcoma: Evaluation using Gd-DTPA. *JCAT* 14:647, 1990.
37. Thakur ML, Vinitski S, Mitchell DG, et al: MR imaging of pulmonary parenchyma and emboli by paramagnetic and suprapara-magnetic contrast agents. *Mag Res Imaging* 8:624, 1990.
38. Vinitski S, Thankur ML, Consigny PM, et al: Use of ferrum in MRI of lung parenchyma and pulmonary embolism. *Mag Res Imaging* 11:499, 1993.
39. Posteraro RH, Sostman HD, Spritzer CE, Herfkens RJ: Cine-gradient-refocused MR imaging of central pulmonary emboli. *AJR* 152:465, 1989.
40. Dinsmore BJ, Gefter WB, Hatabu H, Kressel HY: Pulmonary arteriovenous malformations: Diagnosis by gradient-refocused MR imaging. *JCAT* 14:918, 1990.
41. Richardson DB, MacFall JR, Sostman HD, Spritzer CE: Asymmetric-echo, short TE, retrospectively gated MR imaging of the heart and pulmonary vessels. *J Mag Res Imaging* 4:131, 1994.
42. Remy-Jardin M, Remy J, Wattine L, Giraud F: Central pulmonary thromboembolism: Diagnosis with spiral volumetric CT with the single-breath-hold technique—Comparison with pulmonary angiography. *Radiology* 185:381, 1992.
43. Sinner WN: Computed tomographic patterns of pulmonary thromboembolism and infarction. *JCAT* 2:295, 1978.
44. Breatnach E, Stanley RJ: CT diagnosis of segmental pulmonary artery embolus. *JCAT* 8:762, 1984.
45. Chintapolli K, Thorsen MK, Olsen DL, et al: Computed tomography of pulmonary thromboembolism and infarction. *JCAT* 12:553, 1988.
46. Remy J, Remy-Jardin M, Wattinne L, Deffontaines C: Pulmonary arteriovenous malformations: Evaluation with CT of the chest before and after treatment. *Radiology* 182:809, 1992.
47. Stanford W, Reiners TJ, Thompson BH, et al: Ultrafast CT in peripheral pulmonary embolism: An experimental study. *Radiology* 185(P):362, 1993.
48. Knight LC: Scintigraphic methods for detecting vascular thrombus. *J Nucl Med* 34:554, 1993.

Chapter 10

Magnetic Resonance Angiography of the Thoracic Aorta

Martin R. Prince / John A. Kaufman / E. Kent Yucel

Magnetic resonance imaging (MRI) is particularly well suited for the evaluation of the thoracic aorta.[1-3] The large size of the aorta makes it easy to resolve even with the limited resolution of MRI as compared with plain films and computed tomography (CT). Imaging the aorta allows use of large voxels, which results in high signal-to-noise ratios (SNR). The high flow rate within the thoracic aorta ensures adequate inflow for bright-blood techniques and usually adequate intravoxel phase dispersion for the black-blood techniques. The problems of cardiac and respiratory motion can be compensated by electocardiographic (ECG) gating and by phase reordering techniques. As echoplanar and other fast imaging techniques continue to be developed and disseminated, cardiac and respiratory motion artifacts may be eliminated completely.

Safety is a particularly important advantage of MR, especially once one considers the risk of stroke and other complications associated with catheterization of the aortic arch and ascending aorta. The relatively large volumes of iodinated contrast required to fully opacify large vessels such as the aorta, particularly if there is an aortic aneurysm, can result in contrast-induced renal failure as well as contrast-related anaphylactic reactions and cardiac decompensation. Magnetic resonance is also safer than CT or helical CT, which require ionizing radiation and substantial doses of iodinated contrast.

The applications for which MRI and magnetic resonance angiography (MRA) of the thoracic aorta may be considered include the evaluation of aortic aneurysms and pseudoaneurysms (atherosclerotic, mycotic, traumatic, or related to cystic medial necrosis or aortitis), staging and follow-up of aortic dissection, and congenital abnormalities such as coarctation and vascular rings.[1-11] Important considerations include the size of the aorta, presence of intraluminal thrombus, flow in the false channel, and the relationship of any abnormalities to the brachiocephalic vessels. Generally, a combination of black-blood imaging for overall anatomy and bright-blood imaging for luminal narrowing, intraluminal abnormalities such as plaques and intimal flaps, and patency of the brachiocephalic vessels is required.

PREIMAGING PREPARATION

Sedation is useful in claustrophobic patients. Usually 5 to 10 mg of diazepam is adequate. Properly functioning ECG gating is essential for thoracic MRI/MRA to freeze cardiac motion. The leads should be intertwined and separated from the patient's skin with gauze or cloth to prevent hot leads from burning the patient. Placing the leads close together on the skin also minimizes the risk of a wire loop forming, which might be perpendicular to an oscillating magnetic field and cause the wire to heat up. Unfortunately, placing the leads in a tightly packed configuration leads to poor ECG signal. If the signal is too weak for gating, it can generally be improved by spacing the leads further apart, so that they encircle the heart more. As the leads are spread out, the chance of a loop forming with heating of the wires increases, so greater care must be taken to eliminate wire loops and separate the wires from the patient's skin. This is especially important in sedated patients, who may not notice that they are being burned.

BLACK-BLOOD IMAGING

Spin-Echo Imaging

The most important sequence for imaging large vascular structures is T1-weighted spin-echo imaging with the parameters optimized for allowing intravoxel dephasing within the blood vessels (see Figs. 10-1 and 10-2). This intravoxel dephasing destroys the signal within the flowing blood, producing the so-called "black-blood" effect. This effect creates image contrast between the black vessels and the surrounding tissues, which have the typical contrast of T1-weighted imaging with bright fat and intermediate intensity

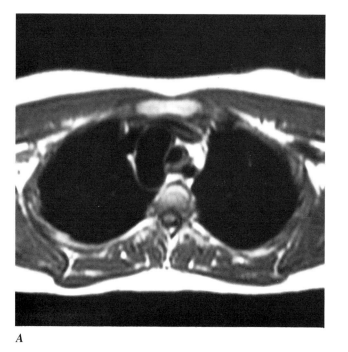

A

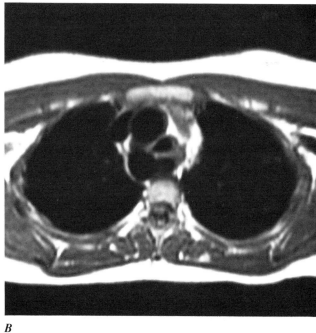

B

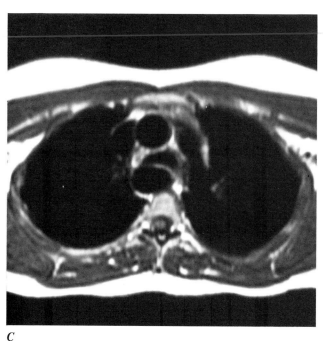

C

FIGURE 10-1 *A–C.* A T1-weighted spin-echo study with respiratory phase reordering, ECG gating, and sufficiently long TE (20 ms) to allow dephasing of the blood. It demonstrates the relationship of the aortic arch to other structures in this patient with a right-sided aortic arch.

of the muscles and organs. Contrast between the black blood, intermediate smooth muscle, and bright adventitial and perivascular fat allows evaluation of the aortic wall. This is especially useful in patients with vasculitis, which may cause thickening of the aortic wall (see Fig. 10-3). Since the signal intensity is high in the surrounding tissues and absent within the blood vessels, this technique shows the relationship between vessels and surrounding structures but is not as good for evaluating luminal anatomy. The technique is also limited

in smaller vessels, which may be completely obscured by volume averaging and phase misregistration artifacts. The ability to see the relationship between the vessels and the surrounding structures, however, is particularly useful for evaluating anatomical variations, whether congenital or acquired.

The best method for ensuring intravoxel dephasing is to use large voxels and make the echo time (TE) sufficiently long for there to be substantial blood flow between the 90°

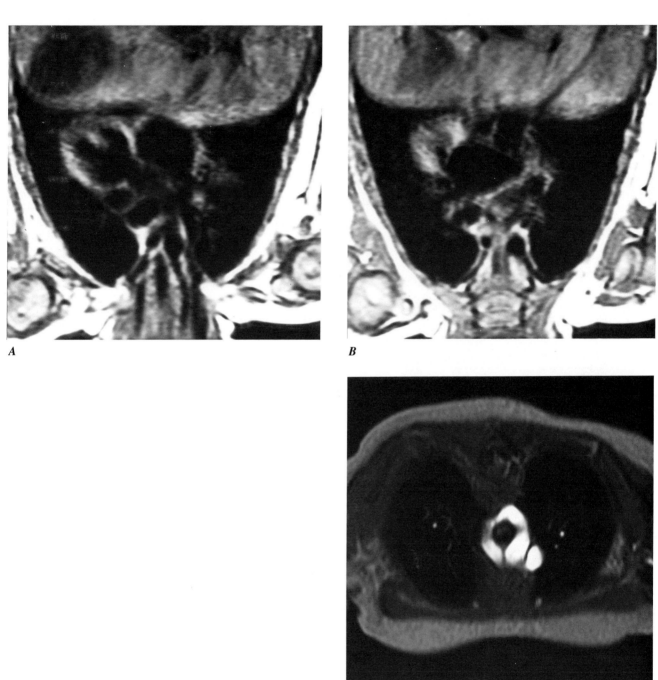

FIGURE 10-2 Spin echo (*A* and *B*) and cine (*C*) images of a double aortic arch.

pulse and the echo. In normal arteries with fast laminar flow, the typical TE required for a full echo of 10 to 12 ms is adequate for the blood to flow away between the 90° pulse and the echo. But in patients with vascular disease (especially aneurysms and dissections) or with poor cardiac output, the flow may be slower or even stagnant. In these patients, a longer TE is required to allow adequate time for intravoxel dephasing. Typically 20 to 30 ms may be required. Often, in the false channel of a dissection, the flow is so slow that

no reasonable TE is long enough to achieve a black-blood effect. It may also be useful to apply saturation pulses or preparatory pulses to further suppress blood signal.

Because of complex curving and unfolding of the thoracic aorta, it must be imaged in at least two and preferably all three cardinal planes. Generally, the easiest approach to imaging the thoracic aorta is to start with a black-blood T1-weighted localizer sequence designed to cover the entire thorax and then to proceed to axial and sagittal images that

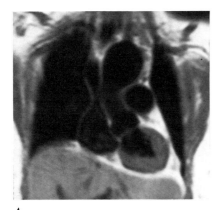

A

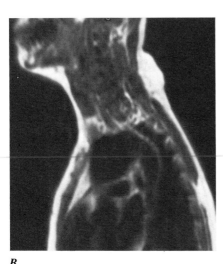

B

FIGURE 10-3 T1-weighted spin-echo images show (*A*) aneurysm of the ascending aorta and (*B*) thickening of the descending thoracic aorta wall and the ''buffalo hump'' from steroid therapy in a patient with giant cell arteritis. This appearance may be indistinguishable from Takayasu's aortitis.

have a smaller field of view but higher resolution. The best localizer sequence is a coronal spin-echo sequence centered (landmarked) high on the xyphoid with the largest possible field of view (e.g., 48 cm), as shown in Fig. 10-1. The following parameters are suggested: repetition time (TR), 1 RR interval; TE, 20 to 30 ms; frequency encoding, S/I; slice thickness, 7 to 12 mm with about a 30-percent gap; ECG gating; and respiratory phase reordering. In patients with a regular rhythm, a trigger window of 10 to 15 percent is adequate. But in patients with a variable heart rate, a longer trigger window is necessary (20 percent) to ensure proper gating. This coronal acquisition shows the arch and aortic valve in cross section and usually extends sufficiently below the diaphragm to demonstrate the inferior extent of any pathology of the thoracic aorta.

This can be followed with axial spin echo with a smaller, 32-cm field of view but otherwise identical parameters. Axial images show the ascending and descending thoracic aorta in cross section. Cross-sectional images are essential for mea-

suring the aortic diameter and for detecting intimal abnormalities, including intimal flaps in aortic dissection (see Fig. 10-4) and intimal thickening in vasculitis. It is important that the bandwidth not be set too narrow. Large chemical shift artifacts, caused by narrow bandwidths, can simulate aortic dissection, leading to false-positive diagnoses. Generally, a bandwidth of 16 kHz is sufficient.

A sagittal acquisition can be obliqued to align with the aortic arch in order to optimally demonstrate the relationship between the arch and great vessel origins. In many older patients, however, the aorta is sufficiently unfolded that a straight sagittal acquisition will be aligned to the arch, and it is not necessary to pick an appropriate obliquity. In our experience, a better sagittal technique is the gadolinium-enhanced three-dimensional gradient echo volume acquisition, which is described below. This gadolinium-enhanced technique allows reformatting into any desired obliquity after the image data have been obtained, which is particularly useful for evaluating the origins of each of the great vessels.

BRIGHT-BLOOD IMAGING

Time of Flight

Standard two-dimensional time-of-flight (TOF) imaging is difficult to implement well in the thoracic aorta because of the problems of respiratory motion, aortic motion, and pulsatility artifacts. These artifacts not only degrade the individual axial images but also make it difficult to avoid misregistration artifacts in coronal or sagittal reconstructions. Using three-dimensional TOF helps to minimize the motion and pulsatility artifacts, but the three-dimensional imaging is limited to a narrow region of interest because of saturation effects. Thus, TOF imaging generally requires some special tricks to adequately image the thoracic aorta.

One useful trick is to use a three-dimensional multislab acquisition. Although time-consuming, the three-dimensional multislab technique is effective in accurately delimitating occlusions, stenoses, and anomalies of the great vessel origins, as shown in Fig. 10-5. This technique can be combined with ramped excitation, in which the flip angle is larger at one end of the slab in order to suppress venous signal and to help minimize the ''venetian blind'' effect of arterial blood saturating as it passes through the slab.

Another useful implementation of TOF imaging is in combination with ECG gating in order to acquire multiple images at the same location at different phases of the cardiac cycle. These cine images can be viewed in sequence like a movie to provide an understanding of the dynamics of the aortic blood flow. These images can be acquired as individual axial images or can be obliqued to show the aortic arch in a single plane, as in Fig. 10-4.

The cine imaging technique can be combined with additional velocity encoding gradients to implement phase-con-

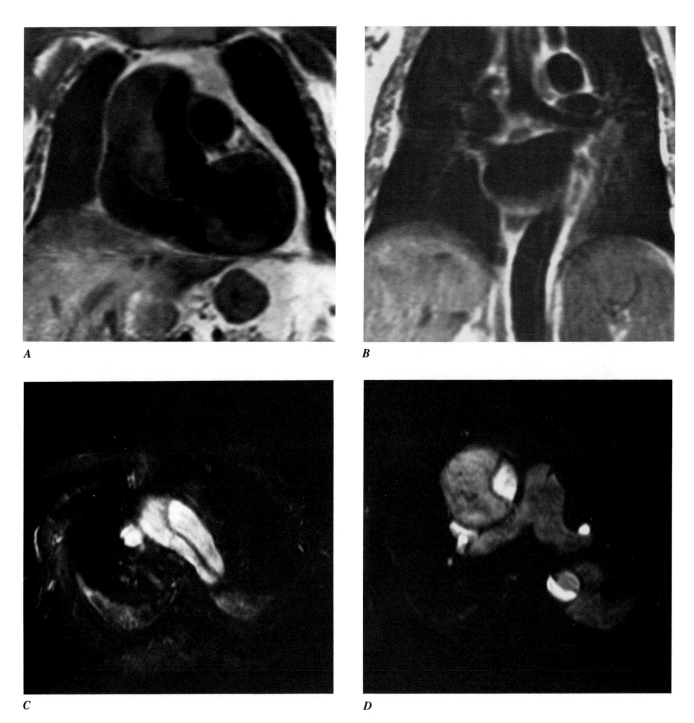

A

B

C

D

FIGURE 10-4   Aortic dissection: T1-weighted axial spin echo (*A* and *B*) and cine images (*C* and *D*).

trast imaging. This can yield a signal which is proportional to blood velocity[12] and is particularly helpful for discriminating between thrombus and slow flow, which may both be comparably bright on TOF imaging. This technique is particularly useful for evaluating aortic dissection to allow assessment of the dynamics of flow in the two different lumens. With phase contrast, it is necessary to pick a maximum velocity representing the range over which the gradients will encode velocity. Aortic blood velocity may exceed 100 cm/s; however, if the velocity encoding is set this high, then slow flow in a false channel will be poorly seen. It is useful to set the velocity encoding (venc) to about 30 to 50 cm/s to better visualize the slower flow near the wall. This will result in aliasing such that high velocity flow during systole and in the center of the aorta will exceed the scale and may be displayed as a reversed image (i.e., black rather than white).

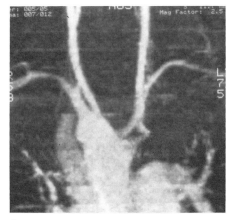

A

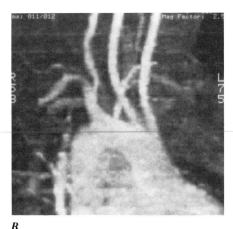

B

FIGURE 10-5 Multislab 3D technique. Anteroposterior (*A*) and left posterior oblique (*B*) projection images in a patient with right aortic arch and aberrant left subclavian artery (non-mirror image branching).

Velocity encoding requires two acquisitions for each flow direction that is encoded or six acquisitions to encode all three flow directions. In order to minimize acquisition time, it is generally adequate to encode only flow in the superior-to-inferior direction for the ascending and descending thoracic aorta.

Numerous additional techniques are being developed that allow preparatory pulses to better suppress fat and other stationary tissue signal (Fig. 10-6). There are also gating techniques which permit acquisition of the image during the period of maximum inflow to further improve TOF imaging. These techniques are discussed more fully in Chap. 13.

Contrast-Enhanced MRA

All of the preceding techniques take advantage of the exquisite sensitivity of MR for detecting motion to differentiate between the moving blood and stationary vessel walls and surrounding tissues. In general, these techniques work well in normal arteries which have normal laminar flow. But in

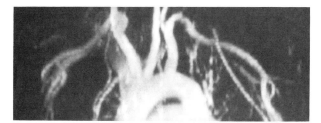

FIGURE 10-6 Right posterior oblique projection image of the aortic arch using a cardiac-gated, segmented fast gradient echo technique. Note the excellent background suppression and absence of pulsatility artifact.

patients with diseased arteries, where the flow is disturbed, these techniques are not as effective. Poor flow is especially problematic in patients with aneurysmal disease, poor cardiac output, or tortuous vessels that may be partially in plane. In these patients, it is useful to image the arteries with a bright-blood technique, which is based on anatomy and does not depend upon blood flow.

Bright-blood images, which are based upon anatomy, are obtained by injecting a sufficient amount of gadolinium to make the blood T1 shorter than the T1 of all of the surrounding tissues. For the three gadolinium compounds currently available—gadodiamide, gadoteridol, and gadopentetate dimeglumine—a dose of at least 0.2 mmol/kg (double dose) is required to reduce the blood T1 to less than that of fat (T1 = 270 ms). In general, the higher the dose of gadolinium, the better the vascular enhancement up to a limit of about 0.5 mmol/kg, where the T2 effects begin to reduce signal on T1-weighted gradient echo images. Only gadoteridol, however, is FDA-approved for these higher doses at the present time.

Once the T1 of blood is shortened with the gadolinium infusion, a T1-weighted sequence optimized to differentiate blood from background tissues is required. One recommended sequence is the three-dimensional volume spoiled gradient-echo pulse sequence. Three-dimensional volume imaging provides high-resolution images with isotropic or near isotropic voxels and minimizes pulsatility and misregistration artifacts. The blurring effect of vessel motion occurring during systole results in the images primarily representing the anatomic appearance during diastole. Surprisingly, the images show minimal cardiac motion artifact, even in the ascending aorta, without the need for ECG or peripheral gating (Figs. 10-7 and 10-8).

The degree of T1 weighting is modulated by adjusting the flip angle. For a TR of about 25 ms with a gadolinium dose of 0.2 to 0.3 mmol/kg, a flip angle of 40° is appropriate. If the TR is substantially reduced, the flip angle may have to be reduced, such that for a TR of 15 ms, a flip angle of 30° is more appropriate. Also, if the dose is increased, better SNR and contrast-to-noise ratio (CNR) may be obtained by increasing the flip angle. Since fat is the brightest background tissue, it is essential to pick a TE that minimizes fat signal.

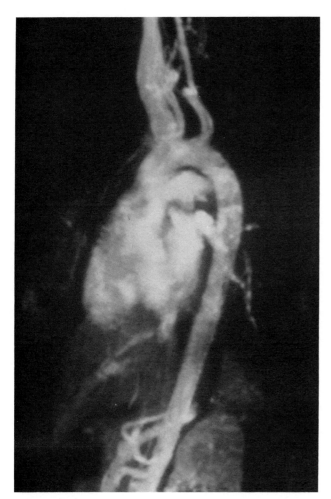

FIGURE 10-7 MIP projection of gadolinium-enhanced MRA. Note excellent depiction of arch and great vessels and absence of pulsatility artifact.

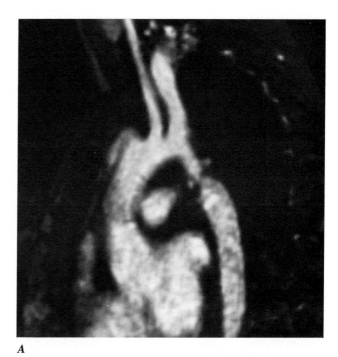

A

B

FIGURE 10-8 Gadolinium-enhanced image of coarctation of thoracic aorta.

Picking a TE where fat and water and are out of phase can substantially reduce the fat signal and thereby improve arterial contrast. At 1.5 tesla, TEs of about 2.3 or 6.9 ms are appropriate. If the TE is longer than 2 to 3 ms, then it is essential to use gradient moment nulling (flow compensation) to minimize flow artifacts and retain the intravascular signal.

One might expect steady-state gradient echo imaging (GRASS) to be preferable to the spoiled gradient-echo imaging for gadolinium-enhanced aortography because the long T2 of blood increases the steady-state blood signal. But this effect enhances veins more than arteries because the fast, pulsatile flow of arterial blood spoils its steady-state component. In theory, this can then have the paradoxical effect of reduced arterial contrast. In practice, however, there is little difference between the spoiled and unspoiled techniques.

By imaging during the infusion of contrast, it is possible to preferentially enhance the arteries more than the veins. This allows evaluation of the aorta and its branch vessels without the confounding effect of excessive venous enhance-

ment. This preferential arterial enhancement is maximized by timing the gadolinium infusion such that the period of maximum arterial-to-venous gadolinium concentration ratio corresponds with the acquisition of the center of k space. In the absence of a pulse sequence tailored to permit controlling the ordering of k space, it is acceptable to simply begin the infusion simultaneous with beginning the acquisition and finishing 30 s before the end of the acquisition, since most three-dimensional sequences acquire k space in a linear fashion, filling the central portion of k space during the middle of the acquisition.

If a dynamic infusion is employed, the infusion rate must be sufficiently fast to maintain a high intraarterial gadolinium level, and it must last for the duration of the acquisition. Thus, it is crucial not to have too long an acquisition time. For a gadolinium dose of 0.2 to 0.3 mmol/kg, an acquisition time of 3 to 5 min is appropriate. The acquisition time for the thoracic aorta can be minimized by acquiring the three-dimensional volume in a sagittal plane. This three-dimensional data set can then be reformatted into any appropriate plane for optimal visualization of the arch, ascending aorta, great vessel origins, or any pathology.

If the gadolinium is not administered dynamically during the acquisition, then both arteries and veins will be enhanced. Since the currently available gadolinium chelates rapidly redistribute into the extracellular fluid compartment, with a half-life of about 11 min, it is important to image as quickly after gadolinium injection as possible to have maximum intraarterial signal and minimal background tissue enhancement. Often, to image the entire aorta, it is possible to image the abdominal aorta during contrast infusion with a coronal three-dimensional volume to include the iliac arteries and then immediately follow this with sagittal three-dimensional volume centered on the thoracic aorta.

REFERENCES

1. Link KM, Loehr SP, Baker DM, Lesko JM: Magnetic resonance imaging of the thoracic aorta. *Semin US, CT, MRI* 14:91, 1993.
2. Webb WR, Sostman HD: MR imaging of thoracic disease: Clinical uses. *Radiology* 182:621, 1992.
3. Link KM, Lesko JM: The role of MR imaging in the evaluation of acquired diseases of the thoracic aorta. *AJR* 158:1115, 1992.
4. Mast HL, Gordon DH, Kantor AM: Pitfalls in diagnosis of aortic dissection by angiography: Algorithmic approach utilizing CT and MRI. *Comp Med Imaging Graphics* 15:431, 1991.
5. Petasnick JP: Radiologic evaluation of aortic dissection. *Radiology* 180:297, 1991.
6. Kersting-Sommerhoff BA, Higgins CB, White D, et al: Aortic dissection: Sensitivity and specificity of MR imaging. *Radiology* 166:651, 1988.
7. Nienaber CA, von Kodolitsch Y, Nicolas V, et al: The diagnosis of thoracic aortic dissection by noninvasive imaging procedures. *N Engl J Med* 328:1, 1993.
8. Cigarroa JE, Isselbacher EM, DeSanctis RW, Eagle KA: Diagnostic imaging in the evaluation of suspected aortic dissection. *N Engl J Med* 328:35, 1993.
9. Mirowitz SA, Lee JKT, Gutierrez FR, et al: Normal signal-void patterns in cardiac cine MR images. *Radiology* 176:49, 1990.
10. Solomon SL, Brown JJ, Glazer HS, et al: Thoracic aortic dissection: Pitfalls and artifacts in MR imaging. *Radiology* 177:223, 1990.
11. Yamada I, Numano F, Suzuki S: Takayasu arteritis: Evaluation with MR imaging. *Radiology* 188:89, 1993.
12. Chang J-M, Friese K, Caputo GR, et al: MR measurement of blood flow in the true and false channel in chronic aortic dissection. *J Comput Assist Tomogr* 15:418, 1991.

Chapter 11

Current Applications of Magnetic Resonance Imaging in Cardiology

Thomas G. Di Salvo / Patrick T. O'Gara

From the vantage point of the clinical cardiologist, magnetic resonance imaging (MRI) has proved both exciting and daunting. Spin-echo MRI permits the study of cardiac morphology in unprecedented detail in a wide array of pathological states. In expert hands, gradient echo cine MRI provides functional assessment of ventricular performance and valvular and congenital heart disease which rivals echocardiography and cardiac catheterization. Noninvasive evaluation of the coronary arteries by ultrafast magnetic resonance angiography (MRA) is a virtual certainty in the not too distant future. Reminiscent of the early stages of echocardiography, each month the leading cardiology journals publish reports of wider applications of MRI techniques in cardiovascular disease.

Unlike the situation for conventional techniques—such as two-dimensional and transesophageal echocardiography, radionuclide ventriculography, contrast angiography, and ventriculography—neither the principles, techniques, nor interpretation of cardiovascular MRI are included in the curriculum of cardiology training. Clinical cardiologists rely heavily on cardiologists specializing in MRI or on radiologists, since MRI is operator-dependent and requires considerable expertise for proper interpretation.

Additionally, clinicians recognize several general limitations of presently available techniques of cardiovascular MRI. It is more expensive than echocardiography or radionuclide ventriculography and takes longer to perform. Patients not infrequently complain about the noise and close quarters of MRI scanners. Since even most large tertiary centers do not have free-standing MRI units dedicated to cardiovascular imaging, scanning often requires scheduling far in advance. Unlike echocardiography, MRI is not portable or office-based. Patients with pacemakers, cochlear implants, brain aneurysm clips, and certain mechanical heart valves cannot be safely imaged. Critically ill patients may be out of view during scanning, and physicians are not physically present in the room. Importantly, unlike echocardiography, MRI at present is not routinely comprehensive: the clinician usually provides specific requests to the imaging physician, who selects appropriate imaging sequences.

In this chapter, the clinical cardiologist's view of the established, evolving, and future indications of MRI in cardiovascular disease is discussed. More detailed discussion of controversial or particularly useful indications for MRI—including aortic dissection, constrictive pericarditis, congenital heart disease, and ischemic heart disease—is provided.

CARDIOVASCULAR MRI: CURRENT INDICATIONS

Diseases of the Aorta

AORTIC DISSECTION

Rapid and accurate assessment of the specific anatomic and functional features of acute aortic dissection is critical for planning definitive management (Table 11-1). Magnetic resonance imaging of aortic dissection was first reported in 1983.[1] Multiple reports have appeared since.[2-9] Compared to computed tomography (CT) and echocardiography, MRI provides distinct advantages and disadvantages to the clinician in imaging acute, subacute, chronic, and surgically repaired aortic dissection (Tables 11-2 and 11-3).[1,10]

Spin-echo MRI is unrivaled in displaying the anatomy of the thoracic aorta.[11] The wide field of view, ability to image in orthogonal and oblique planes, and resolution of MRI permits detailed delineation of the origin and extent of dissection, size of the false lumen, and sites of reentry. In the hands of skilled interpreters, the reported 98 percent sensitivity of MRI for aortic dissection exceeds that of aortography and CT and rivals transesophageal echocardiography (TEE).[9] The reported 98 percent specificity of MRI exceeds that of TEE; with biplane probes in the latter technique, linear or mirror-image artifacts are not uncommon and may

TABLE 11-1   Imaging in acute aortic dissection: Factors in approximate order of importance to the clinician

Accurate and prompt diagnosis
Site of intimal tear (entry site)
Extent of dissection
Pericardial effusion/tamponade
Branch vessel involvement, especially arch/cranial, coronary, visceral and renal arteries
Aortic regurgitation (quantification)
Reentry site
Associated aortic pathology (coarctation, aneurysm)
Status of abdominal, pelvic, and proximal leg vessels for planning surgical femoral vessel cannulation

TABLE 11-3   Disadvantages of MRI in acute aortic dissection

Length of delay to study
Length of study
Distance of scanner from ICU/surgical suite
Lack of close physician monitoring
Exclusion of pacemakers, cochlear implants, brain aneurysm clips, certain mechanical heart valves
Awkward: IV pumps, ECG leads, etc.
Limited assessment of aortic regurgitation
Limited assessment of coronary arteries
Cost

be misinterpreted as intimal flaps or false lumens, respectively.[12] Magnetic resonance imaging detects the site of entry of aortic dissection with a sensitivity of 85 percent and specificity of 100 percent, similar to CT and TEE. Thrombus and pericardial effusion are detected with sensitivity approaching 100 percent. Magnetic resonance imaging is particularly valuable in instances of prior surgery or preexisting aortic disease.[13,14] Atypical MRI patterns of aortic dissection have been described.[15]

Recent studies have suggested that the sensitivity of aortography may be 90 to 95 percent, less than that of MRI.[1] Aortography may fail to disclose an intimal flap not tangential to the x-ray beam. Compared to MRI, aortography is potentially hazardous, since catheter passage into the false lumen can promote further dissection. There may also be contrast-induced depression of ventricular function and contrast-induced nephrotoxicity. Specific advantages of aortography include excellent definition of branch vessel or coronary artery involvement and simultaneous quantitation of aortic regurgitation.

Despite the distinct attractiveness of MRI in aortic dissection, several disadvantages have limited its application in acute aortic dissection.[16] Patients with acute aortic dissection are critically ill and may deteriorate with unexpected swiftness.[10] In many hospitals, MRI suites are geographically distant from intensive care units and operating suites. In

TABLE 11-2   Advantages of MRI in imaging aortic dissection

Wide field of view
Imaging in orthogonal and oblique planes
Excellent soft tissue resolution
Inherent blood-tissue contrast
High diagnostic sensitivity (98%)
High sensitivity for entry site (85%)
High specificity (?100%)
Accurate with prior aortic disease/surgery
No contrast
No ionizing radiation

angiography suites, there are typically more personnel and resources available for resuscitative efforts than in MRI suites. Supervising clinicians are not physically present in the same room with the patient during MRI scanning. The patient may be temporarily out of view during the imaging process. The noise of the MRI scanner may cause elevation of blood pressure, and the surroundings for the patient are more confining than those of a typical angiography suite. Intravenous infusion pumps, intravenous lines, electrocardiographic (ECG) electrodes and wires, arterial lines, or pulmonary artery catheters render MRI scanning awkward. Patients with permanent or temporary pacemakers, cochlear implants, certain mechanical prosthetic heart valves, or aneurysm clips cannot be imaged.[17] By comparison, TEE may be performed at the bedside in the emergency room or intensive care unit.[1]

Time delays in diagnosis are important concerns. In a recent prospective study of patients with suspected aortic dissection, MRI (spin-echo plus cine) itself required 39 ± 16 min.[9] However, the time it took to arrange for the study was not stated, and the hospital, which has specialized services in MRI, offered 24-h imaging. It is unlikely that these prompt results would be duplicated outside of a trial. By comparison, TEE imaging required 13 ± 6 min, CT 5 to 15 min, and angiography 40 ± 16 min.[9] None of these times reflects arranging for the study or calling in necessary personnel. Since it may also require several hours to mobilize a surgical team, the time spent in arranging and performing diagnostic procedures is an important concern.

Although MRI can image the proximal coronary arteries, the specific pulse sequences required may consume extra time.[18] The resolution of images of the coronary arteries is not yet comparable to that of standard coronary angiography.[19–21] Although many surgeons prefer coronary angiography to define coronary artery anatomy, definition of coronary anatomy is likely unnecessary in patients without a history of coronary disease and lacking suggestive ECG abnormalities.[22] Assessment of left ventricular (LV) function is routinely provided by TEE or transthoracic echocardiography but is not yet routine by MRI. Many surgeons require an assessment of LV function prior to repair: operations may be prolonged and myocardial damage may result from lengthy cardiopulmonary bypass times.[10] Cine MRI is less sensitive than echocardiography for the detection of aortic regurgitation.[1,23] Repair with composite valve graft conduits is becoming increasingly popular with surgeons, especially among patients with Marfan's syndrome and annuloaortic ectasia; quantitation of aortic regurgitation may be helpful preoperatively, although the decision regarding valve replacement is not finalized until operation.[24,25] Magnetic resonance imaging is less sensitive than angiography in showing involvement of aortic arch vessels in dissection, the degree of compromise of involved vessels, or vessel origin from the true or false lumen.[1] Thrombosis of the false lumen, either acutely or chronically, may portend better prognosis.[10] On occasion, imaging false lumen thrombosis by MRI is difficult.[26]

Magnetic resonance imaging is not perfectly sensitive in the detection of aortic dissection, particularly in the hands of inexperienced readers (which includes nearly all cardiologists and cardiac surgeons). Inexperienced radiologists may have difficulties in interpretation as well. In one study, radiologists with extensive experience in MRI correctly diagnosed aortic dissection 96 percent of the time, but radiologists with minimal experience diagnosed dissection correctly only 78 percent of the time.[7] Experience in selecting proper MRI pulse sequences and training in recognition of flow artifacts is important in the design and interpretation of studies, particularly in the setting of prior surgery, aortic disease, or thrombosis of the false lumen. Most clinicians have had minimal experience with the technical aspects of image acquisition in MRI and rely more heavily on colleagues for interpretation of these images than for interpretation of angiography or TEE.

Even for experienced readers, interpretive pitfalls exist. The left brachiocephalic vein, arch vessels, superior pericardial recess, motion artifacts, aortic plaques, apposition of the azygos vein with the descending aorta, fibrosing mediastinitis, and subacute thrombus in the false lumen may all occasionally cause difficulty in interpretation.[27] Thin intimal flaps may be difficult to image in spin-echo sequences unless blood in the false lumen is static; gradient echo sequences may be necessary in these instances.[14] Most of the studies of MRI in aortic dissection originate from large centers with specialization in MRI. Such centers provide prompt, superb imaging and expert interpretation. Finally, MRI is more expensive than TEE and contrast CT but cheaper than aortography (Table 11-4).

Given the constraints of MRI in acute aortic dissection, most clinicians presently opt for screening transthoracic echocardiography followed by TEE or angiography. The choice of imaging modality depends to a large extent on the prevalent expertise of a given center. Stable patients with acute dissection may safely undergo MRI in many instances. In patients with subacute or chronic dissections, MRI is the imaging technique of choice.

TABLE 11-4 Relative costs of diagnostic modalities in aortic dissection

Modality	Cost,[a] dollars
Transesophageal echocardiography	798[b]
Contrast CT	842
MRI	1046
Aortography	1792

[a] Base fees at the Massachusetts General Hospital.
[b] Does not include screening transthoracic echocardiogram.

Magnetic resonance imaging is also the imaging modality of choice for serial follow-up of surgically repaired or medically treated aortic dissection, especially complex dissections (Fig. 11-1).[28] During surgery, the entry site and as much of the dissected aorta as possible are resected and the false channel obliterated by oversewing. Patients remain at risk of redissection, progression of dissection, and aneurysm formation. Persistent patency of the false lumen may be a poor prognostic sign.[10] Monitoring the aortic diameter, flow in the false lumen, involved branch or arch vessels, aortic grafts, and coronary ostia (in proximal dissections extending to the root), and surveillance for late reentry sites in cases of residual false lumens are all possible by MRI. Not infrequently, MRI may show aneurysmal dilatation beyond the interposed graft, a residual flap, false luminal patency, and reentry sites postoperatively.[28] Follow-up is critical, especially in the highest-risk patients, such as those with Marfan's syndrome.

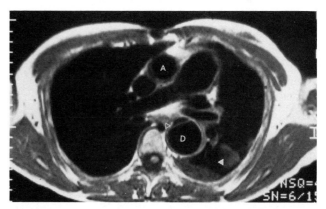

FIGURE 11-1 Spin-echo image of a 36-year-old woman with Marfan's syndrome and previous repair of the ascending aorta (A) following acute aortic dissection with entry site beyond the origin of the left subclavian artery and bidirectional propagation. This 6-month follow-up study demonstrates progressive dilatation of the descending thoracic aorta (D), with enlargement of the false lumen, and a new contiguous pleural effusion (*closed triangle*). An intimal flap (*open triangle*) separating the large false lumen from the compressed true lumen is clearly seen in the descending aorta. The patient underwent successful repair of the descending aorta with resection of the prior entry site.

Magnetic resonance imaging is also useful in the detection of penetrating aortic ulcers and comprehensive assessment of the thoracic and abdominal aorta in stable patients following trauma. The former condition may actually be a variant of aortic dissection. Such ulcers are characterized by intimal rents in areas of severe atherosclerosis, usually in the descending thoracic aorta, with variable penetration of a mural hematoma through the layers of the aortic wall. These hematomas are more likely to spread radially than longitudinally and are more often associated with acute, localized aneurysm or bleb formation than with branch vessel compromise. An intimal flap is not usually seen. Management is highly individualized and depends on the site of the ulceration, size of the associated aneurysm, age of the patient, and other comorbid features.

Deceleration injuries of the aorta are classically associated with partial transection (as distinct from dissection) and false aneurysm formation in the area of the isthmus of the aorta, where the relatively mobile arch becomes tethered to the posterior thoracic cage. Small false aneurysms may be missed by standard MRI, and contrast aortography is preferred in most trauma centers whenever the clinical situation or chest radiography raises the possibility of aortic injury.

THORACIC AORTIC ANEURYSMS

Magnetic resonance angiography is also the modality of choice for serial assessment of thoracic aortic aneuryms.[4,13] Precise assessment of size and three-dimensional reconstruction of the aorta are feasible. The relation of the aneurysm to arch vessels and surrounding structures is readily determined.[11] Magnetic resonance imaging may be of value in the serial assessment of aortitis, such as Takayasu's disease, giant cell arteritis, and syphilis. It is widely used in serial assessment of the aortic root and ascending aorta in Marfan's syndrome and related inherited connective tissue disorders, where progressive enlargement even in the absence of symptoms is considered an indication for surgical intervention.[29] Imaging of congenital anomalies of the arch and coarctation is discussed below.

SUMMARY

Magnetic resonance imaging is the modality of choice for subacute or chronic aortic dissection, follow-up of surgically repaired or medically treated aortic dissection, and surveillance in Marfan's syndrome and related disorders (Table 11-5). It should be considered in stable patients with acute aortic dissection or trauma and in follow-up of aortitis.

DISEASES OF THE PERICARDIUM

Because of its portability, ease, moderate cost, and rapid definition of hemodynamics and ventricular function, echo-

TABLE 11-5   Indications for MRI: Diseases of the aorta

Subacute proximal or distal aortic dissection
Selected stable acute dissection
Surgically repaired or medically treated dissection
Suspected aortic root abscess
Surveillance in Marfan's and related syndromes
Follow-up in Takayasu's and other aortitides
Mural thrombus of abdominal aorta
Diagnosis and follow-up thoracic aortic aneurysm
Congenital anomalies of the aorta and aortic arch

cardiography is routine in instances of suspected pericardial disease. However, the overall sensitivity of transthoracic echocardiography for diverse types of pericardial pathology may be as low as 35 percent.[30] Echocardiography is limited by poor acoustic windows in many patients, obscuring pleural effusion, and inability to distinguish pericardial fluid from hematoma or measure pericardial thickness in some cases. Gated MRI provides exquisite delineation of the pericardium.[31] Except occasionally for the pericardium overlying the right atrium, left ventricular apex, and left ventricular lateral wall, the entire pericardium can be imaged, unlike echocardiography.[32] Normally, the pericardium appears as a low-intensity structure 0.8 to 1 mm thick between the high-intensity mediastinal and subepicardial fat and medium-intensity myocardium. Magnetic resonance imaging is particularly useful in distinguishing constrictive pericarditis from restrictive cardiomyopathy and in imaging pericardial masses.

Constrictive Pericarditis

Constrictive pericarditis results from fibrotic thickening of the pericardium over a protracted period (usually years) following pericardial inflammation or injury.[33] The inflamed, thickened parietal and visceral layers of pericardium adhere, thereby obliterating the pericardial space. Adhesions form between the fused layers of pericardium and the epicardium, effectively encasing the heart within a fibrotic sac. As a result of encasement, ventricular compliance falls sharply, and filling of both ventricles is impeded throughout diastole. Right and left atrial pressures rise, and in advanced stages stroke volume falls, resulting in tissue hypoperfusion, sodium retention, and the clinical syndrome of congestive heart failure. Pericardial thickening is usually global, although focal thickening and constriction by fibrotic pericardial bands have been reported in the atrioventricular groove, aortic groove, pulmonary outflow groove, and around the semilunar valves. Pericardial calcification is apparent in 50 percent of cases of constrictive pericarditis on chest radiographs. Two unusual variants, effusive-constrictive and occult constrictive pericarditis, have been described.[34,35]

In the past, tuberculous pericarditis was the commonest etiology of constrictive pericarditis; at present, the etiology is idiopathic in 50 percent.[33] Constrictive pericarditis may result from viral (coxsackie virus B), bacterial (typical or atypical mycobacteria), fungal (histoplasmosis, coccidiomycosis), or parasitic infections, primary pericardial malignancies (mesothelioma), secondary pericardial malignancies (lymphoma, breast, lung, thyroid), penetrating or nonpenetrating trauma, therapeutic irradiation, uremia (including hemodialysis), amyloidosis, or systemic lupus erythematosus. Rarer causes include cardiac surgery and postmyocardial infarction Dressler's syndrome[36]; rarely, constrictive pericarditis is found in association with atrial septal defect.[33]

In clinical practice, it is crucial to distinguish constrictive pericarditis from restrictive cardiomyopathy. Occasionally these two entities coexist due to amyloidosis, irradiation, or malignancy.[37–39] The correct diagnosis is critical: constrictive pericarditis can be cured by pericardiectomy. Surgical results are very good, with 4 to 6 percent intraoperative mortality and 60 percent 10-year survival.[40–42] Conversely, patients with restrictive disease (most notably amyloid) who are mistakenly taken to surgery do quite poorly.

At present, patients with suspected constrictive pericarditis or restrictive cardiomyopathy undergo diagnostic cardiac catheterization. Unfortunately, even detailed hemodynamic study does not always distinguish the two conditions.[43,44] Endomyocardial biopsy is often necessary, but the results are frequently nonspecific.[45] Neither radionuclide angiographic indices of diastolic filling nor certain echocardiographic Doppler findings are always discriminating.[46–50] The occasional case of focal pericardial bands, loculated effusion, or hematoma resulting in constriction may be missed by echocardiography.

Most patients with suspected constrictive pericarditis have ancillary studies to determine pericardial thickness. In the proper clinical context, pericardial thickness exceeding 2 mm by CT supports the diagnosis of constrictive pericarditis.[51] The overall sensitivity of CT in the detection of pericardial pathology is likely lower than that of MRI, but CT detects pericardial calcification more reliably than MRI. Cine CT, which provides right ventricular (RV) and LV images of enhanced resolution and quantitative assessment of right ventricular systolic and diastolic function, may allow for detailed visualization of the pericardium and evaluation of ventricular diastolic filling.[51]

The precise sensitivity and specificity of MRI in constrictive pericarditis have not been established.[32] In the largest series of 29 patients, the sensitivity, specificity, and accuracy of MRI in the diagnosis of constrictive pericarditis were 88, 100, and 93 percent, respectively.[52] Pericardial thickness in excess of 4 mm in the proper clinical context strongly supports the diagnosis of constrictive pericarditis.[31,53] In chronic constrictive pericarditis, the pericardium is characterized by low signal intensity due to fibrosis and calcification; in sub-

acute or recent constrictive pericarditis, the pericardium is characterized by higher signal intensity (Fig. 11-2).[52] Clinical correlation may thus be important in cases of recent onset. In constrictive pericarditis, the right ventricle is typically diminutive in size and tubular in shape, and the right atrium, inferior and superior venae cavae, and hepatic veins are enlarged. Vena cava flow can be accurately assessed by cine MR velocity mapping.[54]

The ability of MRI to image in all planes is a distinct advantage and makes it possible to detect localized effusions or hematomas undetectable by echocardiography or CT (Fig. 11-3). Although postoperative pericardial constriction occurs in only 0.2 percent of patients following cardiac surgery, those cases that do occur are often effusive-constrictive. In routine postcardiac surgical patients, pericardial thickening is commonplace. Magnetic resonance imaging may be more sensitive than echo or CT in cases of suspected postoperative effusive-constrictive pericarditis and in detecting localized postoperative hematoma or hemopericardium resulting in focal constriction or tamponade[32]; it is particularly useful in visualizing loculated effusions, pericardial adhesions, and hemopericardium. In the latter, signal intensity is markedly increased.

Pericardial Masses

Pericardial masses may be benign or malignant.[32] Pericardial metastases are found in 5 to 15 percent of patients who die of cancer. Malignancies of the lung and breast, leukemia, and Hodgkin's and non-Hodgkin's lymphomas most frequently involve the pericardium by extension from the myocardium or hematogenous or lymphatic spread. Focal pericardial masses, diffuse pericardial thickening and infiltration, pericardial effusion, effusive-constrictive pericarditis, or cardiac tamponade may result. Half of the pericardial effusions occuring in patients with known malignancies are malignant.[32] Primary pericardial tumors are rare; they include mesothelioma, fibrosarcoma, angiosarcoma, teratoma, and pheochromocytoma. Magnetic resonance imaging is useful to confirm the presence of a pericardial mass and to define extent of involvement of the pericardium itself and adjacent myocardial and mediastinal structures (Fig. 11-4). Complete or partial absence of the pericardium and pericardial cysts are readily imaged.

Summary

Magnetic resonance imaging is the modality of choice in suspected constrictive pericarditis when echocardiography is inconclusive regarding pericardial thickening (Table 11-6). It is also indicated when focal constrictive pericarditis is suspected, and in some instances of suspected pericardial hematoma. This modality may be most useful in the evalu-

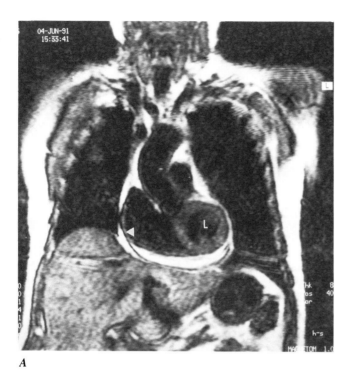

A

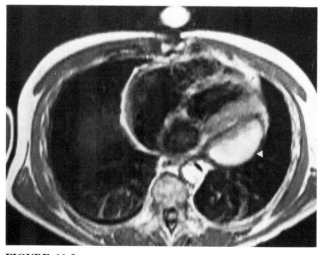

B

FIGURE 11-2 Coronal (*A*) and sagittal (*B*) spin-echo MR images of a 68-year-old man with suspected constrictive pericarditis. The study showed circumferential pericardial thickening (*closed triangle*) and normal left and right ventricular chamber dimensions (L is left ventricle).

FIGURE 11-3 Spin-echo image 14 months following aortic valve replacement for progressive aortic insufficiency reveals a retrocardiac mass not present preoperatively (*closed triangle*). Due to prolonged T2 relaxation time, the mass was presumed liquidlike. Resection of the mass revealed a 7 × 8 × 4 cm liquified, semiorganized hematoma surrounded by a thick pseudocapsule.

ation of pericardial masses and primary or metastatic tumors of the pericardium.

CARDIOMYOPATHY

Broadly speaking, *cardiomyopathy* refers to an intrinsic abnormality of the myocardium not due to ischemia, hypertension, congenital anomaly, valvular or pericardial disease resulting in primary systolic or diastolic dysfunction of the heart.[55] Cardiomyopathies are classified as either dilated, hypertrophic, or restrictive. Impaired systolic function and dilatation of one or both ventricles is characteristic of dilated cardiomyopathy. Early in the course, LV hypertrophy reduces wall tension as LV end-diastolic pressure rises; the increase of LV mass may be less apparent once ventricular dilatation occurs in the late stages. Abnormal, focal hypertrophy of the left ventricle in hypertrophic cardiomyopathy results in decreased LV compliance and impaired diastolic relaxation (lusitropy). Variable degrees of dynamic intracavitary obstruction to blood flow may occur due to exuberant

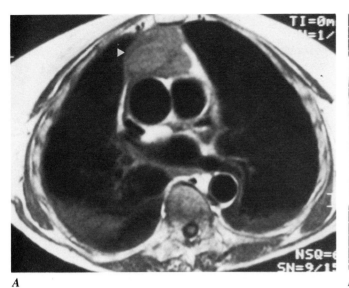
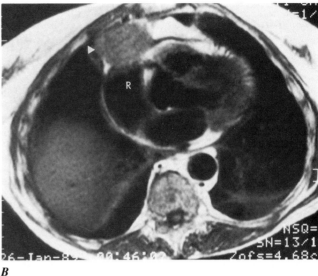

A   *B*

FIGURE 11-4 Transthoracic two-dimensional echocardiography concluded that this mediastinal mass was intrapericardial. MR spin-echo images reveal anterior and superior extensions of the mass (*closed triangle*, panel *A*) into the upper anterior mediastinum and abutment against the anterior pericardium and right ventricular outflow tract (R, panel *B*). Histology of the mass was consistent with thymoma.

focal LV septal and/or free wall hypertrophy. Systolic function is normal or hypernormal until late in the course. In restrictive cardiomypathy, fibrosis or infiltration of the myocardium impedes diastolic relaxation. Systolic function is preserved until the late stages.

At present, the diagnosis and serial assessment of cardiomyopathy are most readily accomplished by echocardiography (to detect chamber size and wall thickness) and cardiac catheterization (to record hemodynamics). Ejection fraction is most accurately assessed by radionuclide angiography; chamber dimensions and segmental wall motion by echocardiography. At present, MRI has a limited role in the assessment of most patients with cardiomyopathy but may provide unique morphological information in selected patients with hypertrophic cardiomyopathy. In the future, MRI may play a crucial role in providing detailed three-dimensional real-time displays of ventricular function, myocardial tissue characteristics, and myocardial metabolism in all varieties of cardiomyopathy.

Dilated Cardiomyopathy

The etiology of dilated cardiomyopathy (DCM) is frequently elusive despite extensive serological, echocardiographic, angiographic, and myocardial tissue analysis. Dilated cardiomyopathy represents a final common pathway of diverse metabolic, toxic, and infectious agents.[55] Although occasional spontaneous remissions occur, the clinical course is typically marked by progressive symptomatic deterioration, with 50 percent mortality within 2 to 4 years. There are no

known distinctive features of DCM by MRI at present, and MRI plays a limited role in etiologic diagnosis except to exclude pericardial, valvular, or congenital heart disease. By MRI, dilatation and depressed systolic function of the left ventricle are readily apparent. Right ventricular dilatation may occur early or late in the course. Ventricular mural thrombi occur frequently in patients with ejection fractions less than 35 percent. Gradient echo MRI is more sensitive than two-dimensional echocardiography and as sensitive as CT and angiography in the detection of apical ventricular mural thrombi.[56,57]

In the future, MRI may play a unique role in the noninvasive serial assessment of ventricular remodeling in DCM and following myocardial infarction.[58] Although the fundamental pathogenetic mechanism of the progression of LV function is not known, deleterious remodeling (progressive cavity dilatation with declining ejection fraction due to the alteration of ventricular geometry, volume, wall stress, and

TABLE 11-6 Indications for MRI: Pericardial disease

Determination of pericardial thickness
Suspected constrictive pericarditis
Effusive-constrictive pericarditis
Suspected focal pericardial constriction/disease
Pericardial adhesions
Pericardial masses
Partial or complete absence of pericardium
Hemopericardium

mass over time) is a potent morphological predictor of prognosis in DCM. Pharmacological interventions such as angiotensin converting enzyme inhibitors attenuate pathological remodeling and improve survival in heart failure.[58] Left ventricular ejection fraction and ventricular volumes may be derived from MRI techniques and are as accurate as those derived from two-dimensional echocardiography. Magnetic resonance imaging is superior to two-dimensional echocardiography in the evaluation of RV size and function.[59,60] Cine MRI can detect ejection fraction, ventricular volumes, mass, and wall stress as well as stress-volume ratio (a load-independent index of myocardial contractility).[61,62] Regional differences in ventricular thickening can be detected.[63,64] The rapid determination of ventricular mass by snapshot gradient techniques is a particular advantage of MRI,[65–67] which also detects ventricular remodeling following myocardial infarction.[68] Currently, such assessment of LV mass and volume is primarily of research interest.

Assessment of diastolic ventricular function is suboptimal by echocardiography, catheterization, or radionuclide angiography. Cine MRI may assess diastolic function by display of diastolic time-volume curves, a technique similar to radionuclide ventriculography.[69] To date, neither radionuclide nor MRI techniques have been shown to be superior to cardiac catheterization in the assessment of diastolic ventricular function.

Radial traction on the mitral annulus resulting from progressive ventricular dilatation frequently leads to nonapposition of the mitral valve leaflets and mitral regurgitation. Velocity-encoded cine MRI provides assessment of mitral valve flow and pulmonary vein velocities, from which transmitral valve flow can be calculated.[70] This technique may permit sensitive, serial, noninvasive quantitation of mitral regurgitation over time. Quantitation of mitral regurgitation by echocardiography is not yet possible.

Right ventricular function is an independent prognostic marker of survival in DCM. Due to the complex three-dimensional configuration of the right ventricle, neither echocardiography nor radionuclide ventriculography, which are limited to imaging in two simultaneous planes, is able to estimate RV size or function. Magnetic resonance imaging provides quantitation of RV mass, volume, and function in patients with DCM or primary pulmonary hypertension.[71–75] Cine MRI, via time-volume curves, may also provide information regarding RV diastolic function.[74,75] Magnetic resonance imaging may prove invaluable in cases of selective RV cardiomyopathy, such as RV dysplasia or fibrosis.[76,77]

Except in select instances, MRI tissue characterization in DCM has not proved widely applicable. In vitro, differences in T1 and T2 relaxation times in adriamycin-induced cardiomyopathy and myocarditis are detectable, but in vivo experience has been conflicting.[59] In hemochromatosis, T1 signal intensity is decreased, as is T2 relaxation time.[59] No characteristic abnormalities have been reported in sarcoidosis, although MRI of the brain frequently detects abnormalities in this condition.[78]

Hypertrophic Cardiomyopathy

Diastolic dysfunction is the primary abnormality in hypertrophic cardiomyopathy (HCM).[79] Several anatomical variants of HCM have been described, including predominant septal hypertrophy (with or without anterior systolic motion of the mitral valve), midventricular free-wall hypertrophy, and apical hypertrophy. The septal and free-wall variants may be associated with dynamic intracavitary pressure gradients and obstruction to LV outflow. In all variants of HCM, LV mass is usually markedly increased. Although RV hypertrophy is common, it generally occurs to a lesser degree than LV hypertrophy. Concentric left hypertrophy is not infrequent in addition to focal, more marked hypertrophy. The LV cavity is usually normal or diminished in size. The apical variant is frequent in Japan, typically lacks an intracavitary gradient, and has a more benign clinical course.[79] Another variant, hypertensive hypertrophic cardiomyopathy of the elderly, is marked by severe LV hypertrophy with systolic cavity obliteration and is commonest in elderly women with long-standing hypertension.[80]

Imaging in HCM should establish the correct diagnosis (given the variation in patterns of hypertrophy in HCM), document outflow or intracavitary obstruction, and define intracavitary pressure gradients (frequently dynamic in nature). Given its wide field of view and ability to image in all planes, MRI has been widely used in HCM. Spin-echo images superbly display the degree, extent, and distribution of hypertrophy,[81] and, not infrequently, MRI reveals more extensive hypertrophy than that apparent by two-dimensional echocardiography (Fig. 11-5).[81] The apical variant of HCM is clearly depicted by MRI.[82–84] In this variant, hypertrophy is confined to the anterolateral LV free wall at the apical level; variable apical myocardial signal intensity may be seen, reflecting a variable degree of ischemic injury.[81] In the other variants, changes in signal intensity and T2 relaxation times may correlate with areas of abnormally ischemic or fibrotic myocardium.[81] Magnetic resonance imaging is not yet able to distinguish the tissue of HCM from normal myocardium, although the myocardium is diffusely abnormal in HCM.[85] However, MRI has demonstrated RV free-wall hypertrophy in HCM.[86] In one study, the pattern of hypertrophy by MRI correlated with the pattern of surface ECG changes.[87] In those patients with suspected HCM who have suboptimal or equivocal echocardiographic studies (approximately 15 percent of unselected cases), MRI is clearly helpful. The benefit of routine MRI imaging in patients with HCM is not yet clear, but it is likely to be substantial in patients who are difficult to image by other modalities.

Accurate quantitation of ventricular mass by MRI may allow for detection of regression or progression of ventricular mass over time in response to therapy. At present, no pharmacological therapy arrests the unpredictable progression of HCM. Patients with marked septal hypertrophy and symptomatic outflow obstruction benefit from partial resection of the septum (myomectomy). Since septal hypertrophy and

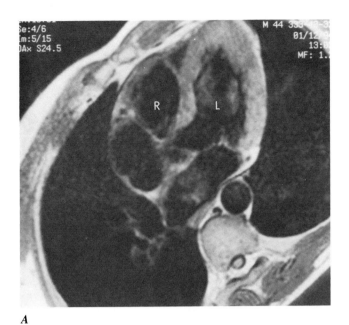
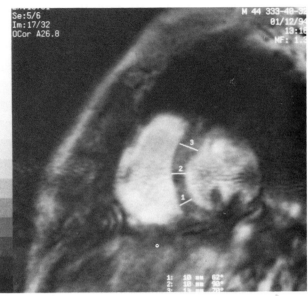

A   *B*

FIGURE 11-5   *A.* Hypertrophic cardiomyopathy (HCM) with apical distribution revealed by spin-echo MR images in a 44-year-old man. HCM was not detected by two-dimensional transthoracic echocardiography. MR image shows thickening of the apical and anterolateral left ventricle with a maximum thickness of 19 mm (L = left ventricle, R = right ventricle).   *B.* Sagittal gradient-echo image shows mild asymmetric hypertrophy of the anterobasal interventricular septum (14 mm at #3).

obstruction may recur following myomectomy, serial assessment is important. Therefore MRI plays an important role in the follow-up of patients in whom echocardiographic acoustical windows are suboptimal following cardiac surgery.

Restrictive Cardiomyopathy

There has not been a great deal of experience with MRI in restrictive cardiomyopathy. The hope that it might provide unique myocardial tissue characterization in several of the more common restrictive myopathies (amyloid, sarcoid, and hemochromatosis) has not been realized to date.[11] It can detect iron overload in hepatic hemochromatosis.[88] Myocardial iron deposition appears to be a late event in the natural history of hemochromatosis; to date, MRI has not been shown to be sensitive for the detection of myocardial hemochromatosis except in the late stages.[89] It detects brain parenchymal abnormalities in high percentage of patients with sarcoidosis: extrapolation to the myocardium has not yet been reported.[78] In amyloidosis, the ventricular myocardium, atrial walls, and atrioventricular valve leaflets may be thickened, although these findings are not pathognomonic.[90] In rare infiltrative glycogen storage disease, like Fabry's disease, MRI may show diffuse increased signal intensity and prolonged T2 relaxation time throughout the myocardium.[91] Generally, in patients with restrictive cardiomyopathy, MRI reveals enlargement of the atria and inferior vena cava in the presence of normal pericardium.[90]

Myocarditis

Inflammatory diseases of the myocardium are notoriously difficult to diagnose by currently available techniques, including endomyocardial biopsy and labeled murine antimyosin antibody scanning. Among inflammatory myocardial diseases, myocarditis and allograft rejection remain the preeminent diagnostic challenges. Only 30 percent of patients with myocarditis have unequivocally positive endomyocardial biopsies.[92] Antimyosin antibody scanning is sensitive but nonspecific in this setting. Reported experience with MRI in myocarditis is scant. It may demonstrate increased mean myocardial to skeletal muscle spin-echo sequence images in myocarditis.[93] Edema may be evident in myocardial regions with segmental wall-motion abnormalities.[94] Neither of these findings is necessarily diagnostic of myocarditis, however.

Allograft Rejection following Cardiac Transplantation

At present, allograft rejection following cardiac transplantation is impossible to detect except with serial endomyocardial biopsy. Initial studies of MRI in non–cyclosporin treated animals with cardiac allograft rejection showed increases in signal intensity and T2 relaxation times throughout the myocardium.[95] Histological severity of rejection and myocardial water content correlated with the degree of increase of T2 relaxation time.[95] In humans, up to 25 days following transplantation, T1 and T2 times are in general prolonged and do not discriminate rejection episodes.[96] Hemodynamically, rejection first results in diastolic dysfunction. Acute rejection is associated with alteration in diastolic twist mechanics, torsional deformation, and a decrease in peak systolic torsion rate.[97] Diastolic noncompliance and decreased lusitropy result from myocardial edema and hemorrhage.[98] Since wall thickness may increase due to edema, both increase in wall thickness and alteration of T1 and T2 relaxation times were used to detect rejection in early studies.[85]

Cyclosporin, a potent immunosuppressive agent now in routine use ot prevent allograft rejection, decreases myocardial edema formation in acute rejection. More recent studies in cyclosporin-treated patients have been unable to show consistent changes in myocardial wall thickness or T1 and T2 relaxation times in acute rejection.[99,100] Not all patients with endomyocardial biopsy-proven acute rejection have evidence of increased wall thickness or abnormal myocardial signal intensity on MRI,[100] and MRI may not distinguish chronic rejection or fibrosis.[100] Current work has focused on the use of contrast agents such as gadolinium-DPTA. Magnetic resonance spectroscopy shows decreased phosphate metabolites during acute rejection; in particular, the ratios of phosphocreatine, phosphomonoester, and beta-adenosine triphosphate to inorganic phosphate are decreased.[101] Presently none of these MRI techniques are sufficiently sensitive to detect allograft rejection.

MR Spectroscopy in Heart Failure

Despite decades of intense investigation, the fundamental biochemical or metabolic "defect" in the failing human heart has not been identified. Magnetic resonance spectroscopy may provide a noninvasive means of assessing the metabolism of the human heart.[102] In particular, 31P MR spectroscopy allows for the monitoring of high-energy phosphate metabolites in congestive heart failure. In excised human hearts, the phosphocreatine concentration is lower in ischemic heart disease than in dilated cardiomyopathy.[103] Magnetic resonance spectroscopy has been used in studies of skeletal muscle metabolism in heart failure.

Summary

Magnetic resonance imaging at present plays a limited role in the morphological evaluation of cardiomyopathy except in selected cases of hypertrophic cardiomyopathy and some restrictive cardiomyopathies (Table 11-7). An exciting future role of MRI may be the noninvasive comprehensive assessment of ventricular volume, mass, wall stress, and three-dimensional geometry of ventricular remodeling in ischemic heart disease and cardiac failure. This modality plays a very limited role at present in the assessment of inflammatory heart disease (myocarditis and transplant rejection). Future

TABLE 11-7   Indications for MRI: Cardiomyopathy

Morphology of HCM
Restriction versus constriction
Ventricular thrombi
Follow-up after myomectomy
Suspected hemochromatosis

studies of myocardial tissue characterization and spectroscopy may provide fundamental insights into the pathophysiology of cardiomyopathy.

CONGENITAL HEART DISEASE

Many common uncorrected congenital heart lesions, including bicuspid aortic valve, small ventricular septal defect (VSD), ostium primum, secundum or sinus venosus atrial septal defects (ASD), coarctation of the aorta, patent ductus arteriosus (PDA), noncritical pulmonic stenosis (PS), corrected transposition of the great arteries, situs solitus with dextrocardia, connections from the vena cava to the left atrium, subaortic stenosis, Ebstein's anomaly, partial anomalous pulmonary veins, sinus of Valsalva aneurysm, and coronary artery fistulas permit adult survival.[104] In addition, the number of adult survivors with cyanotic congenital heart disease is increasing due to spectacular feats of surgical palliation and correction.[104] Palliated or corrected patients present to the adult cardiologist with transformation or distortion of the anatomy and physiology of the original congenital lesion.

Precise definition of anatomy and physiology is paramount in the treatment of congenital heart disease.[105] Prior to palliation or repair, most patients undergo two-dimensional and Doppler echocardiography in addition to cardiac catheterization and angiography. Echocardiography is complementary to catheterization and provides important additional anatomical and functional information. Magnetic resonance imaging possesses several general advantages over echocardiography in imaging congenital heart defects, including a wider field of view, imaging in any plane, precise delineation of three-dimensional anatomical relationships, assessment of the central pulmonary arteries and their anatomical connections, and accurate depiction of surgical patches, grafts, conduits, and baffles.[106–110]

Anomalies of Heart Valves

The sensitivity of spin-echo MRI for the detailed anatomy of cardiac valves is less than that of echocardiography.[107] Although gradient echo MRI sequences reliably distinguished the turbulence associated with valvular regurgitation or stenosis, they provide no clear advantage over adequate two-dimensional Doppler echocardiography at present.[111] Bicuspid aortic and pulmonary valve stenosis, two common congenital valvular lesions, are better assessed by echocardiography. Abnormalities of the mitral or tricuspid valves occur in several congenital lesions—particularly primum ASD (cleft mitral valve), secundum ASD and Marfan's syndrome (mitral valve prolapse), Ebstein's anomaly, and endocardial cushion defect VSDs—and are also better imaged with echocardiography.[105]

ASD, VSD, Intracardiac Shunts

Magnetic resonance imaging is probably as sensitive as two-dimensional echocardiography in the detection of ASD or VSD (Fig. 11-6).[112–115] In one study of gated spin-echo MRI, the sensitivity and specificity of MRI for primum ASD was 100 and 90 percent and for secundum ASD 96 and 90 percent, respectively.[116] Occasional false negatives by MRI arise due to low signal intensity of the interatrial septum and signal dropout in the region of the fossa ovalis, where the atrial septum is thinnest and most mobile.[108,109] The sensitivity of MRI in detecting sinus venous ASD, anomalous pulmonary venous connections, and cor triatriatum probably exceeds that of echocardiography.[116] Spin-echo transverse images reliably detect perimembranous, inlet, atrioventricular (AV) canal, or subpulmonic VSDs of 0.3 cm in diameter or larger.[113,117]

Velocity-encoded cine MRI allows for calculation of stroke flow in the aorta and pulmonary artery and quantification of left-to-right atrial shunts.[118] This technique correlates well with quantification of shunts by standard oximetry during cardiac catheterization and may be useful in noninvasively monitoring shunt volume over time. The significance of shunt flow may be assessed via comparison of right and left ventricular stroke volumes or calculation of shunt flow by phase analysis of gradient sequence images. The reliability of this measure is lessened by valvular regurgitation or change in atrial or ventricular filling pressures. Gadolinium-enhanced ultrafast MRI techniques have also been used to identify the precise site of shunting.[117] Magnetic resonance imaging may provide qualitative assessment of pulmonary vascular resistance in shunt lesions at present, although precise quantitation of pulmonary vascular resistance is necessary for clinical decision making.[119] A great need exists for serial, noninvasive, and accurate assessment of shunt flow, shunt volume, ventricular volume and function, and pulmonary vascular resistance in congenital lesions. In the future, MRI may play a pivotal role in this area.

Anomalies of the Aorta

A distinct advantage of MRI over echocardiography is for imaging abnormalities of the great vessels. It is unparalleled in imaging the aortic root dilatation, aortic aneuryms, and acute or chronic dissections that accompany Marfan's syndrome.[29] Aneurysms of the sinus of Valsalva, supravalvular

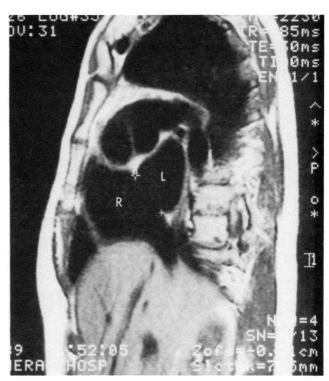

FIGURE 11-6   A 2-cm secundum atrial septal defect (ASD) shown on spin-echo MR image (R = right atrium, L = left atrium). ASD dimensions agreed closely with measurements at cardiac catheterization and operation.

aortic stenosis, and anomalies of the aortic arch are readily identified.[122–124] A most important role of MRI at present is the pre- and post-operative imaging of coarctation of the aorta.

Coarctation of the aorta occurs most often just distal to the origin of the left subclavian artery, opposite the entry of the ductus arteriosus.[105] Associated defects include bicuspid aortic valve (25 percent), anomalies of the aortic arch, and mitral valve prolapse (25 percent). Prior to repair, MRI gated spin-echo sagittal and 60° left anterior oblique (LAO) images are excellent for displaying the anatomy of coarctation.[125] A particular advantage of MRI is the depiction of aortic collateral branches.[14] Serial follow-up examination following surgical repair by resection with end-to-end anastomosis, patch, or conduit is important, since persistent or recurrent coarctation may occur (Fig. 11-7).[104] Echo Doppler may overestimate the degree of recoarctation due to prior vascular procedures or anomalous vessel origin.[126] In recoarctation, reduction in luminal diameter assessed by MRI correlates well with the pressure gradient assessed by catheterization or Doppler ultrasound.[127] Aortic volume flow and peak flow jet velocity measured by MRI phase-shifted velocity mapping correlate with the severity of coarctation stenosis and may provide noninvasive indices for monitoring patients before and after repair.[128]

Not infrequently, MRI soon after surgical repair shows aneurysm or perianastomotic hematomas.[125,127,129] This tech-

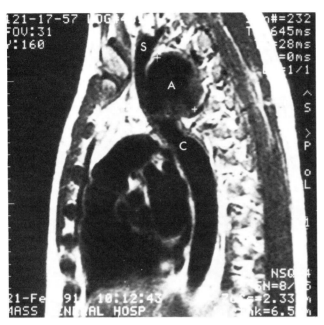

FIGURE 11-7 Sagittal spin-echo image from a 34-year-old man with previous Dacron tube graft repair of a native aortic coarctation. The study clearly delineates recoarctation at the repair site (C) as well as a large false aneurysm (A) distal to the origin of the large left subclavian artery (S).

nique is useful in assessing coarctation restenosis following balloon angioplasty.[130] Obstruction of vascular conduits used for repair of coarctation is detected by MRI spin-echo sequences,[131] and MRI may reliably distinguish pseudocoarctation, a condition in which nonobstructive kinking of the aorta simulates true coarctation.[105] Finally, MRI is excellent for acute dissections or chronic aneurysms which may occur at the site of coarctation.

Vascular Rings

These complex, uncommon lesions include double aortic arch, right-sided aortic arch with aberrant left subclavian, left ductus arteriosus, and pulmonary artery slings (left pulmonary artery passes to the right behind the trachea before supplying the left lung).[105] Preoperative MRI may provide accurate delineation of anatomy in these conditions.[132]

Pulmonary Artery Anomalies

Magnetic resonance imaging provides excellent definition of the main, right, and left pulmonary artery anatomy in right ventricular outflow lesions such as tetralogy of Fallot, pulmonary atresia, tricuspid atresia, and double-outlet right ventricle.[109] In pulmonary atresia, MRI can assess the central pulmonary arteries, systemic collaterals, and surgical shunts; it may obviate the need for diagnostic angiography in some centers.[133] Disadvantages of MRI include the occasional inability to image peripheral pulmonary artery stenoses, the

distal connections of collaterals due to tortuosity and low flow, and in-situ thromboses.[134] Velocity-encoded cine MRI of the main, right, and left pulmonary arteries may provide assessment of differential right and left lung perfusion.[135]

Complex Congenital Heart Disease

Delineation of the right and left ventricular outflow tracts, pulmonary artery anatomy, source or sources of pulmonary blood flow, and atrioventricular valve anatomy is crucial in complex cyanotic congenital heart disease prior to consideration of surgical palliation or repair.[105] In experienced centers, MRI is as precise as angiography and has particular advantages in demonstrating the size and morphology of the ventricles, orientation of the ventricular septum in relation to atrioventricular valves, origin and anatomic relations of the great vessels, visceroatrial situs, bulboventricular loop, and pulmonary venoatrial connections.[106,107] The role of MRI in two complex congenital lesions, tetralogy of Fallot and tricuspid atresia, is discussed below to provide examples.

Tetralogy of Fallot

Tetralogy of Fallot (TOF), the commonest cyanotic congenital heart defect, is characterized by infundibular pulmonic stenosis, RV hypertrophy, a perimembranous VSD which is nearly always large, and an overriding aorta.[105] The pulmonary valve exhibits a variable degree of dysplasia or hypoplasia. Tetralogy of Fallot with absent pulmonary valve, common AV canal, or pulmonary atresia are occasional variants. Anatomy of the pulmonary arteries and right ventricular outflow tract is highly variable and critical to image in detail, since surgical repair is predicated on the source and adequacy of pulmonary blood flow. Collaterals from the descending aorta or bronchial arteries to the pulmonary arteries may be tortuous and bizarre. Associated lesions in TOF include branch pulmonary stenosis (28 percent), patent foramen ovale, right aortic arch (25 percent), additional VSDs (5 percent), obstructive right ventricular outflow tract moderator bands (5 percent), and anomalous origin of the left anterior descending coronary artery from the right coronary artery, the "conus coronary" (5 percent).[105] Preoperative diagnosis of these associated anomalies is important, particularly identification of the conus coronary, which may be transected during right ventriculotomy. Depending on the adequacy of pulmonary blood flow and the anatomy of the outflow tract and pulmonary arteries, repair of TOF involves VSD closure with either infundibulectomy, valvotomy and enlargement of the pulmonic annulus with a transannular patch, or interposition of a conduit from the right ventricle to the pulmonary artery. Patients with pulmonary hypoplasia may undergo shunting procedures (Blalock-Taussig, Glenn) to allow for growth of the pulmonary arteries prior to definitive repair.

At present, patients with TOF undergo catheterization and

angiography prior to repair for definition of the anatomy of the VSD, RV outflow tract, pulmonary arteries, and exclusion of the conus coronary.[105] Catheterization is potentially dangerous, however: in children, infundibular spasm provoked by hypoxia, contrast agents, anxiety, or catheters may result in life-threatening cyanotic "spells." Magnetic resonance imaging correlates excellently with angiography in the definition of anatomy in TOF.[134] T1 spin-echo images may demonstrate collaterals which are often difficult to define by catheterization. Despite its utility in TOF, MRI does not adequately display the pulmonary valve leaflets or coronary arteries and thus has not supplanted echocardiography and catheterization. However, MRI is ideal for studying the central pulmonary arteries in TOF and may play an important ancillary role in preoperative planning.

Magnetic resonance imaging may play an important role in the serial evaluation of patients postoperatively in whom echocardiography is limited or inadequate. Residual RV hypertrophy and progressive dilatation, pulmonary regurgitation due to the transannular patch, patch leak, incomplete VSD closure or residual VSDs, and residual RV outflow tract obstruction may occur. Ventriculopulmonary conduit stenosis frequently occurs over 7 to 10 years and is accelerated in some. Progressive RV dilatation and dysfunction may occur due to pulmonic valve regurgitation. MRI velocity mapping of flow in the main pulmonary artery provides for quantification of pulmonary regurgitation after surgical correction of TOF.[136]

Tricuspid Atresia

Congenital absence of the tricuspid valve and RV hypoplasia characterize this anomaly.[105] Associated anomalies include pulmonic stenosis or atresia (60 percent) or transposition of the great arteries (40 percent).[105] Precise definition of anatomy and pulmonary vascular resistance is crucial to determine candidacy for the Fontan procedure. In this procedure, systemic venous return bypasses a ventricular pumping chamber and is rerouted directly from the right atrium or systemic veins into the pulmonary arteries. Requirements for the Fontan procedure include low pulmonary vascular resistance and pulmonary artery pressure, normal atrioventricular valve morphology and function, preserved pulmonary artery architecture, and normal systemic ventricular function.[105] In a retrospective study of 53 patients considered to be candidates for the Fontan procedure, MRI provided excellent demonstration of the systemic veins and pulmonary arteries and veins.[137] Postoperatively, the most important complication is obstruction of the atriopulmonary connection: MRI may play a role in its diagnosis.[106]

Other Complex Congenital Lesions

Magnetic resonance imaging accurately delineates the anatomy of Ebstein's anomaly, double-outlet right ventricle, truncus arteriosus, transposition of the great vessels, and partial anomalous pulmonary venous connections, and other complex lesions. Situs anomalies including heterotaxia are readily diagnosed.[138]

Postoperative MRI

Although MRI is invaluable in the diagnosis of congenital lesions, its most important role in the future may lie in the noninvasive postoperative evaluation of patients with palliated or repaired congenital heart disease.[106] Magnetic resonance imaging provides information regarding the patency of surgical shunts, the central pulmonary arteries, and pulmonary collaterals.[133] Velocity mapping with MRI is more sensitive than two-dimensional Doppler echocardiography in the detection of obstruction of ventriculopulmonary conduits.[139,140] In the largest study to date, two-dimensional echocardiography satisfactorily assessed the anatomy of conduits in only 17 percent of patients, compared to 90 percent by spin-echo MRI.[140] Echocardiography is limited due to the anterior position of the conduit and inability to define the anatomic levels of obstruction by Doppler techniques.[139] Excellent correlation was reported between the conduit gradients measured by MRI velocity mapping and continuous-wave Doppler echocardiography. Spin-echo and cine MRI provides excellent depiction of anatomy and function following the Mustard or Senning procedures for transposition of the great arteries.[110,141] Magnetic resonance imaging can detect atrial obstruction, baffle leaks, tricuspid regurgitation, and ventricular volume and mass.[106] As discussed, MRI is valuable in imaging postoperative Fontan patients.

Summary

Spin-echo and cine gradient echo MRI provides both anatomic and functional information in congenital heart disease (Table 11-8). At present, MRI is most useful in imaging coarctation of the aorta, anomalies of the great vessels, complex cyanotic lesions, and visceroatrial situs. The role of MRI in congenital heart disease is evolving.[106] The expense, availability, and established roles of echocardiography and catheterization have not yet precisely defined the role of

TABLE 11-8 Indications for MRI: Congenital heart disease

Pulmonary artery anatomy
Visceroatrial situs
Bulboventricular loop
Pulmonary vein anomalies
Vena cava anomalies
Aortic coarctation (pre- and postoperative)
Suspected sinus venosus ASD
Postoperative conduit, shunt, baffle obstruction
Complex cyanotic heart disease

MRI, although its ability to image complex lesions and display the anatomy of the great vessels and pulmonary arteries is unparalleled. Dedicated chest coils, ultrafast imaging, and automated volumetric software will provide increased sophistication of MRI in congenital heart disease.[14]

TUMORS OF THE HEART

Primary tumors of the heart are much less common than metastatic tumors.[142,143] Primary tumors may be either benign or malignant. Atrial myxoma, the commonest intracardiac tumor, accounts for 30 to 50 percent of primary tumors of the heart in large pathological series.[143] The majority of myxomas are benign: 85 percent are found in the left atrium in the region of the fossa ovalis, the remainder are found in the right atrium or are associated with perivalvular structures. These tumors may arise from endocardial sensory nerve tissue.[144] Myxomas may be pedunculated with a fibrovascular stalk and mobile, or they may be sessile. When mobile, left atrial myxomas may prolapse through the mitral valve orifice, producing acquired mitral stenosis; right atrial myxomas may precipitate right-sided heart failure. Mitral or tricuspid regurgitation is not infrequent. Given the gelatinous consistency of these tumors, fragmentation with embolism is a constant risk. Other benign cardiac tumors include papillary tumors of the valves, rhabdomyomas, fibromas, lipomas (including lipomatous hypertrophy of the interatrial septum), angiomas, teratomas, and cystic tumors.[142]

Some 25 percent of all primary cardiac tumors are malignant; thus malignant tumors are second only to myxomas in frequency. Apart from the occasional malignant myxoma, virtually all other primary malignant tumors of the heart are sarcomas (angiosarcomas, rhabdomyosarcomas, fibrosarcomas, lymphosarcomas) (Fig. 11-8).[145] They involve, in decreasing frequency, the right atrium, left atrium, right ventricle, left ventricle, and interventricular septum.[142,143] The clinical course of malignant primary tumors of the heart is one of rapid deterioration due to progressive myocardial infiltration, inflow or outflow obstruction, and difficult-to-manage ventricular arrhythmias.[143] The clinical presentation is nonspecific and includes left- or right-sided heart failure, anginal chest pain, syncope due to ventricular tachycardia, cardiac tamponade, great vessel obstruction, and pericardial effusion.[142]

Systematic imaging of suspected primary cardiac tumors is of critical importance. The origin, site of attachment, size, mobility, and associated infiltration of surrounding myocardium, pericardium, and neighboring mediastinal and vascular structures must be defined prior to attempted resection.[143] Transthoracic two-dimensional echocardiography is used as an effective screening modality. The superior resolution of transesophageal echocardiography permits detailed anatomic study. In some cases, the inhomogeneity of myxomas due to regions of focal hemorrhage may help distinguish them from

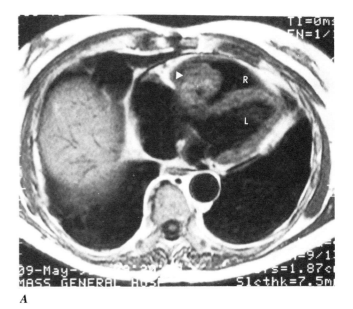

A

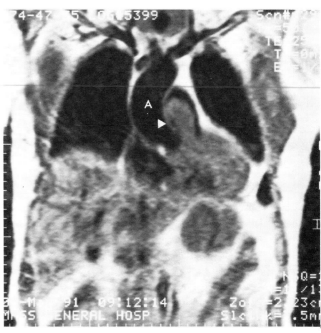

B

FIGURE 11-8 *A.* Transverse image of a large intracardiac mass (*closed triangle*) adherent to the tricuspid valve apparatus (R = right ventricle, L = left ventricle). *B.* On the coronal view, the mass (*closed triangle*) extends into the right ventricular outflow tract (A = aorta). Resection revealed the mass to be a malignant rhabdomyosarcoma.

thrombi. Computed tomography may help exclude mediastinal or pericardial involvement but involves the properly timed administration of contrast and exposure to ionizing radiation.[146] Many patients undergo invasive cardiac catheterization to delineate the anatomical features and hemodynamic effects of mobile tumors.

Multiple studies have documented the utility of MRI in

cardiac tumors.[147–154] In patients referred following echocardiography for suspected cardiac tumors, MRI not infrequently excludes the diagnosis.[143] Thus, MRI is particularly useful to confirm the diagnosis of cardiac tumor suggested by echocardiography, particularly when the echocardiographic findings are equivocal. General advantages of MRI over echocardiography include the inherent natural contrast between intracardiac and intravascular tissues, high soft tissue contrast, imaging in orthogonal or oblique planes, and wide field of view.[143] Magnetic resonance imaging may be superior to echocardiography in delineating the size and shape of myxomas and decreasing the number of false positive identifications of tumor.[153] Magnetic resonance imaging delineates prolapse, valvular obstruction, relative chamber size, and relation of the tumor to nearby intracardiac structures and adjacent extracardiac structures in cases of myxomas.[152,153] However, echocardiography is superior to MRI in demonstrating the motion of myxomas in real time and assessing the degree of valvular obstruction.[11] No large studies have yet appeared directly comparing MRI with TEE.

Magnetic resonance imaging is useful in the serial assessment of tumors, particularly benign rhabdomyomas in children, which may spontaneously regress over time.[155] The distinction between pericardial and intracardiac masses is often apparent by MRI.[156] This modality may be particularly efficacious in imaging predominantly fatty or vascular tumors, since tissue contrast and image resolution are enhanced.[151] Lipomatous tissue has a high signal intensity on T1 images and a moderately low signal intensity on T2 images. Soft tissue tumors may exhibit shorter relaxation times than cystic fluid, and tumors with increased water content may exhibit prolonged T1 and T2 times compared to surrounding tissues.[143] Tissue characterization is complicated by hemorrhage or necrosis into tumor or the presence of dense fibrous or calcified tissue. In such instances, MRI with gadolinium-DPTA contrast may prove useful. At present, distinguishing benign from malignant myocardial tissues by MRI is not possible.

Lipomatous hypertrophy of the interatrial septum not infrequently simulates atrial tumors. By MRI, the readily appreciated bilobed morphology and decreased T1 relaxation time characteristic of lipomatous hypertrophy may help distinguish it from malignant tumors, which characteristically exhibit increased relaxation times.[157] Magnetic resonance imaging may distinguish atrial septal aneurysm from cystic atrial masses,[158] and it is also helpful in imaging cardiac paragangliomas preoperatively.[159]

Excision of tumors of the heart is generally recommended to prevent obstruction, embolization, or arrhythmias.[142] Long-term results of excision of benign tumors, most commonly myxomas, are excellent.[160] However, myxomas recur in 1 to 5 percent of cases and may recur in up to 12 to 22 percent of cases of the rare familial myxomas.[143] Periodic long-term follow-up is essential. Although at present two-dimensional echocardiography is preferred due to ease and

cost considerations, MRI may play an important future role. Excision of malignant tumors is often not feasible; even with palliative resection, survival is poor.[145,160]

Summary

The wide field of view, ability to image in all anatomic planes, resolution by spin-echo imaging, and correlative functional information by gradient echo imaging are distinct advantages of MRI in known or suspected cardiac tumors (Table 11-9). Disadvantages include occasional motion artifacts, flow artifacts, poor ability to image calcification, inability to image patients with irregular heart rhythms, difficulty in distinguishing thrombus or tumor on occasion from slowly moving blood, expense, and protracted scanning times. At present, MRI provides important correlative anatomical and functional information in cases of suspected or confirmed cardiac masses and is widely used by cardiologists and cardiac surgeons.

EVOLVING INDICATIONS FOR CARDIOVASCULAR MRI (TABLE 11-10)

Ventricular Function

In assessing ventricular function, echocardiography is dependent on good acoustic windows, certain geometric assumptions regarding the shape of the left ventricle, and clear endocardial borders. Radionuclide angiography is limited by attenuation factors which render assessment of ventricular volumes unreliable. Contrast ventriculography remains the gold standard, although this technique is invasive and laborious. Magnetic resonance imaging, while not routinely used in the assessment of ventricular function, holds great promise.

TABLE 11-9   Indications for MRI: Cardiac tumors

Definitive diagnosis
Intracardiac, pericardial, mediastinal spread
Follow-up of benign masses
Lipomatous hypertrophy of atrial septum versus tumor

TABLE 11-10   Evolving indications for cardiovascular MRI

Peripheral vascular disease
Regional ventricular function
Left ventricular volume, mass, function
Right ventricular size, volume, mass, function
Ventricular remodeling
Quantitative assessment of intracardiac shunts
Infarct quantification

Ventricular Volume and Mass

Early MRI multislice spin-echo techniques have been replaced by tomographic cine MRI assessment of ventricular volume.[11] Use of the modified Simpson's rule, biplane ellipsoid modeling, and breath-holding with ultrafast imaging significantly decrease cine MRI acquisition time.[161–163] Volume assessment is accurate even when the ventricular cavity has been deformed by infarction, remodeling, or progressive dilatation.[11] Measurement of ventricular mass by a modification of Simpson's rule using contiguous multislice techniques correlates well with the mass of postmortem specimens.[164]

A great advantage of MRI is the accurate assessment of RV volume, mass, and function. Due to complex geometry, the right ventricle is not readily assessed by angiography, echocardiography, or radionuclide angiography.[11] Serial MRI tomograms of the right ventricle can be acquired simultaneously with tomograms of the left ventricle, allowing for assessment of ventricular interaction and interdependence. Either the right or left ventricle can be reconstructed in three dimensions, allowing for accurate ventriclar volume-mass measures without regard to the plane of imaging.[164] The evolution of real-time MRI (via echoplanar or analogous imaging techniques) may eventually rival real-time echocardiography in the assessment of ventricular function.[164]

Regional Ventricular Function

Magnetic resonance imaging reliably detects endocardial motion and systolic wall thickness. Assessment of regional left ventricular function correlates well with contrast ventriculography.[164–166] By "tagging" a predefined section of myocardium by selective radiofrequency saturation prior to cine gradient echo imaging, a myocardial segment can be accurately tracked in three-dimensional space throughout the cardiac cycle.[167–169] Myocardial MRI tagging has provided unparalleled insight into the three-dimensional behavior of ventricular contraction: ventricular shortening, translation, rotation, and torsion-detorsion (or "cardiac twist") are all detectable.[11] This technique has made possible the demonstration of epicardial-to-endocardial shear forces within the myocardium. The velocity of ventricular untwisting during isovolumic diastole has been shown to increase in response to catechols, and the velocity of ventricular untwisting may contribute to diastolic compliance. Measurement of regional and global myocardial strain is possible, and in the future such studies may help eludidate in a fundamental way the relation between myocardial myocyte arrangement and ventricular function.[167]

Valvular Function

Echocardiography is superior to MRI in depicting the detailed anatomy of valve leaflets.[11] In the future, MRI may play an important role in assessing the impact of valvular stenosis or regurgitation on LV or RV volume, mass, and wall stress, particularly in response to medical or surgical therapy. By cine MRI, the turbulence associated with a valvular regurgitation jet produces a signal void due to spin incoherence and signal dephasing; the size of this jet may provide a semiquantitative estimate of the severity of valvular regurgitation.[11] Potential pitfalls include imaging in an improper plane; selection of an improper imaging sequence, echo time or window width; and misidentification of normally present signal voids.[170] Regurgitant fractions may be calculated by cine MRI measures of RV and LV stroke volumes by the modified Simpson formula.[23] More recently, regurgitant volumes have been calculated by analysis of the proximal zone of convergence at the regurgitant valve orifice or by phase velocity mapping.[171,172]

Qualitative stenotic valvular gradients may be assessed by appearance of the transvalvular jet by MRI and more recently by phase velocity mapping.[11,173] In 20 patients with mitral stenosis, cine MRI demonstrated leaflet thickening and decreased diastolic mitral valve opening.[174] Maximum leaflet separation by cine MRI in diastole correlated with mitral valve area calculated by echocardiographic continuous-wave Doppler assessment. The signal intensity of left atrial blood was less than that of right atrial blood, and flow in the left atrium exhibited an abnormal circular motion. In 12 patients with aortic stenosis, MRI velocity mapping measurement of aortic valve area yielded reasonably close agreement to catheterization and echocardiography.[175] Magnetic resonance imaging velocity mapping measurement of cardiac output closely agreed with indicator dilution techniques. Simultaneous quantitation of aortic regurgitation is an attractive feature of MRI imaging. The role of MRI in the assessment of valvular disease will await further larger studies.

ISCHEMIC HEART DISEASE

The ability of MRI to complement or supplant currently existing diagnostic modalities in the assessment of ischemic heart disease will likely determine its ultimate place in cardiovascular imaging. Like other modalities, the goal of MRI in ischemic heart disease is the noninvasive, rapid, accurate imaging of myocardial infarction, hibernating or stunned myocardium, rest- or exercise-induced myocardial ischemia, and the location and composition of coronary artery stenoses.

Myocardial Infarction

Infarcted myocardium is detectable by noncontrast MRI due to increase in myocardial water content with subsequent prolongation of T1 and T2 relaxation times and increased signal intensity on T2-weighted images.[176,177] Quantitation of infarct size by MRI agrees with ventriculography.[177] Without contrast, detection of infarction is limited to regions of edema. Contrast MRI may allow for much earlier detection of infarction. Following the administration of gadopentate dimeglumine (Gd-DPTA) contrast, infarcts show increased signal intensity with fast scanning techniques due to delayed accumulation and clearance of contrast.[11] First-pass images show low signal intensity compared to normal myocardium on T1-weighted images due to delayed uptake.[176] The present role of MRI in quantitating infarct size is unclear, but future goals include distinguishing infarcted from reperfused myocardium, viable versus nonviable reperfused myocardium (stunning), and chronically hypoperfused, dysfunctional but viable myocardium (hibernation).[178]

In patients with known coronary artery disease and chest pain, resting first-pass ultrafast MRI following rapid intravenous injection of Gd-DPTA revealed lower peak signal intensity in myocardial regions subtended by diseased coronary vessels and lower rates of signal increase.[179] Repeat study after revascularization showed increased peak signal intensity in the same regions. In dogs, dipyridamole enhances first-pass assessment of perfusion after Gd-DPTA bolus by turboFLASH sequence imaging.[180] Contrast-enhanced T1-weighted inversion-recovery spin-echo planar perfusion imaging may provide even better image quality and first-pass contrast enhancement.[181] Distinct evaluation of the subendocardial, midepicardial, and subepicardial regions is possible.

Since exercise is not feasible in the MRI scanner, pharmacological stress has been employed in the assessment of coronary artery stenoses.[182] In a study comparing gradient echo cine MRI to thallium 201 during dipyridamole pharmacological stress in 40 patients, segmental wall-motion abnormalities were detected by MRI in 67 percent of myocardial segments with reversible thallium defects.[183] The overall sensitivity of MRI for detecting coronary artery disease was 62 percent. Poor sensitivity resulted from inability to detect small areas of ischemia. Further studies with higher-dose dipyridamole have shown somewhat increased sensitivity.[182] In a later study of dobutamine, pharmacological stress (in doses up to 20 μg/kg/min) in 25 patients, gradient echo cine MRI detected reversible wall-motion abnormalities in 95 percent of those with reversible thallium 201 defects.[184] The overall sensitivity of MRI was 91 percent. There was no difference in this small study in the MRI or thallium detection or location of stenoses.

Coronary Artery Imaging

The small size, tortuous course, and constant motion of the coronary arteries has posed a challenge in MRI. Initial reports of the identification of the ostia and proximal several centimeters of the coronary arteries by spin echo sequences appeared in 1987.[18] Ultrafast gradient echo MRI angiography with breath-holding and standard body coils revealed the feasibility of detecting the coronary ostia and proximal coronary arteries.[21] Fat-suppressed breath-hold MR angiography (MRA) with gradient echo sequences and *k* space augmen-

tation can reveal the proximal portions of the left main coronary artery, left anterior descending artery, circumflex artery, and right coronary artery in 96, 100, 76, and 100 percent respectively.[185] Coronary artery luminal diameter determined by MRA exhibits good correlation with conventional angiography. Another study with similar imaging techniques detected the left main, left anterior descending, right, and circumflex coronary arteries in 95, 91, 95, and 76 percent, respectively.[20] Luminal diameter could be assessed in three-quarters of studies. The coronaries were imaged from between 5 to 30 mm along their respective lengths. Fast spiral imaging and multiple 1-s breath-holds may increase resolution.[186,187]

In a recent blinded comparison of coronary MRA with conventional angiography in 39 patients, the sensitivity and specificity of MRA for detection of stenosis greater than or equal to 50 percent by conventional angiography was 90 and 92 percent, respectively.[20] Only 3 of 149 arteries were not interpretable. Precise quantification of stenosis severity was not possible. A source of potential false-positive examinations is loss of MRI signal due to turbulence at sites of nonstenotic luminal irregularities or vessel ulcerations.

In the near future, MRA may play a role in screening for proximal coronary artery disease in the three major coronary arteries. Other applications may include the diagnosis of proximal coronary artery disease in patients with chest pain, monitoring of proximal stenosis severity, or perhaps even therapeutic decision making.[188] The cost-effectiveness of this strategy will require study. However, MRA will likely not supplant conventional angiography in the near future. Current limitations include the requirement for regular cardiac rhythm, a 12- to 18-s period of breath-holding, and current inability to identify stenoses in branch vessels due to inadequate spatial resolution.[188] Before its use is adopted prior to revascularization procedures, MRA will have to provide high-resolution images of coronary artery branches and patterns of collateral flow. In addition, for use during coronary angioplasty, magnified selective views, imaging of thrombus, and coronary artery dissections will be necessary.

Magnetic resonance imaging can establish the patency of coronary artery bypass grafts. In an early study, spin-echo sequences imaged 91 percent of patent grafts and 71 percent of occlusions.[189] In a later study, the sensitivity of cine gradient echo MRI was 88 percent for patent grafts and 91 percent for occluded grafts.[190] Velocity mapping by MRI of global coronary artery diastolic flow in the ascending aorta may assess coronary flow reserve pre- and postdipyridamole[191] As above, greater resolution will be necessary before widespread clinical use is possible.

CONCLUSION

By comparison with other invasive and noninvasive imaging techniques available at present, MRI provides unparalleled

TABLE 11-11   Accepted indications for cardiovascular MRI

Diseases of the aorta
   Selected stable acute aortic dissections
   Subacute or chronic aortic dissections
   Repaired aortic dissection
   Serial evaluation of Marfan's and related syndromes
   Pre- and postcoarctation repair
   Congenital anomalies of the aortic arch
Diseases of the pericardium
   Constrictive pericarditis
   Masses
Cardiomyopathy
   Hypertrophic cardiomyopathy
Congenital heart disease
   Intracardiac shunts: ASD, VSD
   Pulmonary artery and vein anomalies
   Pulmonary venoatrial connections
   Vena cava anomalies
   Visceroatrial situs
   Ventricular morphology/bulboventricular loop
   Complex cyanotic congenital lesions
   Conduits, shunts, baffles, patches
   Pulmonary and systemic collaterals
   Postoperative assessment (Mustard, Senning, Fontan, etc.)
Cardiac tumors

delineation of cardiac structure. The wide field of view, imaging in orthogonal and oblique planes, and inherent tissue-blood contrast have firmly established the role of MRI as the modality of choice in diverse cardiovascular disorders (Table 11-11). In addition, clinical cardiologists frequently

TABLE 11-12   Future applications for cardiovascular MRI

Cardiomyopathy
   Diagnosis by myocardial tissue characterization
   Myocardial metabolism
   Transplant allograft rejection
   Myocarditis
   Pharmacological remodeling
Valvular heart disease
   Quantitation of regurgitant volumes
   Valve orifice measurement
Ischemic heart disease
   Quantification of infarct size
   Assessment of myocardial viability, stunning, and hibernation
   Rest and stress myocardial perfusion
   Coronary flow reserve
   Noninvasive high-resolution coronary angiography
   Plaque morphology and composition in stable and unstable coronary syndromes
   Detection of postangioplasty restenosis

employ MRI to confirm equivocal results of echocardiography or catheterization.

A great need exists in cardiology for a single noninvasive imaging modality which combines detailed, accurate anatomical and functional assessment of the myocardium, valves, great vessels, and coronary arteries ("one-stop shopping"). Given the impressive achievements to date, MRI is the most likely candidate on the horizon. In the meantime, research applications of MRI techniques may provide insight into fundamental pathophysiological processes in myocardial, valvular, and ischemic heart disease. (Table 11-12).

REFERENCES

1. Cigarroa J, Isselbacher E, DeSanctis R, et al: Diagnostic imaging in the evaluation of suspected aortic dissection: Old standards and new directions. *N Engl J Med* 328:35, 1993.
2. Amparo E, Higgins C, Hricak H, et al: Aortic dissection: Magnetic resonance imaging. *Radiology* 155:399, 1985.
3. Dinsmore R, Wedeen V, Miller S, et al: MRI of dissection of the aorta: Recognition of the intimal tear and differential flow velocities. *AJR* 146:1286, 1986.
4. Dinsmore R, Liberthson R, Wismer G, et al: Magnetic resonance imaging of thoracic aortic aneurysms: Comparison with other imaging methods. *AJR* 146:309, 1986.
5. Geisinger M, Risius B, O'Donnell J, et al: Thoracic aortic dissections: Magnetic resonance imaging. *Radiology* 155:407, 1985.
6. Goldman A, Kotler M, Scanlon M, et al: The complementary role of magnetic resonance imaging, Doppler echocardiography, and computed tomography in the diagnosis of dissecting thoracic aneurysms. *Am Heart J* 111:970, 1986.
7. Kersting-Sommerhoff B, Higgins C, White R, et al: Aortic dissection: Sensitivity and specificity of MR imaging. *Radiology* 166:651, 1988.
8. Nienaber C, Spielmann R, von Kodolitsch Y, et al: Diagnosis of thoracic aortic dissection: magnetic resonance imaging versus transesophageal echocardiography. *Circulation* 85:434, 1992.
9. Nienaber C, Kodolitsch Y, Nicolas V, et al: The diagnosis of thoracic aortic dissection by noninvasive imaging procedures. *N Engl J Med* 328:1, 1993.
10. O'Gara P, DeSanctis R: Aortic dissection, in Loscalzo J, Creager MA, Dzau JV (eds): *Vascular Medicine*. Boston, Little, Brown, 1992, chap 34.
11. Blackwell G, Pohost G: The usefulness of cardiovascular magnetic resonance imaging. *Curr Probl Cardiol* 19:117, 1994.
12. Appelbe A, Walker P, Yeoh J, et al: Clinical significance and origin of artifacts in transesophageal echocardiography of the thoracic aorta. *J Am Coll Cardiol* 21:754, 1993.
13. Cambria R, Brewster D, Moncure A, et al: Spontaneous aortic dissection in the presence of co-existence of previously repaired atherosclerotic aortic aneurysm. *Ann Surg* 208:619, 1988.
14. Mohiaddin R, Longmore D: Functional aspects of cardiovascular nuclear magnetic resonance imaging: Techniques and application. *Circulation* 88:264, 1993.
15. Wolff K, Herold C, Tempany C, et al: Aortic dissection: Atypical patterns seen at MR imaging. Radiology 181:489, 1991.
16. Treasure T, Raphael M: Investigation of suspected dissection of the thoracic aorta. *Lancet* 338:490, 1991.
17. Shellock F, Curtis J: MR imaging and biomedical implants, materials, and devices: An updated review. *Radiology* 180:541, 1991.

18. Paulin S, von Schulthess G, Fossel E, et al: MR imaging of the aortic root and proximal coronary arteries. *AJR* 148:665, 1987.
19. Pennell D, Keegan J, Firmin D, et al: Magnetic resonance imaging of coronary arteries: Technique and preliminary results. *Br Heart J* 70:315, 1993.
20. Manning W, Li W, Edelman R: A preliminary report comparing magnetic resonance coronary angiography with conventional angiography. *N Engl J Med* 328:828, 1993.
21. Edelman R, Manning W, Burstein D, et al: Coronary arteries: Breath-hold MR angiography. *Radiology* 181:641, 1991.
22. Kern M, Serota H, Callicoat P, et al: Use of coronary arteriography in the preoperative management of patients undergoing urgent repair of the thoracic aorta. *Am Heart J* 119:143, 1990.
23. Sechtem U, Pflugfelder P, Cassidy M, et al: Mitral or aortic regurgitation: Quantification of regurgitant volumes with cine MR imaging. *Radiology* 167:425, 1988.
24. Jex R, Schaff H, Piehler J, et al: Repair of ascending aortic dissection: Influence of associated aortic valve insufficiency on early and late results. *J Thorac Cardiovasc Surg* 93:375, 1987.
25. Svensson L, Crawford E, Hess K, et al: Composite valve graft replacement of the proximal aorta: Comparison of techniques in 348 patients. *Ann Thorac Surg* 54:427, 1992.
26. von Schulthess G, Augustiny N: Calculation of T2 values versus phase imaging for the distinction between flow and thrombus in MR imaging. *Radiology* 164:549, 1987.
27. Soloman S, Brown, J, Glazer S, et al: Thoracic aortic dissection: Pitfalls and artifacts in MR imaging. *Radiology* 177:223, 1990.
28. White R, Ullyot D, Higgins C: MR imaging of the aorta after surgery for aortic dissection. *AJR* 150:87, 1988.
29. Schaefer S, Peshock R, Malloy C, et al: Nuclear magnetic resonance imaging in Marfan's syndrome. *J Am Coll Cardiol* 9:70, 1987.
30. Hinds S, Reisner S, Amico A, et al: Diagnosis of pericardial abnormalities by 2D-echo: A pathology-echocardiography correlation in 85 patients. *Am Heart J* 123:143, 1992.
31. Sechtem U, Tshcolakoff D, Higgins C: MRI of the abnormal pericardium. *AJR* 147:245, 1986.
32. Bluemke D, Lund J, Lipton M: Nuclear magnetic resonance assessment of pericardial disease, Marcus ML, Schelbert HR, Skorton DJ, Wolf GL (eds): *Cardiac Imaging: A Companion to Braunwald's Heart Disease*. Philadelphia, Saunders, 1991, chap 52.
33. Fowler N: constrictive pericarditis, in Fowler N (ed): *The Pericardium in Health and Disease*. Futura, Mt. Kisco, NY, 1985, chap 12.
34. Hancock E: Subacute effusive-constrictive pericarditis. *Circulation* 43:183, 1971.
35. Bush C, Stang J, Wooley C, et al: Occult constrictive pericardial disease: Diagnosis by rapid volume expansion and correction by pericardiectomy. *Circulation* 56:924, 1977.
36. Cheung P, Myers M, Arnold M: Early constrictive pericarditis and anaemia after Dressler's syndrome and inferior wall myocardial infarction. *Br Heart J* 65:360, 1991.
37. Hesse A, Altland K, Linke R, et al: Cardiac amyloidosis: A review and report of a new transthyretin (prealbumin) variant. *Br Heart J* 70:111, 1993.
38. Katritsis D, Wilmshurst P, Wendon J, et al: Primary restrictive cardiomyopathy: Clinical and pathologic characteristics. *J Am Coll Cardiol* 18:1230, 1991.
39. Daubert J, Gaede J, Cohen H: A fatal case of constrictive pericarditis due to a marked selective pericardial accumulation of amyloid. *Am J Med* 94:335, 1993.
40. Anand I, Ferrari R, Kalra G, et al: Pathogenesis of edema in constrictive pericarditis: Studies of body water and sodium renal function, hemodynamics, and plasma hormones before and after pericardiectomy. *Circulation* 83:1980, 1991.
41. DeValeria P, Baumgartner W, Casale A, et al: Current indications risks, and outcome after pericardiectomy. *Ann Thorac Surg* 52:219, 1991.
42. Hazelrigg S, Mack M, Landreneau R, et al: Thoracoscopic pericardiectomy for effusive pericardial disease. *Ann Thorac Surg* 56:792, 1993.
43. Vaitkus P, Kussmaul W: Constrictive pericarditis versus restrictive cardiomyopathy: A reappraisal and update of diagnostic criteria. *Am Heart J* 122:1431, 1991.
44. Gasperetti C, Sarembock I, Feldman M: Usefulness of dynamic hand exercise for developing maximal separation of left and right ventricular pressure at end-diastole and usefulness in distinguishing restrictive cardiomyopathy from constrictive pericardial disease. *Am J Cardiol* 69:1508, 1992.
45. Schoenfeld M, Supple E, Dec G, et al: Restrictive cardiomyopathy versus constrictive pericarditis: Role of endomyocardial biopsy in avoiding unnecessary throacotomy. *Circulation* 75:1012, 1987.
46. Gerson M, Colthar M, Fowler N: Differentiation of constrictive pericarditis and restrictive cardiomyopathy by radionuclide ventriculography. *Am Heart J* 118:114, 1989.
47. Aroney C, Ruddy T, Dichero H, et al: Differentiation of restrictive cardiomyopathy from pericardial constriction; Assessment of diastolic function by radionuclide angiography. *J Am Coll Cardiol* 13:1007, 1989.
48. Plotnick G, Vogel R: Noninvasive evaluation of diastolic function: Need for hemodynamically and clinically relevant variables. *J Am Coll Cardiol* 13:1015, 1989.
49. Hatle L, Appleton C, Popp R: Differentiation of constrictive pericarditis and restrictive cardiomyopathy by Doppler echocardiography. *Circulation* 79:357, 1989.
50. Klein A, Cohen G, Pietrolungo J, et al: Differentiation of constrictive pericarditis from restrictive cardiomyopathy by Doppler transesophageal echocardiographic measurements of respiratory variations in pulmonary venous flow. *J Am Coll Cardiol* 22:1935, 1993.
51. Oren R, Grover-McKay M, Stanford W, et al: Accurate preoperative diagnosis of pericardial constriction using cine computed tomography. *J Am Coll Cardiol* 22:832, 1993.
52. Masui T, Finck S, Higgins C: Constrictive pericarditis and restrictive cardiomyopathy: Evaluation with MR imaging. *Radiology* 182:369, 1992.
53. Soulen R, Stark D, Higgins C: Magnetic resonance imaging of constrictive pericardial disease. *Am J Cardiol* 55:480, 1985.
54. Mohiaddin R, Wann S, Underwood R: Vena caval flow: Assessment with cine MR velocity mapping. *Radiology* 177:537, 1990.
55. Wynne J, Braunwald E: The cardiomyopathies and myocarditides: toxic, chemical, and physical damage to the heart, in Braunwald E (ed): *Heart Disease*. Philadelphia, Saunders, 1992, chap. 43.
56. Sechtem U, Theissen P, Heindel W, et al: Diagnosis of left ventricular thrombi by magnetic resonance imaging and comparison with angiocardiography, computed tomography and echocardiography. *Am J Cardiol* 64:1195, 1989.
57. Jungehulsing M, Sechtem U, Theissen P, et al: Left ventricular thrombi: Evaluation with spin-echo and gradient-echo MR imaging. *Radiology* 182:225, 1992.
58. Chatterjee K, Collins P: Ischemic heart failure: Is prevention in sight? *Br Heart J* 70:5, 1993.
59. Buser P, Auffermann W, Holt W, et al: Noninvasive evaluation of global left ventricular function with use of cine nuclear magnetic resonance. *J Am Coll Cardiol* 13:1294, 1989.
60. Gaudio C, Tanzilli G, Mazzarotto P, et al: Comparison of left ventricular ejection fraction by magnetic resonance imaging and radionuclide ventriculography in idiopathic dilated cardiomyopathy. *Am J Cardiol* 67: 411, 1991.

61. McDonald K, Francis G, Matthews et al: Long-term oral nitrate therapy prevents chronic ventricular remodeling in the dog. *J Am Coll Cardiol* 21:514, 1993.

62. Doherty N, Seelow K, Suzuki J, et al: Applications of cine nuclear magnetic resonance imaging for sequential evaluation of response to angiotensin-converting enzyme inhibitor therapy in dilated cardiomyopathy. *J Am Coll Cardiol* 19:1294, 1992.

63. Sechtem U, Sommerhoff B, Markiewicz W, et al: Regional left ventricular wall thickening by magnetic resonance imaging: Evaluation in normal persons and patients with global and regional dysfunction. *Am J Cardiol* 59:145, 1987.

64. Fujita N, Duerinckx A, Higgins C: Variation in left ventricular regional wall stress with cine magnetic resonance imaging: Normal subjects versus dilated cardiomyopathy. *Am Heart J* 125:1337, 1993.

65. Shapiro E, Rogers W, Beyar R, et al: Determination of left ventricular mass by magnetic resonance imaging in hearts deformed by acute infarction. *Circulation* 79:706, 1989.

66. Milliken M, Stray-Gundersen J, Peshock R, et al: Left ventricular mass as determined by magnetic resonance imaging in male endurance athletes. *Am J Cardiol* 62:301, 1988.

67. McDonald K, Parrish T, Wennberg P, et al: Rapid, accurate and simultaneous noninvasive assessment of right and left ventricular mass with nuclear magnetic resonance imaging using the snapshot gradient method. *J Am Coll Cardiol* 19:1601, 1992.

68. Saeed M, Wendland M, Seelos K, et al: Effect of cilazapril on regional left ventricular wall thickness and chamber dimension following acute myocardial infarction: In vivo assessment using MRI. *Am Heart J* 123:1472, 1992.

69. Fujita N, Hartiala J, O'Sullivan M, et al: Assessment of left ventricular diastolic function in dilated cardiomyopathy with cine magnetic resonance imaging: Effect of an angiotensin converting enzyme inhibitor, benazepril. *Am Heart J* 125:171, 1993.

70. Hartiala J, Mostbeck G, Foster E, et al: Velocity-encoded cine MRI in the evaluation of left ventricular diastolic function: Measurement of mitral valve and pulmonary vein flow velocities and flow volume across the mitral valve. *Am Heart J* 125:1054, 1993.

71. Boxt L, Katz J, Kolb T, et al: Direct quantitation of right and left ventricular volumes with nuclear magnetic resonance imaging in patients with primary pulmonary hypertension. *J Am Coll Cardiol* 19:1508, 1992.

72. Doherty N, Fujita N, Caputo G, et al: Measurement of right ventricular mass in normal and dilated cardiomyopathic ventricles using cine magnetic resonance imaging. *Am J Cardiol* 69:1223, 1992.

73. Katz J, Whang J, Boxt L, et al: Estimation of right ventricular mass in normal subjects and in patients with primary pulmonary hypertension by nuclear magnetic resonance imaging. *J Am Coll Cardiol* 21:1475, 1993.

74. Suzuki J, Caputo G, Masui T, et al: Assessment of right ventricular diastolic and systolic function in patients with dilated cardiomyopathy using cine magnetic resonance imaging. *Am Heart J* 122:1035, 1991.

75. Suzuki J, Chang J, Caputo G, et al: Evaluation of right ventricular early diastolic filling by cine nuclear magnetic resonance imaging in patients with hypertrophic cardiomyopathy. *J Am Coll Cardiol* 18:120, 1991.

76. D'Silva S, Kohli A, Dalvi B, et al: MRI in right ventricular endomyocardial fibrosis. *Am Heart J* 123:1390, 1992.

77. Ricci C, Longo R, Pagnan L, et al: Magnetic resonance imaging in right ventricular dysplasia. *Am J Cardiol* 70:1589, 1992.

78. Miller D, Kendall B, Johnson G, et al: Magnetic resonance imaging in central nervous system sarcoidosis. *Neurology* 38:378, 1988.

79. Maron B: Hypertrophic cardiomyopathy. *Curr Probl Cardiol* 18:637, 1993.

80. Topol E, Traill T, Fortuin N: Hypertensive hypertrophic cardiomyopathy of the elderly. *N Engl J Med* 312:277, 1985.

81. Been M, Kean D, Smith M, et al: Nuclear magnetic resonance in hypertrophic cardiomyopathy. *Br Heart J* 54:48, 1985.

82. Casolo G, Trotta F, Rostagno C, et al: Detection of apical hypertrophic cardiomyopathy by magnetic resonance imaging. *Am Heart J* 117:468, 1989.

83. Suzuki J, Watanabe F, Takenaka K, et al: New subtype of apical hypertrophic cardiomyopathy identified with nuclear magnetic resonance imaging as an underlying cause of markedly inverted T waves. *J Am Coll Cardiol* 22:1175, 1993.

84. Weber J, Sasson Z, Rakowski H, et al: Apical hypertrophic cardiomyopathy: Clinical follow-up and diagnostic correlates. *J Am Coll Cardiol* 15:83, 1990.

85. Soulen R: Magnetic resonance imaging of great vessel, myocardial, and pericardial disease. *Circulation* 84 (suppl I):I–311, 1991.

86. Suzuki J, Sakamoto T, Takenaka K, et al: Assessment of the thickness of the right ventricular free wall by magnetic resonance imaging in patients with hypertrophic cardiomyopathy. *Br Heart J* 60:440, 1988.

87. Usui M, Inoue H, Suzuki J, et al: Relationship between distribution of hypertrophy and electrocardiographic changes in hypertrophic cardiomyopathy. *Am Heart J* 126:177, 1993.

88. Kaltwasswe J, Gottschalk T, Schalk K, et al: Non-invasive quantitation of liver iron-overload by magnetic resonance imaging. *Br J Haematol* 74:360, 1990.

89. Johnston D, Rice L, Vick G, et al: Assessment of tissue iron overload by nuclear magnetic resonance imaging. *Am J Med* 87:40, 1989.

90. Sechtem U, Higgins C, Sommerhoff B, et al: Magnetic resonance imaging of restrictive cardiomyopathy. *Am J Cardiol* 59:480, 1987.

91. Matsui S, Murakami E, Takekoshi N, et al: Myocardial tissue characterization by magnetic resonance imaging in Fabry's disease. *Am Heart J* 117:472, 1989.

92. Peters N, Poole-Wilson P: Myocarditis—Continuing clinical and pathologic confusion. *Am Heart J* 121:942, 1991.

93. Gagliardi M, Bevilacqua M, Di Renzi P: Usefulness of magnetic resonance imaging for diagnosis of acute myocarditis in infants and children, and comparison with endomyocardial biopsy. *Am J Cardiol* 68:1089, 1991.

94. Chandrarantna P, Bradley W, Kortman K, et al: Detection of acute myocarditis using nuclear magnetic resonance imaging. *Am J Med* 83:1144, 1987.

95. Aherne T, Tscholakoff D, Finkbeiner W, et al: Magnetic resonance imaging of cardiac transplants: The evaluation of rejection of cardiac allografts with and without immunosuppression. *Circulation* 74:145, 1986.

96. Wisenberg G, Pflugfelder P, Kostuk W, et al: Diagnostic applicability of magnetic resonance imaging in assessing human cardiac allograft rejection. *Am J Cardiol* 60:130, 1987.

97. Yun K, Niczporuk M, Daughters G, et al: Alterations in left ventricular diastolic twist mechanics during acute human cardiac allograft rejection. *Circulation* 83:962, 1991.

98. Kemkes B, Schutz A, Engelhardt M, et al: Noninvasive methods of rejection diagnosis after heart transplantation. *J Heart Transplant* 11:S221, 1992.

99. Smart F, Young J, Weilbaecher D, et al: Magnetic resonance imaging for assessment of tissue rejection after heterotopic heart transplantation. *J Heart Lung Transplant* 12:403, 1993.

100. Revel D, Chapelon C, Mathieu D, et al: Magnetic resonance imaging of human orthotopic transplantation: Correlation with endomyocardial biopsy. *J Heart Transplant* 8:139, 1989.

101. Walpoth B, Tshcopp A, Lazeyras R, et al: Magnetic resonance spectroscopy for assessing myocardial rejection in the transplanted rat heart. *J Heart Lung Transplant* 12:271, 1993.

102. Toyo-oka T, Nagayama K, Suzuki J, et al: Noninvasive assessment of cardiomyopathy development with simultaneous measurement of topical 1H-and 31P-magnetic resonance spectroscopy. *Circulation* 86:295, 1992.

103. Brunotte F, Peiffert B, Escanye J, et al: Nuclear magnetic resonance spectroscopy of excised human hearts. *Br Heart J* 68:272, 1992.

104. Perloff J, Child J: *Congenital Heart Disease in Adults.* Philadelphia, Saunders, 1991.

105. Fyler D: *Nadas' Pediatric Cardiology.* Hanley and Belfus, Inc, Philadelphia, 1992.

106. Link K, Loehr S, Martin E, et al: Congenital heart disease. *Coronary Art Dis* 4:340, 1993.

107. Kersting-Sommerhoff B, Diethelm L, Stranger P, et al: Evaluation of complex congenital ventricular anomalies with magnetic resonance imaging. *Am Heart J* 120:133, 1990.

108. Kersting-Sommerhoff B, Diethelm L, Teitel D, et al: Magnetic resonance imaging of congenital heart disease: Sensitivity and specificity using receiver operating charcteristic curve analysis. *Am Heart J* 118:155, 1989.

109. Didier D, Higgins C, Fisher M, et al: Congenital heart disease: Gated MR imaging in 72 patients. *Radiology* 158:227, 1986.

110. Chung K, Simpson I, Glass R, et al: Cine magnetic resonance imaging after surgical repair in patients with transposition of the great arteries. *Circulation* 77:104, 1988.

111. Kilner P, Firmin D, Rees R, et al: Valve and great vessel stenosis: Assessment with MR jet velocity mapping. *Radiology* 178:229, 1991.

112. Dinsmore R, Wismer G, Guyer D, et al: Magnetic resonance imaging of the interarterial septum and atrial septal defects. *Am J Radiol* 145:697, 1985.

113. Jacobstein M, Fletcher B, Goldstein S, et al: Evaluation of atrioventricular septal defect by magnetic resonance imaging. *Am J Cardiol* 55:1158, 1985.

114. Lowell D, Turner D, Smith S, et al: The detection of atrial and ventricular septal defects with electrocardiographically synchronized magnetic resonance imaging. *Circulation* 73:89, 1986.

115. Sechtem U, Pflugfelder P, Cassidy M, et al: Ventricular septal defect: Visualization of shunt flow and determination of shunt size by cine MR imaging. *Am J Radiol* 149:689, 1987.

116. Diethelm L, Dery R, Lipton M, et al: Atrial-level shunts: Sensitivity and specificity of MR in diagnosis. *Radiology* 162:181, 1987.

117. Didier D, Higgins C: Identification and localization of ventricular septal defect by gated magnetic resonance imaging. *Am J Cardiol* 57:1363, 1988.

118. Brenner L, Caputo G, Mostbeck G, et al: Quantification of left to right atrial shunts with velocity-endcoded cine nucear magnetic resonance imaging. *J Am Coll Cardiol* 20:1246, 1992.

119. Didier D, Higgins C: Estimation of pulmonary vascular resistance by MRI in patients with congenital cardiovascular shunt lesions. *Am J Radiol* 146:919, 1986.

122. Boxer R, Fishman M, LaCorte M, et al: Diagnosis and postoperative evaluation of supravalvular aortic stenosis by magnetic resonance imaging. *Am J Cardiol* 58:367, 1986.

123. Fletcher B, Jacobstein M: MRI of congenital abnormalities of the great arteries. *Am J Radiol* 146:941, 1986.

124. Kersting-Sommerhoff B, Sechtem U, Fisher M, et al: MR imaging of congenital anomalies of the aortic arch. *Am J Radiol* 149:9, 1987.

125. von Schulthess G, Higashino S, Higgins S, et al: Coarctation of the aorta: MR imaging. *Radiology* 158:469, 1986.

126. Marx G, Allen H: Accuracy and pitfalls of Doppler evaluation of the pressure gradient in aortic coarctation. *J Am Coll Cardiol* 7:1379, 1986.

127. Rees S, Somerville J, Ward C, et al: Coarctation of the aorta: MR imaging in late postoperative assessment. *Radiology* 173:499, 1989.

128. Mohiaddin R, Kilner P, Rees S, et al: Magnetic resonance volume flow and jet velocity mapping in aortic coarctation. *J Am Coll Cardiol* 22:1515, 1993.

129. Boxer R, LaCorte M, Singh S, et al: Nuclear magnetic resonance imaging in evaluation and follow-up of children treated for coarctation of the aorta. *J Am Coll Cardiol* 7:1095, 1986.

130. Soulen R, Kan J, Mitchell S, et al: Evaluation of balloon angioplasty of coarctation restenosis by magnetic resonance imaging. *Am J Cardiol* 60:343, 1987.

131. Pucillo A, Schecter A, Kay R, et al: Magnetic resonance imaging of vascular conduits in coarctation of the aorta. *Am Heart J* 117:482, 1989.

132. Bisset G, Strife J, Kirks D, et al: Vascular rings: MR imaging. *Am J Radiol* 149:251, 1987.

133. Rees R, Somerville J, Underwood S, et al: Magnetic resonance imaging of the pulmonary arteries and their systemic connections in pulmonary atresia: Comparison with angiographic and surgical findings. *Br Heart J* 58:621, 1987.

134. Mirowitz S, Gutierrez F, Canter C, et al: Tetralogy of Fallot: MR findings. *Radiology* 171:207, 1989.

135. Caputo G, Kondo C, Masui T, et al: Right and left lung perfusion: In vitro and in vivo validation with oblique-angle, velocity-encoded cine MR imaging. *Radiology* 180:693, 1991.

136. Rebergen S, Chin J, Ottenkamp J, et al: Pulmonary regurgitation in the late postoperative follow-up of tetralogy of Fallot: Volumetric quantitation by nuclear magnetic resonance velocity mapping. *Circulation* 88:2257, 1993.

137. Julsrud P, Ehman R, Hagler D, et al: Extracardiac vasculature in candidates for fontan surgery: MR imaging. *Radiology* 173:503, 1989.

138. Niwa K, Uschishiba M, Aotsuka H, et al: Magnetic resonance imaging of heterotaxia in infants. *J Am Coll Cardiol* 23:177, 1994.

139. Matinez J, Mohiaddin R, Kilner P, et al: Obstruction in extracardiac ventriculopulmonary conduits: Value of nuclear magnetic resonance imaging with velocity mapping and Doppler echocardiography. *J Am Coll Cardiol* 20:338, 1992.

140. Canter C, Gutierrez F, Molina P, et al: Noninvasive diagnosis of right-sided extracardiac conduit obstruction by combined magnetic resonance imaging and continuous-wave Doppler echocardiography. *J Thorac Cardiovasc Surg* 101:724, 1991.

141. Rees S, Somerville J, Warnes C, et al: Comparison of magnetic resonance imaging with echocardiography and radionuclide angiography in assessing cardiac function and anatomy following Mustard's operation for transposition of the great arteries. *Am J Cardiol* 61:1316, 1988.

142. Colucci W, Braunwald E: Primary tumors of the heart, Braunwald E (ed): *Heart Disease,* Philadelphia, Saunders, 1992.

143. Salcedo E, Cohen G, White R, et al: Cardiac tumors: Diagnosis and management. *Curr Probl Cardiol* 17:77, 1992.

144. Krikler D, Rode J, Davies M, et al: Atrial myxoma: A tumour in search of its origins. *Br Heart J* 67:89, 1992.

145. Putnam J, Sweeney M, Colon R, et al: Primary cardiac sarcomas. *Ann Thorac Surg* 51:906, 1991.

146. Jack C, Cleland J, Geddes J: Left atrial rhabdomyosarcoma and the use of digital gated computed tomography in its diagnosis. *Br Heart J* 55:305, 1986.

147. Amparo E, Higgins C, Farmer D, et al: Gated MRI of cardiac and paracardiac masses: Initial experience. *Am J Radiol* 143:1151, 1984.

148. Camesas A, Lichstein E, Kramer J, et al: Complementary use of two-dimensional echocardiography and magnetic resonance imaging in the diagnosis of ventricular myxoma. *Am Heart J* 114:440, 1987.

149. Freedberg R, Kronzon I, Rumancik W, et al: The contribution of magnetic resonance imaging to the evaluation of intracardiac tumors diagnosed by echocardiography. *Circulation* 77:96, 1988.

150. Go R, O'Donnell J, Underwood D, et al: Comparison of gated cardiac MRI and 2-D echocardiography of intracardiac neoplasms. *Am J Radiol* 145:21, 1985.

151. Lund J, Ehman R, Julsrud P, et al: Cardiac masses: Assessment by MR imaging. *Am J Radiol* 152:469, 1989.

152. Menegus M, Greenberg M, Spindola-Franco H, et al: Magnetic resonance imaging of suspected atrial tumors. *Am Heart J* 123:1260, 1992.

153. Winkler M, Higgins C: Suspected Intracardiac Masses: Evaluation with MR imaging. *Radiology* 165:117, 1987.

154. Pizzarello R, Goldberg S, Goldman M, et al: Tumor of the heart diagnosed by magnetic resonance imaging. *J Am Coll Cardiol* 5:989, 1985.

155. Smythe J, Dyck J, Smallhorn J, et al: Natural history of cardiac rhabdomyoma in infancy and childhood. *Am J Cardiol* 66:1247, 1990.

156. Fazekas K, Ungi I, Tiszlavicz L: Primary malignant mesothelioma of the pericardium. *Am Heart J* 124:227, 1992.

157. Applegate P, Tajik A, Ehman R, et al: Two-dimensional echocardiographic and magnetic resonance imaging observations in massive lipomatous hypertrophy of the atrial septum. *Am J Cardiol* 59:489, 1987.

158. Smith A, Panidis I, Berger S, et al: Large atrial septal aneurysm mimicking a cystic right atrial mass. *Am Heart J* 120:714, 1990.

159. Conti V, Saydari R, Amparo E: Paraganglioma of the heart: Value of magnetic resonance imaging in the preoperative evaluation. *Chest* 90:604, 1986.

160. Miralles A, Bracamonte L, Soncul H, et al: Cardiac tumors: Clinical experience and surgical results in 74 patients. *Ann Thorac Surg* 52:886, 1991.

161. Beache G, Wedeen V, Dinsmore R: Magnetic resonance imaging evaluation of left ventricular dimensions and function and pericardial and myocardial disease. *Coronary Art Dis* 4:328, 1993.

162. Dulce M, Nostbeck G, Friese K, et al: Quantification of the left ventricular volumes and function with cine MR imaging: Comparison of geometric models with three-dimensional data. *Radiology* 188:371, 1993.

163. Sakuma H, Fujita N, Foo T, et al: Evaluation of left ventricular volume and mass with breath-hold cine MR imaging. *Radiology* 188:377, 1993.

164. Higgins C: Which standard has the gold? *J Am Coll Cardiol* 19:1608, 1992.

165. Peshock R, Rokey R, Malloy C, et al: Assessment of myocardial systolic wall thickening using nuclear magnetic resonance imaging. *J Am Coll Cardiol* 14:653, 1989.

166. Underwood S, Rees R, Savage P, et al: Assessment of regional left ventricular function by magnetic resonance. *Br Heart J* 56:334, 1986.

167. Zerhouni E: Myocardial tagging by magnetic resonance imaging. *Coronary Art Dis* 4:334, 1993.

168. Zerhouni E, Parish D, Rogers W, et al: Human heart: Tagging with MR imaging-A method for noninvasive assessment of myocardial motion. *Radiology* 169:59, 1988.

169. Axel L, Dougherty L: Heart wall motion: Improved method of spatial modulation of magnetization for MR imaging. *Radiology* 172:349, 1989.

170. Mirowitz S, Lee J, Gutierrez F, et al: Normal signal-void patterns in cardiac cine MR images. *Radiology* 176:49, 1990.

171. Mostbeck G, Caputo G, Higgins C: MR measurement of blood flow in the cardiovascular system. *Am J Radiol* 159:453, 1992.

172. Cranney G, Benjelloun H, Perry G, et al: Rapid assessment of aortic regurgitation and left ventricular function using cine nuclear magnetic resonance imaging and the proximal convergence zone. *Am J Cardiol* 71:1074, 1993.

173. Simpson I, Maciel B, Moises V, et al: Cine magnetic resonance imaging and color Doppler flow mapping displays of flow velocity, spatial acceleration, and jet formation: A comparative in vitro study. *Am Heart J* 126:1165, 1993.

174. Casolo G, Zampa V, Rega L, et al: Evaluation of mitral stenosis by cine magnetic resonance imaging. *Am Heart J* 123:1252, 1992.

175. Sondergaard L, Hildebrandt P, Lindvig K: Valve area and cardiac output in aortic stenosis: Quantification by magnetic resonance velocity mapping. *Am Heart J* 127:1156, 1993.

176. Anderson C, Brown J: Cardiovascular magnetic resonance imaging: Evaluation of myocardial perfusion. *Coronary Art Dis* 4:354, 1993.

177. Johns J, Leavitt M, Newell J, et al: Quantitation of acute myocardial infarct size by nuclear magnetic resonance imaging. *J Am Coll Cardiol* 15:143, 1990.

178. Higgins C: Nuclear magnetic resonance (NMR) imaging in ischemic heart disease. *J Am Coll Cardiol* 15:150, 1990.

179. Manning W, Atkinson D, Grossman W, et al: First-pass nuclear magnetic resonance imaging studies using gadolinium-DPTA in patients with coronary artery disease. *J Am Coll Cardiol* 18:959, 1991.

180. Wilke N, Simm C, Zhang J, et al: Contrast-enhanced first pass myocardial perfusion imaging: Correlation between myocardial blood flow in dogs at rest and during hyperemia. *Mag Res Med* 29:485, 1993.

181. Edelman R, Li W: Contrast-enhanced echo-planar MR imaging of myocardial perfusion: Preliminary study in humans. *Radiology* 190:771, 1994.

182. Pennell D: Magnetic resonance imaging during pharmacologic stress. *Coronary Art Dis* 4:345, 1993.

183. Pennell D, Underwood S, Ell P, et al: Dipyridamole magnetic-resonance imaging: A comparison with thallium-201 emission tomography. *Br Heart J* 64:362, 1990.

184. Pennell D, Underwood S, Manzarea C, et al: Magnetic resonance imaging during dobutamine stress in coronary artery disease. *Am J Cardiol* 70:34, 1992.

185. Manning W, Li W, Boyle N, et al: Fat-suppressed breath-hold magnetic resonance coronary angiography. *Circulation* 87:94, 1993.

186. Meyer C, Hu B, Nishimura D: Fast spiral coronary artery imaging. *Mag Res Med* 28:202, 1992.

187. Doyle M, Scheidegger M, de Graaf R, et al: Coronary artery imaging in multiple 1-sec breath holds. *Mag Res Imaging* 11:3, 1992.

188. Steinberg E: Magnetic resonance coronary angiography—Assessing an emerging technology. *N Engl M Med* 328:879, 1993.

189. White R, Caputo G, Mark A, et al: Coronary artery bypass graft patency: Noninvasive evaluation with MR imaging. *Radiology* 164:681, 1987.

190. Aurigemma G, Reichek N, Axel L, et al: Noninvasive determination of coronary artery bypass graft patency by cine magnetic resonance imaging. *Circulation* 80:1595, 1989.

191. Bogren H, Buonocore M: Measurement of coronary artery flow reserve by magnetic resonance velocity mapping in the aorta. *Lancet* 341:899, 1993.

Chapter 12

Magnetic Resonance Angiography of the Renal and Visceral Arteries

John A. Kaufman / Martin R. Prince / E. Kent Yucel

Magnetic resonance angiography (MRA) of the renal, celiac, superior mesenteric, and inferior mesenteric arteries has many potentially important applications in several patient populations. Magnetic resonance angiography can obtain images of visceral artery blood flow in multiple planes, noninvasively, regardless of renal function, and without iodinated contrast. These qualities set MRA apart from conventional angiography, ultrasonography, and nuclear medicine. Renal artery imaging is the paradigm for visceral artery MRA, as stenosis or occlusion of these vessels is more commonly suspected than celiac or superior mesenteric artery disease, and the renal arteries are the most challenging to image due to their size, course, depth within the body, and anatomic variability. Celiac, superior mesenteric artery, and IMA imaging follow in difficulty and clinical importance.

The role of MRA in the evaluation of the visceral vessels is not yet defined. Controlled comparative studies with more traditional imaging techniques are still in progress. Other new technologies, such as computed tomography (CT) angiography, may prove equal or superior to MRA in some patients. Furthermore, the cost of MRA in comparison to other technologies must be balanced against its impact upon patient management. As techniques improve and become more widely disseminated, the place of MRA in the workup of the patient with suspected visceral vessel occlusive disease may become more apparent. It is our hope that the information presented in this chapter will facilitate this process.

Renal and abdominal visceral vessel MRA is most useful when the abnormality suspected is in the proximal portion of the vessel. Presently, the greatest limitation of visceral artery MRA is inconsistent visualization of the vessels beyond the first several centimeters. Normal vessels in individuals with normal cardiac output can frequently be imaged to second- and third-order branches. As arteries become tortuous and stenotic and flow in the aorta becomes slower and more turbulent, blood inflow is diminished and signal is degraded. The net result is visualization of only the proximal portion of the vessel. When evaluation of branch vessels is essential, as in hypertensive individuals with normal renal function in whom segmental renal artery stenosis is suspected, imaging with MRA may not be satisfactory.

The second most important limitation of visceral vessel MRA is resolution. This is due in part to the central location of the visceral arteries within the body. By contrast with extremity, shoulder, neck, head, breast, and prostate imaging, it it is not possible to construct a renal artery or superior mesenteric artery coil that can be closely applied to the structure of interest. Most centers therefore perform visceral artery MRA in the body coil and attempt to overcome the problem of resolution by employing thin slices, multiple excitations, large matrices, intravenous contrast, and modified pulse sequences. These manipulations result in longer imaging times, increasing the likelihood of patient motion artifacts, which in turn further degrade image quality. Resolution is also constrained by hardware and software, which are presently limited to matrices of 512×512 pixels or less. In contradistinction, state-of-the-art digital subtraction angiography (DSA) units function with matrices of 1024×1024 pixels. An example of the effect of this limited resolution is the difficulty in detecting and evaluating small accessory renal arteries on MRA (Fig. 12-1).

Image postprocessing is an important aspect of renal and visceral vessel MRA. The renal and visceral vessels are central in location in the body and normally follow complex curves. Frequently, MRA data must be reconstructed or reformatted in different planes in order to view the vessels as continuous structures. Careful selection of only the most pertinent images is important during postprocessing. Uncritical reliance upon preprogramed reconstructions will lead to diagnostic errors.

Visceral vessel MRA should never be performed without precise clinical information. As with conventional angiography, familiarity with the patient's history and other imaging studies is necessary to perform and interpret the MR angiogram properly. In particular, lack of knowledge about prior vascular surgery may result in failure to image bypass grafts,

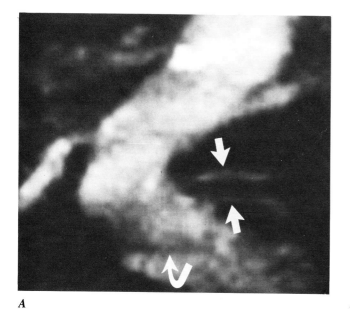

A

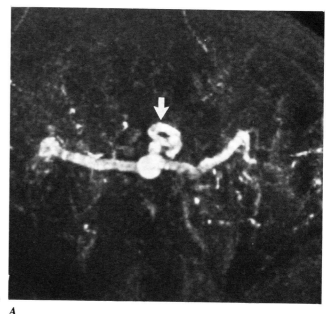

A

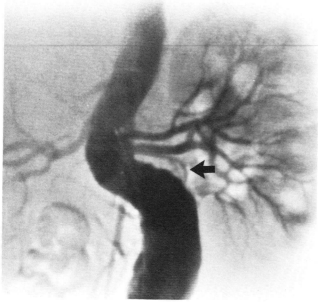

B

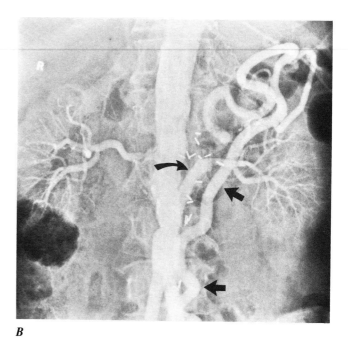

B

FIGURE 12-1   *A*. The detection of small accessory renal arteries can be difficult, especially in the presence of aortic disease. A coronal maximum intensity pixel reprojection of an axial three-dimensional TOF multiple overlapping thin slab acquisition (MOTSA) angiogram in a patient with a known abdominal aortic aneurysm demonstrated a single right and two left (*straight arrows*) renal arteries. The curved arrow identifies the interface between the slabs.   *B*. Conventional digital subtraction aortogram of the same patient reveals a third small left renal artery (*arrow*), missed on the MR angiogram.

FIGURE 12-2   *A*. Axial collapse of a two-dimensional TOF MR angiogram of the pelvis in a patient who has had a prior aortoiliac graft. A large, tortuous vessel is noted anterior to the aorta (*arrow*).   *B*. Conventional abdominal aortogram from the same patient reveals a tortuous graft of the left iliac to the inferior mesenteric artery (*straight arrows*). Also present is a left aortorenal bypass graft (*curved arrow*) surrounded by metallic clips. The imaging of the postoperative patient requires a thorough understanding of the patient's postsurgical anatomy.

which are frequently extraanatomic in location (Fig. 12-2). Although MRA is noninvasive, it remains expensive and time-consuming. Active participation by a physician in the scanning process is generally required to prevent too many repeat or incomplete exams.

RENAL ARTERY MRA

Accurate, noninvasive imaging of renal artery disease is one of the major goals of radiology. Although less than 5 percent of hypertension is thought to be vascular in etiology, hypertension is so pervasive that renal artery disease is suspected in large numbers of patients. The clinical features that suggest renovascular disease include hypertension presenting at a young age, blood pressure that is difficult to control despite multiple medications, an accelerated course, or severe hypertension in combination with azotemia. As the results of percutaneous and surgical intervention for renovascular disease have improved, the priority assigned to establishing this diagnosis has increased. Intravenous digital subtraction angiography (IV DSA), nuclear medicine studies (in conjunction with an angiotensin II blocking agent), ultrasound, MRA, and CT angiography have all been proposed as noninvasive methods of establishing the diagnosis. Conventional angiography remains the "gold standard" in the evaluation of these patients.

Patient selection for renal artery MRA is governed by the size and length of the vessel that can be imaged. Until renal arteries can be routinely visualized beyond the first 3 to 4 cm and accessory vessels identified and evaluated with confidence, the clinical utility of MRA will be limited to patients with suspected proximal renal artery disease. Magnetic resonance angiography cannot yet provide definitive imaging for patients with suspected renal artery fibromuscular dysplasia, branch vessel disease, peripheral emboli, aneurysms, or arteriovenous fistulas. Evaluation of renal transplant donor anatomy still requires conventional angiography because of the critical importance of identifying proximal bifurcations, accessory arteries, and early intimal disease. A good triage rule is that if a patient will require conventional angiography regardless of the results of the MRA, then simply proceed directly to conventional angiography. Furthermore, surgical intervention on the basis of MRA alone is not recommended at this time unless a patient has contraindications to conventional angiography.

The renal arteries can be imaged by all MRA techniques. Selection of a particular protocol is dependent upon available hardware, software, and scheduling constraints. For example, three-dimensional phase-contrast images have the advantage of high resolution, excellent background suppression, and visualization of flow in multiple directions. Disadvantages include the long time required for acquisition and reconstruction of the data and the difficulty in selecting an optimal velocity encoding range.

Development of a reliable but flexible protocol is the key to consistent renal artery MRA. If different techniques or parameters are chosen for each study, results will be inconsistent and frustrating. Conversely, a protocol that does not allow adjustments for such variables as widely spaced accessory arteries or grafts with inferior-to-superior flow (i.e., iliorenal grafts) will lead to diagnostic errors. Renal artery MRA studies should include both anatomic and angiographic series. The anatomic images permit an assessment of the kidneys and the large vascular structures. Frequently one series is sufficient. The MRA sequences address the renal vasculature. In general, two MRA sequences employing different techniques [i.e., two- and three-dimensional time-of-

flight (TOF)] or imaging in two different planes (i.e., axial and coronal two-dimensional TOF) are recommended. A description of each of the elements of a renal artery MRA study follows.

Scout Images

A typical renal MRA study should begin with a T1-weighted spin-echo (black blood) sequences in at least one plane. These are used to evaluate renal parenchyma for size and configuration, assess the number of renal arteries, and inspect the aorta for associated aneurysmal disease. In addition, these images serve as the scouts for the angiographic series. We have found that interleaved 10-mm slices in the sagittal plane [respiratory compensation, no phase wrap, echo time (TE) 12, repetition time (TR) 426, 40-cm field of view (FOV), 24 slices, 256 × 128 pixel matrix, four excitations] frequently provide all of the information necessary to proceed with the study. In particular, the renal artery origins can be identified as black dots as they arise from the aorta or course through the retroperitoneal fat (Fig. 12-3). One should keep in mind that the right renal artery frequently arises from a more anterior location than the left but travels posterior to the inferior vena cava (IVC) (Fig. 12-4). If the arteries are not sufficiently black on this sequence, then the TE can be

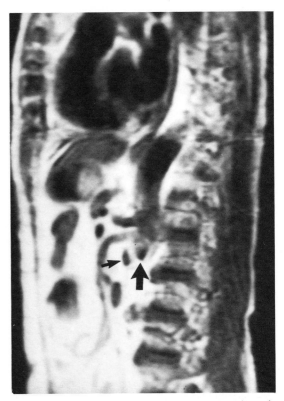

FIGURE 12-3 Sagittal T1 image of the aorta. The left renal artery ostium (*large arrow*) appears as a black flow void arising from the aorta just below the superior mesenteric artery. The left renal vein (*small arrow*) can be seen anterior to the aorta at the same level.

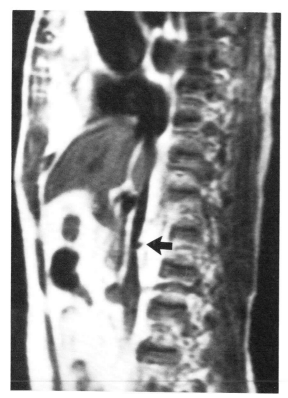

FIGURE 12-4   Sagittal T1 image from the same patient to the right of the aorta demonstrating the right renal artery (*arrow*) posterior to the inferior vena cava (IVC).

increased to 20 or 30 ms in order to provide additional time for intravoxel dephasing.

Approximately 30 percent of the population have supernumerary renal arteries, typically a single accessory vessel, but usually no more than three. These vessels may be submillimeter in diameter or equal in size to the main renal artery. Although accessory renal arteries can arise from as low as the common iliac arteries, they are rarely found to originate above the superior mesenteric artery. Horseshoe kidneys are associated with an especially high incidence of multiple renal arteries. When a low accessory artery or complex renal anatomy is suspected but not convincingly demonstrated on the sagittal T1 images, a coronal T1 weighted series can be added.

Two-Dimensional TOF MRA

Two-dimensional TOF MRA of the renal arteries is fast, allowing imaging during suspended respiration, and sensitive to slow flow, which is advantageous when imaging severely diseased arteries or distal branches. These attributes are counterbalanced by the thick slices required to maintain an adequate signal-to-noise ratio (typically at least 3 mm in the body coil), which limits the ability to resolve small vessels. Two-dimensional TOF renal MR angiograms can be acquired

in the coronal plane with a gradient echo pulse sequence using breath holding for each slice, first-order gradient moment nulling; a flip angle of 30°; TE, 6.7; TR, 22; 32-cm FOV; slice thickness, 2.9 mm; 256 × 192 pixel matrix; two excitations; and frequency encoding in the superior-to-inferior plane.

By centering the slices at the level of the L4 vertebral body, coverage of the abdominal aorta is maximized. If the slices are centered on the renal arteries, the intrathoracic structures will occupy approximately the upper third of each slice. Anterior-to-posterior coverage should favor the retroperitoneum, so that ony two or three slices fall anterior to the aorta. In patients with large abdominal aortic aneurysms (AAA), some coverage of the anterior portion of the aneurysm may have to be sacrificed.

Coronal sequences do not require inferior presaturation bands because the IVC flow becomes relatively saturated simply from being in plane with the slice. However, signal from the renal veins may remain bright, which can make evaluation of the arteries difficult. Some systems allow placement of saturation bands over each kidney to saturate blood flowing into the renal veins (Fig. 12-5A and B). These saturation pulses substantially increase the TR and consequently the scan time. If this makes the scan time too long, an alternative approach is to apply a single coronal oblique saturation pulse graphically prescribed on the sagittal localizer to cover the posterior/inferior aspects of both kidneys and the IVC inferiorly. Careful positioning of these saturation bands is important, because misplacement of the saturation bands may render them either ineffective or detrimental.

Two-dimensional TOF images may also be acquired in oblique coronal or axial planes. In the case of the former, the intent is to image as much of the renal artery in one slice as possible as it courses obliquely through the retroperitoneum. Different sequences are required for the right and left arteries. When imaging in the axial plane, an inferior presaturation pulse is necessary to eliminate signal from the IVC. A bright IVC is not only distracting but can obscure the right renal artery, which lies in close approximation to the posterior surface of the vena cava. Sagittal two-dimensional TOF images are rarely useful in renal artery imaging.

Cardiac gating, when available, is helpful in minimizing pulsatility artifacts but increases scanning time. Cardiac gating also allows reordering the phase encoding such that the center of *k* space is collected during the period of maximum inflow. This helps to minimize in-plane saturation effects.

Two-dimensional TOF images can be acquired in a cine mode, with multiple images collected at one level throughout the cardiac cycle. We have found few applications for this technique when evaluating patients for renal artery stenosis. When involvement of a renal artery by an aortic dissection is suspected, however, cine sequences are very useful. We prefer a phase contrast (PC) two-dimensional axial cine sequence in this situation, for reasons which are discussed below, under "Two-Dimensional Phase-Contrast Imaging."

is possible with two-dimensional TOF MRA. Smaller voxels result in less signal loss from the intravoxel dephasing that occurs in turbulent flow. In addition, the resolution of small vascular structures is improved compared with two-dimensional TOF MRA. Conversely, three-dimensional TOF MRA suffers from insensitivity to slow flow and increased saturation effects, because data are acquired in a large volume or slab rather than a single slice. The degree of saturation will vary depending on patient-specific variables such as blood velocity, direction of flow, and turbulence or imaging parameters such as flip angle, TR, and the size of the volume.

Axial acquisitions positioned such that the renal arteries are roughly at the junction of the top and middle thirds of voume produce the best results (Fig. 12-6). If the renal artery origins are too close to the top of the volume, the vessel may curve up and out of view. However, if the vessels are too low in the volume, saturation effects may become severe, limiting the distance over which renal arteries can be identified. Positioning a three-dimensional TOF volume becomes a logistical problem when the arteries are widely spaced or multiple. In this situation, two or more overlapping volumes may be necessary to provide adequate coverage of the aorta. A typical three-dimensional TOF sequence uses a T1-weighted sagittal image to prescribe the volume, inferior saturation, a spoiled gradient echo pulse sequence (SPGR),

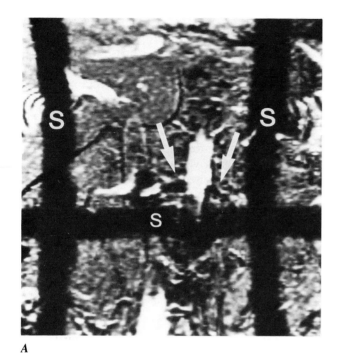

A

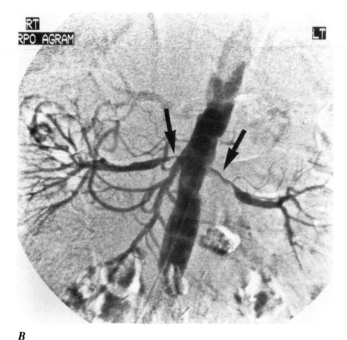

B

FIGURE 12-5 *A.* Coronal two-dimensional TOF MR angiogram of a patient with bilateral proximal renal artery stenoses (*arrows*). Venous saturation bands have been placed over the renal parenchyma (large S) and the IVC (small s). *B.* Conventional digital subtraction angiogram from the same patient confirming the bilateral proximal renal artery stenoses (*arrows*).

Three-Dimensional TOF

Three-dimensional TOF MRA sequences use phase encoding in the slice select direction to achieve higher resolution than

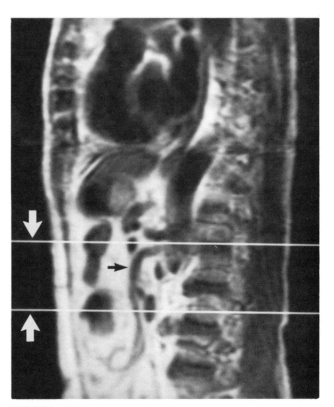

FIGURE 12-6 Sagittal T1 from the same patient as in Fig. 12-3 with an axial volume prescribed to cover the renal arteries (*white arrows*). Note that the top of the volume begins just above the origin of the superior mesenteric artery (*black arrow*).

first-order gradient moment nulling; flip angle of 25°; TE, 6.9; TR, 25; 32-cm FOV; 28 1.5-mm slices; 256 × 256 pixel matrix; two excitations, and anterior-posterior phase encoding.

A number of modifications can be made to the basic three-dimensional TOF sequence to improve visualization of the renal arteries. Availability will vary from site to site, depending on hardware and software configurations. The problem of saturation within a volume can be mitigated by obtaining and interpolating multiple overlapping thin volumes or slabs (MOTSA). This technique permits coverage of a longer aortic segment than is possible with a single slab, but it increases scanning times over single-volume acquisitions. Reprojections and reformations of these images frequently have a faint "venetian blind" artifact (horizontal lines in the imaging plane due to the mismatch in signal intensity where the slabs overlap) (Fig. 12-1). Although usually of minimal consequence, this artifact can be problematic if the junction between slabs falls precisely on the renal artery of interest.

Dynamic contrast-enhanced three-dimensional TOF angiography may prove particularly useful in situations where the flow is especially turbulent, slow, and in plane, such as a stenotic renal artery arising from an aortic aneurysm. Large doses of gadolinium chelates are required, up to 0.3 mmol/kg, injected continuously during the acquisition (Fig. 12-7A, B, and C). The flip angle should be increased to 40° to maximize the signal from the contrast-enhanced blood. Additional modifications include cardiac gating, but this incurs a time penalty. Magnetization transfer pulses dramatically improve the background suppression in intracranial three-dimensional TOF MRA. Applications to visceral artery imaging are not beneficial due to the minimal magnetization transfer effects in fat tissue. Spatially varying the flip angle through the volume reduces saturation effects in single-volume acquisitions (tilted optimized nonsaturating excitation, or TONE), improving the intravascular signal within the slab.

Two-Dimensional Phase-Contrast Imaging

Phase-contrast (PC) imaging has the advantages of short acquisition times, excellent background suppression, and the ability to image selected flow velocities and directions. The ability to view images with directional flow encoding can be valuable when one is trying to distinguish the left renal artery from the left renal vein. Furthermore, in addition to the speed and velocity images, magnitude images are generated that provide an additional opportunity to evaluate the vessels and their surroundings. The major limitations of two-dimensional PC imaging are the requirement to image the entire artery at one velocity sensitization, thick slices, and sensitivity to pulsatility.

Two-dimensional PC sequences can be performed as axial or coronal slices, with breath holding, velocity encoding of 40 cm/s in all directions, graphic prescription from the sag-

ittal scout, first-order gradient moment nulling, a flip angle of 30°, TR of 40, TE of 8.4, 32-cm FOV, 3-mm slices, 256 × 128 pixel matrix, and two excitations. When imaging in the coronal plane, it is important to direct the phase encoding from right to left to prevent pulsatility artifact from the heart from creating phase artifact over the aorta, thus obscuring the renal artery origins. With axial acquisitions, the phase encoding should be directed anterior-posterior to project pulsatility artifacts away from the renal arteries. Most renal arteries can be adequately imaged with 8 to 10 slices in each plane. Accessory vessels may require additional sequences if they arise distant from the main renal arteries. Cardiac gating, when available, will reduce pulsatility artifacts at the expense of increasing scan time.

Involvement of renal artery ostia by an aortic dissection is a clinical concern when patients with dissections develop renal insufficiency or severe hypertension. In this situation we employ a thick-slice (10 mm) cine two-dimensional PC MRA axial sequence with flow encoding in the superior-to-inferior direction at 40 cm/s. The slices are positioned to cover the renal artery ostia, with a flip angle of 30°, minimum TE, 256 × 128 pixel matrix, one excitation, and reconstructions during 12 to 16 phases of the cardiac cycle. The velocity images are useful for identifying the two aortic channels as well as extension of the flap into the renal artery ostia. The magnitude images provide anatomic information but are sometimes limited by an inability to distinguish between slow flow and thrombus in the false lumen.

Three-Dimensional PC Imaging

Three-dimensional PC MRA offers high spatial resolution, an excellent signal-to-noise ratio, and less susceptibility to saturation. The major disadvantage of this technique is the long time required for acquisition and reconstruction. This is because at least four data sets must be acquired to image flow in all three directions as well as a mask for subtraction. With some systems, reconstruction times not only approach scanning times but processing of subsequent acquisitions is not possible during the reconstruction period, effectively "freezing" the scanner. If the wrong velocity sensitization or volume position was chosen at the beginning of the study, this will only become apparent after a long wait for the images. For this reason, three-dimensional PC MRA sequences of the renal arteries are typically employed as the final acquisitions in clinical scanning, in combination with less time-consuming techniques.

In normal individuals three-dimensional PC MR angiograms frequently depict the renal arteries well beyond the bifurcation into the anterior and posterior divisions and not uncommonly to the segmental level. Results are not as consistent in patients with diseased vessels, however, in whom flow velocities may vary between kidneys and may be slow distal to stenoses. In situations where the choice of flow sensitization is not clear, two-dimensional PC MRA images

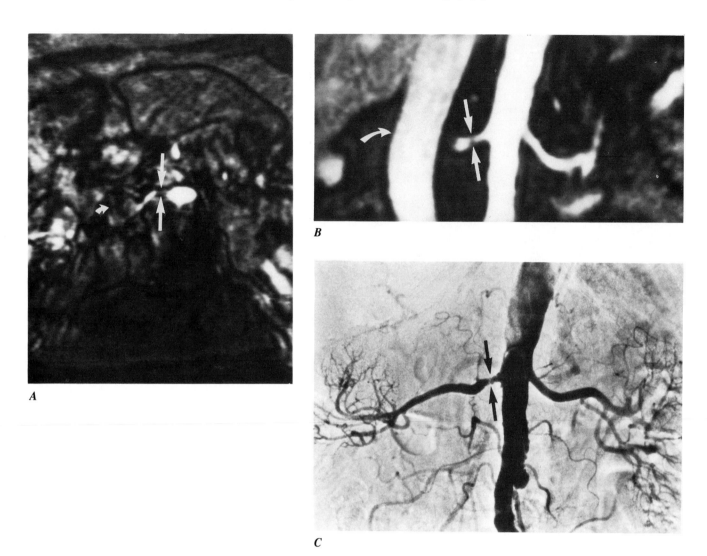

FIGURE 12-7   *A*. Oblique axial reformation of a three-dimensional TOF axial MR angiogram of a patient with hypertension. Signal loss is noted at the origin of the right renal artery (*straight arrows*). Because of an inferior saturation pulse, the IVC flow is not visualized (*curved arrow*).   *B*. Oblique coronal reformation of a dynamic gadolinium-enhanced three-dimensional TOF axial MR angiogram of the same patient, demonstrating that the lesion is a focal, proximal stenosis (*straight arrows*). Dense IVC opacification is present, possibly due to increased cardiac output in this hypertensive individual.   *C*. Conventional contrast angiogram confirming the location and morphology of the right renal artery stenosis (*straight arrows*).

can be quickly obtained to test different velocities. The three-dimensional PC MRA volume can be acquired with an SPGR pulse sequence, 28 axial slices 1.5 mm thick, first-order gradient moment nulling, TR of 34, TE of 10, flip angle of 20°, flow sensitization in all three directions at 30 to 50 cm/s, a 256 × 128 pixel matrix, inferior saturation, phase encoding in the anterior-posterior direction, and one excitation (Fig. 12-8). This particular sequence requires approximately 9 min. Increasing the size of the pixel matrix to 256 × 256 or the number of excitations to two will result in an approximately 18-min scan, not including reconstruction time. When multiple widely spaced vessels are suspected,

the acquisition of additional volumes may become onerous for both patient and imaging staff. However, the diminished saturation through the volume inherent with PC imaging permits effective utilization of larger portions of the volume than three-dimensional TOF MRA.

Modifications of this basic sequence would include, when available, cardiac gating to reduce pulsatility and variable-velocity encoding to improve visualization of smaller vessels. Segmentation of *k* space may benefit image quality in three-dimensional PC and other sequences. If gadolinium is being administered, the phase-contrast imaging can be performed postgadolinium with an increased flip angle (60°) to

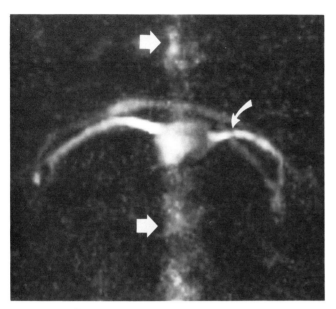

FIGURE 12-8 Axial collapse of a three-dimensional PC MR angiogram of a patient with a mild proximal left renal artery stenosis (*curved arrow*). Note that the phase-encoding direction has been carefully chosen to project the pulsatility artifact (*large arrows*) from the aorta away from the renal arteries. The renal veins and IVC can be faintly visualized anterior to the aorta.

take advantage of the shortened blood T1 conferred by the gadolinium.

Suggested Renal Artery MRA Protocols

The choice of a protocol for renal artery imaging depends on many factors, including hardware and software configurations, prior experience, and the patient population. A useful exercise when initiating a renal artery MRA program is to perform the study on either normal volunteers or patients already scheduled for conventional angiography. This allows testing of protocols in both normal and abnormal subjects, as results may differ in the two populations. Furthermore, correlation of MRA with conventional angiography early in one's experience is important to develop the radiologist's and referring physician's confidence in interpretation.

Most renal artery MRA can be completed within 45 min, utilizing a minimum of three sequences: T1-weighted sagittal, two-dimensional TOF coronal slices with breath-holding, and axial three-dimensional TOF or PC as the final acquisition. A more extensive protocol might add coronal T1-weighted images and axial or oblique coronal two-dimensional TOF breath-hold acquisitions. We routinely perform an axial dynamic gadolinium-enhanced three-dimensional TOF MR angiogram, followed immediately by a coronal three-dimensional TOF acquisition, and then an axial three-dimensional PC MR angiogram. The coronal three-dimensional TOF sequence is included in order to allow evaluation of the celiac artery origin, as hepatorenal and/or splenorenal

bypass surgery is common at our institution. Postprocessed views of the celiac origin allow for more complete surgical planning in these patients. We have also found MOTSA three-dimensional TOF MRA to be a useful technique. In summary, the optimum renal artery MRA protocol remains to be determined.

CELIAC, SUPERIOR MESENTERIC, AND INFERIOR MESENTERIC ARTERIES

Clinically apparent chronic occlusive disease of the celiac and mesenteric arteries is less common than symptomatic renal artery disease due to the rich collateral network that exists among the organs of digestion. The diagnosis of chronic mesenteric ischemia, or "intestinal angina," is frequently delayed because it can mimic many other more common abdominal conditions. Conversely, acute mesenteric occlusions present as abdominal crises that require urgent intervention. Emergent conventional angiography is indicated in this situation. As a result of the incidence and manner in which occlusive disease of the celiac, superior mesenteric, and inferior mesenteric arteries presents clinically, the application of MRA techniques to these vessels, though not difficult, has not paralleled that to the renal arteries.

Knowledge of the multiple anatomic variants that occur with the celiac and superior mesenteric artery is a prerequisite when imaging these vessels. The most common situation (70 to 80 percent) is separate origins of the vessels, with the celiac artery bifurcating into the common hepatic and splenic arteries. The right hepatic artery can arise from the superior mesenteric artery in as many as 15 to 20 percent of individuals. Other important variants include complete replacement of the common hepatic to the superior mesenteric artery, a single celiomesenteric trunk, and separate splenic and hepatic origins from the aorta.

The celiac, superior mesenteric, and inferior mesenteric artery origins can be imaged with the same protocols as the renal arteries, with modifications to account for the anterior location of these vessels. The large size of the celiac and superior mesenteric artery origins is particularly well suited for demonstration by MRA (Fig. 12-9A and B). As with the renal arteries, visualization of the more distal portions of these vessels is inconsistent. Specifically, the celiac vessels are difficult to follow beyond the bifurcation into the splenic and common hepatic arteries. The superior mesenteric artery branches—such as the middle colic, pancreaticoduodenal, jejunal, and ileal arteries—are rarely visualized due to their small size; similarly, the branches of the inferior mesenteric artery are small and rarely seen. Magnetic resonance angiography is not an appropriate technique for patients with suspected distal occlusive disease of branches of the celiac and mesenteric vessels, such as the arteritides, distal atherosclerosis, and small emboli.

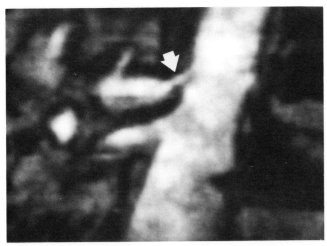

A

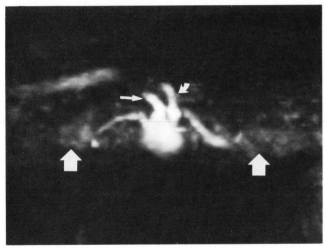

B

FIGURE 12-9 *A.* Sagittal reformation of an axial three-dimensional TOF MOTSA MR angiogram of the celiac and superior mesenteric artery origins. There is a moderate proximal celiac artery stenosis (*arrow*) that was confirmed by conventional angiography. *B.* Axial collapse of a three-dimensional PC MR angiogram of the celiac (*curved arrow*) and superior mesenteric (*small straight arrow*) arteries. Note that the phase-encoding direction was directed from right to left, so that pulsatility artifact (*large arrows*) from the aorta is projected over the renal arteries and away from the mesenteric vessels.

An important current clinical limitation of MRA is the inability to map pathways of collateral flow. This is due to the level of resolution possible with MRA and the tortuous nature of these vessels. For example, an occluded inferior mesenteric artery is reconstituted from the middle colic artery by slow, retrograde flow through the left colic arcade and transmesenteric vessels.

T1-weighted images in the sagittal plane are quite useful for localizing the vessel origins. The anterior location of these arteries is most suitable for two-dimensional imaging in the axial and sagittal planes. In the coronal plane, the origins appear *en face*. Three-dimensional imaging is most effectively acquired axially for the origins, although gadolinium-enhanced three-dimensional TOF sequences in the sagittal or coronal plane may prove useful for depicting the distal superior mesenteric artery. In contrast to renal artery imaging, the phase encoding should be right-left in axial two-dimensional or three-dimensional PC MRA sequences to avoid obscuring the anteriorly located mesenteric vessels with pulsatility artifact. The inferior mesenteric artery can be particularly difficult to image in patients with abdominal aortic aneurysms, in whom this vessel is frequently either occluded or displaced by the enlarged, rotated aorta.

Patient selection for celiac and mesenteric MRA should remain strict at this time. Although the proximal celiac and superior mesenteric artery are easily demonstrated, the distal portions of the vessels are not well seen. Furthermore, because of the extensive collaterals that are usually present but not demonstrated, proximal occlusive disease of these vessels may not explain the patient's symptoms. Nevertheless, this is a promising modality that may achieve wider application as techniques and experience improve.

SUMMARY

Magnetic resonance angiography of the proximal renal arteries and abdominal visceral vessels is a practical application of this technology. Although the "correct" technique has not been established, the protocols described in this chapter can serve as a starting point for individuals interested in pursuing imaging of these vessels. Adjustments will necessarily be required for different sites, but methodical testing in volunteers and careful correlation of findings in clinical cases with other studies, particularly conventional angiography, should permit development of consistent imaging techniques. Finally, the importance of accurate clinical information and careful patient screening should never be underestimated.

BIBLIOGRAPHY

Anderson, CM, Saloner D, Tsuruda JS, et al: Artifacts in maximum-intensity-projection display of MR angiograms. *AJR* 154:623, 1990.

Arlart IP, Guhl L, Edelman RR: Magnetic resonance angiography of the abdominal aorta. *Cardiovasc Intervent Radiol* 15:43, 1992.

Debatin JF, Spritzer CE, Grist TM, et al: Imaging of the renal arteries: Value of MR angiography. *AJR* 157:981, 1991.

Dumoulin CL, Yucel EK, Vock P, et al: Two- and three-dimensional phase contrast MR angiography of the abdomen. *JCAT* 14:779, 1990.

Elster AD: Gradient-echo MR imaging: Techniques and acronyms. *Radiology* 186:1, 1993.

Kim D, Edelman RR, Kent KC, et al: Abdominal aorta and renal artery stenosis: Evaluation with MR angiography. *Radiology* 174:727, 1990.

Kent KC, Edelman RR, Kim D, et al: Magnetic resonance imaging: A reliable test for the evaluation of proximal atherosclerotic renal arterial disease. *J Vasc Surg* 13:311, 1991.

Mistretta CA: Relative characteristics of MR angiography and competing vascular imaging modalities. *J Mag Res Imaging* 3:685, 1993.

Prince MR, Yucel EK, Kaufman JA, et al: Dynamic gadolinium-enhanced three-dimensional abdominal MR arteriography. *J Mag Res Imaging* 3:877, 1993.

Yucel EK, Kaufman JA, Prince MR, et al: Time of flight renal MR angiography in patients with renal insufficiency. *Mag Res Imaging* 11:925, 1993.

Vock P, Terrier F, Wegmuller H, et al: Magnetic resonance angiography of abdominal vessels: Early experience using the three dimensional phase contrast technique. *Br J Radiol* 64:10, 1991.

Chapter 13

Magnetic Resonance Angiography of the Abdominal Aorta and Extremities

E. Kent Yucel

CLINICAL CONSIDERATIONS

Atherosclerotic occlusive disease and aneurysmal disease are the major reasons for performing arteriography of the aorta and lower extremities. Lower extremity occlusive disease causes a range of symptoms—from claudication to rest pain—and can eventually result in tissue necrosis. Occlusive disease of the lower extremities is a significant cause of disability and limb loss in the developed world and will become even more important as the average age of the population increases. At the current time, approximately 100,000 grafts are performed annually for lower extremity occlusive disease, in addition to 50,000 percutaneous angioplasty (PTA) procedures and 100,000 amputations.[1] Occlusive disease occurs at multiple levels, from the infrarenal abdominal aorta through the iliac, femoropopliteal, and tibial arteries.

Occlusive disease falls into two major anatomic groups: inflow disease and outflow disease. Inflow disease involves the aortoiliac segment and is treated with an inflow procedure, such as iliac PTA or an aortobifemoral graft. Outflow disease involves the femoral or popliteal arteries and/or the tibial vessels and can also be treated with PTA or by a femoropopliteal or femorotibial graft. Important considerations in both inflow and outflow disease include the status of the profunda femoris and common femoral arteries, which may require concomitant endarterectomy or profundoplasty. Determining the patency of the tibial vessels is vital, as this determines the level of the distal anastomosis in femoral-distal grafts. At times, combined inflow and outflow lesions may be present and multilevel intervention may be required.

In patients with symptomatic occlusive disease, examination of the peripheral pulses delineates the approximate severity and level of obstruction. Initial testing should involve segmental blood pressure measurements and plethysmography. This noninvasive evaluation objectively measures the severity of obstruction, determines whether the hemodynamic disturbance is severe enough to account for symptoms, and localizes the functional level of disease to the aortoiliac (inflow), femoropopliteal, or tibial arteries.

Conventional arteriography (CA) is pursued only when surgical or percutaneous intervention is warranted clinically, by severely disabling claudication or a threat of limb loss. Conventional arteriography provides essential preoperative information: the precise location of disease, the length of the diseased segment, and the status of the inflow and outflow vessels. This information cannot be obtained from hemodynamic studies alone. The length of the diseased segment is important, because a short segment of disease (<5 to 10 cm), whether it be a stenosis or an occlusion, may be appropriate for PTA, whereas longer diseased segments are preferentially treated with bypass grafts.[2–3] Equally important is the status of the inflow to and outflow from a proposed graft. This information is crucial in predicting the long-term patency of a bypass graft. Prior to surgery, the precise anatomy must be determined so that the surgeon can decide which surgical procedure to perform. For example, obstruction at the level of the common femoral artery and combined disease in the superficial and profunda femoris arteries mimic iliac obstruction on hemodynamic tests but require completely different surgical approaches. In femoropopliteal occlusive disease, the status and level of reconstitution of the popliteal artery and/or tibial vessels determines whether the surgeon will use a prosthetic graft or a vein as well as where the distal anastomosis will be placed.

Given this clinical background, we can look at what role magnetic resonance angiography (MRA) might have in the clinical evaluation of lower extremity occlusive disease. A well-known limitation of current MRA techniques is their tendency to overestimate the length and severity of stenoses. However, determining the exact degree of stenosis is not as important in the extremities as it is in the carotids, for example. The hemodynamic significance of occlusive disease in the extremities is established by the noninvasive evaluation. In marked contrast to the carotids, even the differentiation of severe stenosis from occlusion is not very important, since short occlusions, just like short stenoses, can be treated with PTA. The important data which arteriography provides—the distribution and length of occlusive disease, confirmation of inflow patency, and identification of the level of reconstitution of the outflow vessels—are quite easily obtainable with MRA. Lower extremity arteriography requires a very large area to be imaged, from the infrarenal aorta to the foot. This places severe time constraints on the type of MRA sequence that can be used in practice.

There is an important physiological flow characteristic of the extremity circulation which must be taken into account when attempting to image the arteries of the lower extremity. In the internal carotid and abdominal visceral arteries, blood flow occurs throughout the cardiac cycle. This "low-resistance" flow pattern occurs wherever the metabolic demands of organs are relatively constant. Extremity arteries as well as the mesenteric vessels, where metabolic demands are extremely variable, have a very different or "high-resistance" pattern. Antegrade flow occurs only in systole, often followed by brief flow reversal; essentially no flow occurs during diastole. Certain conditions—for example, atherosclerosis, exercise, vasodilators, and arteriovenous communications, which all reduce peripheral resistance—can convert this high-resistance pattern to a low-resistance one. The normal high-resistance flow pattern in the extremities has important implications for MRA and affects the imaging strategies that should be used in the extremities.

TIME-OF-FLIGHT MRA

The MRA method which has been most widely used in the lower extremities is two-dimensional time-of-flight (TOF) MRA. This approach has adequate spatial resolution, maximizes inflow enhancement, and allows one to prescribe as many slices as necessary to cover the region of interest.[4-8] Three-dimensional (3D) TOF MRA has been used primarily for imaging the carotid and intracerebral circulations.[9-11] Three-dimensional MRA is less useful in the extremities because saturation effects limit the effective field of view. Lower extremity MRA requires the examination of large fields of view; it is routine to cover over 150 cm during a leg MRA study, making standard 3D techniques not generally practical.

In 2D TOF MRA, inflow enhancement of flowing blood increases as the imaging plane becomes perpendicular to the long axis of the artery. For this reason the axial imaging plane is optimal for visualizing the leg arteries. However, it is important to remember that some arterial segments, such as the iliac arteries and the proximal portion of the anterior tibial artery, have a significant in-plane flow vector on axial images, which can substantially decrease vessel contrast. This is especially true in the case of tortuous iliac vessels, where portions of the vessel may be nearly invisible on maximum intensity pixel (MIP) images. In such cases, examination of the source image data becomes essential. Imaging in an oblique plane perpendicular to the course of the tortuous vessel segment can be attempted. Administration of a gadolinium chelated contrast agent may also be of use in such circumstances.[12] Although in general contrast between rapidly flowing blood and stationary tissue increases with the flip angle, the saturation effects in horizontal vessel segments will be more pronounced at higher flip angles. Another disadvantage of high flip angles is a marked increase in pulsatility artifacts, or "ghosting," in the phase-encoding axis. This artifact is due to variations in signal intensity over the cardiac cycle due to the normal triphasic flow in normal extremity vessels and has been shown to increase at higher flip angles.[13,14] Flip angles in the range of 45 to 60° are generally optimal, with the lower value preferred for tortuous segments such as the iliacs and the latter for straight vessels such as the superficial femoral arteries.

Another method for reducing pulsatility artifact is to use multiple averages, although this exacts a substantial price in imaging time. Another solution to the problem of flow variability through the cardiac cycle is to perform cardiac gating, so that images are acquired during systole.[14,15] This method has been found to decrease ghosting and increase arterial signal. It does result in an increase in imaging time proportional to the fraction of the RR interval during which data acquisition is not performed. This time penalty can be reduced with a minimal decrement in image quality by gating only a portion of the MRA acquisition.[15]

Since the arteries and veins in the extremities are in close proximity, it is necessary to eliminate venous signal in order to obtain diagnostic images of the arterial tree. This is accomplished with an inferior saturation pulse located 15 to 20 mm caudal to the 2D slices, which tracks behind them as they are acquired sequentially.[16,17] In addition, the extremity arteries are surrounded by fat, the signal from which must also be suppressed to visualize the vessels. Because the T1 of fat is very short, it cannot be sufficiently saturated simply from the short repetition times (TRs) used in TOF MRA. Additional fat suppression can be achieved by using an echo time (TE) where fat and water protons are out of phase. This occurs at approximately 6.9 ms at 0.5 and 1.5 T and at 10 ms at 1.0 T. Fat-selective presaturation schemes have also been implemented.[18,19]

In order to evaluate atherosclerotic disease of the legs with MRA, one must image the entire lower half of the body from the infrarenal abdominal aorta to the feet. In the abdomen, pelvis, and thighs, a slice thickness of 3 mm in the

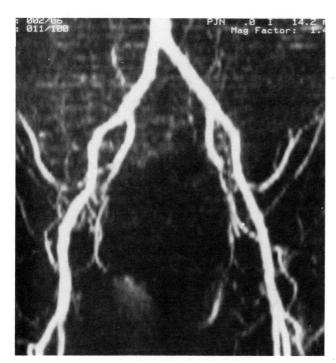

FIGURE 13-1 Two-dimensional TOF angiogram of the iliac arteries. The iliac systems are patent bilaterally. (From Yucel et al.[8] Reproduced by permission.)

body coil provides adequate image quality and allows complete imaging from the aorta to the popliteal artery with a reasonable number of slices (200 to 300) (Fig. 13-1).

The popliteal artery divides below the knee into the anterior tibial, posterior tibial, and peroneal arteries. These vessels may be just 1 to 3 mm in diameter. While a 128 × 256 matrix size is acceptable for imaging the iliac, femoral, and popliteal arteries, it is necessary to increase the resolution to 192 or 256 × 256 to image the tibial vessels in the body coil. As mentioned above, the anterior tibial artery may take a horizontal course at its origin and partial voluming effects may hamper visualization of this segment on MIP projections. Subvolume MIP images and review of the axial source images are often helpful in resolving this area. Alternatively, a 3D TOF study may be performed to image the trifurcation.

Although body coil imaging is acceptable to screen the tibial vessels in most patients, higher-resolution (1.5- to 2.0-mm slice thickness) images obtained in the extremity coil are often necessary, especially in patients who are candidates for femorotibial bypass procedures. With standard extremity coils, two positions are necessary to image the calf, and changing the coil position can be time-consuming. The head coil may be conveniently used to obtain high-quality images of the pedal vessels. The feet should be dorsiflexed to maximize through-plane flow. Coil systems that allow coverage of longer portions of the leg with extremity coil resolution will substantially reduce overall imaging times in the future.[20]

With a typical TR of 20 to 30 ms, the extemity arterial tree from the aortic bifurcation to the foot can be covered in 60 to 90 min. With 300 to 400 images, reconstruction and processing time can become significant. A capability for on-the-fly image reconstruction is very helpful in shortening overall examination time. A powerful work station is essential for MIP image processing. Most of the lower extremity arterial tree can be adequately displayed in a straight antero-posterior projection. Oblique views should be obtained routinely in the pelvis and groins.

Time-of-flight MRA has several advantages, including its relative simplicity and its sensitivity to a wide range of velocities. These can range from normal in patent inflow vessels to virtually stagnant in small reconstituted tibial or pedal vessels. Time-of-flight images do exhibit a small amount of residual background. However, this is itself frequently useful clinically by providing the surgeon with recognizable soft tissue landmarks such as the outlines of the knee and ankle.

Faster gradient echo sequences (fastGRASS, turbo-FLASH, turboFE) have been developed in recent years.[21] These sequences allow TRs on the order of 10 ms. These sequences have several advantages for peripheral arteriography. The rapidity of the sequences allows single slices to be acquired in as little as 1 s rather than the 2 to 3 s required for standard TOF sequences. Alternatively, the increased speed may be utilized in gated studies to acquire a larger proportion of the image in peak systole while maintaining a reasonable acquisition time. Also, these sequences have been implemented with preparation of the stationary tissue magnetization. One method, which involves applying an inversion pulse to eliminate fat signal, has been shown to give significantly improved images of the iliac arteries compared to standard TOF or routine gated TOF MRA acquisitions (Fig. 13-2).[22]

PHASE-CONTRAST MRA

The basis of phase-contrast (PC) MRA is the velocity-dependent phase changes induced in protons as they move through a magnetic field gradient. Like TOF MRA, PC MRA can be acquired as two- or three-dimensional slices.[23–27] A unique feature of PC MRA is the total suppression of background signal. This makes it possible to obtain direct projectional angiograms (without the need for postprocessing of individual slices) through thick slabs or even a single slab encompassing the entire thickness of the body. This capability to bypass multislice acquisition allows cardiac gating to be readily implemented. As in TOF MRA, cardiac gating maximizes vascular signal by allowing direct imaging of systolic flow and reducing pulsatility artifacts. A recent modification of the basic technique varies the velocity-sensitivity of the phase encoding gradients to allow optimal display of flow as blood velocity changes during the cardiac cycle.[28]

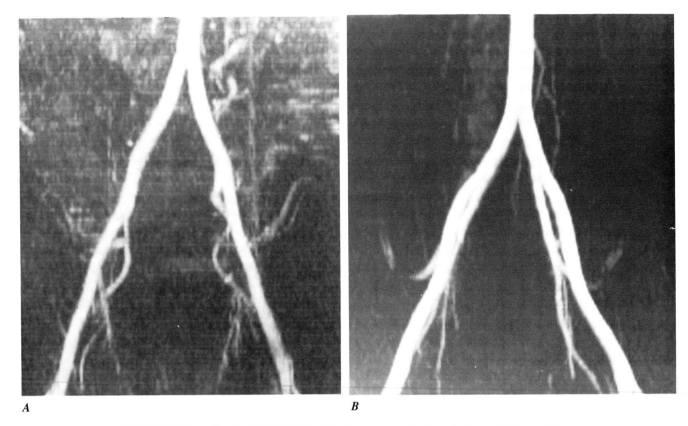

A   *B*

FIGURE 13-2   *A*. Standard 2D TOF MRA of the iliac arteries.   *B*. Turbo field echo MRA acquisition in the same subject as (*A*). An inversion pulse was used to null fat signal. Note the improved background suppression and vessel contrast.

In most cases, only a single flow direction need be acquired for lower extremity MRA, since flow is predominantly in the cephalocaudal direction (Fig. 13-3). However, in the case of tortuous iliac arteries, a second or even third flow direction may have to be added, with a consequent increase in imaging time. An additional feature of direct projectional PC MRA is that only a single projection is acquired at one time. Therefore, as in CA, additional acquisitions must be performed to obtain oblique views. Four 35- to 40-cm coronal fields of view are usually adequate to image both lower extremities.

A unique feature of the PC method is the ease with which quantitative measurements of blood flow and velocity may be obtained.[29] Cardiac-gated PC MRA allows precise quantitative determination of systolic and diastolic flow velocities as well as calculation of flow volumes.[30–32] This capability has the potential to add significant hemodynamic information to that provided by anatomic MRA images. The clinical potential of this capability has been little explored up to now, but one could imagine many applications, such as Doppler ultrasound-like determinations of flow velocity to assess the hemodynamic significance of stenotic lesions or even adding flow determinations at multiple levels during an MRA study

to provide information comparable to that currently provided by plethysmography and segmental pressure measurements. Much work remains to be done in this area.

APPLICATIONS

Occlusive Disease

There are two ways in which MRA can contribute to the evaluation of atherosclerotic occlusive disease of the extremities. The first is by defining the distribution of disease. By characterizing occlusive disease as focal rather than diffuse (Figs. 13-4, 13-5, and 13-6) MRA can identify patients whose symptoms would be treatable by PTA. Providing this information noninvasively can guide the angiographic approach and allow an expeditious combined diagnostic and therapeutic procedure. This can reduce the necessity for a second therapeutic angiographic procedure and shorten the hospital stay. Another consideration is patients who are not candidates for bypass grafting because of the lack of a suitable vein or the presence of complicating medical conditions. Surgeons are often reluctant to subject these patients to the

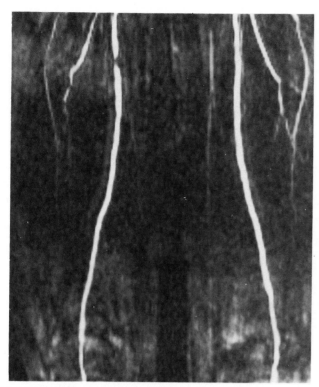

FIGURE 13-3   Phase-contrast MRA of the thighs. There is a proximal superficial femoral artery (SFA) stenosis on the right. (From Yucel EK: Magnetic resonance angiography. *Perspect Vasc Surg* 3:42, 1990. Reproduced by permission.)

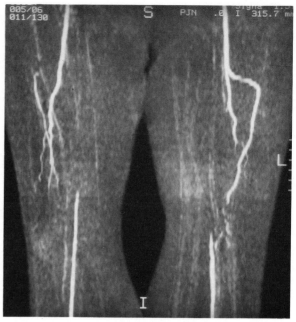

A

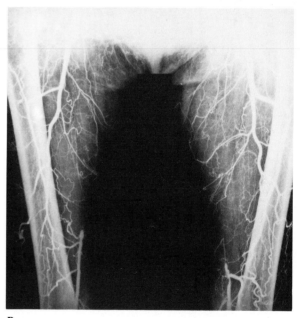

B

FIGURE 13-4   *A*. Two-dimensional TOF MRA.   *B*. Conventional angiogram. Both demonstrate bilateral long SFA occlusions with above-knee popliteal reconstitution. (From Yucel et al.[8] Reproduced by permission.)

risks of CA. In this situation, MRA can identify the patients who would benefit from PTA without performing CA in patients who stand to gain no potential benefit.

The other application of MRA is to provide preoperative anatomy, replacing CA. For preoperative evaluation, the key information is the status of the outflow vessels: the common, superficial, and deep femoral arteries for inflow procedures (Fig. 13-7); the popliteal artery and calf vessels for femoral-distal grafts. This information is needed by the vascular surgeon in order to decide on the placement of the distal anastomosis. Whereas routine noninvasive testing quantitates the severity of runoff disease, it cannot characterize individual runoff vessels. Duplex ultrasound has not been found to be applicable to this problem due to the small size and depth of the tibial arteries. However, MRA can provide such detailed information about the runoff vessels, information previously obtainable only by CA (Fig. 13-8).[4–8] This provides a new and important option for patients with contraindications to CA (e.g., severe contrast allergy, renal insufficiency, prior cholesterol embolization, or difficult arterial access). Published studies have suggested that carefully performed 2D TOF MRA may identify tibial runoff vessels better than CA in patients with severe proximal occlusion.[4]

The techniques of MRA continue to progress rapidly.

Nevertheless, there are some problems which must be solved before it can replace CA routinely. A major limitation of all MRA techniques is their tendency to show signal loss at sites of stenosis due to intravoxel phase dispersion from turbulent flow. This problem is most marked with severe degrees of

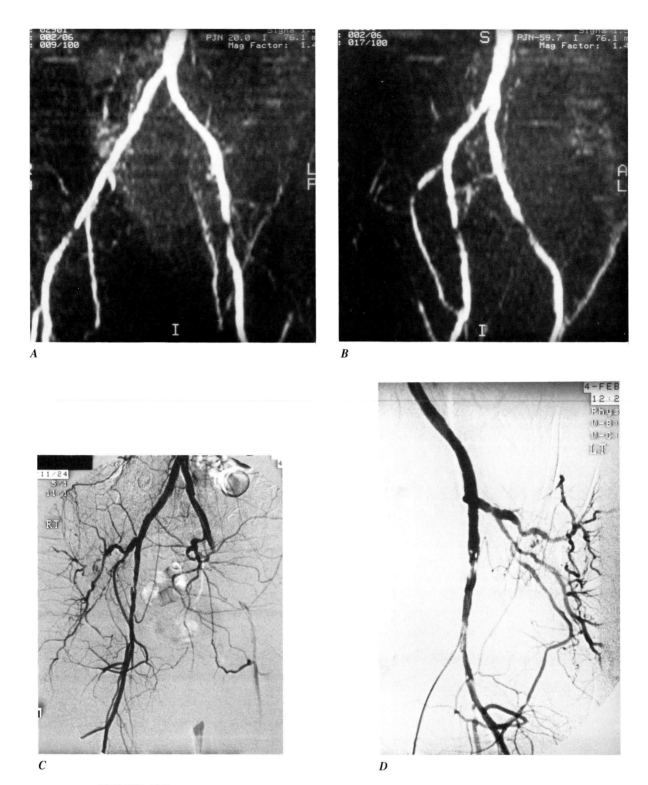

FIGURE 13-5   MRA of the pelvis in the right posterior oblique (*A*) and left posterior oblique (*B*) projections demonstrates bilateral external iliac artery stenoses. Conventional angiogram (*C*) confirms the right-sided stenosis (*arrow*). The left iliac is obturated by the catheter. Angiogram with the catheter pulled down (*D*) identifies the left iliac lesion (*arrow*). (From Yucel et al.[8] Reproduced by permission.)

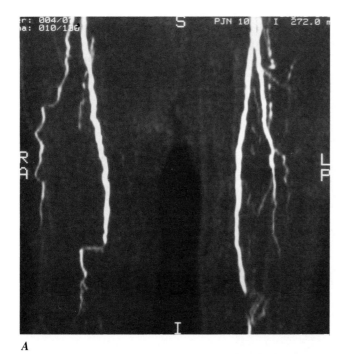

A

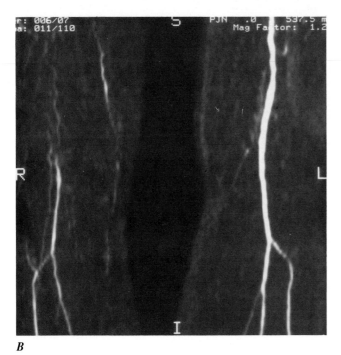

B

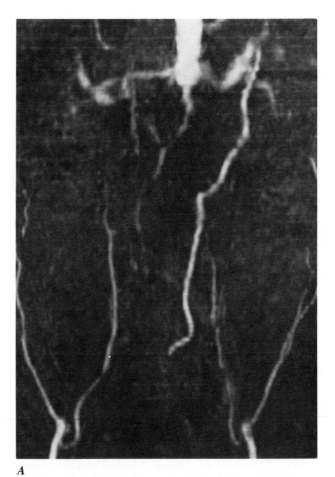

A

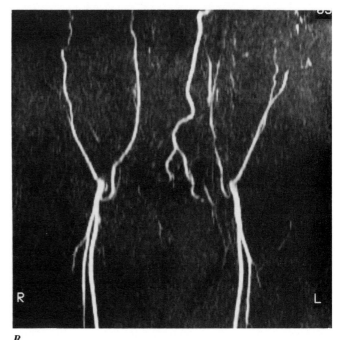

B

FIGURE 13-6 *A*. MRA of the thighs demonstrates a long SFA occlusion on the right, requiring bypass grafting, and a short occlusion on the left (*arrow*), amenable to PTA. *B*. Magnetic resonance angiography at the level of the knees identifies reconstitution of the right popliteal artery (*arrow*), with two-vessel runoff. (From Yucel EK: Magnetic resonance angiography of the peripheral arteries. *MRI Clin North Am* 1:229, 1993. Reproduced by permission.)

FIGURE 13-7 Gated 2D TOF MRA of the abdomen (*A*) and pelvis (*B*) demonstrates infrarenal aortic occlusion with reconstitution of the common femoral arteries bilaterally.

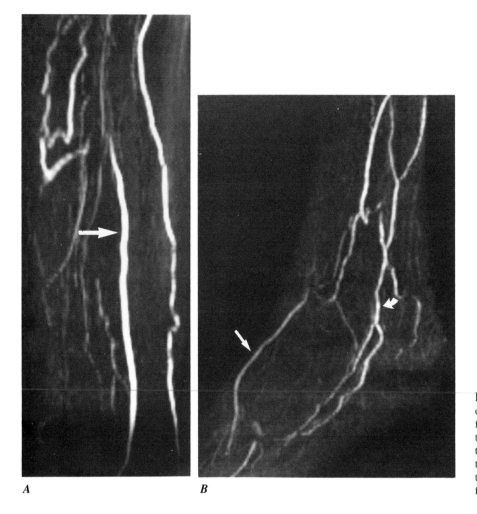

A   *B*

FIGURE 13-8   Two-dimensional TOF MRA of the calf (*A*) in the extremity coil and of the foot (*B*) in the head coil. There is occlusion of the popliteal trifurcation with reconstitution of the peroneal artery (*arrow* in *A*) in the calf and the dorsalis pedis (*straight arrow* in *B*) and posterior tibial (*curved arrow* in *B*) arteries in the foot.

stenosis. Complete signal voids are commonly produced at sites of severe stenosis. As mentioned previously, the differentiation between focal occlusion and severe stenosis is of little clinical importance in the extremities; in fact, this differentiation can sometimes be difficult to make on CA when collateral vessels bypass a severe stenosis and cause it to resemble a focal occlusion.

There are methods to improve the imaging of stenoses. The most important is reducing TE, and this process continues as newer sequences are developed.[33,34] There is a limitation to this effect, however. At less than 6 to 7 ms, fat and water protons start to come into phase, and contrast between fat and water decreases. Intravoxel phase dispersion can also be reduced by decreasing voxel size. This approach is not very practical in MRA of the legs, because going to higher resolution increases scan time. Three-dimensional MRA methods tend to display stenoses with greater accuracy. As mentioned earlier, however, the time demands of 3D acquisitions (due to the tendency of flowing blood to become saturated within the imaged volume) make them impractical for lower extremity MRA. Two approaches could theoretically help to reduce this problem, although experience with

them in the extremities is limited. One is gadolinium enhancement,[35] which lengthens the effective field of view by reducing saturation effects. A side effect of routine bolus gadolinium administration, however, is simultaneous enhancement of veins and arteries. In this situation, overlapping veins can obscure important parts of the adjacent arterial anatomy. This venous enhancement can be dramatically decreased while maintaining arterial enhancement at a high level by administering the gadolinium agent in a dynamic fashion during a 3D scan.[12] Another approach may be to use the multislab 3D technique described in previous chapters. Although this has been described for imaging the aorta, it has not been applied to the evaluation of the extremity vessels.[36]

As mentioned earlier, a major feature of extremity MRA is the tendency to produce ghost artifacts on standard, nongated acquisitions. This ghosting may be very prominent on oblique projections but is not noticeable on straight anteroposterior MIP projections (when phase encoding is set in this direction), since they superimpose on the artery. However, they do decrease the conspicuity of the vessel because the lumen is less bright than it would have been had signal not been lost to the vessel ghosts. Interestingly, ghosting is much less noticeable in diseased vessels than in normal ones. This is because distal to an obstruction, flow changes from high-resistance, pulsatile flow to a low-resistance pattern with flow throughout the cardiac cycle. However, when imaging the inflow vessels to an obstructed segment, a gated method, either TOF or PC, is recommended to produce artifact-free images. Postprocessing algorithms such as surface-rendering or seed-growing techniques can also help to eliminate these artifacts, although these techniques are much more demanding to implement than the standard MIP processing.

A limitation of PC MRA in diseased vessels is its sensitivity to only a small range of velocities. In patients with occlusive disease, a wide range of velocities is present: high velocity at a stenosis, slow flow in reconstituted segments, and intermediate velocities in normal inflow vessels. Other factors, such as cardiac output, also complicate any attempt to estimate flow velocities prospectively.

Aneurysms

Aneurysmal disease represents another promising area for MRA. Aneurysms occur most commonly in the abdominal aorta, followed by the popliteal, iliac, and femoral arteries. Standard spin-echo MR images in multiple planes (Fig. 13-9) are helpful in determining the true diameter of aneurysms, since MRA projection images, like CA, visualize only the patent lumen. In abdominal aortic aneurysms (AAA), multiplanar spin-echo MRI is quite accurate at defining the relationship of the aneurysm to the iliac and main renal arteries

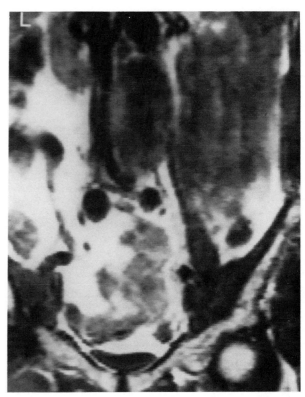

FIGURE 13-10 Coronal T1-weighted image demonstrates the relationship of the renal arteries to an infrarenal abdominal aortic aneurysm. (From Yucel EK, Kaufman JA: Magnetic resonance imaging and magnetic resonance angiography of aortic aneurysms, in Yao JST, Pearce WH (eds): *Aneurysms: New Findings and Treatment*. Norwalk, CT, Appleton and Lange, 1994. Reproduced by permission.)

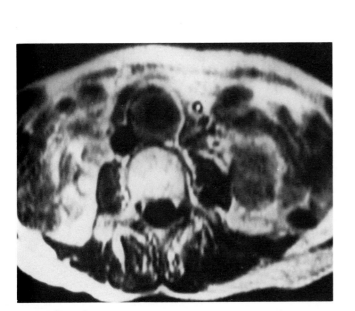

FIGURE 13-9 Axial T1-weighted image of an abdominal aortic aneurysm demonstrates the patent lumen as a signal void and intraluminal thrombus as material of intermediate signal intensity. (From Yucel EK, Kaufman JA: Magnetic resonance imaging and magnetic resonance angiography of aortic aneurysms, in Yao JST, Pearce WH (eds): *Aneurysms: New Findings and Treatment*. Norwalk, CT, Appleton and Lange, 1994. Reproduced by permission.)

(Fig. 13-10).[37–41] However, in the setting of AAA (in contrast to results from patients without aortic aneurysms), standard MRA techniques have been disappointing in their ability to detect accessory renal arteries and establish the patency of the renal and iliac arteries.[41,42] This is due to the flow disturbances that are present in the setting of AAA, which promote signal loss due to intravoxel phase dispersion and saturation effects.

Blood flow in aneurysms is complex and disordered, and forward flow through the aneurysm can be very slow. Therefore, TOF techniques that depend on refreshment of the blood in the slice or volume will not work well because blood remains within the slice for such a long period of time. Phase-contrast techniques depend on flow coherence, so that the same phase change will be imparted to flowing protons by a particular flow-encoding gradient. In aneurysms, however, there is a wide range of blood flow directions and velocities, with consequent degradation in the PC image. One approach which may be helpful, although not adequately investigated, would be to use a cardiac-gated approach, either TOF or PC. A gated PC sequence decreases the intravoxel phase dispersion that occurs as images are averaged over time. In TOF acquisitions, gating allows imaging to be

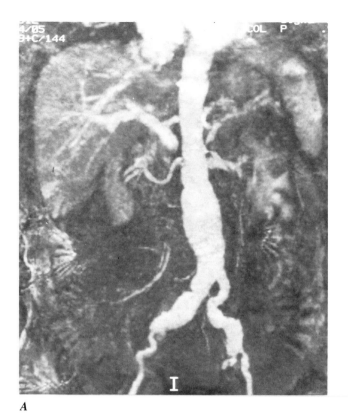

A

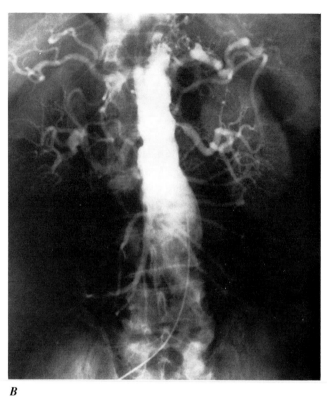

B

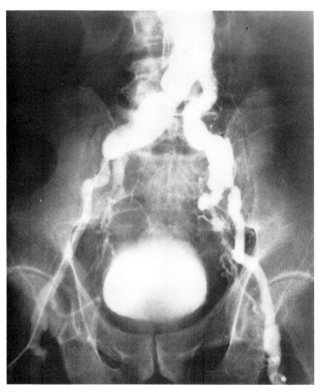

C

FIGURE 13-11 *A*. Gadolinium-enhanced 3D MRA of an aortic aneurysm demonstrates bilateral renal artery stenoses and extension of the aneurysm into both iliacs. *B* and *C*. Confirmatory aortogram. (From Yucel EK, Kaufman JA: Magnetic resonance imaging and magnetic resonance angiography of aortic aneurysms, in Yao JST, Pearce WH (eds): *Aneurysms: New Findings and Treatment*. Norwalk, CT, Appleton and Lange, 1994. Reproduced by permission.)

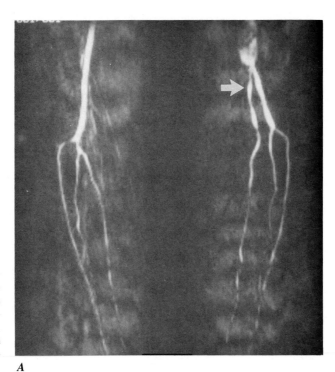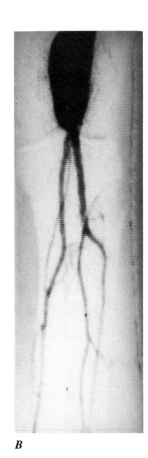

FIGURE 13-12 *A.* Two-dimensional phase-contrast MRA of a popliteal artery aneurysm demonstrates high origin of the posterior tibial artery from the aneurysm (*arrow*). *B.* Confirmatory arteriogram. (From Yucel et al.[5] Reproduced by permission.)

A   *B*

concentrated during the period of the cardiac cycle when there is most forward flow. These sequences can be combined with special postprocessing algorithms, such as seed growing and surface rendering, to further improve both conspicuity of the aneurysm and diagnostic efficacy.

Another approach is the use of gadolinium contrast agents to enhance MRA, which has special advantages in the setting

of AAA. With adequate specific enhancement of the blood pool, refreshment of spins is no longer necessary for imaging of the aneurysm lumen, and consistently bright images of AAA can be obtained.[12] Preliminary work with this technique in the preoperative evaluation of AAA has shown it to be comparable to CA and superior to standard TOF MRA (Fig. 13-11).[41,43]

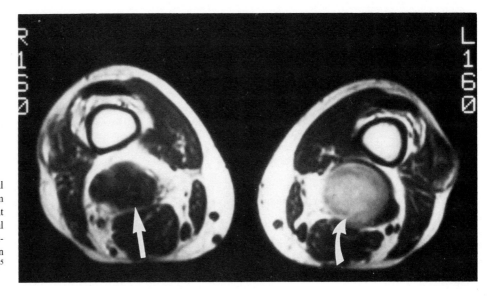

FIGURE 13-13 T1-weighted axial image shows a patent popliteal aneurysm with intraluminal thrombus on the right (*straight arrow*). The occluded popliteal aneurysm on the left (*curved arrow*) exhibits high signal from methemoglobin in subacute thrombus. (From Yucel et al.[5] Reproduced by permission.)

Experience with MRA of peripheral aneurysms has been limited, but, again, gated techniques hold the most promise.[5] The demands on MRA are less in this setting, as there are no branch vessels comparable in importance to the renal arteries. The only requirement is delineation of the patency of inflow and outflow vessels, which should be readily obtainable with cardiac-gated MRA, either PC or TOF (Fig. 13-12). Again, use of spin-echo MR images is mandatory to assess the true diameter of the aneurysm and identify the presence of intraluminal thrombus (Fig. 13-13). Further work will have to be done in this area to establish the optimal techniques before MRA can replace CA.

Other areas in which further investigation is warranted to demonstrate the potential role MRA to replace CA are bypass graft evaluation,[5,44] preoperative evaluation for bone grafts,[45] and arterial trauma.[46]

REFERENCES

1. Martin EC: Transcatheter therapies in peripheral and noncoronary vascular disease: Introduction. *Circulation* 83(suppl I):1, 1991.
2. Hewes RC, White RI Jr, Murray RR, et al: Long-term results of superficial femoral artery angioplasty. *AJR* 146:1025, 1986.
3. Murray RR, Hewes RC, White RI Jr, et al: Long-segment femoropopliteal stenoses: Is angioplasty a boon or a bust? *Radiology* 162:473, 1987.
4. Owen RS, Carpenter JP, Baum RA, et al: Magnetic resonance imaging of angiographically occult runoff vessels in peripheral arterial occlusive disease. *N Engl J Med* 326:1577, 1992.
5. Yucel EK, Dumoulin CL, Waltman AC: Magnetic resonance imaging of lower extremity arterial disease: Preliminary experience. *J Mag Res Imaging* 2:303, 1992.
6. Mulligan SA, Matsuda T, Langer P, et al: Peripheral arterial occlusive disease: Prospective comparison of MR angiography and color duplex US with conventional angiography. *Radiology* 178:695, 1991.
7. Carpenter JP, Owen RS, Baum RA, et al: Magnetic resonance angiography of peripheral runoff vessels. *J Vasc Surg* 16:807, 1992.
8. Yucel EK, Kaufman JA, Geller SC, Waltman AC: Prospective evaluation of two-dimensional time-of-flight MR angiography in lower extremity atherosclerotic occlusive disease. *Radiology* 187:637, 1993.
9. Anderson CM, Saloner D, Lee RE, et al: Assessment of carotid artery stenosis by MR angiography: Comparison with x-ray angiography and color-coded Doppler ultrasound. *AJNR* 13:989, 1992.
10. Masaryk AM, Ross JS, DiCello MC, et al: 3DFT MR angiography of the carotid bifurcation: Potential and limitations as a screening examination. *Radiology* 179:797, 1991.
11. Wesbey GE, Bergan JJ, Moreland SI, et al: Cerebrovascular magnetic resonance angiography: A critical verification. *J Vasc Surg* 16:619, 1992.
12. Prince MR, Yucel EK, Kaufman JA, Waltman AC: Dynamic Gd:DTPA enhanced 3DFT abdominal MR angiography. *J Mag Res Imaging* 3:877, 1993.
13. Pope CF, Dietz MJ, Ezekowitz MD, Gore JC: Technical variables influencing the detection of acute deep venous thrombosis by magnetic resonance imaging. *Mag Res Imaging* 9:379, 1991.
14. DeGraaf RG, Groen JP: MR angiography with pulsatile flow. *Mag Res Imaging* 10:25, 1992.
15. Selby K, Saloner D, Anderson CM, et al: MR angiography with a cardiac-phase-specific acquisition window. *J Mag Res Imaging* 2:637, 1992.
16. Caputo GR, Masui T, Gooding GAW, et al: Popliteal and tibioperoneal arteries: Feasibility of two-dimensional time-of-flight MR angiography and phase velocity mapping. *Radiology* 182:387, 1992.
17. Keller PJ, Drayer BP, Fram EK, et al: MR angiography with two-dimensional acquisition and three-dimensional display. *Radiology* 173:527, 1989.
18. Richardson DB, Bampton AEH, Riederer SJ, MacFall JR: Magnetization-prepared MR angiography with fat suppression and venous saturation. *J Mag Res Imaging* 2:653, 1992.
19. Doyle M, Matsuda T, Pohost GM: SLIP, a lipid suppression technique to improve image contrast in inflow angiography. *Mag Res Med* 21:71, 1991.
20. Rajan SS, Patt RH, Jarso S, et al: An extended-length coil design for peripheral MR angiography. *Mag Res Imaging* 9:493, 1991.
21. Elster AD: Gradient-echo MR imaging: Techniques and acronyms. *Radiology* 186:1, 1993.
22. Yucel EK, Silver MS, Carter AP: MR angiography of normal pelvic arteries: Comparison of contrast for three different inflow techniques. *AJR* 163:197, 1994.
23. Dumoulin CL, Hart HR: Magnetic resonance angiography. *Radiology* 161:717, 1986.
24. Dumoulin CL, Souza SP, Hart HR: Rapid scan magnetic resonance angiography. *Mag Res Med* 5:238, 1985.
25. Dumoulin CL, Yucel EK, Vock P, et al: Two- and three-dimensional phase contrast MR angiography of the abdomen. *J Comput Assist Tomogr* 14:779, 1990.
26. Steinberg FL, Yucel EK, Dumoulin CL, et al: Peripheral vascular and abdominal applications of MR flow imaging techniques. *Mag Res Med* 14:315, 1990.
27. Lanzer P, Bohning D, Groen J, et al: Aortoiliac and femoropopliteal phase-based NMR angiography: A comparison between FLAG and RSE. *Mag Res Med* 15:372, 1990.
28. Swan JS, Weber DM, Grist TM, et al: Peripheral MR angiography with variable velocity encoding: Work in progress. *Radiology* 184:813, 1992.
29. Pelc LR, Pelc NJ, Rayhill SC, et al: Arterial and venous blood flow: Noninvasive quantitation with MR imaging. *Radiology* 185:809, 1992.
30. Dousset V, Wehrli RW, Louie A, et al: Popliteal artery hemodynamics: MR imaging-US correlation. *Radiology* 179:437, 1991.
31. Kerr TM, Cranley JJ, Johnson RJ, et al: Measurement of blood flow rates in the lower extremities with use of a nuclear magnetic resonance based instrument. *J Vasc Surg* 14:649, 1991.
32. Mohiaddin RH, Sampson C, Firmin DN, et al: MR morphological and flow imaging in peripheral vascular disease (abstract). *Mag Res Imaging* 8(suppl 1):312, 1990.
33. Schmalbrock P, Yuan C, Chakeres DW, et al: Volume MR angiography: Methods to achieve very short echo times. *Radiology* 175:861, 1990.
34. Lin W, Haacke EM: Short field-echo sequences with partial Fourier reconstruction to avoid signal loss and blurring in MR angiography (abstract). *Radiology* 177(P):209, 1990.
35. Lossef SV, Rajan SS, Patt RH, et al: Gadolinium-enhanced magnitude contrast MR angiography of the popliteal and tibial arteries. *Radiology* 184:349, 1992.
36. Lewin JS, Laub G, Hausmann R: Three-dimensional time-of-flight MR angiography: Applications in the abdomen and thorax. *Radiology* 179:261, 1991.
37. Koslin DB, Kenney PJ, Keller FS, et al: Preoperative evaluation of abdominal aortic aneurysm by MR imaging with aortography correlation. *Cardiovasc Intervent Radiol* 11:329, 1988.
38. Kandarpa K, Piwnica-Worms D, Chopra PS, et al: Prospective

double-blinded comparison of MR imaging and aortography in the preoperative evaluation of abdominal aortic aneurysms. *J Vasc Intervent Radiol* 3:83, 1992.

39. Pavone P, Di Cesare E, Di Renzi P, et al: Abdominal aortic aneurysm evaluation: Comparison of US, CT, MRI, and angiography. *Mag Res Imaging* 8:199, 1990.

40. Sallevelt PEJM, Barentsz JO, Ruijs SJHJ, et al: Role of MR imaging in the preoperative evaluation of atherosclerotic abdominal aortic aneurysms. *RadioGraphics* 14:87, 1994.

41. Kaufman JA, Yucel EK, Waltman AC, et al: Magnetic resonance angiography in the preoperative evaluation of abdominal aortic aneurysms: A preliminary study. *J Vasc Intervent Radiol* 5:489, 1994.

42. Durham JR, Hackworth CA, Tober JC, et al: Magnetic resonance angiography in the preoperative evaluation of abdominal aortic aneurysms. *Am J Surg* 166:173, 1993.

43. Kaufman JA, Geller SC, Peterson MJ, et al: MR imaging (including MR angiography) of abdominal aortic aneurysms: Comparison with conventional angiography. *AJR* 163:203, 1994.

44. Fillmore DJ, Yucel EK, Briggs SE, et al: MR angiography of vascular grafts in children. *AJR* 157:1069, 1991.

45. Manaster BJ, Doleman DA, Bell DA: Pre- and post-operative imaging of vascularized fibular grafts. *Radiology* 176:161, 1990.

46. Yaquinto JJ, Harms SE, Siemers PT, et al: Arterial injury from penetrating trauma: Evaluation with single-acquisition fat-suppressed MR imaging. *AJR* 158:631, 1992.

Chapter 14

The Vascular Surgeon's Perspective

Richard P. Cambria

In the present chapter, I offer a clinical perspective on the evolving role of magnetic resonance angiography (MRA) in the management of patients with vascular disease in a variety of anatomic locations. Emphasis on the word *evolving* is appropriate, since the ultimate role of MRA in both technical adequacy of imaging and utility in patient management remains to be defined for virtually every anatomic region that the vascular surgeon is likely to treat. Our own efforts in the prospective evaluation of MRA and its potential to replace contrast arteriography in the management of both aortic aneurysm disease and lower extremity occlusive disease continue at the present time. It is appropriate to emphasize that the experience and, admittedly, the prejudices related herein are born of close cooperation and mutual interest between vascular surgeons and vascular radiologists at our hospital. During the course of this experience, I have seen both the scope and quality of MRA advance dramatically over a very short time. Such advances could hardly be expected of those who do not have a background in vascular imaging and/or knowledge of clinically relevant vascular anatomy. It is certainly not possible at the present time for practicing surgeons to obtain MRA of the quality that is available to me, for example, in the realm of lower extremity occlusive disease. Accordingly, widespread use of MRA in a variety of anatomic locations by the practicing surgeon at the moment must be considered inappropriate until prospective evaluation has been carried out in centers with acknowledged expertise in these techniques. It must also be emphasized that there is a distinct difference between determining the role of MRA in patient management and perfecting the technical capabilities of MRA to provide an adequate vascular image. The role of an imaging technique in patient management can be determined only in the context of what particular anatomic information is necessary to plan and execute vascular interventions. In current practice, angiographic imaging is generally not used to make a diagnosis in the treatment of patients with vascular disease but rather to plan the details of an anticipated intervention. In addition, the role of MRA in certain types of vascular lesions will always be different in the hands of different clinicians, just as, for example, con-

trast arteriography is used variably in the preoperative evaluation of patients prior to abdominal aortic aneurysm surgery.

It is clear that the impetus for further development of MRA lies in its potential for replacing contrast arteriography and thereby decreasing both the potential morbidity and cost of interventions for vascular disease. It is also clear that MRA will afford cost savings only if it is used in place of, rather than in addition to, contrast arteriography. This again relates to the importance of establishing the role of MRA in a variety of anatomic locations, so that individual clinicians will have guidelines for the application of MRA, rather than obtaining both studies in a majority of patients who are treated for vascular disease.

Since the demands of any vascular imaging modality, with respect to both resolution and the necessity for an adequate preoperative vascular map, vary substantially in different anatomic regions where vascular intervention may be considered, the remainder of this chapter considers individual anatomic locations and clinical problems that are likely to present for treatment by the vascular surgeon. What follows is a personal perspective based on a developing experience in our own unit rather than a comprehensive review of prospective studies which, at the moment, are only available in the realm of carotid disease imaging. Since technology and experience continue to evolve, it is also possible that the perspective afforded herein will change in the future. One thing, however, is certain: MRA will have an increasing role in the management of the patient with vascular disease, and it will obviate the need for contrast arteriography in a number of as yet undefined clinical and anatomic scenarios.

CAROTID DISEASE

A surgeon's perspective on the role of MRA in the management of carotid disease necessarily considers the role of angiography of any type in the management of such patients. With respect to management decisions in patients with carotid disease, several things are already certain as far as MRA is concerned. First, of the various anatomic regions where the vascular surgeon is likely to intervene, it is clear that MRA has had the greatest impact in the realm of carotid surgery. Second, before the availability of MRA, carotid surgery was, in a variety of centers and clinical circumstances, carried out based on carotid noninvasive studies alone (i.e., without arteriography). Last, it is not possible to separate the role of MRA in the management of carotid disease from broader trends in carotid surgery that have occurred over the past few years. Specifically, performance of endarterectomy in this country declined dramatically in the late 1980s, as increasing questions arose as to the merit of carotid endarterectomy in various patient subgroups. This trend has been largely reversed by the availability of a number of multicenter, randomized, prospective trials that have clearly defined the role of carotid surgery, at least with respect to the treatment of symptomatic patients with high-grade stenoses.[1] In addition, reasonable data are now available with respect to the natural history of patients with high-grade asymptomatic carotid stenoses, and a single prospective randomized study has endorsed the performance of endarterectomy in such patients.[2] In current practice, referral of patients for carotid surgery is increasing, and—because of cost and patient safety considerations—pressures from patients, referring doctors, and, without doubt in the future, third-party payers to eliminate contrast arteriography are increasing.

What general and specific requirements does the angiographic evaluation of carotid disease have to fulfill for the vascular surgeon? It is important to note for nonsurgeon readers that the technical aspects of performing carotid endarterectomy are identical in most patients. Therefore, specific judgments about the technical nature of the operation are generally not made on the basis of arteriography. This could be contrasted with, for example, lower extremity revascularization, where the exact location and nature of the operation is dictated by the preoperative imaging study. Thus, in the realm of carotid surgery, the surgeon generally uses arteriography to determine the degree of stenosis, which is crucial in determining the desirability of operation in most patients. Other anatomic factors which may affect the decision and/or the details of carotid surgery include the length of the stenosis into the distal internal carotid artery, the presence or absence of anterior circulation cross-filling, and the presence of significant arch vessel disease. In addition, anatomic information available from contrast arteriography may be important in the timing of surgical intervention in certain subgroups of patients with carotid disease. For example, in the patient presenting with acute stroke, anatomic features such as the presence of thrombus adherent to the carotid lesion or the carotid "string sign" will lead the surgeon to undertake urgent or even emergent surgery. Thus, in my view, the use of MRA to evaluate carotid disease will be dictated largely by the clinical circumstances accompanying any individual case. Stated in a different way, the resolution available only from a formal contrast arteriogram

is needed only in certain subgroups of patients presenting for treatment of carotid disease.

While a discussion of the role of the noninvasive laboratory in the management of patients with carotid disease is beyond the scope of this chapter, the decision as to whether an MRA or a contrast arteriogram should be obtained prior to proceeding with carotid surgery is greatly influenced by the information available from carotid noninvasive testing. We and others have reported on the feasibility of carotid surgery based on carotid duplex scanning alone, and there is increasing enthusiasm for this approach, particularly in those quarters where long experience and documented reliability with carotid noninvasive testing is present.[3] Physicians and most surgeons have generally considered carotid noninvasive laboratory testing as the first step in carotid artery evaluation, but confirmatory contrast arteriography has generally been considered desirable. Obviously, the necessity for confirmatory arteriography will vary as a function of the accuracy and reliability of any particular noninvasive laboratory. Unfortunately, there is very little quality control among vascular laboratories performing noninvasive carotid studies. In our practice, we have frequently seen grossly inaccurate studies, usually on the side of overestimating the stenoses. Surgeons caring for patients in facilities where the accuracy of noninvasive carotid studies is not clearly documented will be reluctant to proceed without confirmatory angiographic studies, and that would appear to be entirely appropriate.

Despite the fact that an ever-increasing body of literature has indicated a reasonable correlation with MRA and contrast arteriography in defining broad categories of carotid stenosis,[4] my own experience with MRA has permitted the following conclusions. For a truly high-grade or what we would refer to as a preocclusive lesion to be present, there must be a total signal void in the internal carotid artery on the MRA. However, the converse is not true, i.e., a total signal void, since it reflects turbulence, may be seen in arteries with lesser degrees of stenosis. Lesser although still important degrees of stenosis in the 70 to 95 percent range are poorly discriminated with the use of MRA alone. In my own practice, the data available from a carotid duplex scan performed in a laboratory with documented accuracy is more useful in defining the severity of stenoses.

In the contemporary practice of carotid surgery, a number of arguments can be made for or against any algorithm of imaging studies to facilitate judgments about the desirability of surgical treatment. In my view, MRA has an increasing role in the management of patients with carotid disease, but it has in no way eliminated the necessity for contrast arteriography in certain patients. The most important factor in deciding which imaging studies to use relates to the clinical presentation of the patient. Patients discovered to have asymptomatic carotid stenoses may be candidates for surgery based on the severity of the stenoses and their overall suitability for surgical treatment. In such patients, the severity of the carotid stenosis is the single most important factor relating to the desirability of proceeding with carotid endarterectomy. It is therefore desirable to obtain contrast arteriography in such patients to most accurately define the degree of stenosis. In these asymptomatic patients, the detection of significant stenosis on a carotid noninvasive study, and subsequent interrogation with MRA, will inevitably lead to the designation "severe stenosis" and a recommendation for surgery will be forthcoming. It is my belief that patients evaluated with inaccurate noninvasive carotid studies and subsequent MRA may often be judged to have stenoses more severe than are actually present. Accordingly, reliance on the superior resolution of a contrast arteriography prior to recommending surgery for asymptomatic disease is appropriate. Alternatively, in patients with hemispheric transient ischemic attacks corresponding to a lesion identified on duplex scan and/or MRA, precise definition of the degree of the stenosis is unnecessary before proceeding with surgery.

In summary, in current practice, MRA has replaced contrast arteriography prior to carotid endarterectomy in many patients. It is clear that reliance on either MRA or contrast arteriography will vary as a function of the expertise with which noninvasive carotid testing is conducted, and it is also true that carotid surgery after a duplex scan alone is appropriate in certain quarters for certain patients. Last, contrast arteriography remains desirable, if not mandatory, in those clinical situations where precise definition of the degree of stenosis is desirable.

AORTIC ANEURYSMS AND VISCERAL ARTERY OCCLUSIVE DISEASE

It is logical to consider imaging of aortic aneurysms and associated visceral and/or renal artery occlusive disease together for two reasons. First, the single most important piece of data forthcoming from imaging studies with respect to the surgical treatment of abdominal aortic aneurysms is the relationship of the aneurysm and/or its "neck" to the renal arteries. Such information will immediately alert the surgeon to the complexity of the repair required, the location of a proximal aortic cross clamp, and—in the circumstance of a juxta- or suprarenal aneurysm—possibly precipitate referral to a tertiary care center that has considerable experience in the management of complex aneurysm disease. Second, in current practice, the patient presenting for treatment of renovascular disease is typically an older patient with atherosclerotic renovascular disease in addition to a variety of other end-organ sequelae to diffuse atherosclerosis. In these patients, associated aortic disease is the rule rather than the exception, and this has direct implications for the selection of the optimal mode of revascularization of the renal arteries. Indeed, in a recent review of our experience with surgical treatment of renovascular disease, nearly 50 percent of patients underwent combined simultaneous aortic graft placement and aortorenal bypass graft.[5] Thus, in the evaluation

of patients with aortic aneurysm disease, the location and status of the renal arteries are important factors to be determined. In determining the appropriate mode of renal artery reconstruction in patients with renovascular disease, an assessment of concomitant aortic and celiac axis disease (for a potential hepato- or splenorenal bypass) is important.

Any discussion of the role of imaging studies in the preoperative planning for aortic aneurysm surgery must consider the debate about the necessity for angiography prior to aneurysm surgery. While the practice in our unit has generally been to use contrast arteriography routinely in the preoperative evaluation of patients with aortic aneurysms, many surgeons proceed on the basis of a CT scan alone. For example, in the recently reported Canadian multicenter study, where over 600 aortic aneurysm patients were followed prospectively through surgery, 60 percent of patients underwent arteriography preoperatively, with the balance operated upon after a CT scan alone.[6] Advocates of a "proceed with CT scan alone" philosophy argue that a determination of the site of anastomoses is readily made in the operating room. Irrespective of the debate about the merits of arteriography prior to aneurysm surgery, there are certain clinical and/or CT scan markers that most consider to be mandatory indications to proceed with contrast arteriography prior to aneurysm surgery. These include associated aortoiliac occlusive disease, clinical and/or laboratory evidence of renovascular disease, the determination of juxta- or suprarenal anatomy on a CT scan, and any evidence of mesenteric ischemia, including instances of a prior left colon resection, obliterating the meandering mesenteric artery collateral arcade. Simply stated, the role of arteriography prior to aneurysm surgery is to guide the surgeon with respect to the extent of proximal and distal resection, the location of placement of the aortic cross clamp, and the necessity for carrying the reconstruction out onto the iliac or femoral arteries. Last, the surgeon may wish to apply a variety of surgical approaches for the aortic surgery, such as use of the retroperitoneal approach. Certain anatomic and topographic features of aneurysms may lead the surgeon to one particular approach or another. In deciding among these, it has been my practice to opt for complete arteriography.

In an environment where contrast arteriography has been utilized almost routinely prior to proceeding with aneurysm surgery, we have recently evaluated MRA as a potential substitute for contrast arteriography prior to proceeding with aneurysm surgery. Two-dimensional coronal and three-dimensional axial time-of-flight techniques were used, along with gadolinium enhancement. Twenty-seven patients were studied with both MRA and contrast arteriography prior to contemplated abdominal aortic aneurysm surgery.[7] With contrast arteriography and operative findings as the gold standard, MRA was equivalent to contrast arteriography in predicting the proximal extent of the aneurysm and was highly accurate in identifying renal arteries with high-grade stenoses. Attempts to adequately image the inferior mesenteric artery with MRA were not satisfactory. Venous anomalies, specifically the retroaortic left renal vein, are readily displayed on an MRA, but it is equally well shown on CT scan. As experience has accumulated with the use of MRA in aortic aneurysm patients, it is quite clear to me that MRA will supplant contrast arteriography in the majority of patients with uncomplicated aneurysms.

In a referral practice where patients with complex aneurysm disease are frequently seen, we have accumulated considerable experience in the use of MRA to plan the technical components of extensive aortic replacement. In patients with thoracoabdominal aneurysm disease, an important judgment pertains to the extent of proximal aortic resection. These patients will frequently have areas of ectasia but not frank aneurysm formation, and these segments may or may not be contiguous. Furthermore, as long segments of the aorta expand in the transverse diameter, they also elongate in the cephalocaudad direction and frequently buckle in the anterior posterior plane. Because of this, cross-sectional imaging with a CT scan alone is, of necessity, inadequate to evaluate such areas of aortic buckling and, for example, the extent of aneurysm in the transverse portion of the aortic arch. I have found the oblique sagittal cuts available on the MRI study to be particularly useful in determining the extent of proximal aortic resection. In my view, the quality of the proximal aorta wherein a proximal anastomosis needs to be reconstructed is better predicted from the combination of MRI and CT scans than it is with a contrast arteriogram. Frequently, patients with extensive aneurysm disease will have associated renovascular disease and/or varying levels of renal insufficiency. Since the left renal artery is routinely reconstructed and the surgeon has the opportunity to directly visualize the orifice of the right renal artery during the course of thoracoabdominal aneurysm surgery, it may be desirable to eliminate the contrast arteriogram prior to thoracoabdominal aneurysm replacement.

While the utility of MRA in comparison with contrast arteriography for the investigation of renovascular disease is covered in another chapter, a word about the clinical approach to patients with renovascular disease is in order. It is clear that a major impediment to the investigation of these patients until recently has been the lack of an accurate noninvasive imaging modality. Technetium 99 renal scintigraphy can be helpful in the detection of renovascular disease if major asymmetry in renal function is found on the scan. In my experience, this generally occurs only when there has been substantial damage and shrinkage to the kidney on one side and frequently in the circumstance of a total renal artery occlusion. It is well known that renal scintigraphy is a relatively insensitive technique for the detection of nonocclusive but high-grade renal artery stenosis. Thus, the clinician is frequently faced with a management dilemma, in that many patients presenting for investigation of renovascular disease in the modern era will have varying levels of concomitant renal insufficiency. Therefore, contrast arteriogra-

phy is not to be undertaken lightly in these patients; as an invasive technique, it is both too costly and potentially morbid to be used as a screening modality. Furthermore, an imaging modality that at the same sitting gives information referable to the patency of the celiac axis (in order to base a hepato- or splenorenal bypass from it) and potential concomitant aortic pathology would be most desirable. Magnetic resonance arteriography would appear to satisfy all of these requirements and, as experience has been accumulated, I have been very impressed with the accuracy of MRA in detecting high-grade renal artery stenoses with conventional contrast arteriography as a comparative gold standard. In a few patients, clinical findings and information available from a variety of imaging studies was such that the MRA study was sufficient to guide renal artery reconstruction. In each of these cases, intraoperative arterial pressure measurements confirmed the high-grade stenoses in the subsequently reconstructed renal arteries. Thus, I have been impressed with the utility and accuracy of MRA in the evaluation of atherosclerotic renovascular disease and believe that it has been a substantial advance in the management of the patients.

LOWER EXTREMITY OCCLUSIVE DISEASE

Of all the anatomic regions within the purview of the vascular surgeon, revascularization for lower extremity occlusive disease, particularly in those patients requiring very distal bypass grafting, presents the most pressing demands for appropriate arterial imaging. It is certainly true that in the case of abdominal aortic aneurysm repair or carotid endarterectomy, intraoperative decisions can generally be made to facilitate a technically adequate operation even without preoperative angiography of any kind. However, in the circumstance of lower extremity revascularization, advances in surgical techniques have closely paralleled the availability of high-quality angiography, including the vessels in the foot itself. In choosing among a variety of options for infrainguinal revascularization, the vascular surgeon must assimilate clinical information in order first to determine how "complete" or distal the revascularization must be. For example, a patient requiring a femoral popliteal bypass graft for claudication will be adequately treated by bypass to the popliteal level even if significant infrapopliteal disease is present. However, in a patient with necrosis in the foot, who may require local amputation following revascularization, the surgeon generally strives to perform the most distal reconstruction to afford direct pulsatile flow into the foot. Thus, a number of anatomic and technical considerations, aside from the mere patency or occlusion of a vessel, must be considered in making appropriate judgments with respect to bypass grafting in the leg. These include the quality of the vessel used as a recipient for a bypass graft. The surgeon also wants to know how "workable" the outflow vessel is wherein the distal anastomosis will be performed. In addition, complete detail of all the runoff vessels is necessary, since other considerations—such as availability of autogenous vein to perform the bypass—may bear on the decision as to which vessel is used for the bypass. Finally, the degree of distal collateralization or the presence or absence of direct runoff into the foot may be an important factor in deciding on the recipient vessel for a distal bypass graft. While we are in a stage of rapid evolution with respect to the ability of MRA to image these distal vessels, it is worth noting that high-quality conventional arteriography of the runoff vessels may not be universally available. Indeed, a common observation in a referral practice of vascular surgery is an inadequate runoff arteriogram; this becomes an important consideration in comparative studies of MRA and conventional contrast arteriography. Among the important principles of obtaining an adequate runoff arteriogram in the circumstance of a very diseased outflow track, distal catheter positioning and delayed filming are the most important.

Most of the technical considerations relative to imaging long segments of the arterial tree with MRA have been surmounted. This was an initial problem in gaining acceptance from the vascular surgery community relative to MRA of the lower extremities. That is to say, the surgeon making judgments about revascularization of the lower extremities will generally require a complete study from the aorta to at least the ankles and often out into the foot. Even after a careful hemodynamic evaluation, it still may not be possible to accurately determine the relative hemodynamic significance of inflow versus infrainguinal disease. Even in the presence of an apparently adequate femoral pulse and favorable tracing of the thigh pulse volume recording, interrogation of the iliac inflow segments with femoral artery pressure studies is sometimes necessary to adequately determine the hemodynamic significance of aortoiliac disease.[8] Thus, an initial problem with respect to MRA has been overestimation of the significance of iliac stenosis. It remains necessary, in my view, to pursue the severity of iliac stenotic lesions demonstrated on MRA with catheter arteriography and femoral artery pressure study. This is not necessarily an added intervention, since many of these focal iliac lesions will ultimately be treated with balloon catheter angioplasty and will therefore require a concomitant contrast study. Despite this limitation our initial experience with MRA in the evaluation of peripheral occlusive disease demonstrated excellent correlation between MRA and contrast arteriography.[9] In an ongoing prospective evaluation of MRA in patients with lower extremity occlusive disease, I have been impressed with the ability of the vascular radiologist to more precisely define iliac lesions with MRA. My presumption is that we are at the point on the learning curve analogous to that noted a few years ago with carotid MRA, where the initial experience was an overestimation of the severity of stenosis by MRA. This has been at least in part compensated for by vascular radiologists and vascular surgeons interpreting MRAs with a different "mind set" than that with which they might view a conventional arteriogram.

What is the potential role of MRA in the patient with lower extremity occlusive disease? As with other anatomic segments, the replacement of contrast arteriography with MRA is desirable from both cost and patient safety considerations. While it is certainly true that the overwhelming majority of patients with vascular disease are studied safely and effectively with contrast arteriography, we have documented an overall complication rate of 7.5 percent in a large prospective study of patients who underwent catheter arteriography at the Massachusetts General Hospital.[10] It is true that most of these complications are minor and related to the site of arterial puncture; however, we did note an 11 percent incidence of contrast-induced acute renal failure in patients with antecedent renal dysfunction. Again, it is true that the majority of these problems are self-limited and cause no permanent patient morbidity; the cost is generally measured in at least additional hospital days. With respect to risk of conventional contrast arteriography, two distinct groups are recognized. Patients with antecedent renal dysfunction, in particular those with diabetic nephropathy, are at considerable risk for contrast-induced acute renal failure. Second, the patient with diffuse atherosclerotic disease, and in particular patients with an antecedent history of cholesterol emboli syndrome, are at increased risk for further episodes of cholesterol embolization after intraarterial catheter studies. While conventional teaching involves investigation of patients with cholesterol emboli with arteriography to detect a source, in my own practice I prefer to assess the patients with other imaging modalities, such as CT scan and/or MRA if an aortic source of atheromatous emboli is suspected.

The second consideration referable to MRA in patients with lower extremity occlusive disease is its reported superiority in the detection of very distal vessels in patients with severe lower extremity occlusive disease. Owen, et al.[11] reported that MRA was more sensitive than conventional contrast arteriography in the detection of infrapopliteal vessels in patients with critical lower extremity ischemia. They noted an overall 72 percent discrepancy between contrast arteriography and MRA, with the majority of discrepancies being patent infrapopliteal vessels identified by an MRA but missed with conventional contrast arteriography. In their initial study of 23 patients, they found that MRA altered the treatment plan in 17 percent of patients (i.e., a bypass was constructed in situations in which this was thought not feasible on the basis of contrast arteriography alone). While these data look very provocative, no vascular surgeon of experience would accept the fact that 17 percent of patients presenting with advanced ischemia would appear to be "nonreconstructible" on the basis of contrast arteriography. In current practice, it is distinctly uncommon to treat patients who are truly without reconstructive options with respect to placement of a distal bypass and are therefore candidates for primary amputation. We could not confirm that MRA was more sensitive than contrast arteriography in the detection of runoff vessels in our report. We, in fact, found that there was a 98 percent agreement between MRA and contrast arteriography in considering all arterial segments from the aortic bifurcation to the foot.[9]

Discrepancies in the reported accuracy of MRA of the lower extremities will be explained by variations in the reference standard. It is perhaps not surprising that MRA should be more sensitive than contrast arteriography for the detection of runoff vessels in patients with severe distal occlusive disease. The MRA technique images flowing blood directly, rather than depending on reconstituted diluted contrast material in distal vessels after upstream injection. Just as we have disagreed with those who report the necessity for intraoperative prebypass arteriography in up to 70 percent of patients with severe distal occlusive disease,[12] we are also skeptical of discrepancies in the sensitivity of MRA versus contrast arteriography in the detection of diseased distal vessels. Obviously, this will vary in accordance with the adequacy of the preoperative diagnostic arteriogram.

As displayed in Table 14-1, we examined 175 arterial segments in 23 patients and found excellent correlation between MRA and contrast arteriography. This agreement was highly significant when compared with what might be expected by chance alone. Thus, we believe that MRA has great potential to obviate the need for contrast arteriography in certain as yet undefined subsets of patients with lower extremity occlusive disease. Therefore, there is a genuine and very practical need to establish the role of MRA in the management of patients with lower extremity occlusive disease, and such a prospective evaluation is currently under way in our unit. Although experience to date has been modest, certain preliminary conclusions appear justified with respect to the use of MRA in the management of patients with lower extremity occlusive disease. Focal aortoiliac occlusive disease, when detected on MRA, should be pursued with

contrast arteriography and femoral artery pressure study. Alternatively, when the MRA demonstrates severe diffuse disease, and/or long segment occlusions in the aortoiliac segments, aortobifemoral bypass grafting can be performed without confirmatory arteriography. In the circumstance of long-segment superficial femoral artery occlusion, with clear-cut distal popliteal and runoff vessel reconstitution demonstrated by MRA, femoral popliteal bypass can be safely performed based on the results of MRA alone. Experience with bypass to tibial vessels at the moment is limited, and this strategy is currently reserved for those few patients who are at genuinely high risk for complications of contrast arteriography.

SUMMARY

The foregoing must be considered a report on work in progress. In our practice, which considers a large volume of the entire spectrum of vascular surgery, we are applying MRA with increasing frequency and are carrying out a variety of surgical interventions based on MRA without confirmatory contrast arteriography. This recently adopted position remains at the moment an evolving experience. My own position has resulted from very close association with expert vascular radiologists who have both long interest and expertise in vascular imaging and have continued to refine the technical requirements for obtaining an adequate MRA. At the present time, I doubt that most surgeons practicing outside of university centers have this luxury available to them. It therefore becomes crucial for those centers that have both the volume of patients and the available expertise to establish by prospective study the ultimate role of MRA in the management of patients with vascular disease in a variety of anatomic locations.

TABLE 14-1 Correlation between MRA and Contrast Arteriography in 175 Lower Extremity Arterial Segments

		MRA	
		NL	DZ
	NL	107	3
ANGIO			
	DZ	0	65

MRA SENS: 100%
Observed agreement: (172/175): 98%   MRA SPEC: 97%
Expected agreement (chance): 53%   MRA PPV: 95%
Kappa: .96 $p <.001$ MRA NPV: 100%

Abbreviations: MRA = magnetic resonance angiography; ANGIO = contrast arteriography; NL = normal; DZ = diseased; PPV = positive predicted value; NPV = negative predicted value; SENS = sensitivity; SPEC = specificity.
Source: From Cambria, et al.[9] Reproduced by permission.

REFERENCES

1. North American Symptomatic Carotid Endarterectomy Trail Collaborators: Beneficial effect of carotid endarterectomy in symptomatic patients with high-grade carotid stenosis. *N Engl J Med* 325:445, 1991.
2. Hobson RW, Weiss DG, Fields WS, et al: Efficacy of carotid endarterectomy for asymptomatic carotid stenosis. *N Engl J Med* 328:221, 1993.
3. Gertler JP, Cambria RP, Kistler JP, et al: Carotid surgery without angiography: Non-invasive selection of patients. *Ann Vasc Surg* 5:253, 1991.
4. Ackerman RH, Candia MR: Assessment of carotid artery stenosis by MR angiography. *AJNR* 13:1005, 1992.
5. Cambria RP, Brewster DC, L'Italien GJ, et al: The durability of different reconstructive techniques for atherosclerotic renal artery disease. *J Vasc Surg* (in press).
6. Johnston KW, Scobie TK: Multicenter prospective study of nonruptured abdominal aortic aneurysms: I. Population and operative management. *J Vasc Surg* 7:69, 1988.
7. Kaufman JA, Geller SC, Peterson MJ, et al: MR imaging (includ-

ing MR angiography) of abdominal aortic aneurysms: Comparison with conventional angiography. *Am J Roentgenol* 163:203, 1994.

8. Brewster DC, Waltman AC, O'Hara PJ: Femoral artery pressure measurement during aortography. *Circulation* 60(suppl 1):120, 1979.

9. Cambria RP, Yucel EK, Brewster DC, et al: The Potential for lower extremity revascularization without contrast arteriography: Experience with magnetic resonance angiography. *J Vasc Surg* 17:1050, 1993.

10. O'Moore PV, Denham JS, Steinberg FL, et al: The complications of angiography: A prospective study. *Radiology* 169(P):317, 1988.

11. Owen RS, Carpenter JP, Baum RA, et al: Magnetic resonance imaging of angiographically occult runoff vessels in peripheral arterial occlusive disease. *N Engl J Med* 326:1577, 1992.

12. Patel KR, Semel L, Clauss RH: Extended reconstruction rate for limb salvage with intraoperative prereconstruction angiography. *J Vasc Surg* 7:531,1988.

Chapter 15

Magnetic Resonance Venography

E. Kent Yucel

Magnetic resonance venography (MRV) has come to play an important and well-established role in clinical imaging, comparable only to intracranial and carotid magnetic resonance angiography (MRA). In contrast to these applications, however, which are generally complementary to more standard imaging methods such as x-ray angiography and duplex Doppler evaluation, MRV has the potential to replace conventional angiography for several applications.

TECHNIQUES

Standard spin-echo magnetic resonance imaging (MRI) techniques have been applied to the diagnosis of venous thrombosis.[1–4] Signs of venous patency on spin-echo MRI include luminal signal void, which tends to become more marked with longer echo times (TE); even-echo rephasing; marked brightening of intraluminal signal on second echoes, which are even multiples of the first; and venous ghost artifacts in the phase-encoding axis. Conversely, venous thrombosis may be evidenced by a vein with intraluminal signal on all sequences, often higher on the first echo than the second in acute thrombosis, due to the presence of methemoglobin, and the absence of even-echo rephasing or ghost artifacts. While it is true that the presence of a signal void on spin-echo MRI reliably indicates venous patency, the signs of venous thrombosis on spin-echo images are notoriously unreliable. Increased signal in veins may be due simply to stagnant flow or entry slice enhancement rather than venous thrombosis. The widespread use of gradient moment nulling (or flow compensation) to reduce motion artifacts also contributes to increased venous signal as well as reducing the effects of even-echo rephasing and the presence of ghost artifacts. The use of presaturation pulses to help eliminate flow signal is helpful for evaluating veins on spin-echo imaging, but the slow flow in veins makes this technique less reliable for eliminating flow signal than with the arteries.

Gradient echo time-of-flight (TOF) techniques have been most widely applied to clinical MRV. These have been used successfully to image the veins of the lower extremities,[5,6] abdomen,[7–12] and thorax.[13] In the chest and abdomen, optimal images are obtained by utilizing breath-holding. This is accomplished by minimizing the repetition time (TR), so that scan time is as short as possible. Using a TR of 30 ms, a 192×256 matrix, and one signal average, it is possible to obtain one slice in a 6-s breath-hold interval. With smaller TRs or lower matrices, scan time can be shortened even further. Alternatively, two or three slices may be obtained during a single 12- to 18-s breath-hold in cooperative patients, shortening overall scan time. Venous flow is slow relative to that in arteries; in order to use short TRs, the flip angle must be decreased compared to that which would be used for a comparable MR arteriographic examination. Typical flip angles used for venous evaluation are between 25 and 40°. Slice thicknesses of 4 to 5 mm with 1-mm overlap are usually adequate to produce good venograms in a reasonable amount of time. Presaturation of aortic flow is helpful to improve selective visualization of the venous system. For abdominal MRV, an axial presaturation slab can be applied just above the diaphragm. For thoracic MRV, an axial presaturation slab may be applied through the aortic root. However, this can slightly diminish flow signal from the arm veins. An alternative if only one side is of interest is an oblique presaturation slab in a ''sash'' orientation, intersecting the aortic root and the opposite shoulder. This will effectively suppress aortic flow without diminishing flow signal from the arm of interest; it will, however, eliminate flow signal completely in the opposite subclavian vein.

The main limiting factor in TOF MRV is progressive saturation of slowly flowing venous blood. Careful selection of imaging planes to image the venous system of interest is mandatory to achieve an optimal study; saturation effects are minimized by using an imaging plane that is perpendicular to the direction of blood flow in the vessel of interest. For example, the veins of the thorax may be covered most expeditiously using a coronal acquisition; however, this results in in-plane flow in all the veins of interest—subclavian, jugular, innominate, and superior vena cava (SVC)—and diminishes vessel-background contrast. A better MR venogram can be obtained by acquiring slices in the sagittal plane

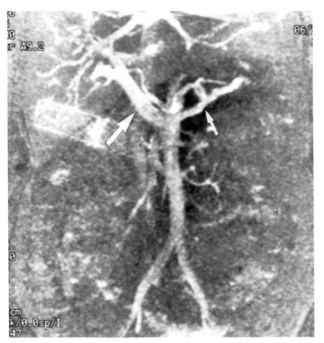

FIGURE 15-1 Two-dimensional TOF coronal image of normal portal (*large arrow*) and splenic veins.

50°) and application of a tracking superior presaturation slab. It is quite straightforward to image in this manner from the popliteal vein to the intrahepatic inferior vena cava (IVC) (Figs. 15-2 and 15-3). Breath-holding becomes necessary for the intra- and suprahepatic IVC. Imaging of the calf veins is complicated by their relatively slow flow in the resting state. Methods that have been used to improve visualization of the calf veins include lengthening of the TR to 100 ms and use of calf compression.[5] However, disadvantages of these techniques include a marked increase in scan time for the former and a decrease in vein size for the latter. Techniques in development may improve our ability to image the slowly flowing blood in the calf veins (Fig. 15-4).

Phase-contrast techniques have also been applied to MRV of the abdomen with success.[14] Both two-dimensional or three-dimensional acquisition modes can be used with phase-contrast MRV. Velocity encoding must, of course, be reduced compared to arterial studies: 10 to 20 cm/s is usually optimal. In contrast, for TOF MRV, only two-dimensional acquisition is possible. This is due to the increased saturation effects present in three-dimensional TOF, effects which tend to completely eliminate inflow enhancement from slowly flowing venous blood after only a few slices. Advantages of

for the subclavian veins and in the axial plane for the jugular and innominate veins and the SVC. This mode of acquisition maximizes inflow enhancement in these veins and produces excellent venographic images of the selected venous systems.

Usually, imaging in standard coronal and axial planes is adequate for visualization of the portal and renal veins (Fig. 15-1). Because of the presence of in-plane saturation, the vessels are usually not bright enough to be visible on maximum intensity projection (MIP) images through the entire abdomen. Restriction of the projection volume is mandatory to obtain the best images, and in most cases review of the source images is necessary. Imaging these veins in standard coronal and axial planes can result in partial saturation of blood flowing in from the splenic or superior mesenteric veins, which may mimic intraluminal thrombus. An oblique acquisition perpendicular to the course of the vein will produce maximal inflow enhancement and allow determination of patency.[9] In patients who are incapable of breath-holding it is also possible to obtain reasonably good MR venograms of the abdomen during quiet breathing.[11] Use of multiple signal averages is helpful in such cases to reduce motion artifact and improve overall signal-to-noise ratio.

Imaging the lower extremity veins is more straightforward due to the relatively straight caudocephalad course of these vessels. Just as in lower extremity MR arteriography the standard approach is to acquire multiple (up to 100) axial slices, which can then be projected using the MIP algorithm to form a venogram. Technical factors are identical to those used for arteriography except for a slightly reduced flip angle (40 to

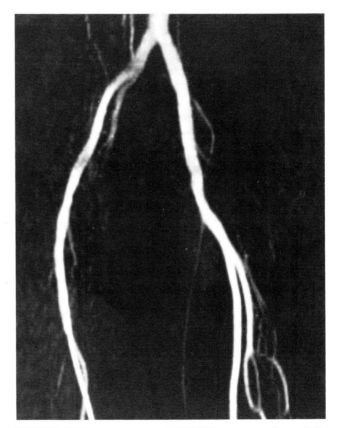

FIGURE 15-2 Two-dimensional TOF MIP venogram of normal iliac veins (axial slice acquisition).

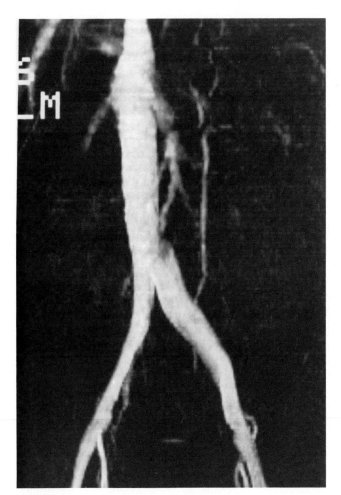

FIGURE 15-3 Two-dimensional TOF MIP venogram of normal inferior vena cava (axial slice acquisition).

ified to provide flow measurements, but this is much more cumbersome to implement in routine practice than the phase-contrast method.[10]

Several new techniques promise to improve the accuracy and speed of MRV in the near future. Gadolinium-chelated intravenous contrast agents in combination with fast gradient echo imaging can be used to increase venous signal and decrease saturation effects.[17] This may be especially helpful in situations with very slow flow—for example, the portal system in patients with severe cirrhosis. Echo-planar imaging, which allows individual images to be obtained on the order of 100 ms, has also been applied with success to imaging the abdominal veins.[18] The greater rapidity of this technique substantially decreases the number of breath-holds required to cover a given anatomical area. In addition to the MIP projection algorithm and viewing of the source images, other postprocessing algorithms are available. One that may have special applicability to MRV is three-dimensional rendering with shaded surface display. In combination with

phase-contrast MRV include the lack of in-plane saturation, the high resolution obtainable with three-dimensional imaging, and the increased contrast-to-noise ratio due to the more complete elimination of background signal. However, in practice, phase-contrast MRV has several major limitations: acquisition times can become prohibitive when all three flow directions or many slices are desired. This can make breath-holding impractical for two-dimensional phase-contrast imaging. Selection of the appropriate velocity encoding may be problematic in disease states with decreased flow or with variable flow in different veins (for example, varices compared to the normal portal vein).

A significant feature of phase-contrast imaging is the ability to obtain quantitative flow measurements in a straightforward fashion.[15,16] In veins such as the portal system, which do not exhibit substantial changes in flow across the cardiac cycle, it is not necessary to implement cardiac gating to obtain flow measurements. Flow measurements can then be obtained in a single breath-hold scan. These measurements can be used to determine both the amount and direction of flow (Fig. 15-5). The TOF technique has also been mod-

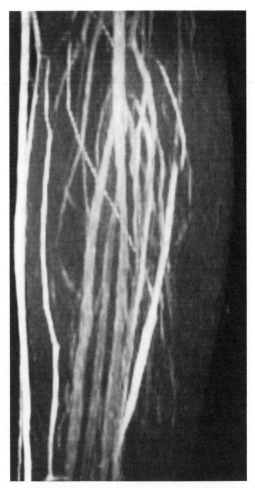

FIGURE 15-4 Calf venogram obtained using an investigational technique involving two-dimensional TOF axial acquisition with chemical-selective fat suppression and magnetization-transfer contrast to improve background suppression.

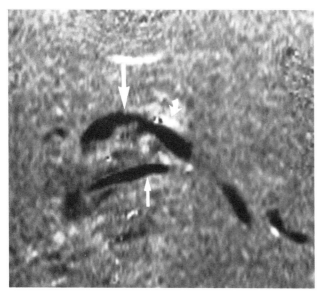

FIGURE 15-5 Two-dimensional phase-contrast image with right-left flow encoding documents normal flow direction in the splenic (*large straight arrow*) and left renal (*small straight arrow*) veins as black signal. Flow in a segment of the splenic artery (*curved arrow*) is encoded as white.

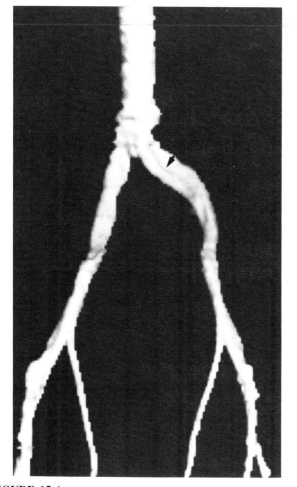

FIGURE 15-6 Shaded surface rendering of normal iliac veins and inferior vena cava. Note the clear delineation of the extrinsic impression from the iliac artery (*arrow*).

seed-growing techniques, this allows the venous system of interest to be completely separated from the background and other vessels (Figs. 15-6 and 15-7). This display method may be especially helpful to clinicians with limited patience for viewing the entire set of images and multiple MIP projections. A disadvantage of this method as currently implemented is the large amount of operator time required to construct the images, although this may decrease as image processing programs become more sophisticated.

CLINICAL APPLICATIONS

The most important role of MRV is in the detection of venous thrombosis involving the lower extremity veins, the portal vein and its tributaries, and the brachiocephalic veins. Generally speaking, venous thrombosis is quite easy to detect, since one is dealing with total or near-total occlusion rather than, for example, trying to grade the degree of a stenosis, which is a much more challenging task. As mentioned above, review of the source data is mandatory. For example, if an intraluminal thrombus is completely surrounded by flowing blood, it may be obscured on the MIP images, which just display the brightest pixels, even though it is readily visible on the original slices. Conversely, an area of the vein with slightly slower flow or more in-plane flow may give the appearance of a focal discontinuity on the MIP projections, while on the source images it will be readily apparent that this is a normal vessel segment with flow throughout. In doubtful cases, repeating the study after intravenous administration of a gadolinium chelate may increase the conspicuity of the blood pool enough to clarify the diagnosis. However, it is even more important to rely on the source images in

FIGURE 15-7 Shaded surface rendering of the normal portal venous system.

such enhanced studies due to the presence of background enhancement, which tends to degrade the quality of the MIP projections. Repeating the acquisition with slices oriented orthogonal to the vein segment of interest may also be helpful in further elucidating problematic areas.

The standard two-dimensional TOF MRV techniques described above can be used to document portal vein patency and delineate the variceal collateral network in cirrhotic patients prior to surgical procedures such as liver transplantation as well as transjugular and surgical portocaval shunts.[9–12] The MRV projection images give a much broader view of the venous anatomy than sonography, which may be of greater assistance to the surgeon. Magnetic resonance venography can be used to supplement sonography in the diagnosis of portal vein thrombosis[19,20] when sonography is limited by body habitus, bowel gas, ascites, or a small liver (Fig. 15-8). Postoperatively, MRV can be used to diagnose surgical shunt patency (Fig. 15-9) noninvasively. This is especially useful in cases where the shunt is not accessible to sonography, e.g., distal splenorenal shunts. Preliminary experience suggests that MRV can characterize the hepatic veins[20] as well as document regional hepatic parenchymal edema in suspected Budd-Chiari syndrome (Fig. 15-10). Either TOF or phase-contrast quantitative flow methods can be used to determine the direction of flow in the portal vein as well as flow velocities and volumes,[10,15,21] but the clinical importance of such information remains to be determined.

In the chest, MRV can be used to diagnose thrombosis of the brachiocephalic veins and SVC[13,22] (Figs. 15-11 and 15-12). Although through most of their course the jugular and subclavian veins can be visualized with ultrasound, the clavicle, manubrium, and sternum obscure the more central venous segments from the sound beam. Spin-echo MR sequences should be added whenever a mediastinal mass or adenopathy is suspected as the cause of central venous thrombosis. Another application for MRV in the chest is to assess central venous anatomy for central line placement in patients who have had multiple prior lines. In such cases, many veins may be thrombosed, and it is very helpful to the physician

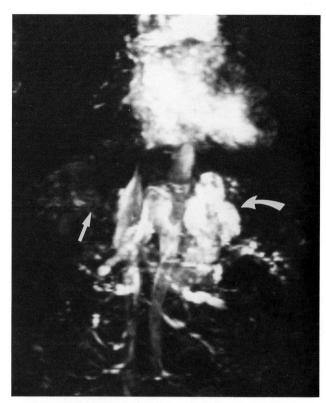

FIGURE 15-8 Two-dimensional TOF venogram of portal vein occlusion. The straight arrow indicates the expected location of the portal vein. Numerous varices are seen in the left upper quadrant (*curved arrow*).

placing the line to know which vessels are patent. Magnetic resonance venography provides a better overall display of the venous system of the chest and neck than any other single modality without the need for contrast material or ionizing radiation (Fig. 15-13). Even conventional venography, which requires injection of both arms to image the venous system bilaterally, cannot visualize the jugular veins.

Magnetic resonance venography is also complementary to sonography in imaging the lower extremities.[4–7] While capable of imaging the femoral and popliteal veins, MRV

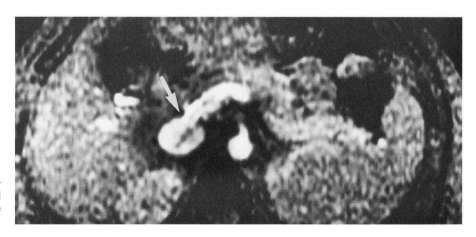

FIGURE 15-9 Two-dimensional TOF axial image of a patient end-to-side portocaval shunt. The anastomosis is indicated by the arrow.

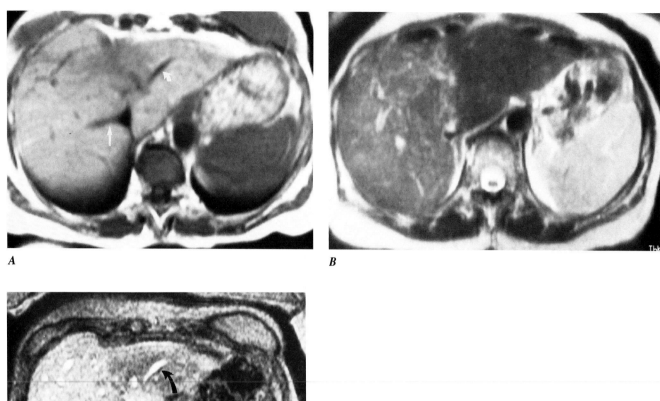

A

B

C

FIGURE 15-10 Budd-Chiari syndrome. *A*. T2-weighted fast spin-echo image demonstrates high signal in the right lobe of the liver due to diffuse edema. *B*. T1-weighted image demonstrates the right (*straight arrow*) and left (*curved arrow*) hepatic veins. No definite conclusion can be drawn about their patency. *C*. TOF axial slice with breath-holding clearly demonstrates patency of the left hepatic vein (*curved arrow*) and thrombosis of the right hepatic vein (*straight arrow*).

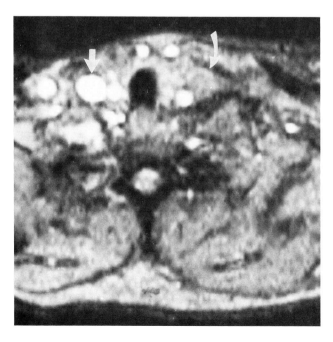

FIGURE 15-11 Two-dimensional TOF axial slice through the neck shows occlusion of the left jugular vein (*curved arrow*). Compare with patent right jugular vein (*straight arrow*).

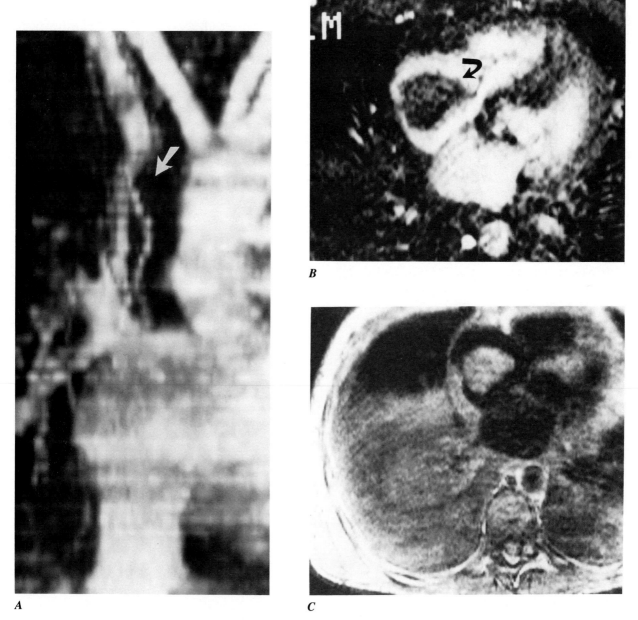

FIGURE 15-12 Superior vena cava thrombosis. *A*. Two-dimensional TOF MRV demonstrates occlusion of the SVC (*arrow*). *B*. Source axial image clearly shows a filling defect extending into the right atrium (*arrow*). This filling defect was obscured on the MIP venogram in *A* because it is completely surrounded by flowing blood. *C*. The atrial filling defect is also seen on the corresponding T1-weighted spin-echo image.

cannot compete with sonography in terms of convenience, availability, and cost. It is in the pelvis and abdomen that MRV has a primary role to play in the diagnosis of lower extremity swelling. Sonography is often suboptimal for visualizing the iliac veins and infrarenal IVC due to the depth of these vessels and the tendency for them to be obscured by overlying bowel gas. Indications for MRV study include unilateral or bilateral leg swelling that extends into the thigh and no evidence of infrainguinal clot by ultrasound. Findings on ultrasound may be normal. Alternatively, diminished

spontaneous flow and lack of respiratory variation may suggest proximal obstruction on duplex Doppler examination of the femoral vein. A high index of suspicion is especially warranted in patients with a history of pelvic pathology or pelvic surgery. Excellent-quality venograms of the IVC and iliac veins can be obtained routinely by using standard two-dimensional TOF techniques (Figs. 15-14 and 15-15). Imaging may be limited in patients with retroperitoneal clips or IVC filters, as the resulting artifact may obscure portions of the venous system. Routine review of the source axial images

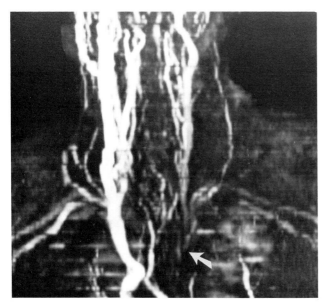

FIGURE 15-13   Magnetic resonance venogram demonstrating occlusion of the right innominate vein (*arrow*). There is excellent central venous access via the right jugular approach.

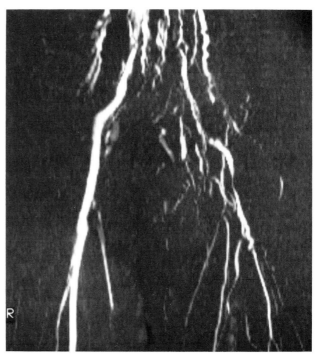

FIGURE 15-15   Left iliac vein thrombosis. Two-dimensional TOF MR venogram.

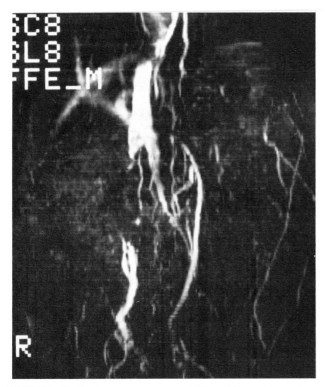

FIGURE 15-14   Inferior vena cava and bilateral iliac vein thrombosis. Two-dimensional TOF MR venogram.

FIGURE 15-16   Two-dimensional TOF MR venogram in a patient with extrinsic compression of the external iliac veins by metastatic adenopathy (*arrows*). ▶

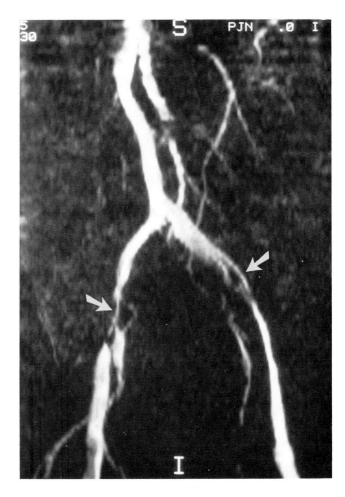

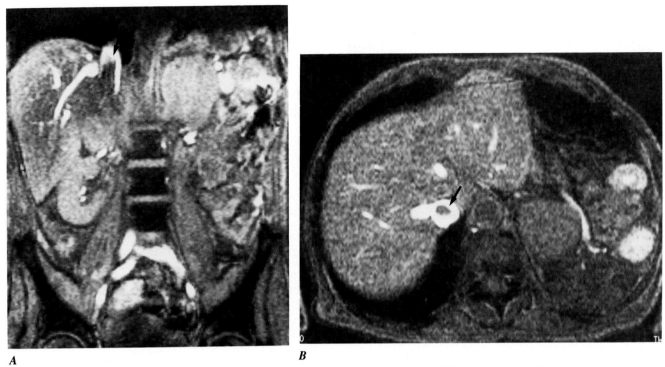

FIGURE 15-17   Renal cell carcinoma with extension into the intrahepatic IVC.   *A*. Coronal two-dimensional TOF image demonstrates the superior extent of the thrombus to just below the diaphragm (*arrow*).   *B*. Axial two-dimensional TOF image shows the filling defect at the level of the hepatic vein confluence (*arrow*).

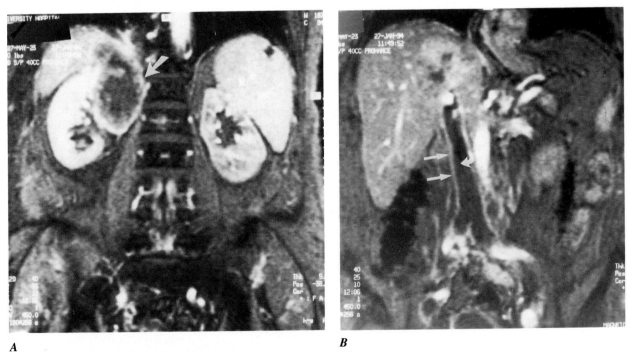

FIGURE 15-18   Renal cell carcinoma with IVC thrombosis. Two slices from a coronal two-dimensional TOF MR venogram obtained after administration of 0.2 mmol/kg gadoteridol.   *A*. The tumor is seen as a peripherally enhancing mass arising from the upper pole of the right kidney (*arrow*).   *B*. The nonenhancing thrombus (*curved arrow*) in the IVC can be clearly delineated from the slowly flowing blood at the periphery of the vessel (*straight arrows*).

is mandatory to detect small intraluminal thrombi as well as to differentiate intraluminal thrombosis from extrinsic compression or encasement as the cause of venous occlusion (Fig. 15-16). In cases of extrinsic involvement by, for example, tumor, it is also very helpful to obtain T1-weighted spin-echo images to complement the MRV study. Magnetic resonance venography has limited value for the evaluation of the calf veins at the current time due to the high spatial resolution requirements and slow spontaneous flow in these veins, and the utility of MRV has not been demonstrated for isolated calf vein thrombosis.

Similar considerations apply to imaging the renal veins. This is most commonly requested for staging renal cell carcinoma.[8] T1-weighted spin-echo images are often satisfactory for assessing possible invasion of the renal veins and IVC by tumor. However, MRV images can be helpful in differentiating extrinsic compression from intraluminal tumor thrombus as well as in assessing the full cephalocaudal extent of the IVC involvement. Coronal images are very helpful in delineating the relationship of the tumor to the suprahepatic IVC and right atrium (Fig. 15-17). Gadolinium enhancement may be helpful in selected cases to differentiate tumor from stagnant blood pool (Fig. 15-18). The role of MRV in the diagnosis of nonmalignant renal vein thrombosis—as, for example, may occur with membranous glomerulonephritis—has not been determined.

In summary, MRV has established itself as an important diagnostic modality for the evaluation of venous disease involving the abdomen, pelvis, and chest. It is most cost-effective when used in conjunction with ultrasound to visualize areas that are not accessible to sonography in patients with high clinical suspicion of central venous obstruction. Review of source images is mandatory to identify intraluminal abnormalities, and spin-echo images are complementary to MRV in the evaluation of extrinsic abnormalities affecting the veins. In many cases, MRV can replace conventional venography for central venous evaluation.

REFERENCES

1. Horan JJ, Robertson CH, Choyke PL, et al: The detection of renal carcinoma extension into the renal vein and inferior vena cava: A prospective comparison of venocavography and magnetic resonance imaging. *J Urol* 1989; 142:943.
2. Zirinsky K, Markisz JA, Rubenstein WA, et al: MR imaging of portal venous thrombosis: Correlation with CT and sonography. *AJR* 1988; 150:283.
3. Levy HM, Newhouse JH: MR imaging of portal vein thrombosis. *AJR* 1988; 151:283.
4. Erdman WA, Jayson HT, Redman HC, et al: Deep venous thrombosis of extremities: Role of MR imaging in the diagnosis. *Radiology* 1990; 174:425.
5. Evans AJ, Sostman HD, Knelson MH, et al: Detection of deep venous thrombosis: Prospective comparison of MR imaging with contrast venography. *AJR* 1993; 161:131.
6. Carpenter JP, Holland GA, Baum RA, et al: Magnetic resonance venography for the detection of deep venous thrombosis: Comparison with contrast venography and duplex Doppler ultrasonography. *J. Vasc Surg* 1993; 18:734.
7. Colletti PM, Oide CT, Terk MR, Boswell WD: Magnetic resonance of the inferior vena cava. *Mag Res Imaging* 1992; 10:177.
8. Roubidoux MA, Dunnick NR, Sostman HD, Leder RA: Renal carcinoma: Detection of venous extension with gradient-echo MR imaging. *Radiology* 1992; 182:269.
9. Finn JP, Kane RA, Edelman RR, et al: Imaging of the portal venous system in patients with cirrhosis: MR angiography vs. duplex Doppler sonography. *AJR* 1993; 161:989.
10. Edelman RR, Zhao B, Liu C, et al: MR angiography and dynamic flow evaluation of the portal venous system. *AJR* 1989; 153:755.
11. Hubbard AM, Meyer JS, Mahboubi S: Diagnosis of liver disease in children: Value of MR angiography. *AJR* 1992; 159:617.
12. Finn JP, Edelman RR, Jenkins RL, et al: Liver transplantation: MR angiography with surgical validation. *Radiology* 1991; 179:265.
13. Finn JP, Zisk JHS, Edelman RR, et al: Central venous occlusion: MR angiography. *Radiology* 1993; 187:245.
14. Dumoulin CL, Yucel EK, Vock P, et al: Two- and three-dimensional phase contrast MR angiography of the abdomen. *J Comput Assist Tomogr* 1990; 14:779.
15. Applegate GR, Thaete FL, Meyers SP, et al: Blood flow in the portal vein: Velocity quantitation with phase-contrast MR angiography. *Radiology* 1993; 187:253.
16. Mohiaddin RH, Wann SL, Underwood R, et al: Vena caval flow: Assessment with cine MR velocity mapping. *Radiology* 1990; 177:537.
17. Rodgers PM, Ward J, Baudouin CJ, et al: Dynamic contrast-enhanced MR imaging of the portal venous system: Comparison with x-ray angiography. *Radiology* 1994; 191:741.
18. Goldberg MA, Yucel EK, Saini S, et al: MR angiography of the portal and hepatic venous systems: Preliminary experience with echoplanar imaging. *AJR* 1993; 160:35.
19. Silverman PM, Patt RH, Garra BS, et al: MR imaging of the portal venous system: Value of gradient-echo imaging as an adjunct to spin-echo imaging. *AJR* 1991; 157:297.
20. Arrive L, Menu Y, Dessarts I, et al: Diagnosis of abdominal venous thrombosis by means of spin-echo and gradient-echo MR imaging: Analysis with receiver operating characteristic curves. *Radiology* 1991; 181:661.
21. Tamada T, Moriyasu F, Ono S, et al: Portal blood flow: Measurement with MR imaging. *Radiology* 1989; 173:639.
22. Hansen ME, Spritzer CE, Sostman HD: Assessing the patency of mediastinal and thoracic inlet veins: Value of MR imaging. *AJR* 1990; 155:1177.

Chapter 16

Contrast Agents for Magnetic Resonance Angiography

Ralph Weissleder

Magnetic resonance (MR) contrast characteristics are determined by tissue relaxation times (T1, T2, T2*), proton density, magnetic susceptibility, and flow. Parenteral MR contrast agents (Table 16-1) primarily alter relaxation times of tissues to which they are distributed, which ultimately results in a change in MR signal intensity. Magnetic resonance angiographic sequences are obtained by minimizing signal of stationary tissues and maximizing signal of flow, relying either on differences in longitudinal magnetization [time-of-flight (TF) techniques] or transverse magnetization [phase contrast (PC) techniques].

Although non–contrast-enhanced magnetic resonance angiography (MRA) techniques are currently of sufficient quality to yield images for clinical imaging, the concomitant use of optimized contrast agents usually improves anatomic resolution and image quality (improved signal-to-noise ratio, SNR). In addition, contrast agents increase the SNR of vessels with slow flow or turbulent flow and of vessels not perpendicular to the imaging plane. The intent of this chapter is to review the different types of MR contrast agents suitable for MRA.

CLASSIFICATION

Contrast agents for MRA are best classified according to their pharmacologic behavior.[1–4] There are basically two categories of agents: those with a prominent extravascular distribution and those with a prominent intravascular distribution (Fig. 16-1). *Extravascular (extracellular) agents* are chelates of low molecular weight that contain a paramagnetic metal ion such as gadolinium (Gd). These agents rapidly distribute into the extracellular fluid (ECF) space with no permanent increase in vessel/background signal intensity ratio. On the first pass through the capillary bed, approximately 50 percent of circulating gadopentetate dimeglumine (Gd-DTPA) diffuses from the blood into the extravascular com-

partment, and the plasma concentration of Gd-DTPA declines by 70 percent within 5 min of administration.

Because of the inability of these agents to cross an intact blood-brain barrier, they can be used for MRA of intracranial vessels or alternatively for first-pass imaging of peripheral vasculature. *Blood pool agents,* on the other hand, have a long plasma half-life and more unique biodistribution to the vascular system, so that they can be used for equilibrium imaging at later time points. Agents in this class include Gd-DTPA–labeled proteins, macromolecular polymers or polysaccharides, and particulates.

The success of a MRA contrast agent lies primarily in its pharmacologic profile, and it is not surprising that ECF agents have little to add to noncontrast MRA. The development of nonimmunogenic blood pool agents is at a stage where their safety profile warrants further preclinical and ultimately clinical trials.

MECHANISM

Contrast agents for MRA act mainly by reducing the T1 relaxation time of blood. Because of the enhanced longitudinal relaxation of blood, there is less saturation of spins, especially in three-dimensional acquisitions, where saturation effects are most prominent. Among other techniques that reduce such saturation effects are reducing the three-dimensional slab thickness (multiple overlapping thin-slab acquisitions, or MOTSA) or varying the magnitude of the radiofrequency (RF) pulse through the three-dimensional volume (tilted optimized nutation angle, or TONE). However, unlike contrast agents, these techniques result in a decreased SNR, decreased contrast-to-noise ratio (CNR), or both.

Magnetic resonance imaging parameters must be optimized if imaging is to be performed after the administration of contrast agents. Typically, repetition times can be reduced to the minimum achievable, reducing the acquisition time.

TABLE 16-1   Classification of parenteral MR contrast agents

Extracellular	Intracellular or cell bound
Positive enhancers	
Low molecular weight	Hepatocyte-directed
Gd-DTPA	Gd-BOPTA
Gd-DOTA	Gd-EOB-DTPA
Gd-HP-DO3A	Mn-DPDP
Gd-DTPA-BMA	Fe-HBED
Nitroxides	Fe-EHPD
Macromolecular/blood pool	Lymph-node directed
Albumin-(Gd-DTPA)$_x$	PL-(Gd-DTPA)$_x$-dextran
Dextran-(Gd-DTPA)$_x$	Adrenal-gland directed
Polylysine-(Gd-DTPA)$_x$	PL-(Gd-DTPA)$_x$-NH$_2$
PEG-PL(Gd-DTPA)$_x$	RES-directed
Paramagnetic liposomes	Paramagnetic liposomes
MION-46	Tumor-directed
USPIO	Metalloporphyrins
	Antibody-(Gd-DTPA)$_x$
	Calcification-directed
	Gd-DTPA-diphosphonate
Negative enhancers	
Low molecular weight	Hepatocyte-directed
Dys-DTPA	AG-USPIO
Dys-DTPA-BMA	MION-ASF
Macromolecular/blood pool	RES-directed
PION	SPIO, USPIO,
USPIO	MION
Albumin-(Dys-DTPA)$_x$	Superparamagnetic
	liposomes
	Lymph-node-directed
	USPIO
	MION-46
	Antigen-directed
	MION-immunoglobulin
	MION-Fab

Source: Modified from Brasch and Weissleder.[2] Reproduced by permission.

As in non–contrast-enhanced MRA, short echo times (TE) or "fractional echo" and smaller voxels decrease signal loss due to intravoxel dispersion. The use of small flip angles (10 to 30°) is typical with standard three-dimensional MRA, but flip angles can be increased with contrast agents, improving background suppression as well as vessel-to-background contrast-to-noise. Future improvements are expected from altered pathways for traversing k space (e.g., centric or helical).

EXTRACELLULAR AGENTS

Types of Agents

A variety of extracellular agents are available for clinical MR imaging (Table 16-2). These agents differ mainly in

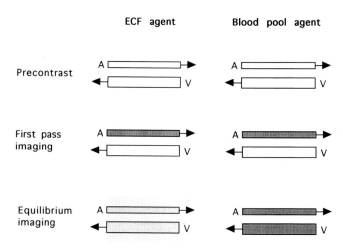

FIGURE 16-1 Types of MRA contrast agents. The efficacy of contrast agents for MRA depends primarily on the pharmacologic properties—extravascular extracellular fluid (ECF) agents versus intravascular "blood pool" agents—and the time at which imaging is performed. Blood pool agents allow delayed imaging, whereas ECF agents usually require rapid MRA sequences. (A, artery; V, vein.)

their formulations and chelates.[1,2] The first agent to be used in clinical trials was Gd-DTPA, whose favorable benefit-to-risk ratio has been firmly established in more than 5.5 million administrations. The pharmacokinetic properties of the four agents are quite similar. The apparent volume of distribution is 20 to 30 percent of the body weight, similar to that of the ECF space; hence the term *ECF agent*. In humans, the elimination half-life from the ECF space is roughly 1.5 h, primarily by glomerular filtration. The intravascular blood half-life is much shorter, as rapid equilibrium with the ECF is the rule (Table 16-2).

A second class of ECF agents characterized by a short intravascular half-life comprises hepatobiliary agents such as GD-ethoxybenzyl-DTPA (Gd-EOB-DTPA) (Schering A.G., Berlin, Germany) or manganese dipyridoxal diphosphonate (Mn-DPDP, Salutar, Sunnyvale, CA), which are primarily cleared by the liver rather than the kidney. Currently there are no reports in the literature describing the use of these agents for MRA.

TABLE 16-2   Extravascular agents

Generic name	Trade name	Formula	Ionic	Mol. wt.	$T_{1/2}$ (min)[a]
Gadopentate	Magnevist	Gd(DTPA)$^{2-}$	Yes	938	14.4
Gadodiamide	Omniscan	Gd-DTPA-BMA	No	573	3.7
Gadoteridol	Prohance	Gd-HP-DO3A	No	559	12
Gadoterate	Dotarem	Gd(DOTA)$^-$	Yes	752	7.1

[a] Distribution phase half-life is the time required for the agent to decrease to one-half in the central compartment of a two-compartment model.

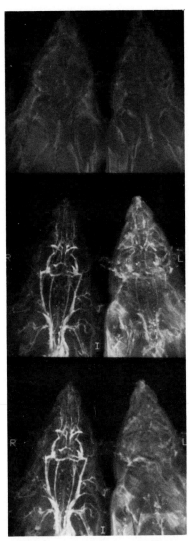

FIGURE 16-2   Comparison of ECF and blood pool agents. Sequential spoiled GRASS MIP images (*top row:* precontrast; *middle row:* 15 min; *bottom row:* 40 min after administration) of a blood pool agent (*left column: MPEG-PL-Gd-DTPA*) or an ECF agent (*right column: Gd-DTPA*). There are obvious differences in quality of the MR angiograms, reflecting the different pharmacologic behaviors of the two types of contrast agents. (Reprinted from *Radiology* 187:701, 1993, with permission.)

Imaging

Because of their rapid clearance from the intravascular space, ECF agents are only useful for MRA if they are either combined with fast imaging sequences or the agent is administered continuously during imaging (see Fig. 16-2). In an attempt to maintain high blood levels, biphasic injections have been utilized for MRA of the brain, with half of the dose injected as a loading dose while the remainder is infused during the scan. Because of the intact blood-brain barrier (BBB) limits the agents to the intravascular space, ECF contrast-enhanced MRA of intracerebral vasculature has been

shown to result in higher-quality images. Clinical trials also suggest that more vessels and vessels with slower flow are more easily detected. This may be particularly helpful in the assessment of the venous drainage of arteriovenous malformations, vascular tumor supply, and aneurysms with slow flow.

Two caveats of ECF-enhanced MRA have been reported. First, enhanced images routinely increase the signal of both arteries and veins (Fig. 16-1). Separation of vessels has been attempted by a postacquisition vessel tracking algorithm.[5] Alternatively, first-pass imaging can be performed in which images are acquired during the early arterial phase.[6] Second, nasal mucosa enhances after administration of ECF agents. This phenomenon obscures vascular detail of cranial maximum intensity pixel (MIP) images unless excluded from the reconstruction algorithm.

BLOOD POOL AGENTS

Blood pool agents are being developed to more selectively enhance the intravascular space (the "blood pool"), assess flow, and detect abnormalities of capillary permeability (Figs. 16-3, 16-4, and 16-5). Optimally, intravascular agents should meet two primary requisites: first, to have a molecular size large enough to escape filtration in glomeruli, and, second, to escape rapid recognition by receptor systems or RES (long blood half-life). Two groups of agents are useful for MRA: macromolecular Gd-DTPA agents and particulate agents.

Macromolecular Gd-DTPA Agents

Macromolecular agents (Table 16-3) tested preclinically have in common a molecular weight generally greater than 50 kDa, which is chosen to minimize renal excretion and to prolong intravascular retention. Most macromolecular agents are either derivatives of proteins, polysaccharides, or synthetic polymers to which varying amounts of Gd-DTPA are covalently attached. For example, albumin-(Gd-DTPA)$_{30}$, dextran-(Gt-DTPA)$_{15}$, polylysine-(Gd-DTPA)$_{60}$, and polyethyleleimine-(Gd-DTPA) have been used. Undoubtedly, future research will result in modification of such backbones with other chelates. Each of these polymers demonstrates high T1 relaxivity, from 40 to 200 times higher than Gd-DTPA on a per mole basis (Table 16-3). This high dose efficiency is due to the multiplicity of gadolinium ions (reported to be as high as 110 Gd/molecule) attached to each polymeric molecule and to the slowing of molecular rotation of each paramagnetic subunit. The slower rotational correlation time of gadolinium complexes bound to macromolecules, compared to Gd-DTPA alone, more closely approximates the tumbling rate of water. Because of the limited volume of distribution

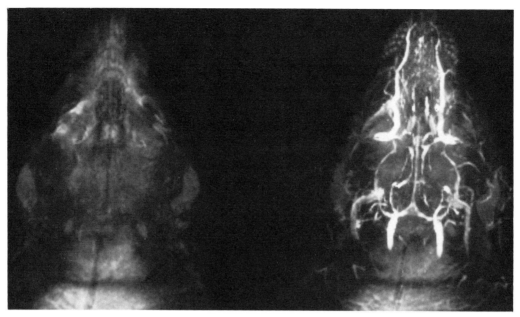

FIGURE 16-3 MPEG-PL-(Gd-DTPA). Pre- (*left*) and postcontrast (*right*) maximum signal intensity projection (MIP) images of a rat head using MPEG-PL-(Gd-DTPA), a macromolecular contrast agent incorporating multiple Gd-DTPA and methoxypolyethyleneglycol (MPEG) groups on a polyaminoacid backbone. Postcontrast: both venous and arterial anatomy is clearly defined, even of vessels as small as 100 μm. (Reprinted from *Radiology* 187:701, 1993, with permission.)

(roughly the intravascular space), lower Gd concentrations are required than with ECF agents.

A concern raised with the use of macromolecular contrast agents is their potential toxicity (due to intracellular distribution), longer retention in the body, and possible immunogenicity. In order to improve the toxicity profile and decrease the dose, a chemical variation of these agents has recently been suggested in which methylpolyethylene glycol (MPEG) residues are attached to a Gd-DTPA bearing backbone.[7] The well-hydrated MPEG side groups mainly serving to minimize recognition of the agent as a foreign molecule. The MPEG shields the backbone from phagocytic cells and decreases the adsorption of C3 complement component onto the backbone, and initiator of antigenic response.

Particulate Agents

Nonpolymeric particulate or colloidal formulations also have the potential to enhance the blood pool. These agents include small iron oxide colloids such as monocrystalline iron oxide (MION), which have a pronounced T1 effect[3]; paramagnetically labeled liposomes[8]; or paramagnetically labeled erythrocytes. Most particulate substances and liposomes administered intravenously are cleared from the blood by

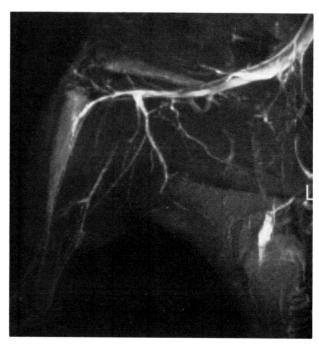

FIGURE 16-4 Peripheral vasculature. MPEG-PL-(Gd-DTPA)-enhanced image of a rat hind leg (three-dimensional TOF MIP image) demonstrates femoral artery and vein as well as peripheral branches. Note that the FOV is only 4 cm. (Reprinted from *Radiology* 187:701, 1993, with permission.)

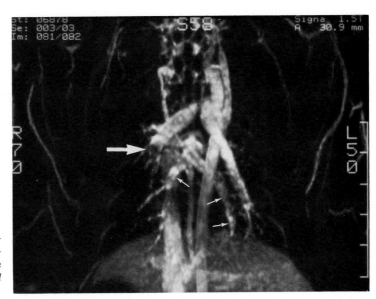

FIGURE 16-5 Pulmonary embolism. MPEG-PL-(Gd-DTPA)-enhanced image of a rabbit chest (three-dimensional TOF MIP image) demonstrates occlusion of the right main pulmonary artery due to an embolus (*arrow*). Pulmonary veins are also visible (*small arrows*).

phagocytic cells of the reticuloendothelial system (RES) at variable rates. The clearance rate and the blood half-life depend primarily on the chemical composition of the individual agent.

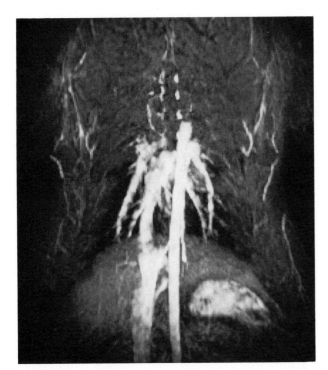

FIGURE 16-6 Iron oxide–enhanced MRA. MIP image of a 3D spoiled GRASS sequence 30 min after the IV injection of 2 mg Fe/kg of MION-46, a monocrystalline iron oxide. Precontrast images are similar to those shown in Fig. 16-2 (*top row*). Image quality appears comparable to that of macromolecular T1 agents.

Liposomes are assemblages of one (unilamellar) or several (multilamellar) concentric lipid bilayers with internal aqueous spaces. Several of the physical parameters can be altered, including size, change, and membrane structure. Of interest in the context of MRA are attempts to load liposomes with paramagnetic labels.[8] The paramagnetic label may either be placed in the inner space of the liposome or attached to the lipid bilayer. With internalized compounds, water flux across the membrane bilayer may be limiting for contrast enhancement in vitro. In vivo, however, this may not be an issue, as liposomes decompose rapidly after internalization into cells, thus liberating their contents.

A prototype particulate of an iron oxide with a long blood half-life and pronounced T1 effect is MION-46.[9] The agent has a plasma half-life of 180 min in rodents. Vascular signal enhancement is dose-dependent and is typically maximum at doses of 1 to 3 mg Fe/kg (Fig. 16-6). The agent is essentially cleared by macrophages of liver, spleen, and lymph nodes. Intracellular degradation of the iron oxide does occur and iron is ultimately incorporated into the body's total iron pool. Because intracellular toxicity of iron is less of an issue than that of Gd, such iron oxides may well become preferred macromolecular imaging agents for MRA.

Imaging

After IV administration of blood pool agents, MRA can be performed at any time point during first pass or in the equilibrium phase and still result in high vessel-to-background CNR (Fig. 16-1). The efficacy of the different agents depends mainly on their pharmacologic profile—more specifically their volume of distribution (the more closely it resembles that of the intravascular space, the better) and their

TABLE 16-3   Macromolecular Gd-DTPA agents

	Gd-DTPA	Albumin-Gd-DTPA	Dextran-Gd-DTPA	Polylysine-Gd-DTPA	MPEG-PL-Gd-DTPA
Gd ions/molecule	1	30	15	60	110
Molecular weight (Da)	538	~92,000	~75,000	~50,000	~400,000[b]
T1[a] per Gd $(mmol\ s)^{-1}$	3.7	14.4	10.5	13.1	19.0
T1[a] per molecule $(mmol\ s)^{-1}$	3.7	432	157	786	1770
Half-time in rat plasma (h)	<0.3	>3.6	>1.5	>1	14–24
LD_{50} mice (mmol Gd/kg)	7.5	—	—	>17	—
Volume of distribution (L/kg)	0.16	—	—	0.25	0.30

[a] Relaxivities at 0.25 to 0.47T and 37°C.
[b] Calculated molecular weight (note that the molecular weight of 110 Gd-DTPA groups alone is approximately 60,000).

plasma half-life. Preclinical trials of these agents have corroborated that peripheral vascular anatomy is improved and that vessels with slow and nonorthogonal flow are better visualized because of the reduced T1 of blood. In one study, even arterioles and venules as small as 100 μm could be resolved because of the high vessel-to-background CNR.[7]

The use of blood pool agents may be particularly useful in assessing slow-flow systems (pulmonary vasculature, peripheral arterial disease) or small vessels such as coronary arteries. Animal studies in our laboratory indicate that contrast-enhanced MRA of pulmonary vessels improves the detectability of pulmonary emboli, even small peripheral emboli in fourth-order branches.

SUMMARY

A large variety of contrast agents are available that may potentially be used for MRA. These agents all decrease the T1 relaxation time of blood. Agents vary considerably in their molecular structure and pharmacologic behavior. Extravascular agents (prototype: Gd-DTPA) have a short plasma half-life and are readily distributed to the extracellular space; furthermore, these agents can be used for MRA of intracranial vessels where an intact BBB limits their diffusion into brain parenchyma. Blood pool agents, on the other hand, are desirable for MRA of the extracranial vasculature because

of their unique distibution and lack of imaging time constraints. Irrespective of the agent used, contrast agents increase vessel-to-background SNR, improve anatomic resolution, and facilitate visualization of a broader range of flow velocities.

REFERENCES

1. Brasch RC: New directions in the development of MR imaging contrast media. *Radiology* 183:1, 1992.
2. Brasch RC, (ed): *MRI contrast enhancement in the central nervous system: A case study approach.* Raven, 1993, p 301.
3. Weissleder R, Papisov M: Pharmaceutical iron oxides. *Rev Mag Res* 4:1, 1992.
4. Weissleder R, Bogdanov A, Papisov M: Target-specific superparamagnetic contrast agents. *Mag Res Qu* 8:55, 1992.
5. Lin W, Haake EM, Smith AS, Clampitt ME: High-resolution MR angiography with gadopentate dimeglumine: Preliminary results in the intracranial circulation. *JMRI* 2:4, 1992.
6. Prince MR, Yucel EK, Kaufman JA, et al: Dynamic gadolinium-enhanced 3-dimensional abdominal MR arteriography. *JMRI* 3:877, 1993.
7. Bogdanov A, Weissleder R, Frank H, et al: Macromolecular complexone as a contrast agent for MR angiography: Preparation, properties and animal studies. *Radiology* 187:701, 1993.
8. Unger EC, Shen D, Fritz TA: Status of liposomes as MR contrast agents. *JMRI* 3:195, 1993.
9. Shen T, Weissleder R, Papisov M, et al: Monocrystalline iron oxide nanocompounds (MION): Physicochemical properties. *Mag Res Med* 29:599, 1993.

Chapter 17

Helical Computed Tomography Angiography

Lorraine K. Skibo

A number of competing modalities exist for noninvasive vascular imaging. Duplex ultrasound (US) is well suited to peripheral vascular work where the vessels are relatively superficial, but it is much less accurate in deeper vessels, such as those supplying the viscera. Other limitations of ultrasound include obscuration of intravascular signal in heavily calcified vessels and limitation to two-dimensional images. Three-dimensional reconstruction of US images is possible but is still a research tool.

Magnetic resonance imaging (MRI) of vascular structures is tremendously appealing because it is noninvasive, exquisitely flow-sensitive, and well suited to three-dimensional reconstruction. It can provide a large field of view compared to US or computed tomography (CT) techniques but is limited by its cost and availability. Resolution of small or moving vessels (pulmonary) is reduced. Flow artifacts can confound all but the most experienced reader. Motion from bowel peristalsis or magnetic field distortions induced by metallic surgical clips can seriously degrade images. Calcification is not detected. Claustrophobic or unstable patients are difficult to scan.

Computed tomography has traditionally evaluated pathology of large vessels such as the central pulmonary arteries and the thoracic and abdominal aorta. In these vessels, CT is especially valuable in the concomitant assessment of the surrounding soft tissues—for example, in diagnosing leakage from an abdominal aortic aneurysm by increased x-ray attenuation in the periaortic fat.

Computed tomography in the helical mode provides continuous anatomic data without respiratory artifact or misregistration. The resulting data set provides the best circumstances for reconstruction of images in three dimensions. Rapid scanning times (no need to wait for table movement or breathing instructions) allow for volume acquisitions of data in 30 to 42 s during a single breath-hold. Appropriate timing of intravenous contrast administration allows tracking of the contrast bolus in arterial or venous phases. The images can be viewed in the usual axial plane to evaluate the surrounding soft tissues and organs. Alternatively, two-dimensional reformatting in orthogonal planes or a three-dimensional reconstructed angiogram can be performed. Depiction of the high-attenuation vessels is possible by excluding surrounding structures with maximum-intensity projection (MIP) multiplanar reconstruction programs. These images are known as helical computed tomographic angiography (CTA).

TECHNICAL FACTORS

Hardware

Conventional axial CT data are obtained section by section, each 360° projection being acquired sequentially. This is because cables attach the x-ray tube and detector assembly to the reconstruction processor and high-voltage power source in the conventional design. Therefore, the source-detector assembly has to oscillate to allow for a finite cable length, causing a 5- to 10-s delay for the assembly to return to the starting position for the next scan. With the introduction of slip-ring technology (source-detector assembly without cables) in the 1980s, simultaneous patient transport through the gantry with continuous 360° data acquisition became possible. The first description of helical CT came in 1989.[1] The x-ray beam traces helical path. Data acquisition is done during a single breath-hold, so there is no respiratory variation to cause misregistration or respiratory movement artifacts (especially important for multiplanar or three-dimensional reconstructions). Acquisition times are decreased further with no interscan delay for table feed and breathing commands.

Slice thicknesses of 1 to 10 mm are possible, with table feeds of 1 to 10 mm/s. Pitch is the table feed distance per 360° rotation (usually one 360° rotation per second) divided by the section collimation. The pitch is usually set to 1, but can be made greater than 1 to permit greater coverage at some expense in resolution. Maximum scan time is dependent on tube heat capacity and amount of computer memory, but 24- to 50-s scans are possible. The limiting factor in scan time is often the breath-holding ability of the patient. Imaging a large volume requires either a long breath-hold or preprogramming of multiple spiral scan sequences to allow for breathing between sequences.

A 25- to 40-s continuous scan generates a considerable amount of heat in the x-ray tube. Conventional CT tubes must be operated at lower milliampere-seconds (mAs) in order to tolerate the long scans. This reduces the number of photons available for imaging. Tubes are being developed which will allow conventional mAs settings to be used.

For a pitch of 1 and equivalent mAs settings, the radiation dose to the patient is the same as in conventional CT. If a pitch of greater than 1 is used, the dose is lower.[2]

It is the continuous anatomic information without respiratory misregistration provided by a helical CT (as opposed to contiguous or conventional CT) that allows a near-anatomical three-dimensional display of vascular structures. Even with a pitch greater than 1, the scanning is still continuous; in no case will gaps result (or can a lesion be excluded from the data). When vessels or lesions smaller than the section are present, their contrast will be decreased due to partial volume effect. The speed of acquisition of the helical scan allows a well-timed bolus of contrast material to be tracked and imaged entirely in the arterial or venous phase.

For each helical scan, the radiologist must consider and determine several scanning parameters; scan collimation, table speed (and their ratio, pitch), total scan (or breath-hold) time, and image reconstruction intervals. The scan must cover the length of the vessel(s) of interest during maximum opacification with contrast. Vessel size and position will determine collimation and reconstruction intervals.

Software

Conventional CT images are reconstructed from the raw data by a filtered back-projection algorithm. Direct reconstruction of images from the data obtained over any 360° segment in helical CT would show motion artifacts due to the continuous patient transport through the gantry. Therefore, the data are synthesized point by point for all projections over the 360°. After interpolation of data between adjacent turns, a filtered back-projection algorithm is applied as in conventional CT to obtain transaxial images.[2]

Image quality parameters of spatial resolution, image homogeneity, and image contrast are identical to those of conventional CT scanning.[3]

The section sensitivity profile (SSP) defines voxel dimensions and characteristics along the z axis (direction of table motion) and serves as a measure of resolution in the longitudinal plane. Even in conventional CT, the resolution in the longitudinal plane is usually inferior to that in the x or y image plane. Broadening of the section sensitivity profile is

not detectable unless the table feed per revolution is greater than the slice thickness. In spiral CT, even when the pitch is 1, the SSP is broadened with programs for data reconstruction that interpolate data over 360°.[4]

Broadening of the SSP is less when the data are interpolated over 180° segments instead of 360°, so that with a pitch of 1, no broadening is seen.[5] At higher pitches, broadening still occurs with 180° reconstructions, but not as much as with the 360° reconstructions. The 180° interpolation programs are not available universally as yet.

Image noise is the standard deviation of pixel values in a homogeneous region of interest. Using the 180° interpolation algorithm increases the image noise (since only half the photons are available compared to the 360° interpolations). Compared to conventional CT, noise is increased when the algorithm is combined with the lower rate of mAs used.[5] This becomes a problem only when the contrast between different tissues of interest is low.

Postscan processing of the data set can add a significant amount of physician time to the examination. There are several software approaches to reformatting and viewing contrast-enhanced vasculature for helical CTA.

The MIP approach is a volume-rendering technique first used with MRA. A two-dimensional image is obtained by projecting a mathematical ray through a stack of reconstructed sections. The intensity of pixels in the resulting image is the maximum intensity encountered along the ray in its course through the volume. Projections can be displayed singly or grouped together in a cine-type loop. With MIP, mural calcification can be distinguished from contrast. Vessels adjacent to bone are obscured and must be manually excluded by the operator prior to reconstruction. Because it is a two-dimensional rendering, depth perception is absent. In preliminary studies, it has been shown to be more sensitive and accurate in detecting renal artery stenoses than shaded surface displays.[6]

Shaded surface displays depict a model of the surface of a volume that connects all pixels with a Hounsfield unit above a user-prescribed threshold. Pixels below the threshold are eliminated from the image. Different views are created by rotating the three-dimensional image. The gray scale in the resulting image encodes shading as if illuminated from a single-point light source. Problems with this method of display result from the single Hounsfield unit threshold. Calcium cannot automatically be eliminated from the final image. Also, nonuniform contrast in vessels—due to poor mixing, suboptimal timing, or decreased flow due to stenosis—may cause segments to be excluded from the image and therefore to be mistaken for stenoses or occlusions.

Connectivity algorithms can be used to assist the standard programs to follow contrast-opacified vessels. The operator selects a "seed point" in the vessel of interest and causes all voxels above a selected Hounsfield unit threshold and spatially connected to the seed point to be included in the final image.

Curved planar reformations are available on some scanners. This program generates a curved coronal or sagittal section based on an arc drawn with a track ball on one axial section. This feature can be used to render a nonplanar vascular structure in one planar image. For example, the aorta and both renal arteries can be depicted in one image, one voxel thick, thus removing overlaping vessels.

Despite all the three-dimensional manipulations available, one group has found the axial multiplanar reconstructed images to be superior for diagnosis.[7]

Contrast

Iodinated contrast material (300 mg/mL iodine, 90 to 150 mL) is used to opacify the vessel(s) of interest. For most studies, it is given intravenously, through a 20-gauge or larger catheter placed in the antecubital fossa. Because of patient-to-patient variability in the flow of contrast out of the arm to the central circulation and differences in cardiac output, timing of the arrival of the contrast bolus in the vessel(s) of interest is often required.

The duration of the contrast bolus determines the approximate time length of arterial opacification. In general, a 30-s bolus is assumed to provide 30 s of arterial opacification. For longer imaging times or multiple sequential helical scans, longer or repeat boluses would be required (Fig. 17-1). Flow rates of 3 to 4 mL/s are optimal in providing a rapid appearance of contrast, a long plateau, and minimal early venous opacification. The amount of contrast opacification of veins will vary with the time into the bolus, so that early images will have very little venous contrast whereas late scans may display a significant amount.

Timing of the helical scan is critical in the abdomen. A small bolus (3 mL/s for 6 s) is given intravenously, and scanning is performed continuously at a level just cephalad to the vessel(s) of interest, noting the time of contrast opacification of the aorta by measuring its attenuation in a small region of interest. The final helical scan is prescribed so that the vessel of interest is in the center of the volume of the scan and after a delay calculated from the timing scan.[8] Table feed and collimation is based on the resolution required for the examination but limited by the volume required, because resolution is best preserved by maintaining a pitch of 1. For example, a 3-mm/s table feed with 3-mm collimation during a 30-s scan images 9 cm of the abdomen. More volume can be scanned if slice thickness, table speed, or pitch is increased. For example, collimation of 3 mm with table speed of 5 mm/s results in a pitch of 1.67 and a scanned volume of 15 cm.

With a pitch greater than 1, the section sensitivity profiles are widened, but there are no data as yet to determine a significant threshold where clinically important data would be lost in CTA by using pitches greater than 1.

When portal venous opacification is required, the bolus timing is done with the region of interest in the superior mesenteric vein and scanning is performed in a caudad-to-cephalad direction.

Timing in the thoracic aorta and the brachiocephalic vessels can in most cases be standardized because of the prox-

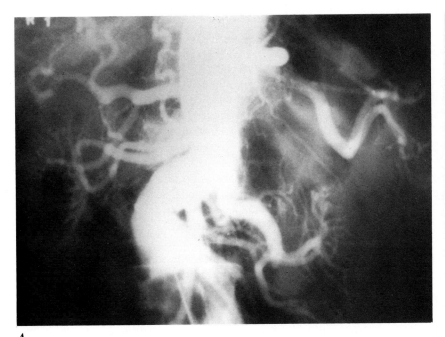
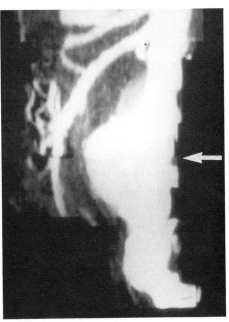

A　　　　　　　　　　　　　　　　　　　　　　　　　　*B*

FIGURE 17-1　Two separate intravenous boluses and helical scans were prescribed to visualize the entire abdominal aortic aneurysm seen at anteroposterior aortography (*A*) and in the lateral-view helical CTA (*B*). The slight difference in opacification of the aorta marks the level of the separate scans (*arrow*).

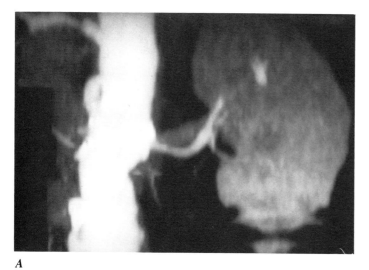

A

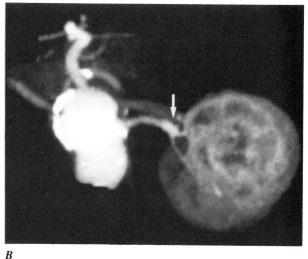

B

FIGURE 17-2   In this patient with a solitary left kidney and lower pole mass, CT was requested to evaluate the mass. Helical CTA at the same time demonstrates the bifurcation of the main renal artery in the renal hilum (*arrow*) in the anterior view (*A*) and inferior view (*B*). The inferior view gave a better perspective regarding the relative position of the mass.

imity. To image the proximal aorta, only 60 mL of contrast is typically used (3 mL/s for 15 s, then 1 mL/s for the remainder). If additional disease is present at the diaphragm, then a second spiral scan and injection can be performed.

To cover the entire pulmonary vascular tree, 5-mm collimation with 5 mm/s table feed is typically used. The scan is started at the level of the aortic arch and continues caudad. Higher injection rates (5 to 7 mL/s) and more dilute contrast (12 to 30% iodine) are utilized so that high opacification of vessels can be obtained without producing streak artifact from poor mixing of a more concentrated agent. Breath-hold times should be kept lower (24 s) to accommodate a generally dyspneic patient population.

For imaging the carotid bifurcation, an uninfused scout scan is first obtained to locate the bifurcation. Contrast is injected at 2.5 mL/s for a total of 75 ms. The scan is started 20 s following the start of the injection. This results in some opacification of veins (especially at the caudad extent of the scan). Collimation and table speed is set at 2 to 4 mm. Scan times can be as long as possible, as respiration need not be suspended, but there must be no swallowing.

Patient Preparation

Prior to the long breath-hold scans, patients should be thoroughly coached in the breathing sequences. They should be allowed to hyperventilate just prior to the scan to achieve longer breath-holds. Ideally, identical breath-hold volumes should be obtained for both the scout and the final contrast spiral scans. This is to prevent the edges of a volume of interest from being displaced out of a tightly coned imaging volume. The target anatomy should always be placed in the center of the imaging volume.

APPLICATIONS

Abdomen

ABDOMINAL AORTIC ANEURYSM

Conventional CT has played a major role in evaluating patients preoperatively for aortic aneurysm repair. It can accurately determine the size of the aneurysm and the relative positions of major arterial branches. The most critical information is the position of the neck of the aneurysm with respect to the renal and mesenteric arteries. It is likely that helical CTA, compared to conventional CT, will improve visualization of visceral artery branches, accessory branches, and their pathology in addition to displaying the aneurysm. It has been found that CTA is superior to conventional aortography in displaying the lumen, presence of thrombus, and calcified plaque. Compared to MRA, CTA can better assess wall calcification. The aim is to use helical CTA as the only preoperative study for abdominal aortic aneurysms. However, there are no data as yet assessing CT as a full substitute for aortography. One potential advantage of CTA is the ability to display the anatomy from any angle, giving a theoretical preview of the operative approach and assuring that overlapping structures are well resolved (Fig. 17-2).

In postoperative graft evaluations, most complications (infection, pseudoaneurysm, thrombosis) are readily evident on axial images.

Dissections of the abdominal aorta are usually continuations of thoracic dissections. The CTA technique can easily visualize the origins of the visceral vessel from the true or false lumens (Fig. 17-3). Display of the true lumen is usually depicted in the arterial phase of the scan. Opacification of the false lumen can occur late and can be demonstrated if

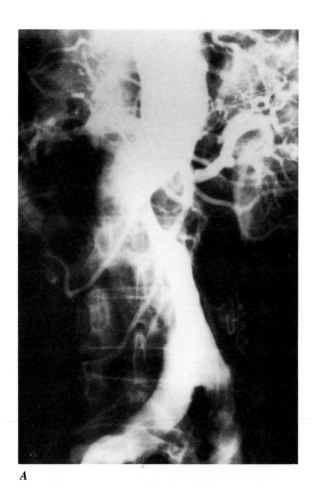

A

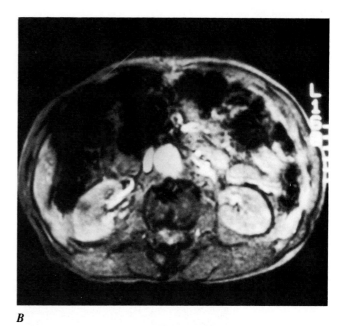

B

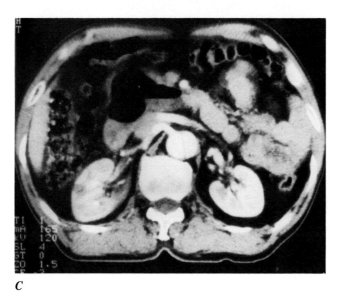

C

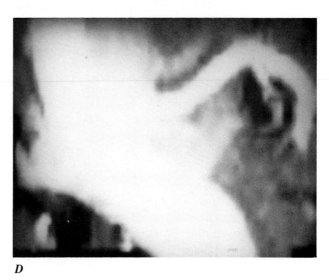

D

FIGURE 17-3 (*A*) This aortogram was performed to evaluate the renal arteries in a patient with aortic dissection and new renal insufficiency, but it failed to clearly display the renal artery origins with respect to the true and false lumens. Note poor arterial opacification of the celiac branches and the right renal artery. Magnetic resonance angiography was performed (*B*), but neither right nor left renal artery origin was clearly displayed. Axial image (*C*) from helical CTA shows the right renal artery arising from the false lumen, with slightly delayed opacification of the parenchyma. The MIP image from the scan (*D*) closely resembles the aortogram. The axial images were superior to the reconstructed images for actual diagnosis.

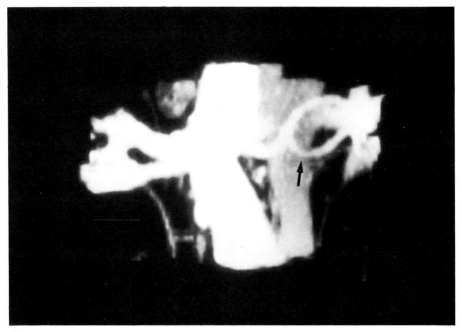

A

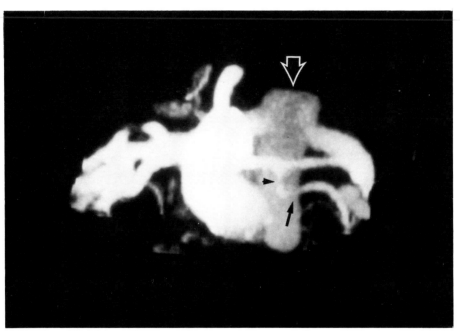

B

FIGURE 17-4   Maximum-intensity-projection images from helical CTA of the renal arteries in a patient with hypertension. Right renal artery, posterior view (*A*) shows suspected stenosis (*arrow*) of the posterior division, which becomes more obvious as the image is rotated for a more superior view (*B*). A second stenosis is uncovered (*arrowhead*). Note opacification of the inferior vena cava (*open arrow*), interfering somewhat with the image.

the helical scan is repeated provided that the false lumen is not thrombosed.

RENAL VASCULAR DISEASE

The search for an accurate, noninvasive anatomical screening test for renal artery stenosis continues (Fig. 17-4). Preliminary work comparing CTA of the renal arteries to conventional angiography shows success in visualizing main and accessory renal arteries and 92 percent sensitivity in diagnosing severe renal artery stenoses using MIP algorithms for display.[6] Some authors have found reading directly from the axial images and multiplanar reformatted images superior to MIP images.[7] Other evidence of renal artery stenosis should be searched for, such as poststenotic dilatation or decreased opacification of distal renal vessels. No work has been published as yet in evaluating transplant renal arterial disease. CTA may prove most valuable in evaluating renal artery stent function. The renal vessels are usually too deep for reliable evaluation with US, and the stent itself interferes with signal on MRA. The length of stent and its position with respect to the renal artery ostium in the aorta can also be visualized with CTA.

MESENTERIC VASCULAR DISEASE

Most significant atherosclerosis of the mesenteric arteries occurs in the proximal 3 to 6 cm, an area well seen with CTA. To date there is no other widely applicable screening test for mesenteric ischemia. Ultrasound in this area is highly dependent on the skill of the operator and the habitus of the patient, so it cannot be applied universally. Visceral artery aneurysms due to atherosclerosis or pancreatitis can be visualized with conventional CT and can also be expected to be well displayed using helical CTA.

Preoperative mesenteric studies to document common vas-

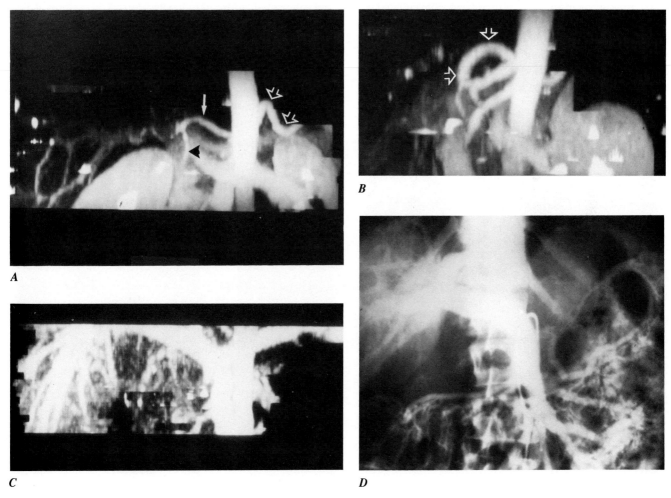

FIGURE 17-5 Preoperative assessment for left-lateral-segment liver donor. Helical CTA MIP anterior (*A*) and lateral (*B*) views shows the common hepatic (*arrow*), gastroduodenal (*arrowhead*), and looping splenic (*open arrow*) arteries. Portal venous phase of the spiral CT confirms patency and demonstrates anatomy (*C*) similar to that seen at the portal venous phase of the superior mesenteric arteriogram (*D*).

cular anomalies are often performed prior to liver transplantation. For potential left-lateral-segment liver donors, a full workup—including mesenteric angiography and conventional CT—is usually done. At least third-order aortic branches can be demonstrated by CTA, which can also show the replaced right hepatic artery and confirm portal venous patency.[8] Whether these data are sufficient to replace conventional angiography has not been determined (Fig. 17-5).

Thorax

THORACIC AORTA

Currently there are several imaging modalities that can image dissections of the thoracic aorta. All modalities—including CT, MRI, transesophageal echocardiography, and aortography—are highly accurate, though the gold standard is still considered to be aortography.[9] The hospital and clinical setting usually determine the order of examination. The additional improvements helical CT adds to conventional CT include the lack of respiratory misregistration and artifacts and a decrease in the amount of contrast used.[10] Three-dimensional reconstructions can aid in the visualization of the true and false lumens with respect to the origins of the coronary and brachiocephalic arteries.

Other diseases of the thoracic aorta well evaluated by CT include atherosclerotic aneurysms, congenital anomalies, and vasculitis. Computed tomography can also serve to assess grafts postoperatively. For most of these applications, the axial imaging plane is preferred.

The utility of CT or CTA in assessing traumatic aortic disruption is to date limited to the adjacent soft tissue changes. Time will tell whether CTA will supplant aortography for this indication.

PULMONARY VASCULATURE

Preliminary studies have demonstrated pulmonary thromboemboli well in second- to fourth-division pulmonary arteries.[11] False positives occurred because of adjacent lymph nodes and/or asymmetrical perfusion. The only series published claims minimal respiratory artifact even in patients unable to suspend respiration.[11] Axial images displayed the anatomy and pathology best.

Reconstruction programs may only serve to obscure thromboembolism by introducing artifacts. Currently, CT is indicated for patients who would be at high risk for complication during pulmonary angiography, where central vessel embolism is suspected.

The final role CT will play in the workup of pulmonary embolism has not been determined.

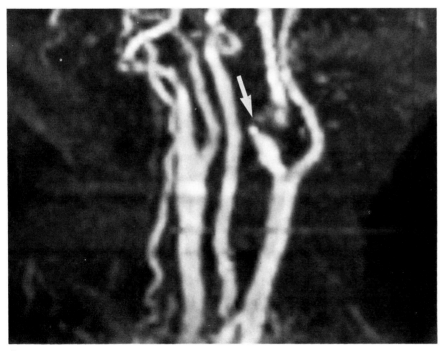

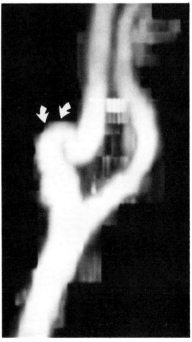

A   *B*

FIGURE 17-6 Magnetic resonance angiography image (*A*) of the left carotid artery bifurcation shows signal void in the internal carotid (*arrow*), which could be due to high-grade stenosis. The MIP image from helical CTA (*B*), demonstrates looping of the vessel (*arrowheads*), with no underlying stenosis. This technique provides good visualization of calcified or tortuous vessels as compared to ultrasound or MRI. (Images courtesy of Dr. Richard B. Schwartz, Department of Radiology, Brigham and Women's Hospital, Boston, MA.)

Peripheral Vasculature

CAROTID ARTERIES

Internal carotid endarterectomy in severe stenosis has recently been shown to be protective against stroke in symptomatic patients.[12] Accurate assessment of the degree of stenosis is required if a noninvasive imaging modality is to be clinically effective. Conventional angiography remains the gold standard. Ultrasound is the dominant screening modality but is difficult or impossible when vessels are heavily calcified or in very high bifurcations. Magnetic resonance imaging can be limited by flow artifacts and patient conditions that prohibit examination. Helical CTA can image a contrast-enhanced lumen despite calcification, tortuosity, or position (Fig. 17-6). Bony or cartilaginous landmarks can be left in the images to assist the surgeon. The bifurcation can be viewed from any angle or orientation, including its cross section.

Results of the first studies published indicate that carotid CTA is accurate with correlation with angiography seen in 92 percent of 20 patients.[13] In another series, correlation of stenosis category was present in 41 of 50 carotid arteries.[14] Ulcers, aneurysms, and loops were also well displayed.

Extremities

In the evaluation of vascular disease of the extremity, CTA cannot cover a sufficient length of the arteries to be comprehensive. To date CT has been limited to evaluating complications of bypass grafts such as pseudoaneurysm and infection. Since the axial resolution is 0.8 mm, the potential exists to evaluate the peripheral arteries with focal disease, such as trauma or tumor.

FUTURE DIRECTIONS

The drawbacks of helical CTA will always be the use of iodinated contrast and radiation. Because it is minimally invasive (only an intravenous catheter is required), its role in screening for vascular disease has great potential. There is hope that CTA may be the only modality necessary to evaluate abdominal aortic aneurysms preoperatively.

Another drawback is the amount of postscan processing time required to generate satisfactory three-dimensional angiograms. As software becomes more sophisticated, it is hoped that this will be reduced.

The infinite manipulations of the three tools of intravenous contrast, scan timing, and patient anatomy promise that refinements of current applications and new indications will occur.

REFERENCES

1. Kalender WA, Seissler W, Klotz E, Vock P: Spiral volumetric CT with single-breath-hold technique, continuous transport, and continuous scanner rotation. *Radiology* 176:181, 1990.
2. Heiken JP, Brink JA, Vannier MW: Spiral (helical) CT. *Radiology* 189:647, 1993.
3. Kalender WA, Polacin A: Physical performance characteristics of spiral CT scanning. *Med Phys* 18:910, 1991.
4. Brink JA, Heiken JP, Balfe DM, et al: Spiral CT: Decreased spatial resolution in vivo due to broadening of section-sensitivity profile. *Radiology* 185:469, 1992.
5. Polacin A, Kalender WA, Marchal G: Evaluation of section sensitivity profiles and image noise in spiral CT. *Radiology* 185:29, 1992.
6. Rubin GD, Dake MD, Napel S, et al: Spiral CT of renal artery stenosis: Comparison of three-dimensional rendering techniques. *Radiology* 190:181, 1994.
7. Galanski M, Prokip M, Chavan A, et al: Renal arterial stenoses: Spiral CT angiography. *Radiology* 189:185, 1993.
8. Rubin GD, Dake MD, Napel SA, et al: Three-dimensional spiral CT angiography of the abdomen: Initial clinical experience. *Radiology* 186:147, 1993.
9. Cigarroa JE, Isselbacher EM, DeSanctis RW, Eagle KA: Medical progress. Diagnostic imaging in the evaluation of suspected aortic dissection: Old standards and new directions. *AJR* 161:485, 1993.
10. Costello P, Ecker CP, Tello R, Hartnell GG: Assessment of the thoracic aorta by spiral CT. *AJR* 158:1127, 1992.
11. Remy-Jardin M, Remy J, Wattinne L, Giraud F: Central pulmonary thromboembolism: Diagnosis with spiral volumetric CT with the single-breath-hold technique—Comparison with pulmonary angiography. *Radiology* 185:381, 1992.
12. North American Symptomatic Carotid Endarterectomy Trial collaborators: Beneficial effect of carotid endarterectomy in symptomatic patients with high-grade carotid stenosis. *N Engl J Med* 325:445, 1991.
13. Schwartz RB, Jones KM, Chernoff DM, et al: Common carotid artery bifurcation: Evaluation with spiral CT. *Radiology* 185:513, 1992.
14. Dillon EH, van Leeuwen MS, Fernandez MA, et al: CT angiography: Application to the evaluation of carotid artery stenosis. *Radiology* 189:211, 1993.

Index

Index

In this index, page numbers in *italics* refer to illustrations; page numbers followed by the letter ''t'' refer to tables.

ISBN 0-07-072695-7

9 780070 726956

90000>